THE ART OF MUSIC

*A Short History of
Musical Styles and Ideas*

THE ART
OF MUSIC

A Short History of
Musical Styles and Ideas

BEEKMAN C. CANNON

ALVIN H. JOHNSON

WILLIAM G. WAITE

Yale University

THOMAS Y. CROWELL COMPANY

New York · Established 1834

PREFACE

THIS BOOK has grown from the authors' long collaboration in teaching an introduction to the history of music. Many of the ideas contained in it were suggested by colleagues present and past. In the development of these ideas individual contributions were made which can no longer be traced to the original author. To these unacknowledged friends we express our gratitude.

The authors wish to thank the Copenhagen National Museum for the photograph of the Greek vase reproduced in Plate 1; the Biblioteca Medicea-Laurenziana, Florence, for the photograph of the manuscript reproduced in Plate 2; and the libraries of Yale University for the remaining plates, as well as for the illustration appearing on p. 144. For the quotations from *Source Readings in Music History* we are indebted to Professor Oliver Strunk and W. W. Norton & Company.

The authors are deeply aware of the many special debts owed to those who assisted in the preparation of this book. Dean Luther Noss, Chairman of the Music Department of Yale University, made funds available which enabled us to multilith the text for trial use in the classroom. Dr. Carl A. Rosenthal and Mrs. Riki Levinson were lavish with their skills in the copying of the musical examples. Mr. Alfred B. Kuhn performed the exacting task of preparing the index. It has been a particularly gratifying experience to work with the staff of the Thomas Y. Crowell Company. Our editor, Mr. Philip Winsor, offered countless valuable suggestions and has been a patient counsellor in the preparation of the manuscript. We also express our appreciation for the interest and encouragement of Mr. Robert L. Crowell.

BEEKMAN C. CANNON   ALVIN H. JOHNSON   WILLIAM G. WAITE

Yale University

24938

This book is the product of more than ten years of fruitful cooperation and experience in teaching an *Introduction to the History of Music* at Yale University. For the ideas contained in it its three authors are individually and collectively responsible. For the time and skill William G. Waite has spent in reconciling the literary idiosyncrasies of its authors the other two authors wish to record their gratitude and appreciation.

CONTENTS

PLATES

THE ART OF MUSIC

A Short History of
Musical Styles and Ideas

INTRODUCTION

The history of music must be seen not as a large portrait gallery
of individual composers, but as a history of styles, and the latter
in turn must be seen as a history of ideas.

MANFRED BUKOFZER, *The Place of Musicology in
American Institutions of Higher Learning*, p. 30.

WHAT IS MUSIC? In every age a different answer has been
found. Today music may be the art of organizing tones so that an aesthetic
experience may result. It was once held to be sound related to number,
and at another time the union of word and tone. Two thousand years
after Plato, Johannes Kepler still adhered to Plato's idea that music was
a force regulating the universe through the mathematical relationships
inherent in musical intervals. For a man of the Enlightenment music was
matter in motion, while a man of the nineteenth century would have
described it as the language of the emotions, an irrational form of speech
capable of expressing the inexpressible.

The variety of answers is in itself an indication of the complex role
that music has played in man's experience. The power of music to evoke a
response in man has led him to make it a part of his most important activities. It has been employed in his religious rituals; it has accompanied him
at work and at leisure; and it has been used as a means of education down
to the present day. The mysterious capacity of music to arouse physical
and psychological reactions has also made it a matter for speculation since
the earliest times. It has been woven into myth and it has inspired philosophers and scientists.

There is another reason why music has been such an important aspect
of human thought. For millennia music was held to be not only an art,
but a science. Tradition ascribes to Pythagoras, a Greek thinker of the
sixth century B.C., the discovery that the relationships of musical tones

are measurable by specific mathematical proportions. Although the earliest makers of musical instruments, such as the man who bored holes in a wooden pipe to produce different tones, must have had some knowledge of these numerical relationships, it was not until the fifth or sixth century B.C. that they were formulated mathematically.

This discovery, that sound is subject to the rational laws of number, was one of the first intimations the Greeks had that nature is an orderly process. If the harmony which exists between tones is the product of mathematical proportions, could it be possible that other aspects of the world are regulated by the same numbers? May not the succession of the seasons, the ebb and flow of the tides, the balance and discords of the human spirit all be related through the same proportions? May not music be the foundation of the universe? As a result of such speculations music became the companion of arithmetic, geometry, and astronomy as a science that measures and explains the causes and relationships of the universe. In subsequent centuries the evolution of music as an art was continually to be influenced by the premises of music as a science. Even today the mathematical aspect of music is an important element in the theories of many composers.

The complexity of the tradition of music is also to be explained by the fact that of all the arts, with the exception of the dance, music has had the least historical continuity. The monuments of ancient Greece can still be seen; the wall paintings of primitive cave men, ancient Chinese art, the artifacts of past civilizations are still here to remind us of the painter's mode of expression. Shakespeare is as valid a literary experience today as is T. S. Eliot. But musical works of art have quickly disappeared from the memory and experience of man. Music to be known must first be performed. As new works have engaged the attention of the performer, the music of preceding generations has lapsed into desuetude and finally oblivion. In this process even the systems of notation of earlier composers were forgotten. Their compositions were embalmed in hieroglyphs indecipherable to later generations. As a result, the life of a musical composition was until very recent times little more than a century unless some special tradition or sanction preserved it beyond its normal span, as, for example, when the Catholic church canonized the sixteenth-century contrapuntal idiom of Palestrina as the true style for religious music.

Ignorance of musical styles of the past has had both a fructifying and a debilitating effect upon music. His familiarity with only the immediate musical past has enabled the composer to develop new styles in comparative freedom. At the same time the composer and the listener have been denied their rightful heritage. Until historians of music in the latter part of the eighteenth century began to rediscover the music of previous epochs and until devoted groups of musicians in the nineteenth century began to perform them, masterpieces lay unheard in dusty libraries. The revival of music written before the eighteenth century has not been an easy task and it has gained impetus only in recent decades. Unfamiliarity with our musical heritage still makes it difficult for most of us to appreciate the great music of a Guillaume de Machaut or a Jacob Obrecht. It has also made it difficult to fit music within the framework of a general aesthetic. Only too often it is assumed of music that it begins only with Bach, or that music contemporary with Michelangelo and Raphael is primitive or "gothic."

But musical styles and forms are not accidents, nor are they processes divorced from all other aspects of man. Music is created by men for other men; its mode of expression must be comprehensible. In any age the artist must work with the complex of ideas shared by his contemporaries, to whom he naturally speaks. James Joyce's *Ulysses* could not have been written in the age of the first Elizabeth; *The Rake's Progress* of Stravinsky could only have been written in the twentieth century. Like the man of letters, the musician's perception of the world will be conditioned by the intellectual and spiritual climate of his day and this in turn will be reflected in his style. The style of a work of art thus enables us to understand the spirit and ideals of the past, and, conversely, familiarity with the past may illuminate our understanding of a work of art. Thus the task that lies before us is to examine the manifestations of musical style in the light of ideas.

I THE LEGACY OF GREECE AND ROME

OUR STORY of Western music begins with the Greeks. The genius of ancient Hellas is usually thought of in terms of the plastic arts or literature, but even in the prehistory of Greece music was pre-eminent among the arts. In the earliest Hellenic times before the establishment of laws, it was the poet-musician who preserved and guided the traditions of his people through the recitation of the deeds of the heroes of his race. For the early Greeks music was not simply tone as such. It was a composite art: word and music united in the utterances of the bards. The poet, composer, and singer were one, the lawgiver who guided his primitive political society through the examples of proper action recited in his songs. Through the force of his thought, ennobled by musical expression, the musician could move his audience to emotions and actions. This power of music was felt to be of divine origin, and it was said to have come into the possession of mortals as a gift of the gods who had invented musical instruments.

Poetry and music were the transmitters and the mainstay of culture. The first form of education was "musical," by which the Greeks meant an indoctrination into the arts of music and poetry as well as the assimilation of the examples and laws furnished by poetry. Music was considered to be necessary for the preservation of the community and it was inextricably interwoven with the life of the state. All public occasions were graced by music, often performed by the populace. Contests were established in which both singers and instrumentalists participated to win public acclaim.

The role of music in Greek life was enlarged when Pythagoras, the leader of a religious sect in the sixth century B.C., discovered the mathematical principles underlying this art. Passing by a forge one day—so the story goes—Pythagoras became aware of the musical sound of the five hammers being used by the blacksmiths. Four of the hammers, which sounded harmoniously together, weighed respectively 12, 9, 8, and 6 pounds; the weight of the fifth, whose sound was discordant, was not a whole number. Observing these measurements, Pythagoras concluded that harmonies must arise only from the relationship of whole numbers. He then ascertained from the fact that the interval of the octave was formed by the two hammers weighing 12 and 6 pounds that the proportion determining this interval was two to one. The two hammers weighing 12 and 8 pounds, and the two weighing 9 and 6 pounds, being in the proportion of three to two, produced the interval of a fifth. The proportion four to three in the two hammers of 8 and 6 pounds and also in the two of 12 and 9 produced the interval of a fourth. The hammers weighing 8 and 9 pounds yielded the interval of a whole tone.*

The knowledge of the proportions inherent in musical intervals played a significant part in the thought of the followers of Pythagoras, who believed in the immortality and the transmigration of the soul. These beliefs led the Pythagoreans to seek an explanation of the universe in terms of immortal, immutable, suprasensible things. The orderly world of number, which had manifested itself in the discovery of the numerical basis of musical relationships, provided them with the necessary key. They concluded that all phenomena, spiritual and physical, were manifestations of the all-embracing laws of numerical proportions. Number determined not only the quantities, but also the qualities of objects.

It was held, for example, that the numbers 1, 2, 3, 4, constituted the nature of magnitudes. Greek mathematicians frequently represented numbers by points. The number one is symbolized by a point, and two by two points from which a line, the first dimension, is produced. With three points a triangle or surface appears, and with four a pyramid or solid. The number four also included the elements: fire, air, earth, and water; the four seasons of the year; and the ages of man: infancy, youth, manhood, and old age. Through such associations mathematics was raised from the level of a practical science of counting and measuring to the level of philosophical speculation. Music, as a mathematical science, explained and ruled the universe.

* This account of Pythagoras's discovery must be apocryphal, since the mere weight of an object does not determine its pitch. Nevertheless it gives the mathematical proportions governing the relationship of tones correctly. Sound is a form of vibration and any tone can be measured by the number of vibrations per second. A tone which sounds as the octave to another tone is actually vibrating just twice as fast: the proportion is 2:1.

The orientation of music towards mathematics increased the reverence in which it was already held. Music, which had acted as the binding force of society, was now seen to link all phenomena. Thereafter the Greek attitude towards music became highly complex. Music was not only the composite art of poetry and music, but also a primary element of philosophy: it was the mirror of the mathematical universe. Music may consequently be assessed according to its effects upon human activities or as a symbol of the natural and supernatural world.

The importance of music as an educational and speculative element was upheld in the philosophy of Plato. Plato's utterances on music are to be found primarily in two sources, *The Republic* (380–370 B.C.) and *Timaeus*, a dialogue written subsequently. In the *Republic* Plato is concerned with the problem of what is just. Concluding that justice ultimately resolves into the relationship between individuals, Plato held that this virtue could exist only in a society founded upon sound principles. Consequently he was moved to outline the requisites of an ideal state in which justice could flourish. It was to be a state in which every class was to have its own function. Living in an age when war was ever-present, Plato saw the necessity of a well-trained class of warriors who were to be the guardians of the state. Since such a class would inevitably be the most powerful force within the Republic, it was foreseen that the warriors might easily pervert their power and thus destroy the very state that they had been appointed to guard. It was imperative that the soldiers should be properly educated and indoctrinated with right principles, so Plato devoted a considerable portion of his work to the problems of the substance and form of education.

In the *Republic* Plato inquires of Adeimantus,

"What, then, is our education? Or is it hard to find a better than that which long time has discovered? Which is, I suppose, gymnastics for the body and for the soul music." "It is." "And shall we not begin education in music earlier than in gymnastics?" "Of course." "And under music you include tales, do you not?" "I do." "And tales are of two species, the one true and the other false?" "Yes." "And education must make use of both, but first of the false?" "I don't understand your meaning." "Don't you understand," I said, "that we begin by telling children fables, and the fable is, taken as a whole, false, but there is truth in it also? And we make use of fable with children before gymnastics." "That is so." "That, then, is what I meant by saying that we must take up music before gymnastics." *

The education envisioned here by Plato is, as he says, one of long tradition. It is the "musical" education of hoary antiquity coupled with

---

* This and the following quotation are from Plato, *The Republic*, tr. Paul Shorey. The Loeb Classical Library.

gymnastics to train and develop the body. Music is to be instilled in the child from its earliest years, even before its body is trained through gymnastics. Through the words, be they fable or true, the child learns the code of moral behavior which he is to imitate. For this reason it is most important that the words should present only proper examples. Plato accordingly devotes the best part of one book to the discussion of what subjects are proper for such fables and poetry. But words are only one aspect of musical art, and Plato eventually takes up the problem of its tonal side.

"After this, then," said I, "comes the manner of songs and tunes?" "Obviously." "And having gone thus far, could not everybody discover what we must say of their character in order to conform to what has already been said?" "I am afraid that 'everybody' does not include me," laughed Glaucon; "I cannot sufficiently divine offhand what we ought to say, though I have a suspicion." "You certainly, I presume," said I, "have a sufficient understanding of this—that the song is composed of three things, the words, the tune, and the rhythm?" "Yes," said he, "that much." "And so far as it is words, it surely in no manner differs from words not sung in requirement of conformity to the patterns and manner that we have prescribed?" "True," he said. "And again the music and rhythm must follow the speech." "Of course." "But we said we did not require dirges and lamentations in words." "We do not." "What, then, are the dirge-like modes * of music? Tell me, for you are a musician." "The Mixolydian," he said, "and the tense or higher Lydian, and similar modes. . . ."

In the continuation of this passage Plato proceeds to exclude certain modes and instruments which are not conducive to the propagation of the virtues required of the guardians.

It should be noticed first of all that Plato accepts the ethos of the modes unquestioningly. For him the individual character of each scale is self-evident. Consequently the same criteria are to be applied to tones as to words; both must represent only those qualities desirable for the development of moral character. The subject matter of poetry and its musical expression are to be chosen for a specific purpose, namely to form the proper character in a particular class of citizens. The exclusion of certain forms of poetry and music is not due, as is frequently claimed, to Plato's bias against the arts in general, but to the fact that these do not conform to the purpose at hand.

The second important conclusion to be drawn from this passage is that words and music as an inseparable unit share the same task: the expression of an idea. Melody, in other words, must be framed in a mode

---

* The modes are the Greek scales. Unlike modern scales, they were sung downward from the highest note to the lowest. Each scale bore the name of a Greek tribe and was supposed to possess a specific character or *ethos*. See below, pp. 19 f.

and rhythm that conform to the idea of the words. Thus the composer is not free to work according to his own arbitrary precepts. Instead his art must be conditioned by the end to be achieved, the presentation of an idea suitable for the molding of character.

Despite the limitations which Plato imposes upon musical types, music is the sine qua non of education. Without it education and the state could not exist. Music is thus thrust into a position of extraordinary importance in the Platonic scheme of things. The emphasis accorded here to the role of music is not idle theorizing on the part of Plato. It is maintained also by his pupil, Aristotle, and must be an accurate reflection of the status of music in Greek society. However, music in this form of education cannot as yet be properly termed science or knowledge. It is a formative principle, guiding and molding the character of the young. The children subject to this educative process are indeed shaped by it, but they do not understand the reason for such an education, nor do they know the reasons for the choice of the specific examples given to them. The next step in education must be, then, the development of intellectual awareness.

While the musical education is sufficient for the guards, a higher form of knowledge is required for the rulers of the state. The men who were to be the leaders of the community were to be drawn from the guardian class; to them was to be entrusted the power of final decisions. Since they must understand the principles upon which the state has been founded, it is necessary that they be more than molded by education. They must see beyond the examples provided by music to the truths which lie behind them. They must, in other words, be philosophers—philosopher kings. They must be given an education that will lead them above empiric observation and obedience to experience to the realm of ultimate causes.

The first step in the progress to this goal is for Plato the mastering of the mathematical arts, of which he names five: arithmetic, plane geometry, solid geometry, music, and astronomy. These disciplines are related to each other in that they are different aspects of the general art of number. By formulating laws and principles, which may be viewed in the abstract at the same time that they are perceptible to the senses, the various branches of mathematics direct the mind to first causes. They reveal for the first time the principles underlying the concrete manifestations of nature. Through mathematics the philosopher moves toward his goal, the contemplation of the eternal rather than the transitory, the causes rather than the effects. Music, then, is an essential part of higher education. At this level, however, music is studied not as an art but as a science. It is the mathematical laws discoverable in music that make it a subject worthy to guide the mind to philosophy. Manifestly the position accorded to music in the *Republic* of Plato is one of paramount importance, exceeding by far the status of any other art. It is the means through which the character of the state is sustained and it is one of the roads by which the ruler attains philosophical knowledge.

In the later *Timaeus* Plato soars to a vision of the creation of a universe regulated by musical proportions. He relates how the Maker of the universe fashioned a perfect, spherical body from the matter of the four elements of fire, air, earth, and water, and animated it with a soul destined to be its ruler. Since the model for this universe is the eternal idea of a perfect creature, Plato maintains that the world soul, which rules it, must partake of the nature of such a creature. According to Plato, we may make three forms of assertions about a thing: that it *exists*, that it is the *same* as itself, and that it *differs* from any other form. Therefore the prototype of the soul, if it is truly perfect, must exist eternally and indivisibly and must be ever the same as itself and ever different from all else. As a being created after such a model, the world soul must share these qualities of Existence, Sameness, and Difference. But since it owes its existence to a Maker who may terminate it when he so desires, the world soul does not possess these qualities in the same degree of perfection as its model. Furthermore, since it contains within itself the possibility of all that has bodily existence, the soul must possess an Existence that is divisible and a Sameness and a Difference that are likewise divisible. The soul of the world is thus a blend of indivisible and divisible Existence, Sameness, and Difference. It occupies an intermediate position between eternal idea and the transitory forms of idea realized in matter.

Having created the substance of the soul out of these three forms, the Maker divided and distributed it throughout the whole universe. Plato describes this process as follows:

And when He had mixed them, and had made of them one out of three, straightway He began to distribute the whole thereof into so many portions as was meet; and each portion was a mixture of the Same, of the Other, and of Being. And He began making the division thus:

First He took one portion from the whole (1);

then He took a portion double of this (2);

then a third portion, half as much again as the second portion, that is, three times as much as the first (3);

the fourth portion He took was twice as much as the second (4);

the fifth three times as much as the third (9);

the sixth eight times as much as the first (8); and

the seventh twenty-seven times as much as the first (27).

After that He went on to fill up the intervals in the series of the powers of 2 and the intervals in the series of powers of 3 in the following manner:

He cut off yet further portions from the original mixture, and set them in between the portions above rehearsed, so as to place two Means in each interval,—one a Mean which exceeded its Extremes and was by them exceeded by the same *proportional part* or *fraction* of each of the Extremes respectively (the "harmonic mean"); the other a Mean which exceeded one Extreme by the same *number* or *integer* as it was exceeded by its other Extreme (the "arithmetical mean").

And whereas the insertion of these links formed fresh intervals in the former intervals, that is to say, intervals of 3:2 and 4:3 and 9:8, He went on to fill up the 4:3 intervals with 9:8 intervals. This still left over in each case a fraction, which is represented by the terms of the numerical ratio 256:243 (the semitone).*

What Plato visualizes in this difficult passage is the division of the world soul into related parts organized according to the principles of a musical scale. First of all he divides the substance of the soul into portions which produce the series 1, 2, 3, 4, 8, 9, 27. In terms of musical proportions this would give us the notes in Illustration 1 (assuming that Plato

ILLUSTRATION 1

was thinking of the Dorian scale ranging downward from E and that the numbers represent the length of strings). From this example it may easily be seen that the proportion 1:2 produces an octave; 2:3, a fifth; 3:4, a fourth; 4:8, another octave; 8:9, a whole tone; and 9:27, a twelfth or an octave plus a fifth. Next the intervals of the octave and twelfth are filled in with tones obtained through the arithmetical progression 2:3:4 and the harmonic progression 3:4:6. By applying these two progressions to the original series (whose numbers we multiply by six in order to avoid fractions), still more tones are formed. In the example in Illustration 2 the tones of the original series are written as whole notes and the ones derived from this second step are written as quarter notes.

ILLUSTRATION 2

* Plato, *Timaeus*, tr. R. G. Bury, The Loeb Classical Library.

Finally the scale is completed by filling in the fourths with two whole steps and a half step. The first fourth thus becomes the *tetrachord*, or series of four notes, EDCB, while the second becomes the tetrachord AGFE, and so on. Some inconsistencies arise in the latter part of the series, particularly at the end where fifths rather than fourths occur. This is of no great moment, since Plato is concerned not with a literal but a poetic conception of the constitution of the scale.

After imposing order upon the material of the soul, which is imagined by Plato to be a length gradated by the various musical proportions, the Maker of the world split this fabric lengthwise into two halves. These he formed into a cross, joining them in their centers. Then he bent each into a circle with the ends meeting opposite their first point of contact. The outer circle became the sphere of the fixed stars having but one motion. The interior circle, however, was subdivided into seven other circles which were the individual orbits of the seven planets. The first circle's motion is the motion of the Same while that of the second is the motion of the Different. Weaving these heavenly motions of the soul together with material of the four elements, the structure of the entire universe is finally completed.

It should be apparent that music is here raised to the region of metaphysics. Music lies at the very beginning of the universe; through it order is brought into the world. Thus at every level of existence music is a controlling factor. It is one of the ultimate truths of a universe framed in the beginning by its Maker in musical proportions. At a lower level it is the science of number, leading away from the purely physical and temporal to the contemplation of the abstract and intelligible world. Lastly it is the union of word and tone, an art which in everyday life is the means by which the character of the citizens is formed. In this way music encompasses every phase of human life. It is the precondition of man's very existence; a key to the knowledge of ultimate truths; and the trainer and conditioner of man's earthly life.

The lofty position of music in the philosophy of Plato was not maintained in the system of his pupil and ultimate opponent, Aristotle. The diminished role accorded to music by Aristotle is to be attributed not to any anti-musical bias on his part but to a fundamental disagreement between Plato and Aristotle on first principles. For Plato the true goal of knowledge was the archetypal Idea lying behind all perceptible things. It is not then the shadowy world of physical reality that should engage our attention but the luminous heaven of pure Ideas. Nevertheless, in the last two decades of Plato's life his Academy at Athens was increasingly preoccupied with the problem of how the physical universe is connected with the Idea upon which it was modelled. Plato had answered in the *Timaeus* that it is by means of the power of number which is both a substance and an abstraction. His disciples therefore busied themselves with the classification of natural objects, seeking to find their relationships and proportions.

The discussions of this question were at their height when Aristotle came to the Academy in 367 at the age of seventeen. It is probable that the trend towards scientific investigation during the years of Aristotle's training in the Academy helped form his mind. Becoming insatiably curious about the phenomena of this world, he eventually grew dissatisfied with Plato's explanation of number as the determiner of the form of all things, for number failed to take into account the phenomenon of motion. In Plato's cosmology motion had not been imparted to the universe through any power inherent in number but by the creator who set the spheres spinning in their appointed directions with a push of his hand. Aristotle, seeking some first cause that would account for motion, was led to transform Plato's static Idea into a dynamic Eidos, Form that is forever realizing itself in matter, causing motion in this very act. He thus set up an eternal antithesis between Form, the determiner and quality of all things, and Matter, an undifferentiated chaotic substance which is determined by Form. Whereas Plato's Idea had presupposed the ultimate unity of all things, Aristotle conceived of a multiplicity of forms to explain the manifold objects of nature. He assumed, furthermore, that these forms exist only insofar as they *are* materialized. Plato's Idea remains independent of material existence and would lose nothing if it were never to be imitated in the physical world. But the forms of Aristotle are destined from the beginning to be imposed upon matter. Without this act of becoming concrete they would have neither function nor meaning. Form and Matter may be antipodal but they can exist only in terms of each other. The flux and change of the natural world are the result of the process of Form forever infusing itself into Matter.

Aristotle in his philosophy abstracts and intellectualizes the multiplicity of forms, organizing them through the rigorous application of logic. It is well to remember, however, that no matter how intellectual his view of the world may appear in his philosophy, it is always assumed to be grounded in physical reality. When Aristotle's approach to philosophical truth is compared with Plato's it is not difficult to see why the importance of music is inevitably diminished. No longer is music the organizing force of the universe, as it was for Plato. It is now only one of innumerable natural phenomena, a physical rather than a metaphysical object. Music is a particular form realized in a particular matter and its numerical basis is stripped of any metaphysical implications for the rest of the universe. Consequently in dealing with this art Aristotle directs his interest primarily to how music manifests itself and its uses and action.

Aristotle's most extensive discussion of music is to be found in his *Politics*. Like Plato's *Republic*, this book outlines the requisites of an ideal state. While Aristotle differs with Plato in admitting that there may be more than one form of the ideal society due to differences in natural conditions and the like, he agrees with him that the state must be formulated with some end in view. For Aristotle this end is the attainment and exercise of virtue.

Let us acknowledge then that each has just so much of happiness as he has of virtue and wisdom, and of virtuous and wise action. God is a witness to us of this truth, for he is happy and blessed, not by reason of any external good, but in himself and by reason of his own nature. And herein of necessity lies the difference between good fortune and happiness; for external goods come of themselves, and chance is the author of them, but no one is just or temperate by or through chance. In like manner, and by a similar train of argument the happy state may be shown to be that which is best and which acts rightly; and rightly it cannot act without doing right actions, and neither individual nor state can do right actions without virtue and wisdom. Thus the courage, justice, and wisdom of a state have the same form and nature as the qualities which give the individual who possesses them the name of just, wise, or temperate.*

It is important to note that for Aristotle virtue is not just the passive possession of virtuous qualities. Virtue must realize itself in right actions; it is a form which must be imposed upon matter. Since virtue and virtuous action are the goals of both the individual and the state, it follows that the legislators must see to it that the citizens are formed in the stamp of virtue. The education devised to attain this end must, furthermore, take into account the nature of the human soul because virtue is a property of the spirit.

Now the soul of man is divided into two parts, one of which has a rational principle in itself, and the other, not having a rational principle in itself, is able to obey such a principle. And we call a man in any way good because he has the virtues of these two parts. In which of them the end is more likely to be found is no matter of doubt to those who adopt our division; for in the world both of nature and of art, the inferior always exists for the sake of the better or superior, and the better or superior is that which has a rational principle. This principle, too, in our ordinary way of speaking, is divided into two kinds, for there is a practical and a speculative principle. This part, then, must be similarly divided. And there must be a corresponding division of actions; the actions of the naturally better part are to be preferred by those who have it in their power to attain to two out of the three or to all, for that is always to every one the most eligible which is the highest

* This and the following quotation are from Benjamin Jowett's translation of the *Politics*.

attainable by him. And the whole of life is further divided into two parts, business and leisure, war and peace, and of actions some aim at what is necessary and useful, and some at what is honourable. And the preference given to one or the other class of actions must necessarily be like the preference given to one or the other part of the soul and its actions over the other; there must be war for the sake of peace, business for the sake of leisure, things useful and necessary for the sake of things honourable. All these points the statesman should keep in view when he frames his laws; he should consider the parts of the soul and their functions, and above all the better and the end; he should also remember the diversities of human lives and actions. For men must be able to engage in business and go to war, but leisure and peace are better; they must do what is necessary and indeed what is useful, but what is honourable is better. On such principles children and persons of every age which requires education should be trained.

The system of education accordingly must be based upon the divisions of the faculties of the soul. In the young child the lower faculty must first be trained. After this, studies must be provided to prepare him for the practical activities of life and for the exercise of his highest rational faculty. Not all practical subjects are to be taught, however, or rather they are to be pursued only insofar as they are indispensable for the necessary activities of life. Preoccupation with a practical subject would imply a concern for some end other than virtue, such as financial gain or the praise and applause of others. Such studies are unworthy of a free man; they are illiberal rather than liberal arts. What then is the position of music? Is it a liberal or an illiberal art? Is it a subject to be pursued only as a practical art, or is it worthy to occupy the hours of leisure which are to be spent in the exercise of the highest faculty of the mind?

At the first stage of education, according to Aristotle,

there are perhaps four customary subjects of education, reading and writing, gymnastics, music, and fourth, with some people, drawing; reading and writing and drawing being taught as being useful for the purposes of life and very serviceable, and gymnastics as contributing to manly courage; but as to music here one might raise a question. For at present most people take part in it for the sake of pleasure; but those who originally included it in education did so because, as has often been said, nature itself seeks to be able not only to engage rightly in business but also to occupy leisure nobly; for—to speak about it yet again—this is the first principle of all things. For if although both business and leisure are necessary, yet leisure is more desirable and more fully an end than business, we must inquire what is the proper occupation of leisure. For assuredly it should not be employed in play, since it would follow that play is our end in life. But if this is impossible, and sports should rather be employed in our times of business (for a man who is at work needs rest, and rest is the object of play, while business is accompanied by toil and exertion), it follows that in introducing sports we must watch the right opportunity for their employment, since we are applying them to serve as medicine; for the activity of play is a relaxation of the soul, and serves as recreation because of its pleasantness. But leisure seems itself to contain pleasure and happiness and felicity of life. And this is not possessed by the busy but by the leisured; for the busy man busies himself for the sake of some end as not being in his possession, but happiness is an end achieved, which all men think is accompanied by pleasure and not by pain. But all men do not go on to define this pleasure in the same way, but according to their various natures and to their own characters, and the pleasure with which the best man thinks that happiness is conjoined is the best pleasure and the one arising from the noblest sources. So that it is clear that some subjects must be learnt and acquired merely with a view to the pleasure in their pursuit, and that these studies and these branches of learning are ends in themselves, while the forms of learning related to business are studied as necessary and as means to other things. Hence our predecessors included music in education not as a necessity (for there is nothing necessary about it), nor as useful (in the way in which reading and writing are useful for business and for household management and for acquiring learning and for many pursuits of civil life, while drawing also seems to be useful in making us better judges of the works of artists), nor yet again as we pursue gymnastics for the sake of health and strength (for we do not see either of these things produced as a result of music); it remains therefore that it is useful as a pastime in leisure, which is evidently the purpose for which people actually introduce it, for they rank it as a form of pastime that they think proper for free men.*

Entertainment and relaxation are to be found both in listening to and performing music. But while these forms of recreation are beyond doubt admissible, music, if it is to be construed as a liberal art, must do more than this. It must have the ability to move the soul and lead it to virtue. Aristotle concedes this ability to music and so admits it to the rank of the liberal arts. His reasons for doing so become clear in the following passage:

But nevertheless we must examine whether it is not the case that . . . it is proper not only to participate in the common pleasure that springs from it, which is perceptible to everybody (for the pleasure contained in music is of a natural kind, owing to which the use of it is dear to those of all ages and characters), but to see if its influence reaches also in a manner to the character and to the soul. And this would clearly be the case if we are affected in our characters in a certain manner by it. But it is clear that we are affected in a certain manner, both by many other kinds of music and not least by the melodies of Olympus; for these admittedly make our souls enthusiastic, and enthusiasm is an affection of the character of the soul. And moreover everybody when

* This and the following quotation are from the translation of the *Politics* by H. Rackham. The Loeb Classical Library.

listening to imitations is thrown into a corresponding state of feeling, even apart from the rhythms and melodies themselves. And since it is the case that music is one of the things that give pleasure, and that virtue has to do with feeling delight and love and hatred rightly, there is obviously nothing that is more needful to learn and become habituated to than to judge correctly and to delight in virtuous characters and noble actions; but rhythms and melodies contain representations of anger and mildness, and also of courage and temperance and all their opposites and the other moral qualities, that most closely correspond to the true natures of these qualities (and this is clear from the facts of what occurs—when we listen to such representations we change in our soul); and habituation in feeling pain and delight at representations of reality is close to feeling them towards actual reality (for example, if a man delights in beholding the statue of somebody for no other reason than because of its actual form, the actual sight of the person whose statue he beholds must also of necessity give him pleasure); and it is the case that whereas the other objects of sensation contain no representation of character, for example the objects of touch and taste (though the objects of sight do so slightly, for there are forms that represent character, but only to a small extent, and not all men participate in visual perception of such qualities; also visual works of art are not representations of character but rather the forms and colors produced are mere indications of character, and these indications are only bodily sensations during the emotions . . .), pieces of music on the contrary do actually contain in themselves imitations of character; and this is manifest, for even in the nature of the mere harmonies (modes) there are differences, so that people when hearing them are affected differently and have not the same feelings in regard to each of them, but listen to some in a more mournful and restrained state, for instance the harmony called Mixolydian, and to others in a softer state of mind, for instance the relaxed harmonies, but in a midway state and with the greatest composure to another, as the Dorian alone of harmonies seems to act, while the Phrygian makes men enthusiastic; for these things are well stated by those who have studied this form of education, as they derive the evidence for their theories from the actual facts of experience. And the same holds good about the rhythms also, for some have a more stable and others a more emotional character, and of the latter some are more vulgar in their emotional effects and others more liberal. From these considerations therefore it is plain that music has the power of producing a certain effect on the moral character of the soul, and if it has the power to do this, it is clear that the young must be directed to music and must be educated in it.

From this argument it is apparent that Aristotle, like Plato, accepts without question the ethos of the modes. Indeed it is because music has this ethical, moral character that it is a suitable activity for the free man. There is, however, an essential distinction in the reasons given by Plato and Aristotle for the existence of moral qualities in this art. Where Plato would in all likelihood have maintained that this phenomenon is in some way related to the power of number, Aristotle explains it in quite another manner. Music is one of the imitative arts and the subject which it imitates is men in action. In other words, music imitates the character of men as it manifests itself in some action. Through this imitative representation of moral states music can arouse a similar or related emotion.

Granted that music is an art which imitates men in action, the question remains of how this is to be accomplished. What quality does music possess that enables it more than any other art to represent such actions? Aristotle's response is that actions are a form of motion and must exist in a temporal succession. In his 27th Problem he states: "[The motions experienced in the soul from music] participate in the regularity that exists in the rhythms, as well as in the successive order of high and low tones. The impressions of the other senses present nothing equal to this. As to the motions produced by musical perception, these lead men to action; and acts are a manifestation of the moral state." The fact that music consists of melodic and rhythmic succession makes it more akin to real states of the soul than other arts, such as painting and sculpture, which can only represent one immovable moment of an entire action.

Aristotle's conception of imitation as a formative principle was not new with him but was derived from a long tradition. Plato too had seen art as a form of imitation which he did not wholly favor. For Plato the ultimate truth was the pure Idea, and the natural world was but an imitation of it. Since art imitated the natural world, it was imitation twice removed from the original. Hence it was not a very elevated approach to the realm of the Ideal. But while Plato's interest was concentrated upon the world of Being, the eternal Idea, Aristotle dwelt upon the realm of Becoming. The world for Aristotle was not a pallid imitation of an ultimate reality, but a direct manifestation of the first principle of all things, form realizing itself in matter. This dynamic principle is also to be found in the human organism; the faculty of thought is in a sense form which constantly manifests itself in action. Thus Aristotle maintained that the subject matter of art is man in action: the moments when the state of the soul reveals itself in concrete form. Granted this principle, it is obvious what the function of the artist must be. He too must impose form upon the material of his art. He must first of all have something material, something palpable to the senses such as colors, marble or tones, upon which to work. Having chosen his subject, some action of man, he derives a form from it by which he organizes his material. In the case of music he establishes an orderly series of rhythms and tones analogous to his subject matter. These, through their quality of motion, have a special affinity with the souls of men. It is not, however, the tone itself, the raw material of music, that gives music its meaning. It is rather the form imposed upon the tone which enables music to reproduce or induce states of the soul. In the act of creation the artist is employing the very principle which governs all manifestations of the universe. For this reason Aristotle gives art an importance far greater than that accorded to it by Plato.

It seems remarkable to us that the Greeks could attribute such extraordinary powers to an art that did not use the resources of harmony. So conditioned are we by harmonic thinking that we find it difficult to believe that Greek music achieved its effect relying only upon melodic and rhythmic organization. But there is no evidence that the use of simultaneously sounding tones played anything other than a nonessential role in Greek music. The lack of harmony was nevertheless compensated for by melodic and rhythmic nuances lacking in our music.

For the Greeks, as for us, music exists within a definite area of sound determined, for all practical purposes, by the range of instruments and voices. Our musical space ranges from the lowest note of the double bass to the topmost note of the piccolo. The Greeks circumscribed musical space within the span of only two octaves that extended from the A above middle C down to the second A below middle C.* This greater perfect system of the Greeks, as it was called, consisted of fifteen tones, of which the A below middle C acted as a tonal center. Because of its central position within the double octave, this A was called the *mese*, meaning middle. The other tones were grouped around the mese in the following manner:

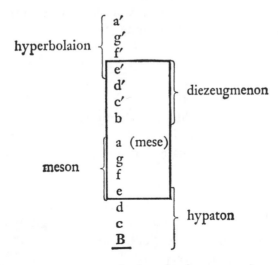

A (proslambanomenos)

* The exact pitch of these notes does not necessarily agree with our modern pitches, but we equate the notes of the Greek scale with ours for the sake of convenience. Actually the Greek range more nearly approximates the double octave a third lower, that is, from the F above middle C down to the second F below middle C. This is about the range of the male voices for whom the music was written.

The intervals within the two octaves were derived from a characteristic arrangement of tones within a perfect fourth. The braces in the diagram mark off these groups of four notes called tetrachords, each of which has the same order of two whole tones and a half tone. To round out the full two octaves low A has been added—*proslambanomenos* meaning literally "the added tone." The four tetrachords are arranged in two conjunct pairs: the lowest tone of one tetrachord is at the same time the highest of the next. Each tetrachord bears a name relating to its function within the greater perfect system. The *tetrachordon hyperbolaion* is the extra tetrachord; the *diezeugmenon* is the disjoined tetrachord, for it is not joined to the tetrachord below it by a common tone. The *tetrachordon meson* is the middle tetrachord, and the *hypaton* is called the highest tetrachord because of its position on the lyre.

By means of this system of tetrachords musical space is divided into two identical octaves, from a′ to a, and from a to A proslambanomenos. It would be a mistake, however, to assume that the Greeks thought of the arrangement of the eight notes within these octaves as the foundation of their musical system. To the contrary, they maintained that the characteristic octave is that which comprises the two tetrachords grouped around the mese. This octave, which is boxed off in the diagram, ranges from e to E and is constructed of two disjunct tetrachords. Its tonal center a is also the center of the totality of musical space contained in the greater perfect system. This species of octave was called the Dorian mode after a Greek tribe. A melody written in this mode gravitates not only towards the e's which determine its limits but also towards the mese, the center of all musical sounds. In this way a subtle relationship between tones is established: there is an interplay of tension and relaxation as the melody moves towards or away from these points of orientation.

The Greeks at the height of their musical development employed seven other species of octave. Each preserved the basic structure of the Dorian scale, but began on a higher or lower tone. To make the sequence of intervals identical with that of the Dorian, it was necessary to alter the pitch of some of the tones of the greater perfect system. Thus the Mixolydian mode, beginning on a′, reads a′ g f e d c b♭ a. The first four notes follow the pattern of the Dorian tetrachord, but in the second tetrachord the b must be lowered half a step in order that the sequence whole step, whole step, half step may be reproduced. The eight modes are in fact nothing but transpositions of one basic scale. The use of the eight modes corresponds somewhat to our use of key signatures, which indicate the tones to be altered in order to reproduce the characteristic succession of intervals of the C major scale beginning on any tone other than C. The modes are presented here with their individual pitches; parentheses surround the note corresponding to the mese of the Dorian scale.

Hypermixolydian *	b′	a′	g	f♯	(e)	d	c	b							
Mixolydian		a′	g	f	e	(d)	c	bb	a						
Lydian			g♯	f♯	e	d♯	(c♯)	b	a	G♯					
Phrygian				f♯	e	d	c♯	(b)	a	G	F♯				
Dorian					e	d	c	b	(a)	G	F	E			
Hypolydian						d♯	c♯	b	a♯	(G♯)	F♯	E	D♯		
Hypophrygian							c♯	b	a	G♯	(F♯)	E	D	C♯	
Hypodorian								b	a	G	F♯	(E)	D	C	B

The internal structure of the scales is the same in all cases. However, the pitch of the notes differs, and the difference in the relative position of the scales gives each one its characteristic emotional association or, as the Greeks termed it, its ethos. Manifestly a melody written in a scale above or below the Dorian will seem more excited or more subdued because of its relatively high or low tonal range.

The ethos of a scale is determined by more than pitch. Greek music, though essentially a vocal art, was accompanied by an instrument, primarily the lyre, which duplicated and reinforced the vocal line. The number of the lyre's strings varied in different periods, but in the "classical" age of Greek music the number was six. The player, starting from a mese, tuned the strings in relation to this central tone in one of three ways:

1.   e d   b a G   E
2.   e d c   a G   E
3.   f   d c   a G F

With the exception of the third tuning, which was resorted to for purely technical reasons, the range of the lyre was that of the Dorian octave. The instrumentalist produced the missing tones in the scale series by stopping or shortening the string with his finger, causing it to sound at a higher pitch. To reproduce the full Dorian scale he would use the first tuning and supply the missing c by stopping the b string, and the missing F by stopping the E string. The Mixolydian, which contains a bb, would require the second tuning, in which the flat is sounded by stopping the a string. In the same manner all of the eight modes can be reproduced.

The lyre can duplicate the tones of the singer as long as the vocalist remains within the limits of the Dorian octave. When the singer's voice

* The first note is fictional, because it lies outside the greater perfect system.

exceeds this range, the instrumentalist must either pause or play the singer's tones an octave higher or lower. The limited range of the lyre within the Dorian span emphasizes the centrality of this octave. At the same time the listener becomes aware of the quite different space occupied by the real scale of the composition. Thus one becomes conscious of the interrelationship of musical space. This relationship, furthermore, is intensified by the fact that each scale has its own mese. In the tuning of the lyre, no matter the mode being used, the primacy of the a mese is always sensed, but the melody itself will nevertheless have as a point of reference the mese of its particular key. In effect, there arises a tension, an interplay of forces, between the immutable mese of the greater perfect system, called the thetic or stationary mese, and the dynamic or mobile mese of the individual scales. Only in the Dorian octave do the two forces coincide. The relationship between two mesae therefore becomes an individual characteristic of each scale. The Hypermixolydian and Hypodorian scales, ostensibly the same since both are B octaves, actually differ in the relationship of their mese to the thetic mese.

This phenomenon of opposing and yet related centers of gravity must have been a decisive factor in attributing ethos to the modes. It also helps to explain the position of esteem that the Dorian mode occupied in Greek thought. Only in the Dorian scale are the mobile and stationary centers the same; all is serenity, repose, and balance. Its ethos therefore is one of virtue and moderation; it is simple but manly and vigorous. It is not surprising that Plato preferred the Dorian for the education of the citizens of his Republic.

Greek melody possessed still other nuances. The intervals which we have seen in the greater perfect system were by no means the only ones utilized. There were three ways, or *genera*, of subdividing a tetrachord. The subdivision into two whole tones and a half tone, which we have already examined, was called the *diatonic* genus. The *chromatic* genus consisted of a minor third and two semitones; the *enharmonic* genus was built out of a major third plus two intervals of roughly a quarter tone each. Every scale had a diatonic, chromatic, or enharmonic form, and its ethos was modified accordingly. Such fine gradations of tone, common in Oriental as well as Greek music, are almost unknown in Western music. They help to explain how the Greeks drew such spiritual sustenance from melody alone.

We have discussed thus far the tonal aspects of Greek music, but music does not live, in a manner of speaking, until it is animated by rhythm. Temporal relationships guide and unify a melody as it pursues its course. For the Greeks it was the text that established the rhythm of a composition; rhythm was thus the link between language and music.

The metrics of Greek poetry rested upon the quantitative measurement of syllables. Syllables are long or short, a long syllable being equal to two short ones. Long and short syllables were variously combined to yield many different meters or feet. The trochee consisted of a long syllable followed by a short one; an anapest was built of two shorts and a long; a spondee of two longs, etc. By combining different feet a subtle and complex rhythmic motion was achieved. Even purely instrumental music used metrical rhythms at times. The *nomos trochaios*, for example, was an instrumental form which employed the meter of the trochee.

Only eleven fragments of Greek music are still extant. One of the most interesting of these is the *Hymn to the Sun* written by Mesomedes in the second century A.D. (Illustration 3). The meter of the poem, except at the end of each phrase, consists mainly of anapests and spondees, producing an alternation of 8/8 and 7/8 measures. Written in the Mixolydian mode, which has d as its mese, the melody stresses the thetic mese a by constantly beginning or ending its phrases on it. The compass of each melodic phrase (the phrase length coinciding with the line of text) is relatively small. The voice moves within the range of a fourth or fifth, and never more than a sixth. Furthermore, in each phrase one or two tones are repeated. The repetition gives each phrase its special quality. The first phrase stresses a, the second dwells upon c. The melody, having emphasized the thetic mese in the first phrase, gradually utilizes the dynamic mese more and more (notice the third and fourth phrases). A tension is thus built up between the two tones. The melody proceeds in steps, employing no large melodic leaps. Such melodic progression is typical of vocal music—at least until quite recent times when vocal melody began to model itself upon instrumental melody.

When Greece submitted to Rome's rising power, its rich musical heritage was not destroyed. On the contrary the Latins absorbed the culture of the race they had conquered. As Rome's military might welded the Mediterranean world into one political unit, the musical thought of the Greeks was carried throughout the length and breadth of the Empire. Though the Romans made few, if any, original contributions to music, the importance of Rome in the history of music lies in the fact that it is through the agency of Latin civilization that Greek musical speculation was transmitted to modern Europe. Even after the military collapse of the Roman Empire, the power of its political and social institutions continued to exercise an influence upon the barbarian tribes who came to pillage, but who remained to become Latinized. In this process of assimilation the pure light of Greek thought flickered and grew dim, but never wholly vanished. From time to time it shone forth again in the periods spoken of as Renaissances.

ILLUSTRATION 3

Hymn to the Sun

Father of the bright-eyed Dawn, who dost drive thy rosy chariot with the winged courses of thy steeds, delighting in thy golden hair, over the boundless vault of heaven shedding thy far-piercing ray and turning over all the earth the farseeing fount of splendor: thy streams of immortal fire bring forth the lovely day. Before thee the gentle chorus of the stars dance over lord Olympus, ever singing their unrestrained song, rejoicing in the lyre of Phoebus. And before thee the silvery Moon in due season leads the way amid throngs of white kine; and thy mild spirit is glad as it speeds through the richly clad firmament.

II THE CHRISTIAN FOUNDATIONS OF WESTERN MUSIC

Part I. Gregorian Chant

THE STUDENT of Western civilization retracing the meandering paths to the past discovers that all converge ultimately upon the institution of the Catholic church. Whatever remains to us of the thought of Greece and Rome has survived largely because it was salvaged by the church. But the church did more than act as a repository for fragments of the past. Borrowing whatever it needed from other traditions, it shaped them to its own purposes. Thus the church created many of the ideas and institutions upon which Western civilization is based.

The period in which the Christian church emerged coincides with the centuries in which Roman power reached its apogee. Indeed the rapidity with which the new faith spread is partly to be explained by the fact that Rome had removed all political barriers from one end of the Mediterranean to the other and had established a unified culture within its dominions. In the years following the Crucifixion small bands of Christians appeared in city after city within the Roman Empire. At first the Roman authorities, traditionally tolerant of new gods, did not welcome the God of the Christians because He demanded that all other divinities be abandoned. Nevertheless the new religion gradually gained ascendancy over its rivals until it became in 313 a legitimate faith through an edict of toleration of the Emperor Constantine. By the end of the century the Christians had become the majority and their religion the official one of the State.

When Christianity changed from a despised and persecuted sect into a state religion, it became necessary to modify the structure of the church itself. In its earliest stages the Christian fellowship had consisted of small bands of believers, each administering unto its own needs. But as a state religion it was imperative that the scattered churches should be ad-ministered by a central organization that could maintain and enforce uniformity in belief and religious practices. In time an ecclesiastical hierarchy developed paralleling the administrative organization of the Roman Empire. The bishops of provincial capitals came to possess a prestige over other local bishops just as the governor of a province was supreme over other officers within his jurisdiction. At the same time there were certain bishoprics which by tradition enjoyed a pre-eminence over all others. These were the sees which had been founded by the Apostles or their immediate disciples. Such were Antioch, Alexandria, Jerusalem, and Rome.

When the Empire was divided into two administrative sections governed from Rome and the newly founded city of Constantinople (consecrated in 330), these two cities came to claim spiritual as well as temporal authority for themselves. The subsequent cleavage between East and West, unforeseen when the Empire was first partitioned, was reflected eventually in the church itself, which divided into the Greek-speaking Eastern Orthodox church and the Latin-speaking Roman Catho-lic church headed by the Bishop of Rome as Pope and Supreme Pontiff. The Roman bishops asserted their primacy over all others, for they were the direct successors to St. Peter to whom Christ had addressed the words: "And I say also unto thee that thou art Peter, and upon this rock I will build my church . . . and I will give unto thee the keys of the Kingdom of Heaven" (Matthew, 16:18–19). By the end of the fourth century the simple faith of the Christians had become an institu-tion, whose strength was such that it has outlived the political forms of the civilization upon which it was based.

During the same years in which the character of the old Roman world was being transformed by the advent of the new church, the very existence of the Roman Empire was threatened by the untamed tribes who lived beyond its northern ramparts. In the course of the fourth century, as Roman resources diminished, the alien peoples encroached upon ter-ritories over which Rome had once held undisputed sway. In successive waves came the Alemanni, Goths, and Huns. At times they came peacefully; more often they entered by force, sacking and pillaging wherever they roved. But even as the barbarians became the actual rulers of the Western Empire, they submitted to the superior civilization which they had conquered. They chose to govern within the existing framework of civil institutions, selecting as their advisers and administrators men from Rome's ancient ruling class. Thus, in the very process of disintegration, the Latin Empire of the West began to form a new civilization, one in which Germanic, Roman, and Christian elements were interwoven to form the basis of the modern European world. It is impossible to say at what point the ancient civilization ceased to exist. Various attempts were made to restore the political hegemony of the Empire, but all ended in failure. After the death of the Emperor Justinian in 565, the decline of the West gained momentum. The Imperial territories were dismembered into ever smaller fragments ruled by barbarians; Roman institutions disappeared; and the Western world slipped ever deeper into darkness, ignorance, and anarchy.

Rome, the city which had given its name to the greatest state yet known to man, never recovered from the effects of the sieges to which it was subjected in the course of the wars of the sixth century. No longer did it have economic or military significance. But the claim to universality once made by Rome as the capital of the civilized world was now taken over by Rome as the seat of spiritual authority. In the centuries of the slow collapse of the Empire, the institution of the church had increasingly assumed the functions abandoned by the state. Not infrequently the bishop of a city became the head of the municipal administration as well, acting in the name of Rome's authority. Judicial powers granted to the church as early as the reign of Constantine were now oftentimes the only means of obtaining justice. The mingling of religious and secular interests, which later gave rise to dissensions and abuses, provided in this period of transition almost the only continuity and stability in a disorganized society. Moreover, the institution of the church became the only force binding upon all the nations emerging from the wreckage of the Roman Empire. The prestige of the church was international; its customs and beliefs were universally accepted; in its rituals the Latin language lived on to become the only means of communication between men of different nations where the vernacular tongues were making their appearance.

One of the functions assumed by the church was education and the conservation of knowledge. This it did because of an inherent need in the Christian faith. Unlike most religions of the period, Christianity was a faith revealed to man through Scriptures. The gods of the Greek and Roman pantheon had manifested themselves in no such sacrosanct writings. They had been worshipped as representatives of the forces of nature with no fixed dogma or specific creed. The God of the Christians on the other hand had made Himself known through the Old Testament and through Christ the Son, the meaning of whose life and teachings were to be found in the New Testament. The Bible, then, was the Word of God. Only through its pages could man learn of his promised salvation and the way to achieve it. The Holy Scriptures alone could provide man with the key to redemption and the blessed life of the hereafter. For this reason the ability to read and interpret the Bible was absolutely necessary to the propagation of the Christian faith.

The work of interpreting the Scriptures began in the earliest days of Christianity, continuing a practice of the Hebrews. At first the followers of Christianity were unsophisticated men drawn from the lowest classes of society. Their faith was direct and untroubled by the doubts and scruples of men of higher education. As the new religion won converts in the higher classes, it became necessary to reconcile the philosophy of the Greeks and Romans, a body of knowledge erected upon firm principles of logic, with the Biblical conception of the universe. It became necessary, in other words, to refute conflicting doctrines, and where this was impossible, to prove that the Scriptural and philosophical statements were but different aspects of the same truth. Accordingly the men of the church, at first contemptuous of the learning of the secular world which they viewed as a hated symbol of pagan evil, were eventually compelled to master and assimilate the vast body of knowledge built up by non-Christians.

In the third and fourth centuries Christian writers still went to secular schools where they received the traditional training of the Romans. There they encountered a curriculum based upon the seven liberal arts. These included the "trivium" or three arts of language: grammar, dialectic, and rhetoric; and the "quadrivium," the four mathematical arts of arithmetic, geometry, music, and astronomy. At these schools they also absorbed the doctrines of the neo-Pythagoreans and neo-Platonists whose speculations about number dominated the philosophy of the first centuries A.D.

As the secular schools and libraries disappeared before the onslaught of the barbarians, the store of knowledge dwindled alarmingly. Manuscripts in libraries and private homes were destroyed by violence or by neglect. Greek was gradually abandoned as the language of learning and the writings of Greek philosophers became unknown unless they had been translated into Latin. By the seventh century there remained of Plato's works only a translation of part of the *Timaeus;* of Aristotle only minor treatises on logic survived. A few Latin treatises dealing with one or another of the liberal arts also remained to become the principal text-books of the Middle Ages. Most notable of these were the grammatical works of Donatus and Priscian and the treatises on arithmetic and music by Boethius.

Attempts were made to salvage some of the accumulated wisdom of the past by compiling encyclopedic summaries of all knowledge. It was in these abstracts that the mediaeval world found most of its learning and its knowledge of the seven liberal arts. There are three of these encyclopedias. One is *The Marriage of Mercury and Philology* by Martianus Capella (early fifth century), an allegory that culminates in a summary of the subject matter of the seven liberal arts. The second is the *Institutiones divinarum et humanarum lectionum* (*The Foundations of Sacred and Secular Readings*) written by Cassiodorus some time after 551. This is a summary and catalog of important sacred and secular books "extremely useful, since through them one learns the indicated origin of both the salvation of the soul and secular knowledge." The third is the *Etymologiarum sive originum libri XX* (*The Twenty Books of Etymologies or Origins*) compiled by Bishop Isidore of Seville between 622 and 633. In this work knowledge is reduced to principles of interpretation of words. "The power of a word or name is gathered together by means of interpretation," the Bishop wrote. "When you see from whence a name is derived, you will more rapidly understand the power of this word." The method of symbolic and rhetorical interpretation found in these encyclopedias left its impress upon the mediaeval mind and in time exerted an influence upon the development of music.

By the end of the sixth century the pattern of mediaeval learning had emerged. Education henceforth was to be carried on in monastic establishments sheltered from the unending wars by their situation in hidden valleys and wildernesses. It was to be a wholly Christian education with secular subjects taught only as an aid to the interpretation of the Scriptures. The instruction provided by the monks for the young boys, who were themselves to become clerics, was in the darkest days of the decline of the West little more than a smattering of the elements of language, such as reading, writing, and grammar, as well as arithmetic and music. These subjects were the necessary minimum for the preservation and execution of the rites of the church. Thus even in this ebb tide of human history music remained an indispensable part of education.

The idea of music as a speculative science belonging to the seven liberal arts was transmitted to the Middle Ages by the early doctors of the church as well as by the encyclopedists. The writings of St. Augustine (354–430), whose theology dominated the early Middle Ages, are full of the symbolism of number derived from the neo-Pythagoreans. In a treatise devoted to music the great saint demonstrated how the knowledge of the numerical relationships that regulate rhythm may lead one to an understanding and contemplation of the order and system with which God has invested the universe. The most influential musical treatise, however, was written by Boethius (470–80; 524–26). His *De institutione musica* (*Concerning the Science of Music*) remains incomplete, for it discusses only the theoretical, numerical basis of music. But this very restriction is important because it led the men of the Middle Ages to think of music primarily in terms of its mathematical structure. Boethius, furthermore, passed on the Pythagorean and Platonic conception of music as the ordering force of nature. Like Plato, he sees music existing at three different levels. He speaks of these as *musica mundana*, the music of the universe and the elements of nature, *musica humana*, the proportions of the soul and its harmonious relation to the body, and *musica instrumentalis*, sounding music in either its vocal or instrumental forms. This tripartite division of music was subsequently brought into line with Christian premises by making *musica mundana* the eternal song of praise rising to the Creator from the revolving spheres of the heavens and the angelic hosts inhabiting them.

Though the role of music as a theoretical science won for it an honored place in mediaeval learning, the knowledge of this science shrank to pitiful proportions. Few men knew anything more about it than was to be found in the writings of the encyclopedists. How meager this knowledge was may be seen from the following exposition of music taken from the *Institutiones* of Cassiodorus.*

1. A certain Gaudentius, writing of music, says that Pythagoras found its beginning in the sound of hammers and the striking of stretched strings. Our friend Mutianus, a man of the greatest learning, has translated the work of Gaudentius in a manner attesting his skill. Clement of Alexandria in his *Exhortation to the Greeks* declares that music received its origin from the Muses, and takes pains to make clear for what reason the Muses themselves were invented: they were so named *apo tou mosthai*, that is, from inquiring, because, as the ancients would have it, they were the first to inquire into the power of songs and the modulation of the voice. We find also that Censorinus, in his treatise *De die natali*, addressed to Quintus Cerellius, has written things not to be overlooked concerning musical discipline, or the second part of mathematics, for which reason it is profitable to read him, in order to implant those things more deeply in the mind by frequent meditation.

2. The discipline of music is diffused through all the actions of our life. First, it is found that if we perform the commandments of the Creator and with pure minds obey the rules he has laid down, every word we speak, every

* Translated by Oliver Strunk, *Source Readings in Music History*.

pulsation of our veins, is related by musical rhythms to the powers of harmony. Music indeed is the knowledge of apt modulation. If we live virtuously, we are constantly proved to be under its discipline, but when we commit injustice we are without music. The heavens and the earth, indeed all things in them which are directed by a higher power, share in this discipline of music, for Pythagoras attests that this universe was founded by and can be governed by music.

3. Music is closely bound up with religion itself. Witness the decachord of the Ten Commandments, the tinkling of the harp, the timbrel, the melody of the organ, the sound of cymbals. The very Psalter is without doubt named after a musical instrument because the exceedingly sweet and grateful melody of the celestial virtues is contained within it.

4. Let us now discuss the parts of music, as it has been handed down from the elders. Musical science is the discipline which treats of numbers in their relation to those things which are found in sounds, such as duple, triple, quadruple, and others called relative that are similar to these.

5. The parts of music are three: harmonics, rhythmics, metrics.

Harmonics is the musical science which distinguishes the high and low in sounds.

Rhythmics is that which inquires whether words in combination sound well or badly together.

Metrics is that which by valid reasoning knows the measure of the various meters; for example, the heroic, the iambic, the elegiac.

6. There are three classes of musical instruments: instruments of percussion, instruments of tension, wind instruments.

Instruments of percussion comprise cup-shaped vessels of bronze and silver, or others whose hard metal, when struck, yields an agreeable clanging.

Instruments of tension are constructed with strings, held in place according to the rules of the art, which upon being struck by the plectrum delightfully soothe the ear. These comprise the various species of cithara.

Wind instruments are those which are actuated to produce a vocal sound when filled by a stream of air, as trumpets, reeds, organs, pandoria, and others of this nature.

7. We have still to explain about the symphonies. Symphony is the fusion of a low sound with a high one or of a high sound with a low one, an adaptation effected either vocally or by blowing or striking. There are six symphonies: [here Cassiodorus names the fourth, fifth, octave, octave plus fourth, octave plus fifth, and the double octave, giving their numerical ratios, not, however, without error].

8. Key is a difference or quantity of the whole harmonic system, consisting in the intonation or level of the voice. There are 15 keys: [here Cassiodorus gives the names of Greek modes, and their relative pitches].

From this it appears that the Hyperlydian key, the highest of all, exceeds the Hypodorian, the lowest of all, by seven tones. So useful, Varro observes, is the virtue displayed in these keys that they can compose distraught minds and also attract the very beasts, even serpents, birds, and dolphins to listen to their melody.

9. But of the lyre of Orpheus and the songs of the Sirens, as being fabulous matters, we shall say nothing. Yet what shall we say of David, who freed Saul from the unclean spirit by the discipline of most wholesome melody, and by a new method, through the sense of hearing, restored the king to the health which the physicians had been unable to bestow by the virtues of herbs? Asclepiades the physician, according to the ancients a most learned man, is recorded to have restored a man from frenzy to his former sanity by means of melody. Many other miracles have been wrought upon the sick by this discipline. It is said that the heavens themselves, as we have recalled above, are made to revolve by sweet harmony. And to embrace all in a few words, nothing in things celestial or terrestrial which is fittingly conducted according to the Creator's own plan is found to be exempt from this discipline.

10. This study, therefore, which both lifts up our sense to celestial things and pleases our ears with melody is most grateful and useful. Among the Greeks Alypius, Euclid, Ptolemy, and others have written excellent treatises on the subject. Of the Romans the distinguished Albinus has treated it with compendious brevity. We recall obtaining his book in a library in Rome and reading it with zeal. If this work has been carried off in consequence of the barbarian invasion, you have here the Latin version of Gaudentius by Mutianus; if you read this with close attention, it will open to you the courts of this science. It is said that Apuleius of Madaura has also brought together the doctrines of this work in Latin speech. Also St. Augustine, a father of the church, wrote in six books *De musica*, in which he showed that human speech naturally has rhythmical sounds and a measured harmony in its long and short syllables. Censorinus also has treated with subtlety of the accents of our speech, declaring that they have a relation to musical discipline. Of this book, along with others, I have left a transcript with you.

The oldest music still in widespread use today is that of the Catholic church, the so-called Gregorian chant. An enormous body of compositions, organized into a highly complex and artistic repertoire, it is obviously not the work of one man, nor even a single generation of composers. Just as centuries were required before the church was firmly established, so too the liturgy and music of the divine service were evolved only slowly and painstakingly. With the Edict of Milan in 313, the Emperor Constantine granted to the new church liberty and official approval. The church could now move in freedom to establish for itself a permanent foundation. One of the first steps taken was the erection of the basilicas as permanent houses of worship. With the establishment of permanent buildings where the Christian community might congregate openly without fear of persecution, more carefully regulated forms of worship slowly began to evolve.

In general, the forms of the Christian services were the result of adapting Jewish rites to the doctrinal demands of the new religion. The spoken word was of utmost importance, but there was also a place for music, as there had been in the liturgy of the Jewish synagogue. Only vocal music was admitted, sung to prescribed Biblical texts. In the establishment of a uniform rite numerous difficulties were encountered. The lack of communication and the relatively low standards of literacy attendant upon the break-up of the Roman civilization prevented the diffusion of a universal liturgy with regulated forms of worship and prescribed texts. The absence of a written form of notation—the Greek system having disappeared from practice—made the dissemination of the music of the service from one community to another, as well as from generation to generation, dependent upon oral transmission. For centuries, therefore, local practices continued to dominate the liturgy. In the period from the fourth through the sixth centuries there were established several regional rites observed in different locales: the Ambrosian in Milan, the Gallican in France, the Mozarabic in Spain, the Beneventan in lower Italy, and the so-called Gregorian in Rome, the seat of the Papacy. Of these only the Roman need concern us, for ultimately all the others were supplanted by it.

Before proceeding to the chant, the forms of the liturgy must be sketched in broad outline, for the music of the church is at all times conditioned by the liturgical purposes it aims to serve. The chant, being music sung to a prescribed text, would seem to have come into being only after the texts for the service had been established. But the selection of these texts, in turn, was determined both by the season of the church year and by the type of service in which they occur. For this reason our discussion must begin with a brief description of the church calendar.

For Christianity Christ is the center of worship. It is only natural, therefore, that the events of His life should form the basis of the church calendar. By fixing the times of Christmas and Easter on the calendar, all other events could be arranged around these two most important feasts. Four Sundays before Christmas the season of Advent begins, a period of anticipation and expectancy of the birth of Christ. The forty days before Easter comprise the season of Lent, a time of mourning and penitence for the death of Christ upon the Cross with which He bought the salvation of mankind. Other days related to the life of Christ are fixed by their relation to the days of His birth and death. In addition to these central observances, the church in its long history has added to the calendar other feasts in honor of the saints. These commemorative services are fitted into the order of the church year without interfering with the feasts celebrating the life of Christ. The church year, then, begins with the fourth Sunday before Christmas, the First Sunday in Advent, and proceeds through Christmas, Lent, Easter, Ascension Day, Pentecost and on through the summer and fall months, to begin again with the next Advent season.

Not all services held during the church year are of the same kind, for there are different purposes to be served within the general mode of worship. In the Catholic church there are two basic types of worship service—the Mass and the Daily Offices or Hours. Of the latter, which are devoted to prayer and praise, there are eight, beginning in the very early morning and continuing until after sundown: Matins, Lauds, Prime, Terce, Sext, None, Vespers, and Compline. Of these Offices only Matins and Vespers are observed by the laity; all, however, are part of the daily exercises of monastic orders.

The Mass, which is also a daily service coming between Terce and Sext, is distinguished from the other observances because of its special form of worship. In it the Communion is celebrated, commemorating the Last Supper. The faithful of the church who partake of the bread and wine, which by Divine Grace have been miraculously changed into the body and blood of Jesus, achieve a mystical union with Christ. Obviously, this is a service which outranks all others in solemnity and importance. Because of its pre-eminent position in the order of divine worship the Mass has called forth the greatest artistic efforts of composers down through the ages.

As a form of worship, the Mass is divided into two consecutive parts: the Preparation and the Sacrifice. In the first part, confessions, prayers, and readings from the Scriptures prepare the worshippers for their participation in the act of communion. Originally this part of the Mass was a separate service. It was called the Mass of the Catechumens because it was intended for the uninitiated who were receiving instruction in the tenets of Christianity. It is followed in the second part by three successive acts: first, the Offertory, the offering of the bread and wine; second, the Consecration, during which the bread and wine are changed into the body and blood of Christ; and finally the Communion, the receiving of the sacred offering.

If the order of service for a particular day, for example, Easter, is followed step by step, the significance of the liturgy will emerge. The service opens with a group of preparatory prayers said before the altar, after which the choir sings the *Introit*. Originally this chant was a Psalm with an *antiphon* or refrain sung as the priests entered the church in procession from the sacristy, but it has been curtailed so that all that now remains are the antiphon, one verse of the Psalm and the *doxology*, with the antiphon repeated after the doxology. The text for the Introit varies from day to day. For this reason it is called "proper" because it has been selected for its appropriateness to the season or feast being celebrated.

Introit

ANTIPHON: [pieced together from phrases of the 18th, 5th, and 6th verses of Psalm 138] Resurrexi, et adhuc tecum sum, alleluia: posuisti super manum tuam, alleluia: mirabilis facta est scientia tua, alleluia, alleluia.

VERSE: [Psalm 138:1, 2] Domine probasti me, et cognovisti me: tu cognovisti sessionem meam, et resurrectionem meam.

DOXOLOGY: Gloria patri et filio et spiritui sancto, sicut erat in principio, et nunc et semper et in saeculum saeculorum. Amen.

ANTIPHON: Resurrexi, et adhuc tecum sum, etc.

ANTIPHON: I arose, and am still with thee, alleluia: thou hast laid thy hand upon me, alleluia: thy knowledge is become wonderful, alleluia, alleluia.

VERSE: Lord, thou hast proved me, and known me: thou hast known my sitting down, and my rising up.

DOXOLOGY: Glory be to the Father, the Son and Holy Ghost, as it was in the beginning, is now, and ever shall be. Amen.

ANTIPHON: I arose, and am still with thee, etc.

Following the Introit there is sung the *Kyrie eleison* and directly thereafter the *Gloria*. These two texts, in contrast to the Introit, are said to belong to the Ordinary of the Mass, for they remain unchanged throughout the year, unaffected by the season or feast being celebrated. The texts for these chants are as follows:

Kyrie

Kyrie eleison, Kyrie eleison, Kyrie eleison.
Christe eleison, Christe eleison, Christe eleison.
Kyrie eleison, Kyrie eleison, Kyrie eleison.

Lord, have mercy, Lord, have mercy, Lord, have mercy.
Christ, have mercy, Christ, have mercy, Christ, have mercy.
Lord, have mercy, Lord, have mercy, Lord, have mercy.

Gloria

Gloria in excelsis Deo. Et in terra pax hominibus bonae voluntatis. Laudamus te. Benedicimus te. Adoramus te. Glorificamus te. Gratias agimus tibi propter magnam gloriam tuam. Domine Deus, Rex caelestis, Deus Pater omnipotens. Domine Fili unigenite, Jesu Christe. Domine Deus, Agnus Dei, Filius Patris. Qui tollis peccata mundi, miserere nobis. Qui tollis peccata mundi, suscipe deprecationem nostram. Qui sedes ad dexteram Patris, miserere nobis. Quoniam tu solus sanctus. Tu solus Dominus. Tu solus Altissimus, Jesu Christe. Cum Sancto Spiritu, in gloria Dei Patris. Amen.

Glory be to God on high, and on earth peace to men of good will. We praise thee; we bless thee; we adore thee; we glorify thee. We give thanks for thy great glory, O Lord God, heavenly King. God the Father almighty. O Lord Jesus Christ, the only-begotten Son; O Lord God, Lamb of God, Son of the Father, who takest away the sins of the world, have mercy upon us; who takest away the sins of the world, receive our prayers; who sittest upon the right hand of the Father, have mercy upon us. For thou only art holy; thou art Lord; thou only, O Jesus Christ, art most high, together with the Holy Ghost, in the glory of God the Father. Amen.

Immediately we notice that, in contrast to the Introit, these texts (with the exception of the first two phrases of the Gloria) have not been adapted from the Holy Scriptures. The Kyrie eleison, retaining as it does the Greek language, harkens back to the first centuries of the Christian era before the Latin language superseded Greek in the Western church. We may also note that the Gloria is often called the greater doxology in contrast to the lesser doxology used after the verse of the Introit.

Following the Gloria come the *collects*, short prayers proper to the season that are intoned or uttered by the priest. The collects ended, one of the assisting clergy goes to the lectern to read or recite the Epistle lesson. For Easter Day, the reading is a selection from the Apostle Paul's first letter to the Corinthians, Chapter five, verses seven and eight. Since the Epistle lesson is chosen for its appropriateness to the season of the year, it too is designated as part of the Proper of the Mass. After the lesson has been concluded, the choir sings the *Gradual* and the *Alleluia*, two chants whose texts are proper to the day.

Gradual

RESPOND: [Psalm 117:24] Haec dies, quam fecit Dominus: exsultemus, et laetemur in ea.

VERSE: [Psalm 117:29] Confitemini Domino, quoniam bonus; quoniam in saeculum misericordia ejus.

RESPOND: This is the day which the Lord hath made; let us be glad and rejoice therein.

VERSE: Give praise to the Lord for he is good: for his mercy endureth forever.

Alleluia

Alleluia, Alleluia.

VERSE: [I Corinthians 5:7] Pascha nostrum immolatus est Christus.

Alleluia, Alleluia.

VERSE: Christ our paschal lamb is immolated.

The Gradual originally encompassed more than the single verse which now remains. Like the Introit, it consisted of an alternation of the respond with succeeding verses of a Psalm. The Alleluia, on the other hand, consisted of a lengthy florid melody sung only to the word alleluia. This long flourish of melodic enthusiasm was an expression of unutterable religious ecstasy which St. Augustine called the *jubilus:* "a certain sound of joy without words." The verses associated with the Alleluias appear to be later additions. Because of the joyous nature of its musical expression the Alleluia is omitted in seasons of mourning and penitence. In its place is sung the *Tractus,* a chant of considerable length and undoubtedly of great antiquity.

As the liturgy of the Mass is constituted today, the *Sequence, Victimae paschali laudes,* is sung after the Alleluia on Easter Day. The sequence was a poetic text composed and introduced into the liturgy in great numbers after the ninth century. However, by decree of the Council of Trent in the sixteenth century only four sequences were retained in the liturgy; in the eighteenth century a fifth, the famous *Stabat Mater dolorosa,* was readmitted into the Mass. *Victimae paschali laudes,* which dates from the first half of the eleventh century, is presented in modern books of the chant in the version approved by the Council of Trent. In the revision one stanza, *V*a, was omitted and the order of others rearranged. Since this version obscures the structure of the poem, the sequence is given below in its original form.

1. Victimae paschali laudes
immolent Christiani.

iia. Agnus redemit oves,
Christus innocens Patri
reconciliavit
peccatores.

iib. Mors et vita duello
conflixere mirando,
dux vitae mortuus
regnat vivus.

iiia. Dic nobis, Maria,
quid vidisti in via?

iiib. Angelicos testes,
sudarium et vestes.

iva. Sepulcrum Christi viventis,
et gloriam vidi
resurgentis.

ivb. Surrexit Christus, spes mea;
praecedet suos in
Galilaeam.

va. Credendum est magis soli
Mariae veraci,
quam Judaeorum
turbae fallaci.

vb. Scimus Christum surrexisse
a mortuis vere,
tu nobis, victor
Rex, miserere.

1. Let Christians dedicate their praises to the Easter victim.

iia. The lamb has redeemed the sheep; the innocent Christ has reconciled the sinners with the Father.

IIb. Death and life have fought in wondrous conflict; after death the leader of life, living, reigns.

IIIa. Tell us, O Mary, what thou sawest upon thy way?

IIIb. The angelic witnesses, the veil and the garments.

IVa. I have seen the sepulchre of the living Christ, and the glory of Him rising.

IVb. Christ, my hope, has arisen, he goes before his own into Galilee.

Va. Truthful Mary is more to be believed than the false crowd of Jews.

Vb. We know in truth that Christ has arisen from the dead: be merciful unto us, O victorious king.

The second of the scripture readings, the Gospel lesson, follows the singing of the Sequence. For Easter Day the lesson is selected from the Gospel according to Mark, Chapter 16, verses 1–7. Then, as a conclusion to the Mass of the Catechumens, the *Creed* is sung. This part of the Ordinary is a late addition to the liturgy, having been introduced shortly after the year 1000.

Credo

Credo in unum Deum, Patrem omnipotentem, factorem caeli et terrae, visibilium omnium, et invisibilium. Et in unum Dominum Jesum Christum, Filium Dei unigenitum. Et ex Patre natum ante omnia saecula. Deum de Deo, lumen de lumine, Deum verum de Deo vero. Genitum, non factum, consubstantialem Patri: per quem omnia facta sunt. Qui propter nos homines, et propter nostram salutem descendit de caelis. Et incarnatus est de Spiritu Sancto ex Maria Virgine: Et homo factus est. Crucifixus etiam pro nobis: sub Pontio Pilato passus, et sepultus est. Et resurrexit tertia die, secundum Scripturas. Et ascendit in caelum: sedet ad dexteram Patris. Et iterum venturus est cum gloria, judicare vivos et mortuos: cujus regni non erit finis. Et in Spiritum Sanctum, Dominum, et vivificantem: qui ex Patre Filioque procedit. Qui cum Patre et Filio simul adoratur, et conglorificatur: qui locutus est per Prophetas. Et unam sanctam catholicam et apostolicam Ecclesiam. Confiteor unum baptisma in remissionem peccatorem. Et exspecto resurrectionem mortuorum. Et vitam venturi saeculi. Amen.

I believe in one God, the Father Almighty, Maker of heaven and earth, of all things visible and invisible. All in one. Lord Jesus Christ, the only-begotten Son of God. And born of the Father before all ages: God of God, light of light, true God of true God, Begotten, not made, consubstantial with the Father; by whom all things were made. Who for us men, and for our salvation, descended from heaven; and was incarnate by the Holy Ghost, of the Virgin Mary: and was made man. He was crucified also for us, suffered under Pontius Pilate, and was buried. And the third day He rose again, according to the Scriptures; And ascended into heaven. He sitteth at the right hand of the Father; And again He shall come with glory to judge the living and the dead; His kingdom shall have no end. And in the Holy Ghost, the Lord and giver of life, Who proceedeth from the Father and the Son; Who together with the Father and the Son is adored and glorified; Who spake by the prophets. And one, holy, Catholic and apostolic church. I confess one baptism for the remission of sins. And I await the resurrection of the dead, And the life of the world to come. Amen.

At this moment the second part of the Mass begins, which treats of the commemoration of the Lord's Supper. As an accompaniment to the placing of the Elements—the Bread and Wine—upon the altar, the *Offertory* is sung. Originally it was an antiphon and a psalm; now only the antiphon remains. Like the Introit, the Offertory text is chosen for its appropriateness to the particular feast celebrated and is therefore part of the Proper of the Mass. For Easter Day the Offertory text is verses 9 and 10 of Psalm 75.

Offertory

Terra tremuit, et quievit, dunc resurgeret in judicio Deus, alleluia.
The earth trembled and was still, when God arose in judgment. Alleluia.

After the choir has concluded the singing of the Offertory, the priest alone offers a group of prayers which mark and accompany the various stages of the offering of the Host and Chalice. At the conclusion of these prayers and the reciting of the Twenty-fifth Psalm during the washing of the priest's hands, the priest in a low voice offers a prayer called the Secret—a prayer like the collects—in which God is asked to accept the offerings of the people (the bread and wine) and to grant His grace unto the believers.

The Preface, which leads into the *Sanctus*, is appropriately selected from a small group of texts—about fifteen at present. The Sanctus, part of the Ordinary of the Mass, is interrupted before the words *Benedictus qui venit* have been sung, for it is at this moment that the miracle of the changing of the bread and wine into the body and blood of Christ takes place.

Sanctus

Sanctus, sanctus, sanctus Dominus Deus Sabaoth. Pleni sunt caeli et terra gloria tua. Hosanna in excelsis. Benedictus qui venit in nomine Domini. Hosanna in excelsis.

Holy, holy, holy, Lord God of hosts. Heaven and earth are full of thy glory. Hosanna in the highest. Blessed is He that cometh in the name of the Lord. Hosanna in the highest.

Another group of prayers called the Canon of the Mass is uttered by the celebrant during the singing by the choir of the Sanctus. It is during his recital of prayers that he repeats the words of Jesus as He officiated at the Last Supper.

Immediately after the final Amen of the Canon the priest sings the Lord's Prayer, and then the act of breaking the bread and the com-mingling of the consecrated Elements takes place, accompanied by appro-priate prayers. The choir follows these prayers with the singing of the *Agnus Dei*, part of the Ordinary of the Mass.

Agnus Dei

Agnus Dei, qui tollis peccata mundi, miserere nobis.
Agnus Dei, qui tollis peccata mundi, miserere nobis.
Agnus Dei, qui tollis peccata mundi, dona nobis pacem.

Lamb of God, who takest away the sins of the world,
have mercy upon us.
Lamb of God, who takest away the sins of the world,
have mercy upon us.
Lamb of God, who takest away the sins of the world,
grant us peace.

The prayer which follows is a prayer for peace and is succeeded by the kiss of peace. The celebrant now partakes of the communion accom-panied by several prayers. Then the choir sings the *Communion*, a proper chant which, like the Offertory, has been shortened from a complete Psalm with an antiphon to the antiphon alone.

Communion

[I Corinthians 5:7, 8] Pascha nostrum immolatus est Christus, alleluia: itaque epulemur in azymis sinceritatis et veritatis. Alleluia, alleluia, alleluia.

Christ our Paschal Lamb is immolated, alleluia: therefore let us feast with the unleavened bread of sincerity and truth. Alleluia, alleluia, alleluia.

This chant originally had to be of considerable duration for it accom-panied the partaking of communion by the congregation. The reduction of the chant to its present size was made when the communion act was limited to a select few and the need for a chant of protracted length ceased to exist. After the Communion, the priest says aloud a final prayer, the Post-communion, which is followed by the dismissal:

Ite, missa est, alleluia, alleluia.
RESPOND: Deo gratias, alleluia, alleluia.

Go, you are dismissed, alleluia, alleluia.
RESPOND: Thanks be to God, alleluia, alleluia.

The word *missa* (in English, Mass) of this concluding formula has given its name to the entire service.

In this outline of the Mass only those texts normally set to music have been quoted. Certain of these have been designated as "proper," others as "ordinary." Generally the texts of the Ordinary are not drawn directly from the Bible, while the texts of the Proper for the most part are excerpted from the Psalms. The items of the Ordinary, whatever prior history they may have had, were admitted into the liturgy of the Mass later than those of the Proper, and they have never been organically necessary to the liturgy. As a consequence, their position has not been so securely established as those of the Proper. During certain seasons of the church year the Gloria and Credo are excluded from the Mass. On the other hand, the items of the Proper are functionally necessary to the very meaning of the rite.

The chants of the Proper may be divided into two types. Chants of the first type are the Introit, originally a Psalm sung by the choir during the procession of the clergy from the sacristy into the church; the Offertory, likewise in its earliest form a Psalm, sung to accompany the bringing of the offerings to the altar; and finally the Communion, also at one time a complete Psalm, sung by the choir during the distribution of the Sacred Elements. These then are compositions introduced into the service to occupy time taken by the performance of ceremonies. The fact that all have been much abbreviated is the result of changes made in the performance of the ceremonies for which they provide a musical accompaniment.

The second type of proper chant includes those which are not subordinate to another act; nothing else occurs in the liturgy during their performance. These chants, the Gradual and the Alleluia (and at certain seasons, the Tract and Sequence), are sung between the reading of the Epistle and Gospel lessons. Originally, three lessons were read (a reading from the Prophets preceded the Epistle lesson) and the Gradual and Alleluia were chants sung by the choir between the readings. After the reading from the Prophets was excluded from the service, the two chants were still retained, directly following each other between the two remaining lessons.

In addition to the different functions of the chants of the Proper and Ordinary, their methods of performance also serve to distinguish them. The chants of the Ordinary were intended for performance by the congregation or the officiating clergy. As might be expected, the chants intended for untrained singers were simple, unadorned melodies. Later, when the choir became responsible for the performance of the Ordinary, changes took place in the melodies reflecting the greater capacities of the professional singers.

The various chants of the Proper, on the other hand, were intended from the beginning for the choir. There are, however, different manners of performing these chants. The Introit, Offertory, and Communion are called *antiphonal* chants; the Gradual and Alleluia, *responsorial* chants. In antiphonal chants, the choir is divided into two equal parts, which sing alternate sections of the chant. Originally, the antiphonal chants encompassed an entire Psalm and an antiphon which introduced and concluded the Psalm and could also serve as a refrain between the verses. The two bodies of singers sang alternate verses of the Psalm, or one group sang all the verses while the second responded to each verse with the antiphon.

In the Introit text quoted above vestiges of the older practice are present, despite the omission of all but one verse of the Psalm. The abbreviation of the Introit was accomplished in two stages. When the number of Psalm verses was reduced to one, the antiphon preceded and followed the lone verse; then the doxology was sung, and finally the antiphon was repeated as a conclusion. Thus the antiphon was sung three times in the following order: Antiphon—Verse—Antiphon—Doxology—Antiphon. The present arrangement of the Introit resulted when the repetition of the antiphon between the verse and the doxology was omitted. In the Offertory and Communion of the Easter Day service not even a single verse remains, the text having been reduced to the antiphon alone, and one can no longer recognize in these chants their original antiphonal form.

Responsorial chant is similar to antiphonal chant in that it also proceeds in alternation between divisions of the choir. But now the division involves a solo singer or singers to whom the remainder of the choir responds. Thus there is introduced into the service a place for the soloist. In the earliest times the Gradual was a complete Psalm with a respond. The oldest records indicate that in the performance of this and other responsorial chants the soloist first sang the respond after which the choir repeated it; then he sang a verse of the Psalm and the choir responded by repeating a second time the respond, and so forth. Thus the Gradual had the form: Respond (soloist)—Respond (choir)—Verse (soloist)—Respond (choir) and so forth. Vestiges of the older practice may still be found in the liturgy of Easter Week. There the respond of the Gradual, *Haec dies*, is retained throughout the week but with a different verse on each day. No doubt, these Graduals of Easter Week were originally a single composition, which has since been split up and distributed over the entire week.

When the number of verses was reduced, the method of performing responsorial chants was altered. The soloist now sings the respond to a point marked by an asterisk in modern chant books where the choir enters singing the remainder of the respond. Then the soloist sings the verse to the asterisk at which point the choir enters and concludes the chant. Thus the alternation of soloist and choir has been retained, even though the principle of a recurrent refrain has been abandoned.

From the preceding description of the church calendar, the forms of worship, and the structure of the individual items of the liturgy, one could surmise—correctly—that the melodies to which the texts are sung must be conditioned by the structure of the text and its function in the liturgy. A chant, for this reason, should not be viewed as a work of art leading an independent existence by virtue of its artistic merits alone. On the contrary, it lives completely only when it fulfills the function for which it was created—the artistic adornment of the rites of the church. Whatever artistic merit it may possess, a chant is still subordinate to the liturgy and is created in conformity to the structure and purpose of its text. Individual expression, vain artistic display or idle decoration are suppressed. The great achievement of the composers of the chant, whoever they may have been, was to create a repertory of liturgical music, universal in its expression and decorous in its artistry.

Because of their different purposes and their great variety of texts, the chants of the church possess a wide range of melodic forms and types. We must distinguish first of all between those chants which are no more than melodic formulae suitable for a variety of texts and those melodies created for a specific text. In the description of the Mass it was noted that the lessons were read or intoned. If the solemnity of the Mass calls for the second, more artistic method of rendering the lesson, the cleric intones it according to a musical formula called a *Lection Tone*, either the Epistle or Gospel Tone as the case may be. A Lection Tone consists of nothing more than a recitation upon a fixed pitch, the *reciting tone*, with an occasional raising or lowering of the pitch reflecting normal speech inflections determined by the punctuation of the text. One and the same formula may be used for any number of texts intended for such a recitation.

More highly developed melodic formulae are the *Psalm Tones*, used for singing the Psalms in the Offices. These are more sensitive to normal speech inflections than the Lection Tones. They are essentially a stylization of the narrative tones of the speaking voice, which rises at the beginning of a sentence, sustains itself on a tonal plateau as the thought is continued, and drops only at the end of a phrase or with the final period. The Psalm Tones regularly begin with a group of notes rising to a reciting tone and conclude with a descent to a point of rest. They also reflect in their structure the characteristic division of each verse of a Psalm into two parts. The example in Illustration 1 illustrates how the first two verses of Psalm 109 are sung to the first Psalm Tone. The remaining verses of this Psalm, which is the first of five Psalms prescribed for the Vesper Service on Christmas Day, are fitted to the same formula in a similar manner.

ILLUSTRATION I

Di-xit Do-mi-nus Do-mi-no   me-o: Se-de a dex-tris me-is.

Do-nec po-nam in-i-mi-cos tu-os,   sca-bel-lum pe-dum tu-o-rum

The gradually rising tones of the word *Dixit* translate into precise pitches the natural speech inflection of an opening word in a sentence. The last of these three tones, *a*, is the reciting tone on which the next word *Dominus* is sustained. With the words *Domino meo* a slight rise and fall preparatory to the end of the first part of the verse brings the music to a point of momentary rest. By stopping on the reciting tone, the melody suggests that this is only a slight caesura in the middle of the verse. This little turn of phrase and the pause on the reciting tone translate into music the speech inflections induced by the colon which divides the verse into two members. In the second half of the verse, which commences on the reciting tone, the final words *dextris meis* have a turn of phrase that suggests in its falling tones the completion of a thought. A sense of finality not present at the end of the first part of the verse is achieved by concluding at a pitch below that of the reciting tone.

Though the Psalms are to be performed by a choir, the initial phrase of the first verse is always sung by a soloist. This is done for a practical reason—to establish the pitch for the other performers. Since the Psalm is sung in its entirety, the continuity of the verses is emphasized by beginning the second and all the remaining verses on the reciting tone instead of using the initial formula of rising tones. This practice corresponds to the natural intonation of the speaking voice which tends to begin successive sentences on the pitch level at which most of the discourse is delivered.

A few comments on the notation of the chant are in order. Chant melodies are of such limited range, rarely encompassing more than an octave, that a four-line staff is usually sufficient for them. The pitches of the staff are determined by clef signs. ▮ marks the line representing Middle C. The only other clef used in chant notation ▮▮ identifies the

F below Middle C. Single tones are represented by the forms ■ and ◖. The notes joined together in groups are called *ligatures*. They are used to indicate a succession of tones sung to a single syllable.

The most common ligatures are read according to the following rules: when one note is written directly above another ▐, the lower note is sung first; when two notes are joined together in this form ▙, they are read from left to right; and the ligature of two notes, one above the other with a stem extending downward from the upper note ▐, is read from top to bottom. The figure ◪ is a ligature of three notes. The uppermost part of the heavy oblique line represents the first note, the end of the line the second, and the square note above, the third. At one time the various note shapes may have had rhythmic values associated with them, but they no longer signify precise durations of time. Nevertheless, in fairly recent years the monks of Solesmes have devised a method of rhythmic measurement which has received the official approval of the church. Their system does not rest upon indisputable historical evidence, however, and it is the subject of considerable controversy among scholars.

Psalms performed in the Offices are invariably introduced and concluded by the singing of a prescribed antiphon. Furthermore, the doxology is sung after the Psalm before the repetition of the antiphon. Each of its two lines is sung to the Psalm Tone. The complete performance of a Psalm therefore follows the form: Antiphon, Psalm, Doxology, Antiphon. The antiphon, in contrast to the pliable melodic formula of the Psalm, is a composed melody and consequently has a fixed and unchangeable form. Since musical continuity from the antiphon to the Psalm and from the doxology to the antiphon is desired, the melodic characteristics of the antiphon will determine which of the various Psalm Tones is selected for the performance of the Psalm and doxology. The chant in Illustration 2, *Tecum principium*, is the antiphon for Psalm 109 sung at Vespers on Christmas Day.

ILLUSTRATION 2

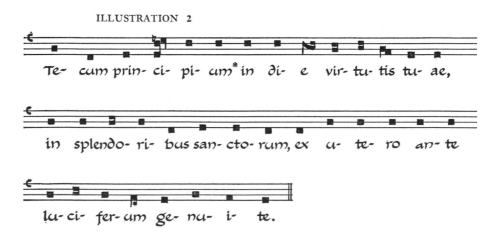

Te- cum prin- ci- pi- um* in di- e vir- tu- tis tu- ae,

in splendo- ri- bus san- cto- rum, ex u- te- ro an- te

lu- ci- fer- um ge- nu- i- te.

This antiphon is said to be in the first or Dorian mode. What is a mode? Everyone is familiar with the usage of describing scales as major or minor. These two terms in reality describe two different modes, two different patterns of whole and half steps within the scale. The mediaeval modes are also patterns of whole and half steps, but they include other characteristics as well. Each mode, of which there are eight, has three principal features. One is the *final*, the note on which the mode rests. In any composition the final is the note on which the piece normally ends. The second feature of a mode is its range or *ambitus*. Theoretically only an octave range is assigned to each mode, but slight extensions above and below the theoretical limit are admitted. The third characteristic of a mode is the reciting tone. In a melodic formula such as a Psalm Tone the reciting tone is easily detected. In a composed melody, however, it plays a less prominent role and the use made of it will be less obvious. The reciting tone is, nevertheless, the note around which much of the composition normally is centered. The eight mediaeval or church modes are arranged schematically in the table below. The underscored letter represents the final, and the letter placed in a box is the reciting tone.

ɪ Dorian	D̲ E F G a̅ b c d
ɪɪ Hypodorian	A B C D̲ E F̅ G a
ɪɪɪ Phrygian	E̲ F G a b c̅ d e
ɪᴠ Hypophrygian	B C D E̲ F G a̅ b
ᴠ Lydian	F̲ G a b c̅ d e f
ᴠɪ Hypolydian	C D E F̲ G a̅ b c
ᴠɪɪ Mixolydian	G̲ a b c d̅ e f g
ᴠɪɪɪ Hypomixolydian	D E F G̲ a b c̅ d

Though their names are obviously borrowed from the Greek modes, the church modes do not correspond to those of the earlier Greek system, for the musicians of the Middle Ages had misunderstood the ancient theorists. For one thing, the mediaeval modes were viewed as ascending scales, while the Greek modes were descending scales. Moreover, the eight modes of the mediaeval system are true modes, each having an internal structure differing from the others, while the Greeks had only one mode shifted to higher or lower levels of pitch.

It is apparent from the table that no one feature of the modes is sufficient to distinguish them. Although there are eight modes, only four tones, D, E, F, and G, serve as finals. Modes I, IV, and VI, furthermore, have the same reciting tone, a, and modes III, V, and VIII use c as the reciting tone. Finally, the Dorian and Hypomixolydian modes share the same range from D to d. Therefore to define the modes all three characteristic features are essential. The Dorian and Hypodorian modes, for example, though they have the same final, are still distinguishable one from another by their different ranges and reciting tones. In the case of the Dorian and Hypomixolydian modes, their ambitus may be the same, but they differ in their finals and reciting tones.

Without doubt the complete system of modes was the product of theorists who abstracted them from the features of existing melodies as a means of classifying the chants. However theoretical the system may be, it exerted a strong influence upon later composers and upon those responsible for the preservation of the music of the liturgy. Old melodies have often been revised to bring them into agreement with the modal system, and compositions of later vintage conform to the modal system in greater degree than do the oldest chants.

To return to the antiphon *Tecum principium*, it may now be observed that its final D conforms to the normal ending of Dorian melodies. The reciting tone, a, of the Dorian mode is not prominent; only the first phrase, after the initial rising figure, centers around it. Nevertheless, coming near the beginning of the chant it places its stamp upon the melody and identifies the chant with the Dorian mode. Finally, the range of the antiphon, from C to b♭, lies within the Dorian octave D to d, with the exception of the C. The C, called the *subfinal*, is so often present in Dorian chants that it has come to be an integral part of the mode.

The melodic characteristics of this Dorian antiphon, it can be seen, agree with those of the first Psalm Tone illustrated in the first example. Both melodies employ the same reciting tone and lie within the same range. These two factors insure a substantial degree of musical agreement between the antiphon and the Psalm. Usually, in performing the antiphon before the Psalm, it is cut off at the point of the asterisk, the remainder being omitted. The reason for this practice may be deduced from the antiphon *Tecum principium*, where this portion of the chant ends on a, the reciting tone, and so provides an excellent introduction to the Psalm Tone which follows immediately. During the performance of the verses of the Psalm and the doxology, no decisive cadence is reached at the end of the melodic formula; it provides only a point of rest for the voice at the end of the phrases. This dip in the melodic line also serves as a smooth transition to the concluding rendition of the entire antiphon, which brings the whole performance to a satisfying close as the melody descends for the last time to the final of the mode. Thus a coherent and artistic structure has been created through the skillful use of the properties of the mode. It clearly conveys the idea of a beginning (the initial antiphon), a sustained central portion (the Psalm and doxology), and a final resolution (the concluding antiphon).

In the Psalm Tones and Lection Tones each syllable of the text is normally sung to a single note. Occasionally ligatures, in which a syllable is carried through a group of notes, break the regularity of the declamation and help to place emphasis upon particular words. These occur regularly at the beginning and ending of the formula. This type of singing in which there is generally only one note for each syllable is described as *syllabic*. The syllabic style is not limited to Psalm and Lection Tones, but is also found in other types of chant. The antiphon *Tecum principium*, for example, is predominantly a syllabic chant.

In this antiphon ligatures are introduced at important moments in the melodic line. The first ligature in the opening phrase leaps from D, the final of the mode, to the reciting tone, a, and pushes on to the b♭ above. The upward thrust of the melody is finally halted on the next syllable as it comes to rest momentarily on the reciting tone. This ligature contains a most important melodic phrase because in it the two most essential notes of the mode are emphatically introduced. The leap from the final to the reciting tone at the very beginning of the chant is significant for another reason as well. Here the high point and climax of the melody are suddenly reached.

After this almost dramatic beginning the tension created by the upward leap of the first ligature is relaxed in the four successive, smoothly flowing ligatures on the syllables (*di*)*e virtutis*, and the melody comes to rest at the final on the word *tuae*. The opening words of the text have formed a complete musical phrase in which all the characteristics of the mode are sharply defined. From this point the chant flows along at a lower level of pitch in a quieter, more subdued vein. Two more sections of text are set forth in clearly articulated musical phrases. The ligatures here give stress to the accented syllable of words of four syllables: *splen-dó-ri-bus, lu-cí-fe-rum*. Although the antiphon possesses a higher degree of artistry than the Psalm Tone, it nonetheless adheres to the syllabic style of the psalm formula. This it does of necessity, for its function within the liturgy is to frame the Psalm. The appropriateness of the antiphon to the Psalm is evidence of the taste and artistic judgment of the ecclesiastical musician.

There are other chants, such as the Gloria and Credo, which utilize a predominantly syllabic style because their texts are so long. The performance of these chants would be unduly protracted unless their texts were treated syllabically. In the example of a Gloria in Illustration 3 most of the syllables are sung to a single note; those provided with ligatures are usually stressed syllables of polysyllabic words.

This Gloria is in the seventh, or Mixolydian mode. In previous examples of the chant the entire range of the mode was not employed, but here the range has been fully utilized. Indeed, slight extensions beyond the normal range occur from time to time. Occasionally, as at the cadence of the first phrase on the word *Deo,* the melody dips down to E before returning to the final. The subfinal, F, also appears frequently. The upper limit of the mode is exceeded only once, near the end of the chant, but this deviation falls at an appropriate moment within the phrase *Tu solus altissimus* (Thou only art most high). The two pivotal notes of the mode, the final, G, and the reciting tone, d, are the only ones used as points of rest at the end of the phrases of the text. Even the short caesuras within phrases employ only these two notes to pause on momentarily. The constant recurrence of the characteristic notes of the mode at all cadential points and at the beginning of the majority of the phrases forcefully emphasizes the modality of the entire chant.

In addition to modality, another factor contributing to the unity

ILLUSTRATION 3

Glo-ri- a in ex- cel- sis De- o. Et in ter- ra pax

ho-mi- ni- bus bo-nae vo- lun- ta- tis. Lau-da-mus te.

Be-ne- di- ci-mus te. A-do- ramus te. Glo-ri-fi- camus te.

Grati- as a- gi-mus ti- bi propter magnam glori-am tuam.

Domi-ne De- us, Rex cae- le- stis, De-us Pa-ter omnipotens.

ILLUSTRATION 3 (*continued*)

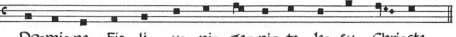

Do-mi- ne Fi- li u- ni- ge- ni- te, Je- su Chri-ste.

Do-mi- ne De- us, A- gnus De- i, Fi- li- us Pa- tris.

Qui tol-lis pec-ca- ta mundi, mi- se- re- re no- bis. Qui tol-lis

pec-ca- ta mun-di, sus- ci- pe de-pre-ca- ti- o-nem nostram.

Qui se-des ad dex-te-ram Pa- tris, mi- se- re- re no- bis.

Quoni- am tu so- lus san-ctus. Tu so-lus Do-mi- nus.

Tu so- lus Al- tis- si-mus, Je- su Chri-ste. Cum Sancto

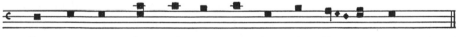

Spi- ri- tu, in glo-ri- a De- i Pa- - tris.

A- - - - men.

of the chant is the use of melodic correspondences. These are often suggested by the text itself, if it possesses balanced phrases or rhymes. But prose texts, such as the Gloria, generally contain few such symmetries. When they do occur, the composer often avails himself of the opportunity they present for musical repetitions. Some of the simpler settings of the Gloria are replete with examples of this device. In the Gloria illustrated above, the composer has disguised the musical repetitions by slight variations. Thus in the repetition of the words *Qui tollis peccata mundi*, he has established a relationship between the two phrases by repeating the melody of the words *Qui tollis* one step higher, which serves at the same time to intensify the expression of the text. Another manner of handling musical repetitions is to transfer a melodic figure from one phrase to some other position within another phrase. The rise and fall of the melody on the words *in excelsis* in the opening phrase of the chant is repeated in the following phrase over the words *pax hominibus* to mark an internal cadence. Such musical correspondences, woven subtly through the chant, create a sense of cohesion and unity while avoiding the obviousness of a literal repetition.

In the responsorial chants involving solo performers we meet with melodies which in their ornateness are far removed from the schematic formulae of the Psalm Tones or the predominantly syllabic chants of the Credo and Gloria. Indeed, from a purely musical point of view, the elaborate melodies of the Gradual and Alleluia make the syllabic chants seem somewhat pedestrian by comparison. The Alleluia for Easter, shown in Illustration 4, illustrates the extent to which single syllables could be drawn out in long musical flourishes.

The group of notes provided for any one syllable is called a *melisma*, and a composition in which such groups predominate is said to be written in a *melismatic* style. If this chant seems unduly long in relation to the brevity of the text, it must be remembered that the time taken up by the performance of the Alleluia was not limited or restricted in any way by the liturgy. The Alleluia and the Gradual preceding it represent the *musical* high point of the Mass and it is to be expected that the purely melodic element of the chant should overshadow the text. Nevertheless, the text establishes the basic structure of the composition: the division into two parts, Alleluia and Verse, and the phrasing reflect the syntactical elements of the text. But the music goes beyond these formal elements to clothe the words with a highly ornamental song.

The Alleluia is performed by a soloist alternating with the choir. The soloist sings the short introductory passage terminated by the asterisk. The choir then repeats the phrase sung by the soloist and continues to the end of the first part of the chant. The long melisma on the final syllable is called the jubilus or jubilation. After the choir has finished, the soloist sings the verse up to the point indicated by the asterisk. The choir then sings the remainder of the verse.

In melismatic chants the long vocalizations are virtually independent

ILLUSTRATION 4

of the text and must be governed by purely musical considerations. Here the modality of a composition provides the general set of conditions within which the composer's artistic inventiveness operates. The Easter Alleluia is in the seventh, or Mixolydian mode. The range of the melody includes the subfinal, F, as well as an extension beyond the normal upper limit. As in the Gloria, all the important cadences fall on either the reciting tone, d, or the final, G. The larger divisions of the chant are marked by points of rest on the final, while the reciting tone is used for less crucial and only momentary caesurae.

The alleluia with its long jubilus is divided into four phrases, the first ending on d and all the others on G. In reality, the first two phrases are subdivisions of a larger phrase. Taken together, they describe a gradual ascent from the final to the reciting tone, followed by a downward glide to the point of origin. The third phrase hovers climactically about the reciting tone, oscillating between d and e, before falling again to the final. A link to the preceding phrase exists in the use of the same descent to the final. The last phrase of the jubilus, in contrast to the immediately preceding section, is centered around the final, thereby stressing its cadential function. The importance of the pivotal notes of the mode for the construction of the melody is graphically demonstrated by the manner in which the melody gravitates around them.

The individual phrases of the Alleluia and Verse, though shaped by characteristics of the mode, have also been subjected to a larger musical design. Musical form is to a large extent created by repeating recognizable musical phrases. One of the most common of musical forms is built out of two contrasting sections followed by a repetition of the first. This symmetrical structure is usually represented by the schema: ABA, and it is called the *ternary form*. Though the text of the Alleluia does not suggest the use of this form, it is nonetheless present in this composition, for the final melisma on the word *Christus* repeats the greater part of the Alleluia melody. One may designate the Alleluia as A, the music of the verse up to the asterisk, B, and the concluding melisma on the word *Christus*, A.

This larger musical design is embellished by other more subtle correspondences within the chant. One such has been seen in the jubilus where the second and third phrases use the same melodic fragment to return to the final. In the verse the climax is reached when the soloist soars to the uppermost regions of the vocal range on the syllable *la*. Once having reached this exalted level, the melody is loath to leave it, and the climax is protracted by a repetition of the initial part of the melisma. Then the tension of this moment is slowly released as the melody ebbs in undulating curves back to the final. In the last notes of its descent the melisma recalls the fragment heard before in the second and third phrases of the Alleluia. The exuberance and subtlety of this melody are typical of the artistry which composers lavished upon the responsorial chants, the musical high point of the Mass.

Another melismatic chant offers us an example of how the text and the music may combine to produce a structure of striking beauty. In Illustration 5 is given a Kyrie for Feasts of the Blessed Virgin Mary. (Although the text is from the Ordinary of the Mass and therefore unchangeable, certain Kyrie melodies are associated with special feasts and thus are proper to that feast. This fact need not obscure the classification of the Kyrie as an item of the Ordinary, for it is on the basis of the text, not the music, that the classification has been made.)

The simplest setting of the Kyrie text would require only two musical phrases: one for *Kyrie eleison*, thrice repeated, and another for *Christe eleison*, also thrice repeated. The first musical phrase would be used again for the final threefold *Kyrie eleison*. In the chant before us a musical organization of much greater complexity has been superimposed upon the simple repetitive order of the text. The fact that each of the implorations is repeated three times suggested to the composer that the

ILLUSTRATION 5

principle of ternary form might be applied to them. The thrice repeated exclamation, *Kyrie eleison*, at the beginning is provided with two musical phrases, A and B, in the order ABA. Furthermore, the melody for the three utterances of the word *eleison* (placed in brackets marked x), remains the same in each phrase. The three cries, *Christe eleison*, are treated similarly. The first and third are sung to a new melodic phrase, C, while the middle *Christe eleison* brings back the musical phrase A in an almost exact repetition—only the first three notes are changed. The composer is carefully binding the composition together by means of repetitive elements arranged in a complex design.

The final Kyries also have a ternary relationship. The first starts off with what appears to be a new musical idea, but after six notes reverts to phrase C used in the *Christe eleison*. The seemingly new material of its opening is, however, derived from the first few notes of phrase B raised to the upper octave. Here the chant reaches its first high point. The penultimate *Kyrie eleison* is a repetition of the music sung to the second *Christe eleison*. The last *Kyrie* is much longer than any of the others; in it the composer recasts material previously used to bring the composition to a brilliant close. The climax reached earlier is recaptured and sustained as the choir sings phrase C′ twice in direct succession. The chant then draws to a close with a repetition of Phrase A as it had appeared in the second *Christe*. In this composition the involved relationships of the melodic material go far beyond anything suggested by the text. The composer has used a formal structure created of musical elements to embellish and enhance the basic simplicity of the text.

The history of the chant, its origin and evolution, is still full of mysteries. Little is known of its earliest stages and no manuscript preserving the chant in notation exists which was written before the ninth century. A very old tradition credited Pope Gregory the Great (590–604) with the composition of a substantial part of the chants. This claim has since been modified to limit his contribution simply to a codification of the chants. More recently even this activity has been assigned to a succession of pontiffs throughout the sixth and seventh centuries. Whatever its origin, the so-called Gregorian chant became official in the late Middle Ages. This did not mean that the musical heritage of the church did not continue to grow, or that local differences no longer existed. As musical ideals changed, the chant was altered to satisfy the demands of new conditions.

At the end of the sixteenth century an attempt was made to establish the repertoire of the chant in a fixed, officially sanctioned form. But the task was badly bungled, and the Medicean edition of the music for the Mass, rather than restoring the chant according to the most reliable sources, altered the melodies in such a way that they reflect the late sixteenth-century concepts of melodic invention. Not until the late nineteenth century was the task of the restoration of the chant successfully undertaken with the tools of a precise historical method. All chants have not been restored to their original form. In some cases this is impossible, because written records go no farther back than the ninth century. In other cases the chant has not been restored to the earliest mediaeval forms because the ceremonies have been altered or abbreviated, and the chant is no longer functionally related to present rituals. Although the entire body of music thus far discussed was composed by men whose names have not been preserved or at least cannot be identified with specific compositions, the Roman chant remains a living testimony to the creative artistry of the musicians of the early church.

III THE CHRISTIAN FOUNDATIONS OF WESTERN MUSIC

Part II. The Outgrowth of the Chant

ON CHRISTMAS DAY of the year 800 Pope Leo III bestowed the crown of the Roman Empire upon Charlemagne, King of the Franks. By this act the Catholic church recognized Charles's sovereignty over the lands of Western Europe which he had won by his military prowess. The coronation marks the beginning of a regrouping of the forces of civilization after the alarming disintegration of society in the preceding centuries, for, in accepting the imperial crown, Charles assumed more than an empty title; he also assumed the responsibility of restoring to the West the stability and justice that had existed in the days of Roman authority. Thus the Roman ideal of a state founded upon universal political and social institutions was revived. Charlemagne's efforts to reinstate the forms of Roman administration and law are frequently spoken of as the first "Renaissance." They represent the first stage in the reassimilation of the classical past by northern civilization, a process subsequently completed by the restoration first of ancient philosophy and then of classical art and literature.

From the very first, Charles had recognized that the strength of his empire depended upon finding capable individuals to act as administrators. At the same time he was aware that educated men qualified to fill such positions were scarce. For this reason he turned to the church as the only available source of literate men. His government was thus sustained by the double authority of an ecclesiastical and secular ruling class. The equality of the two estates is illustrated by the fact that the *missi* of Charlemagne, agents appointed to travel throughout the kingdom to supervise the local administration, always functioned in teams of two, one of whom was invariably a cleric. In this way the church became the instrument of Charles's political and social reforms.

Among the duties assigned to the church was that of providing a rudimentary education for the populace. To this end Charlemagne ordered the churches and monasteries to open schools for the laity as well as for those who were training for the priesthood. It was difficult, however, to carry out this injunction, since the church itself was only barely literate. Charles alternately commanded and exhorted the officials of the church to raise their standards of education. He also strove to make the Palace school an example for others to follow and his most significant step in this direction was the installation of the Englishman Alcuin as director of the school in 782.

It was under Alcuin's tutelage that the ancient ideal of a systematic education was revived. Instruction, which had shrunk to the barest essentials of learning, was now expanded to include the full range of the trivium and quadrivium. The seven liberal arts, which represented for Alcuin the totality of secular knowledge, were held by him to be necessary for the attainment of the highest knowledge of all, the study of the divine word. "Wisdom is sustained by the seven columns of the liberal arts," he wrote. "Nor may anyone be led to perfect knowledge unless he has been elevated by these seven columns of grammar, rhetoric, dialectic, arithmetic, geometry, music, and astronomy. Through these philosophy contrives all its tasks and activities." Thus Alcuin, devout churchman and champion of learning, made the seven liberal arts the handmaidens of theology. Through his inspiration the study of the theoretical aspects of music was revived and placed in the service of the wisdom of the church.

Although Alcuin and Charlemagne wished for a revival of all the liberal arts, they placed a special emphasis upon the literary arts of the trivium. This emphasis was the result of a mental predisposition formed by Christian modes of knowledge. The church had long since accepted the premise that the function of reason and knowledge is to assist faith in attaining an understanding of God and His ways towards man as they are revealed in the Biblical Word. The primary purpose of learning was to interpret and explain Biblical texts as well as the official doctrines and liturgy of the church.

To plumb the meaning of these texts the interpreter must employ the disciplines of the trivium: grammar, rhetoric, and logic. For this reason Charlemagne in a letter to one of his churchmen, Baugulf the Abbot of Fulda, urged him "not only not to neglect the study of letters, but to acquire this knowledge zealously with a most humble exertion pleasing to God, so that you may more easily and correctly penetrate the mysteries of the Holy Scriptures. For inasmuch as phrases and verbal figures and tropes are to be found in the divine pages, no one may doubt that anyone reading these will understand them in his spirit more rapidly if he has first been given fuller instruction in the literary disciplines." This tradition of amplification of meaning through exposition and interpretation was to have an immediate effect upon the evolution of music.

The same tireless energy and passion for detail that led Charlemagne to supervise the educational curriculum of his kingdom and even to participate actively in the classes of the Palace school also moved him to institute reforms in the chants of the church. During the previous reign of the Merovingian kings the ties between the Roman and the Gallican churches had become so tenuous that the rites and chants of the Gallican church had become quite distinct from those of Rome. The discrepancies between the two liturgies had been forcefully brought to the attention of Charlemagne's father, King Pepin, when Pope Stephen II visited Gaul in 754, bringing with him the singers of the papal chapel. So marked was the contrast between the practices of the Frankish and Roman singers that Pepin resolved to ameliorate it by introducing the Roman rite in the churches under his jurisdiction. To accomplish this he procured chant books from Rome to serve as models for the Gallican liturgy. He also endeavored to improve the singing of the chant by sending for Roman singers to teach the proper execution of the Gregorian melodies to the Franks, and he dispatched singers to Rome that they might learn the authentic chant at its very source.

Pepin's attempt to substitute the Roman for the Gallican liturgy was not entirely the product of an exceptional piety but was motivated rather by political expediency. The unification of the ritual of the church was in a sense a guarantee of the alliance between Gaul and the Pope against their common enemies. Charlemagne saw the necessity of continuing his father's reforms, for if the church was to be the instrument of his policies, it was most essential that it should be united in a common ritual. Consequently he turned to the task of purifying the liturgy with increased ardor. The old chant books were ordered to be destroyed and to be replaced by those of the Roman rite; edicts were issued, commanding the clergy to devote the utmost attention to the proper execution of the chant; and the *missi* on their rounds of inspection were charged with the task of checking up on the fulfillment of these decrees. The Palace chapel was of course to be a model for all other churches and, whenever his duties permitted, Charlemagne himself tested the abilities and proficiency of the singers. Despite many objections and inevitable hesitancies, the Gallican chant gradually succumbed before the obstinate insistence of Pepin, Charlemagne, and their descendants. By the end of the ninth century the Roman rite, somewhat modified to be sure, prevailed throughout the Carolingian empire.

The result of this reform was not, however, something that Charlemagne could have anticipated. Unwittingly, in his efforts to create a stable administration through the agency of the church, he had unleashed two opposing forces. The introduction of a uniform liturgy was, on the one hand, a conservative and restrictive influence: the acceptance of a prescribed ritual could only mean that the creative efforts of musicians and literary men were deprived of their normal outlet. It was now seldom possible to introduce new hymns and chants except under such special circumstances as the formation of a new office for a newly canonized saint. On the other hand, the stimulus of the renewal of higher learning was an expansive force which roused the dormant mind to seek outlets for a reawakened interest in artistic creation. Since submission to the authority of the Roman chant, and intensified intellectual activity with its inevitable renewal of interest in artistic expression, were both official policies of church and state, there was only one possible solution to the dilemma brought about by these opposing doctrines: the artist must find a means to indulge his fantasy in ornamenting and amplifying the chant while still preserving its integrity. He must place his Muse in the service of the ordained liturgy.

In response to this need new modes of expression evolved in the ninth century. The desire to enrich the liturgy found its outlet in the phenomenon of *troping*, a process whereby the chant was ornamented through the interpolation or addition of textual and musical material. In this manner the artist could create original texts and music which at the same time were dependent upon the original chant. In the trope, as an artistic process, the dominant intellectual interests of the ninth century meet. The renewal of literary studies is reflected in this outpouring of poetic and prose texts created to embellish the original texts of the liturgy. The new emphasis upon the artistic aspects of language is revealed in the very term "trope," a word borrowed from rhetoric, signifying ornamented speech or a figure of speech. The belief that the function of learning is to plumb the meaning of the Word of God is seen in the fact that the tropes are literary reformulations of liturgical texts or religious doctrines. They are didactic as well as literary works.

In the trope the artist endeavors to enrich the original meaning of a given text through the devices of his art, clothing it in poetic form, ornamenting it with the figures of rhetoric, or embellishing the melody of the chant by juxtaposing one of his own invention. Just as the jeweler reveals the latent beauty of a gem by cutting and polishing, so the mediaeval artist sought to illuminate the truths of Christianity with flashing facets of rhetoric. The threefold imploration, *Kyrie eleison*, becomes for example:

> Omnipotens genitor, Deus omnicreator: eleyson.
> Fons et origo boni, pie luxque perennis: eleyson.
> Salvificet pietas tua nos, bone rector: eleyson.

Omnipotent Father, Lord creator of all: have mercy upon us. Fount and source of good, kindly light eternal: have mercy upon us. May thy mercy save us, O good leader: have mercy upon us.

Here the simple invocation of the Lord has been colored and transformed by the addition of his attributes. (For the complete trope and its relationship to the original Gregorian chant the reader is referred to Davison and Apel, *Historical Anthology of Music*, I, p. 13.)

Though troping may seem a rather barren procedure, it actually possessed an extraordinary vigor and fertility. Through this process the liturgy of the church gave birth to many of the secular arts of today. It stimulated a new Latin poetry which in many ways was the progenitor of the yet unborn vernacular poetry. From the trope emerged the mediaeval drama culminating in the mystery and morality plays which are the distant ancestors of the modern stage. Finally the musical manifestation of the trope is one of the most important steps in the development of Western music. Not only were new melodies created as additions or interpolations to the original chant melody, they were also created to be sung *simultaneously* with the original melody. The acceptance of the harmonic combination of tones which begins at this time has ever since been a characteristic of Western music as opposed to that of other cultures.

For the musician few places within the repertoire of the chant presented greater opportunities for the exercise of his creative talents than the jubilus of the Alleluia. This had been from the very first the place wherein the composer was most free, under no limitations imposed by the text or by the ceremonial rituals. Indeed, for the musician, the Alleluia had always been the supreme moment in the liturgy of the Mass. In most Masses the chant is concluded by a repetition of the Alleluia section after the singing of the verse. It is this Alleluia refrain that attracted the attention of the composer. Instead of merely repeating the Alleluia after the verse musicians seized the opportunity to extend the jubilus to even greater lengths, adding optional melodies at this moment. The added melody at first was simply called a *melodia*, but later the term *tropus* or trope was applied to it. Though originally the trope was a musical phenomenon, the analogy made with a rhetorical ornament is indicative of the way in which the musician viewed his invention. The trope was a free embellishment of the chant, a compromise between obedience to the law of the established chant and the demands of creative freedom.

The melody added to the Alleluia is called a *sequence* because it follows the chant. Other tropes may appear as melodic passages interpolated within an established chant. Because the sequence developed into an independent and highly artistic form in the ninth through the twelfth centuries, it has become customary to use the term trope only for those additions to the chant which are not sequences.

Since the melody added to the end of the alleluia was nothing more than an elaborate and lengthy extension of the jubilus, it obviously had no text other than the final vowel of the exclamation "Alleluia." But we have already seen (Chapter II, p. 38) that the sequence *Victimae paschali laudes* has a long poetic text. How did it come about that the protracted, wordless melody has lost its melismatic qualities and has become instead a syllabic chant? The answer to this question still remains in the realm of hypothesis. One explanation was given by a monk from the Monastery of St. Gall, Notker Balbulus (c. 840–912), who was actively engaged in the composition of sequences in the early years of its history. Though there are many who are unwilling to accept his simple account, it still remains a document of central importance for knowledge of the origins of the sequence.

In 884 or 885 Notker prefaced a collection of his sequences with an account of how he came to write them. As a young man, he relates, he had sung the very long melodies, *longissimae melodiae*, attached to the Alleluia, but because of their great length he had had difficulty in memorizing them. Then a monk, fleeing from the monastery of Jumièges after it was destroyed by the Normans, brought to St. Gall a book of chants which included sequence melodies to which verses had been fitted. Notker immediately recognized in this practice a solution to the problem of memorizing the melodies, for the addition of words to the tune made the melody easier to fix in the mind. However, he was not pleased with the quality of the verses, and he resolved to invent more suitable texts. Notker makes no claim to be the inventor of the sequence. Rather, it would appear from his statements that the melodic additions to the Alleluia had been supplied with texts as early as the middle of the ninth century.

The sequences found in ancient manuscripts rarely exhibit the degree of association with the melody of the Alleluia which their origin would suggest. Nevertheless, some of the oldest examples maintain a melodic connection to the Alleluia. One such is Notker's sequence *Christus hunc diem* (printed in Davison and Apel, *Historical Anthology of Music*, I, p. 13). Its first verse is sung to the melody of the Alleluia prescribed for the Feast of the Ascension, though slight modifications of the chant have been made in fitting the text to the melody. After the first verse, the melody for the remainder of the sequence makes no further reference to the chant of the Alleluia. Even the mode changes; for the Alleluia is in the eighth, or Mixolydian Mode and the new melody is in the Phrygian Mode. But the relationship of the sequence to the Alleluia is maintained in its text which takes the text of the Alleluia as its point of departure. It is so clearly an amplification and extension of the thought briefly stated in the Verse of the Alleluia that it may be described as a trope of the Verse. Both texts are given here for the sake of comparison.

Alleluia

Alleluia, alleluia.

VERSE: Dominus in Sina in sancto, ascendens in altum, captivam duxit captivitatem. (The Lord is in Sinai, in the holy place: ascending on high, he hath led captivity captive.

Sequence

I. Christus hunc diem jocundum cunctis concedat esse Christianis amatoribus suis.

IIa. Christe Jesu, fili Dei, mediator naturae nostrae ac divinae,

Terras, Deus, visitasti aeternus, aethera novus homo transvolans.

IIb. Officiis te Angeli atque nubes stipant ad patrem reversurum

Sed que mirum, cum lactanti adhuc stella tibi serviret et Angeli?

IIIa. Tu hodie terrestribus rem novam et dulcem dedisti, domine, sperandi coelestia.

IIIb. Te dominum non fictum levando super sidereas metas regum, domine.

IVa. Quanta gaudia tuos replent apostolos,

IVb. Quis dedisti cernere, te coelos pergere.

Va. Quam hilares in coelis tibi securrunt novi ordines.

Vb. In humeris portanti diu dispersum a lupis gregem unum.

VI. Quem, Christe, bone pastor, dignare custodire.

I. Christ grants this day for rejoicing to his assembled loving Christians.

IIa. O Christ Jesus, son of God, mediator between our nature and the divine, Thou hast visited the places of the earth, a new man flying through the ether.

IIb. The angels with their ministrations and the clouds crowd about thee as thou art rising to thy Father;
But who should wonder that the stars and the angels serve thee?

IIIa. This day thou gavest to earth-born men a new and sweet thing, O Lord, a heavenly hope:

IIIb. Thou thyself, O Lord, a true man, rising above the starry limits of the kingdom.

IVa. How great are the joys that fill thy apostles

IVb. To whom thou hast granted that they might perceive thee rising to the skies.

Va. What joyous new ranks meet thee in the heavens

Vb. As thou bearest upon thy shoulders a flock for a long time dispersed by the wolves.

VI. This flock, O Christ, good shepherd, deign to guard.

The author, it must be remembered, presumably had the task of fitting his text to a pre-existent melody conceived quite independently of a text. Under these conditions, he could hardly succeed in imposing upon the melody a metrical, poetic structure; he could only compose prose lines equal in length to the phrases of the melody. As the lines of the text are presented, we see that except for the first and last stanzas, they form successive pairs. The pairing of lines probably represents an attempt to create the semblance of a poetic structure (it has been suggested that this pattern was derived from a secular poetic form, the *lai*). The form of this sequence in both its text and music, is schematically represented as *a bb cc dd ee f.*

Each pair of lines is sung to the same musical phrase, and this symmetry led to a method of performance contrasting with the responsorial singing of the Alleluia. The Alleluia after the Verse had been sung by the choir. Because the sequence is a substitute and extension of that repetition, its performance quite naturally was entrusted to the choir. After the first stanza, however, the singers are divided into two equal groups, each singing one of the paired lines. At the conclusion the choir reunites to sing the last, unpaired stanza. Thus an antiphonal method of chanting the sequence grew out of the responsorial Alleluia.

Once the sequence gained a foothold in the liturgy of the church, the unwieldy task of accommodating a text to a pre-existing melody was soon circumvented. New compositions, melodically independent of the Alleluia, were written in which the melodies and the texts were conceived for each other. The paired lines or double versicles were still retained, but metrical poetry of an accentual rather than quantitative nature gradually replaced the earlier prose. Frequently it employed rhyme as an added ornament. Once again the musician's free flights of melodic fancy came under the regulation of the text, as the melodies began to reflect the metrical, regulated order of the poetry. The Easter sequence, *Victimae paschali laudes* (Illustration 1), from the first half of the eleventh century, is a composition in which poetic order is only beginning to make itself felt. (A translation of the text appears in Chapter II, p. 38.)

ILLUSTRATION I

Vi- cti-mae pas-cha-li lau-des im-mo-lent Chri-sti-

a- ni. A- gnus re- de-mit o- ves: Chri- stus in- no-

cens Pa- tri re- con-ci- li- a- vit pec- ca- to- res.

Mors et vi- ta du- el- lo con- fli- xe- re

mi- ran-do: dux vi- tae mor- tu- us, re- gnat vi- vus.

Dic no- bis Ma- ri- a, quid vi- di- sti in vi- a?

ILLUSTRATION I (*continued*)

Se- pul- crum Christi vi- ven- tis, et glo- ri- am vi- di

re- sur-gen-tis: An- ge- li- cos tes-tes, su- da- ri- um, et

ve- stes. Sur- re- xit Christus spes me- a: prae- ce- det

su- os in Ga- li- lae- am. Sci- mus Christum sur- re-

xis- se. a mor- tu- is ve- re: tu no- bis, vi- ctor

Rex, mi- se- re- re. A- men. Al- le- lu- ia.

The lines of regular length in stanzas IIa, IIb, IIIa, and IIIb, and the rhyming end syllables in stanzas IIIa, IIIb, IVa, Va, and Vb cast a powerful sense of poetic order over this poem. But the independent stanza at the beginning and the unequal dimensions of the double versicles are vestiges of the older sequence. The music of *Victimae paschali laudes*, which was later adapted for the Lutheran hymn *Christ lag in Todesbanden*, is justly famous. Using the combined ranges of the Dorian and Hypodorian modes, the melody dips below the final in the midst of soaring flights to the upper limits of the vocal range. As impressive as the boldness of its sweeping range is the captivating irregularity of the melody—a feature which stems directly from the poetry.

In the twelfth century the irregularities of verse structure begin to disappear: lines tend to be of equal length and rhyme schemes are prominent features of the stanzas. The independent verses at the beginning and end vanish, leaving a poetic structure of equal stanzas not unlike the strophic hymn. The bold, imaginative poetry of a *Victimae paschali laudes* is superseded by a refined elegance typified in the sequences of Adam of St. Victor. (His *Jubilemus Salvatori* is printed in Davison and Apel, *Historical Anthology of Music* I, p. 14.) The melodies naturally reflect the regularity of the poetry and tend to flow smoothly in symmetrical patterns.

Tropes other than sequences may be dealt with more briefly because in general they did not, like the sequence, free themselves from the compositions they embellished. A notable exception to this statement are the tropes in the form of dialogues which evolved into independent dramas. Tropes are of two classes: (1) those that are added to the antiphonal chants of the Mass, Introits, Communions, and Offertories, and (2) those that are embellishments of the parts of the Ordinary of the Mass. An example of a troped Kyrie, *Omnipotens genitor*, has been cited on page 61. With regard to the troped Kyrie it is not certain that a melismatic form of the chant, that is, a form without the troped text, ever existed independently prior to the addition of the trope. The chants of the Ordinary of the Mass are generally later additions to the repertory, and it may be that the Kyrie melodies which are now melismatic were originally conceived to be sung syllabically with a troped text. An indication of the erstwhile prevalence of tropes is the fact that most of the Kyrie chants in current use are still identified by the first words, the *incipit*, of the trope that was once associated with them. It is worth noting that the tropes at times brought the text of the Ordinary into a close relation to a particular feast, giving the Ordinary of the Mass something of the nature of the Proper. After the Council of Trent, the tropes were deleted, and the melodies are now sung as melismatic chants.

The methods of troping discussed thus far have taken the form of additions or interpolations to the existing chants and their texts. A momentous step in the history of Western music, one which set it on a new and hitherto untrodden path, was taken when a melody was added to be sung *simultaneously* with the existing chant. At first the added melody was not the creation of a composer but was improvised by a singer. The added part was merely a duplication of the chant at a fixed interval below it. Our earliest precise knowledge of this revolutionary new music comes from theoretical treatises. The *Musica Enchiriadis* written in the last half of the ninth century describes several manners of producing this new complex of musical sound, called *organum*. In the examples cited in this treatise the voice singing the original chant is called the *vox principalis*, while the voice duplicating the chant at a prescribed interval below it is called the *vox organalis*. The anonymous author quotes a phrase from the *Te Deum* as it would be sung in the new manner at the interval of a fourth.

ILLUSTRATION 2

Illustration 2 demonstrates that the part added to the chant is not at all a newly composed melody, for it merely reproduces the chant at a lower level of pitch. The interval chosen may be the fourth or the fifth, but the one selected is maintained throughout the performance. In addition to this simplest form of organum, which is termed *parallel organum*, there was a more complicated type that grew directly out of this elementary method of improvisation. By adding to the simple type of organum just described a third voice singing the chant an octave below the vox principalis and a fourth voice duplicating the vox organalis in the upper octave, a harmony of four parts is produced. The example in Illustration 3 shows this procedure. The basic interval chosen is the fifth, seen between the vox principalis, singing the chant at its original pitch, and the vox organalis.

If these first essays in multivoiced or polyphonic music seem primi-

ILLUSTRATION 3

tive, we must keep in mind that this is only an improvised form of singing in parts. The performers did not have their individual melodies written out for them and therefore they moved slowly, maintaining with a conscious effort a set interval from the pitch of the chant. The intervals prescribed in these elementary forms of organum are those sanctified by the musical speculations of the Greeks: the perfect fourth, fifth, and octave. Only these intervals, which are determined by the simplest mathematical proportions, were regarded as consonant, a view that was to be maintained throughout the Middle Ages.

To maintain the improvised interval of the perfect fourth or fifth is not as simple as it might seem, for there are certain difficulties inherent in the nature of the scale itself. In the first example, when the vox principalis sings b the vox organalis, in order to maintain the relationship of a perfect fourth to it should sing F♯. This was an irregular note, requiring an emendation of the scale generally employed. To avoid this modification it would also be possible for the chant to lower the b to b♭, enabling the vox organalis to sing an F. But this creates still another difficulty, for it involves an alteration of the chant itself, and, since the chant was the foundation upon which the other voices rested, it could not be emended without confusing the other parts. Furthermore, the authority residing in the traditional chants of the church was such that singers were reluctant to alter them arbitrarily. It was therefore incumbent upon the improvising voice to accommodate its part to the original chant.

The intervals of the augmented fourth or diminished fifth, which failed to live up to the mathematical perfection of the normal fourth or fifth, aroused such feelings of horror in the mediaeval musician that he was moved to call them *diabolus in musica*, the devil in music. So strong was the aversion to this imperfection in music that another means, pregnant with unforeseen possibilities for future development, was devised to avoid it. This solution appears in another example from the *Musica Enchiriadis*, part of the sequence *Rex coeli Domine* (Illustration 4).

ILLUSTRATION 4

Rex coe- li Do- mi- ne ma- ris un- di- so- ni,
Ti- ta- nis ni- ti- di squa- li- di- que so- li,

Te hu- mi- les fa- mu- li mo- du- lis ve- ne- ran- do pi- is.
Se ju- be- as fla- gi- tant va- ri- is li- be- ra- re ma- lis.

In the musical scale advocated by the author of this treatise, the b below middle c is always natural, while the B an octave below that is always flatted. Thus augmented fourths exist between B♭ and E, and between F and b. This means that the singer improvising his part a fourth below the vox principalis would encounter the devil's music on the third and the last tones of the first phrase. In the example the augmented fourth has been avoided at these points, but only at the cost of introducing intervals other than the fourth between the two parts. The vox organalis starts in unison with the chant melody and clings to this first tone until the troublesome E has been passed, when it begins to move in the customary parallel fourths. For the same reason it returns to unisons for the last two notes of the phrase. Other instances of the same practice are to be discerned in the second phrase of the example. Imperfect intervals have in this way been admitted into harmonic usage. Though regarded as dissonances, they were tolerated and even preferred to the augmented fourth.

The feature of this method of circumventing the tritone that is significant for the future development of music is the relative freedom of movement gained by the added voice. In addition to parallel movement, two other kinds of motion are introduced. At the beginning of the first phrase, where the upper part rises while the lower voice remains stationary, the relationship of the direction of these two parts is described as *oblique*. The definition of oblique motion is also satisfied when one voice moves downward while the other remains on a fixed pitch. Near the end of the example the chant moves downward from F to D, a movement which coincides with a rise from C to D in the lower voice. This relationship of movement between the parts is called *contrary* motion. In contrast to parallel motion, contrary and oblique movement free the voices from dependence upon each other.

The freedom offered by these different kinds of motion soon attracted the creative musician to the composition of polyphony. The oldest extant collection of *composed* organum dates from the first half of the eleventh century and originated in England. In France, where the main development of polyphonic music took place, a group of polyphonic compositions from the eleventh century is preserved in two manuscripts at Chartres. In the first are five Alleluias for the Christmas and Easter seasons, and in the second, eight Alleluias for Easter, Ascension Day, and Pentecost, completing a cycle of compositions for the main feasts of the church year. The Alleluia in Illustration 5 is for Easter Monday.

In this organum many of the most characteristic features of mediaeval polyphony are already present. The chant is now placed below the added melody instead of above it as in the examples from the *Musica Enchiriadis*. This throws the composed voice into greater prominence.

ILLUSTRATION 5

The chant continued to be placed in the lowest position throughout the Middle Ages. The newly composed melody is fitted only to the portions of the chant normally sung by the soloist. Apparently the difficulty of singing in parts prompted the composer to write organum only for the most highly trained musicians, the solo performers. The practice here instituted of composing polyphonic sections for soloists rather than for the choir is to continue throughout the Middle Ages. Not until the fifteenth century does choral, as opposed to soloistic, polyphony make its appearance.

The rendition of the Alleluia begins with the soloists (there must be at least two: one to sing the chant, the other to sing the added melody) singing the organum on the word Alleluia, followed by the choir singing in unison the repeat of the Alleluia and its appended jubilus. The soloists re-enter, singing the organum section of the Verse, after which the choir completes this part of the chant. The Alleluia refrain is then sung by the choir, concluding the composition. This method of performance is a complete reversal of present day practice which customarily assigns the singing of part music to the choir and reserves a single line of melody for the soloist. But as we have seen, there are practical reasons for restricting the singing of organum to the soloists.

A distinctive feature of this composition lies in the extensive use of contrary motion, which has a strange fascination for the listener. In contrast to parallel progression which produces the effect of an intimate agreement between the voices, contrary motion produces a sense of the independence of the parts within certain necessary limits. Occasionally, the voices even cross, with the part normally lying above momentarily dropping down below the chant. Although the intervals of the fourth, fifth, octave and unison prevail, other intervals, seconds, thirds, and sixths, considered dissonant, are freely employed. The dissonant intervals, however, are usually passed over lightly and only consonances are used at stressed, important points in the composition. For instance, at the cadences only the octave and unison relationships occur, and at the beginning of each phrase only perfect intervals. This handling of the harmony remains a characteristic of mediaeval polyphony. It rests upon the acceptance of the mathematically perfect intervals as consonant. In contrast to these primary intervals, all others were regarded as imperfect and dissonant and were to be used only in passing between perfect intervals.

As in improvised organum, the composer of this Alleluia has added his melody to the chant in a note against note (*punctum contra punctum*) fashion. It is from this Latin phrase that the word *counterpoint* is derived. This simple method of combining the two parts may have been retained to facilitate the synchronizing of the two parts, for the note forms still did not have mensural significance and the composition is sung in a free rhythm. Despite its simplicity, this Alleluia is one of the boldest and most imaginative creations of the mediaeval musician, a flower of the seemingly sterile and unoriginal process of troping.

IV THE MIDDLE AGES

Part I. The Triumph of Time
1150-1300

IN THE TWELFTH and thirteenth centuries mediaeval civilization reached its apogee. This climax had been prepared by the Carolingian Renaissance, but it was attained only after many vicissitudes. The Empire of Charlemagne had rapidly melted away under the administration of his incompetent descendants. The military and administrative districts into which Charlemagne had divided his realm passed into the hands of their governing officials and became hereditary kingdoms, duchies, and even smaller units. These small domains proved, however, to be more manageable than the vast agglomeration of territories welded together by Charlemagne. They became increasingly stable during the tenth century and around their rulers there gradually crystallized a form of society known as feudalism.

The feudal system evolved from the political structure of Charlemagne's empire. He had appointed counts, marquises, and dukes to govern portions of his lands. They were expected to remain loyal to their king and to perform whatever services he might require of them. In return they were recompensed by the revenues from the lands which they administered. When these offices became hereditary and virtually autonomous during the reign of Charlemagne's weak heirs, their possessors made grants of land to their own retainers in return for loyal

73

service. A bewildering number of such overlapping fiefs soon appeared, some of vast power and prestige, others little more than fortified manors. All, however, were linked by the bond of loyalty between vassal and lord and ultimately to the king. The strength of the relationship depended, of course, upon the power of the lord and his ability to exact service from his vassals. Tenuous as this bond might be, the oath of loyalty remained the sole title to political legitimacy. By gathering up this slender thread, stronger monarchs, such as Philip the Second of France, began in the twelfth and thirteenth centuries to form the great national states of modern Europe.

In this feudal society each castle and manor was self-supporting, deriving its sustenance from the land. Isolated and independent, the rural castles of the lords of the land became the centers of social life. Here, as conditions ameliorated in the course of the tenth and eleventh centuries, a new society took form. An aristocratic culture appeared, worldly but deeply religious, sophisticated and idealistic, but at the same time vigorous and forceful.

Although the castle and manor were the pivots around which the feudal world revolved, other centers began to emerge during this same period. The relative peace and stability provided by the institution of feudalism had encouraged the growth of trade, moribund since the collapse of the Roman Empire. Towns began to develop at important junctions along the trade routes to house the commercial establishments of merchants and traders. A new urban population of manufacturers and artisans made its appearance. By the twelfth century many of these towns had achieved a certain measure of independence and self-government, and a lively society of city-dwellers, the bourgeoisie, had been established.

The church had also been undergoing changes in these centuries. After the death of Charlemagne the discipline which he had imposed upon the monastic houses disintegrated and for a time the Papacy was unable to restore it. But in the eleventh century a series of great Popes re-established the authority of the church. They even laid claim to temporal power, asserting that secular rulers held their thrones only through the sanction of the Pope. The growing strength of the church coupled with the new economic prosperity initiated a period of magnificent church building. In the twelfth and thirteenth centuries the soaring arches and buttresses of Gothic cathedrals began to dominate the urban landscape. These grandiose churches required a large complement of clerics to conduct their services and to administer their affairs. The clergy associated with a cathedral were organized in a chapter subject to a rule or canon ordering their way of life. Under the supervision of the bishop and other specified officers, the chapter was a self-sufficient unit responsible for all the activities of the cathedral.

One of the functions of the chapter was to provide a school for the choristers and other young boys. Gradually these cathedral schools usurped the educational role formerly occupied by the monasteries. In response to the need of the revitalized church for able and enlightened servants, young men flocked to the new urban centers of education where instruction was offered not only in the rudiments of learning but in higher studies as well. The arts of the quadrivium, philosophy, theology, medicine, and law, were expounded to eager listeners in one or another of the new schools. Unable to meet the needs of the ever-growing throngs of students from their own resources, the chapters were ultimately compelled to grant licenses to teach to masters other than members of their own body. These men, setting up classrooms in the shadow of the cathedrals, lectured on their chosen subjects to students drawn from every country and from every walk of life. Before long it became necessary to formalize this flourishing activity and thus the universities were born. By 1215 the University of Paris was a well-defined institution with legal rights and privileges and had become the leader and model for a host of other evolving universities.

The expansion of learning characterized by the rise of the universities was accelerated by the rediscovery of the works of Aristotle. Rediscovery is perhaps not the correct word for this event, for Aristotle had never really vanished except in Christian Europe. His writings had passed into the hands of Arab scholars who had copied them and commented upon them during a brilliant intellectual era that coincided with the centuries of Europe's greatest ignorance. Early in the twelfth century at points where Christian and Arabian civilization met, such as Sicily and Spain, the learning of the Arabs began to be translated into Latin. The cathedral schools had much to do with this movement, particularly that of Toledo where a group of men were employed to translate the works of Aristotle and the Arabian philosophers.

Until this moment Europe had known only two of the treatises of Aristotle, the *Categories* and *De interpretatione*, which had formed the basis of the teaching of dialectic. To these works there were now added his other treatises in the same field, his writings on natural science, and finally his *Metaphysics*, *Ethics*, and *Politics*. In addition to the works of Aristotle numerous other Greek treatises on mathematics, astronomy, optics, and medicine were brought to light. Strangely missing in this revival were the works of Plato. Although two of his dialogues were translated in the twelfth century, they seem to have been almost totally ignored. Only the *Timaeus*, already known to the Middle Ages, continued to enjoy a wide currency. Thus the flood of new ideas sweeping into the West via the work of the translators was predominantly Aristotelian in color. It was Greek natural science and the philosophical method of Aristotle which the twelfth century restored to Europe in this second stage of the rebirth of Classical knowledge. It remained for the thirteenth century to reconcile this mass of new ideas to Christian dogma, a process that culminated in the great philosophical syntheses of Albertus Magnus and Thomas Aquinas.

The castle, the cathedral, and the university: these were the background for the music of the twelfth and thirteenth centuries. Each contributed something to the profound changes in the musical art of this period. A new secular art came into being, the poetry and music of the feudal courts. However, this form of musical expression remained apart from the swelling tide of polyphony. Stubbornly it clung to the older tradition of monody and not until the second half of the thirteenth century did it begin to mingle with the polyphonic music nurtured by the church. While the emergence of secular forms was of importance for future developments in music (see Chapter V), even more significant were the changes in the music of the church. Following the trend already noted in the case of education, the center of musical activity shifted from the monastery to the cathedral. It was in the cathedral of Notre Dame in Paris that a major revolution in musical style was born in the second half of the twelfth century. An important part in this revolution was taken by the universities, for the new musical idiom was rapidly disseminated throughout western Europe by the teachings of composers and theorists associated with the University of Paris.

The new musical epoch began with the innovations of two composers of Notre Dame, Leonin (fl. 1160–1170) and Perotin (fl. 1190–1220). These two men decisively altered the course of musical evolution by introducing a coherent system of rhythm and a form of notation capable of expressing this rhythm. Until this moment the music of the church had not employed a precisely measured rhythm but had been performed in a succession of free, flexible time values. It was Leonin who first ordered the succession of tones in his polyphonic works by imposing upon them time values which were in an exact mathematical relationship with one another. Simultaneously he indicated this rhythm in his notation by grouping the tones in distinctive patterns of individual notes and of groups of notes in the form of ligatures.

Although we do not possess a theoretical exposition of their rhythmic practice by either Leonin or Perotin, its basis is known to us through the writings of musical theorists of the thirteenth century. And though we have no firsthand evidence of the genesis of this theory of rhythm, it was derived apparently from principles enunciated in the fourth century by St. Augustine in his *De musica*. According to this father of the church, rhythm is an organization of temporal values found in all arts that make use of succession or motion. These include poetry, music, and the dance. As its basis rhythm presupposes an exact relationship between two units of time, one having one beat and the other, two. These are, of course, the short and long values employed in the scansion of classical poetry. The two values, in the form of syllables or notes or gestures, are combined into patterns or feet of from two to four syllables, ranging from the pyrrhic foot of two short syllables to the dispondee of four long syllables.

Each foot is assumed to be divisible into two parts, which are measured by beating the time with an upward motion of the hand (*levatio*) and a downward motion (*positio*). No matter how many syllables the foot contains, its total value will be indicated by only these two motions. For example, the dispondee would be represented by a levatio equal to two longs or four times, while the remainder of the foot would be marked by a positio of the same length. The trochee (long, short) would have a levatio of two times and a positio of one, and the iamb (short, long) a levatio of one time and a positio of two.

In combining long and short values into feet a numerical relationship, a proportion, has been established between the two parts of the foot which is regarded as an entity in itself. This does not as yet constitute rhythm. Rhythm does not come into being until a succession of feet has been established. Furthermore all the feet in a rhythmic progression must be measured in the same way. Thus a succession of spondees (two longs) is a rhythm, because the levatio and positio are the same in all the feet. It is also possible to introduce dactyls and anapests within this spondaic series, for both the dactyl (a long and two shorts) and the anapest (two shorts and a long) are measured in the same way as the spondee by a levatio and positio, each having two times. Conversely, it is impossible to combine feet which are measured differently. The numerical relationship between the levatio and positio would have to be changed for each foot with the result that no orderly succession would be found.

Rhythm in the Augustinian sense of the word is a succession of feet measured in the same manner and theoretically stretching into infinity. In practice this infinite rhythm must be subdivided into poetic lines or musical phrases. This can only be achieved by ending each verse of poetry or phrase of music with a rest that will separate the preceding phrase from the following one. The silence or rest must have an exact mensural value, otherwise the orderly flow of rhythm would be disrupted. To maintain the rhythmic pulse, each phrase must end preferably with a syllable or musical tone equivalent to the duration of the levatio, while the following rest will be equal in time to the positio.

A musical composition written in a trochaic rhythm might have the following phrases (the long being represented by a quarter note and the short by an eighth note):

♩ ♪♩ ♪♩ ＇ ♩ ♪♩ ＇ ♩ ♪♩ ♪♩ ♪♩ ＇

The first phrase consists of two and a half feet with a rest equivalent to the positio of the last foot. The next two phrases contain respectively one and a half feet and three and a half feet with corresponding rests. It is possible to replace the long value in any one of these feet by two shorts. In such a case a tribrach (three shorts) would be substituted for the trochee. This would not be an infraction of the laws of rhythm, for the tribrach may be beaten with a levatio of two times and a positio of one. Hence its measurement would be the same as that of the trochee.

It is this conception of rhythm that was taken over by Leonin and his successors. By the end of the twelfth century all polyphonic music had submitted to this form of rhythmic measurement. In practice six rhythmic patterns or modes were employed. These were:

MODE I: ♩ ♪   MODE III: ♩. ♪♩   MODE V   ♩. ♩.

MODE II: ♪♩   MODE IV: ♪♩ ♩.   MODE VI: ♪♪♪

Three of these modes, the first, second, and sixth, are equivalent to the metrical trochee, iamb, and tribrach. The other modes seem at first glance to be unrelated to metrics since they make use of a dotted quarter note, a value of three times, while in metrics only a long of two times is admitted. But if we accept the dotted quarter note as analogous to the long of metrics, it is apparent that the fifth mode consists of two equal longs and is thus the equivalent of the spondee. In the case of the third and fourth modes the dotted quarter or long is accompanied by two shorter notes whose total value equals that of the long. This is the characteristic relationship of the dactyl and anapest of metrics. The reason for this distortion of metrical feet is to be found in the musical practice of early measured polyphony. At first only the upper part was performed in a rhythmic mode, while the lower part sustained its tones for the duration of one or more feet. As a consequence a long value of three or more times came into being. Subsequently it was rationalized and codified into the forms of the third, fourth, and fifth modes.

The introduction of this system of rhythm created a sharp distinction between contemporary musical practice and the older tradition of Gregorian chant. But the teachers associated with the University of Paris, while enthusiastically accepting the new art, endeavored to fit it within the framework of inherited musical thought. The ancient trilogy of musica mundana, humana, and instrumentalis was made to accommodate the new polyphony by subdividing musica instrumentalis into unmeasured music, i.e. the Gregorian chant, and measured polyphony. In this way the new musical practice was reconciled with the mediaeval conception of music as a branch of mathematics, the science of number related to sound. If anything, the introduction of measured rhythm only intensified this idea, for rhythm is still another way of relating number to sound.

The remarkable developments in polyphonic music taking place in the twelfth century were facilitated by the advances that had been made in the notation of music. Even before the need for a precise notation of rhythmic measurement had arisen, more exact ways of indicating levels of pitch had been devised. At first the written symbols were arranged at approximate distances above and below an imaginary or dry-point line. This approximate representation of the level of pitch, with the line representing a norm, was sufficient to recall for the singer melodies he had learned by oral transmission. From the moment of the appearance of a single line designated as a specific pitch from which all others were to be measured, it was inevitable that parallel lines, each indicating a precise pitch would be added. Naturally this meant that the spaces also acquired meaning as specific levels of pitch. The pitch of a line was at first indicated by its color, but later a letter was affixed at the beginning of the line. That letter, because it was the key to the pitch of all notational symbols on the staff, was called the clef. The perfection of this system of pitch notation is credited to Guido of Arezzo (c. 995–1050). Although he has often been described as its inventor, it has been proven that his role was limited to the systematization of practices not yet standardized.

Guido may not have been the inventor of the staff, but he is the originator of the solmization syllables which, with some modifications, continue in use today. Everyone knows the syllables: do, re, mi, fa, sol, la, ti (si), do. In Guido's system there were only six syllables: ut (do), re, mi, fa, sol, and la, comprising a *hexachord*, a span of six successive ascending notes. The relationship of the pitches represented by these syllables to each other was permanently fixed. Between mi and fa there is always a half step and between any other two successive syllables there is a whole step. Guido derived the names of the syllables and the fixed relationship of the pitches they represent from the hymn *Ut queant laxis* (Illustration 1).

ILLUSTRATION I

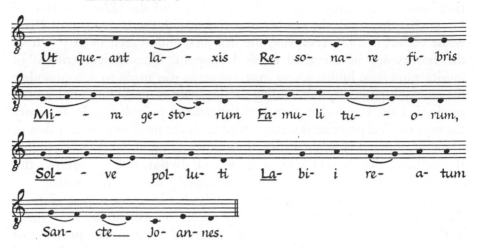

The solmization syllables are the first syllable of all but the last line of the hymn, and the rising progression of notes to which they are sung produces the hexachord. To this "natural" hexachord Guido added two others of identical structure. One extended from G to E and was called the "hard" hexachord because the B contained in it is natural. The other ranges from F to d and was called the "soft" hexachord because the b was flatted. If the singer, after having firmly fixed in his mind the solmization syllables and the pitch relationships they represent, properly identifies them with written musical notation, he can translate into sound at sight any notated melody, whether it be new or previously unknown to him. Guido boasted that after he "began teaching this procedure to boys, some of them were able to sing an unknown melody before the third day, which by other methods would not have been possible in many weeks."

The impetus behind the developments in symbols of notation and the invention of the mediaeval solmization system was above all the emergence of the new polyphonic art. Polyphonic music involved so many new and complicated features unknown to the chant that its diffusion and preservation could not possibly have been effected by anything less precise than the notation the mediaeval musician created for it. With the aid of this efficient musical script, the composers could begin to explore the possibilities of polyphony. It is primarily in France that the new art was consistently developed, reaching its first great climax in the work of Leonin and Perotin at Notre Dame in Paris, the cultural and intellectual center of all Europe.

The last polyphonic composition examined, the Alleluia from Chartres (Chapter III, p. 71), still demonstrates the *nota contra notam* style characteristic of improvised polyphony. The next step in the evolution of polyphony introduced a new complication, for the simple note against note relationship of the parts is supplanted by a style in which the composer juxtaposes long melismata to each note of the chant.

ILLUSTRATION 2

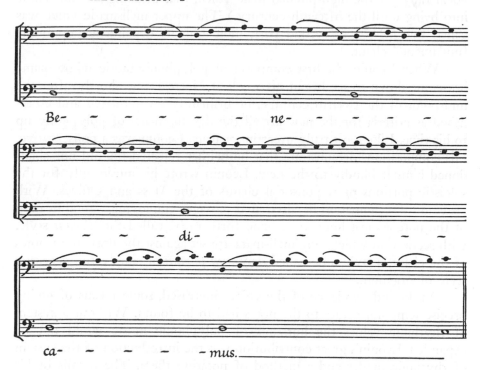

This organum (Illustration 2) from the first half of the twelfth century was composed at the Abbey of St. Martial at Limoges, in southern France. By adding a florid melody to the individual tones of the chant, the musician has found a way to create flowing melodies, less restricted in their sweep, and free from the limitations of declamatory speech. But within this rediscovered freedom the established concepts of harmony based on the perfect intervals as consonant prevails. At the beginning of each note of the chant, the harmonic relationship of the voices always rests upon a perfect interval: the unison, fourth, fifth, or octave. In the course of each melisma the composer freely introduces intervals regarded as dissonant, but these are made to appear as merely passing, momentary harmonies between the pivotal perfect intervals.

The addition of long, arching melismata to each note of the chant greatly extends the length of the composition. In contrast to organum written in the nota contra notam style where the duration of the chant melody was not appreciably altered, the melismatic organum caused the

chant to be protracted to such enormous lengths that its identity as an
integral melody is virtually lost. With this new style of organum new
names for the voice parts were introduced. Because the chant was drawn
out to inordinate lengths, it was now called the *tenor*, from the Latin
tenere, to hold. (At this time the term tenor had no association with the
vocal range of the high-pitched male voice; that meaning did not come
into being until the fifteenth century.) The upper melismatic voice was
called the *duplum* or second part, indicating its dependence upon the
fundamental chant.

When Leonin, the first composer of polyphonic music whose name
has come down to us, began his work at Notre Dame shortly after the
mid-point of the twelfth century, he brilliantly recapitulated and established as criteria for the new art all the developments of polyphony up
to his time. Like most truly great innovators, Leonin was a conservative.
His compositions demonstrate that he neither rejected the old nor abandoned himself blindly to the new. Leonin wrote his music only for the
soloistic portions of responsorial chants of the Mass and Offices. With
taste and discrimination he alternated passages employing a modification
of the note against note style, henceforth to be called the *discant* style,
with sections in which long melismata are set against the drawn out notes
of the chant, a style now called *organum purum* or simply the *organum*
style of organum.

As the independence of the voices increased, some means of giving
precise temporal values to the notes had to be found. Without a system
of rhythmic values the horizons of polyphonic music could not be
expanded. Leonin's great contribution was the introduction of the system
of rhythmic modes and a method of notating them. The details of his
notational practices are technical matters outside the scope of this book.
For our purposes a simple statement must suffice: to the note forms used
in the writing of chant melodies Leonin imparted rhythmic values with
the result that the symbols of notation placed upon a staff now designated
both pitch and duration. From this innovation the entire development of
musical notation in Western civilization unfolds. By the end of the Middle
Ages, the system in use today was all but completed.

A relatively short section of one of Leonin's compositions will illustrate all the salient features of his style. The example in Illustration 3 is
the organum section, that is, the soloistic portion, of the respond of the
Gradual for the Feast of the Assumption of the Blessed Virgin Mary,
celebrated on August the fifteenth. (The remainder of this work consists
of the concluding section of the Respond sung in unison by the choir,
a long organum section for the soloists comprising the greater part of
the Verse, and the conclusion of the Verse given over to the choir.)

ILLUSTRATION 3

In order to gain an understanding of the creative processes underlying the composition of a piece of organum, it may be instructive to follow the composer in the practice of his art step by step. The example above embraces only the first two words of the Gradual and, as is invariably the case, the melody of the chant is assigned to the tenor. This melodic phrase Leonin undoubtedly copied from a book of chant where it appeared in approximately the form in Illustration 4.

ILLUSTRATION 4

Pro- pter ve- ri - ta-   ~   ~   tem

Because the chant contains an extensive melisma on the syllable *ta* this section of the chant is of considerable length despite the fact that only two words are sung; for only six syllables there are, in all, twenty notes. If a long melisma were to be added in the duplum for each note of the chant in the tenor, the composition would grow to enormous proportions. Leonin solved this problem by employing one style for the syllabic sections of the chant and another for the melismatic sections. When the chant proceeds in an essentially syllabic manner, as on the word *propter*, the duplum is provided with a melismatic melody, thereby protracting this section of the chant. When the chant is melismatic, as on the syllable *ta*, the duplum is written in the nota contra notam style, or more precisely in Leonin's modification of it, the discant style, thereby allowing the chant to proceed at a more normal pace. While this solution brought the composition within moderate dimensions, it introduced what appears to be an unfortunate mixture of two widely divergent musical styles within one and the same composition. The reconciliation of these styles was Leonin's great achievement: by introducing a uniform rhythm for the entire composition he brought the opposing styles under the spell of a single but variously articulated rhythmic pattern.

As in almost all of Leonin's compositions, it is the first rhythmic mode that orders the flow of the melody. Even when subdivided into smaller units or replaced by larger ones, the unmistakable succession— long, short—prevails. It is significant that the rhythmic pattern is altered most freely in the organum purum section (on the word *propter*), for by introducing irregularities in the pattern at this point the freedom characteristic of the older form of organum purum still seems to exist. In fact, the tenor in this section still remains outside the prevailing rhythmic pattern, for it derives its measurement only indirectly from the duration of the melismata of the duplum.

In the section on the word *veritatem* we encounter the most dramatic demonstration of the organizing power of a rhythmic pattern. The tones of the tenor are laid out in a repeated pattern of three dotted quarters followed by a dotted quarter rest, an example of the fifth rhythmic mode. The monotonous reiteration of this pattern in the tenor sets up a regular motion that provides a firm rhythmic foundation for the duplum which moves in the quicker pace of the first mode. This passage typifies Leonin's modification of the nota contra notam style into discant style. Instead of singing only one note against each note of the tenor, the duplum normally has two, the result of combining the first rhythmic mode in the duplum with the fifth in the tenor. Nevertheless, the parts move together in closely related rhythmic phrases. For each statement of the rhythmic pattern of two measures in the tenor, the duplum has a group of notes of corresponding duration. At this point in the composition, the tenor has reasserted its primacy. Through the power of its rhythmic pattern, it has compelled the duplum, which had moved at will in the preceding section of organum purum, to submit its phrasing to that of the tenor.

Not only does the rhythmic pattern of the tenor control the phrasing of the duplum, it also determines to a large extent the actual tones of the added melody. As each note of the tenor is intoned, the duplum is forced to form a perfect interval with it. Only on the second of the two notes of the duplum's pattern, the positio, is it allowed a dissonant note. There are only two instances in this discant section where the duplum does not obey this rule, in the second half of measures 29 and 33. But these exceptions still conform to the same general law, for they occur on the second note, the positio, of the tenor's pattern. It is evident that in the new art of measured polyphony rhythm has become a decisive factor in creating both harmony and melody.

The manuscripts in which Leonin's works are preserved name no composers. Were it not for the mention of his music by an anonymous writer in the thirteenth century, we would know neither his name, nor the extent of his works. This Englishman, who studied at the University of Paris about 1280, wrote that "Master Leonin was the best composer of organum, who made the *Magnus liber organi de Gradali et Antiphonario* (a great book of organum for the Gradual and Antiphonal) in order to increase the divine service." The Gradual and Antiphonal referred to are chant books for the Mass and Offices. It has already been observed that Leonin set only the responsorial forms of the chant. In the Mass these would be the Gradual and Alleluia. Leonin's *Magnus liber* includes the principal responsorial chants both for the Mass and the Offices throughout the church year. In this volume we witness an expansion of the principle of a cyclic arrangement of organum, first seen in the small collection of Alleluias at Chartre, into proportions rivalling those of the great philosophical *summae* of Thomas Aquinas and Albertus Magnus in the next century. The vastness of such an undertaking bespeaks a boldness and limitless confidence on the part of the composer that still excites our wonder. Never again in the history of Western music was a composer in a position to create singlehandedly a repertory spanning the entire church year with music for both the Mass and the Offices. Early in the sixteenth century a comparable task was undertaken by Heinrich Isaac, who limited his work to the music for the Mass, but death overtook him before he had finished his labors.

In a typically mediaeval manner Leonin's successor, Perotin, chose to work within the framework of inherited tradition. Seeing in Leonin's music an authoritatively sanctioned repertory of liturgical music, Perotin devoted himself primarily to a revision of the *Magnus liber organi*. He wished to keep the monumental achievement of his predecessor alive and vibrant by substituting newly composed sections for passages that seemed old-fashioned. The greatest opportunity for modernization by means of further rhythmic refinements lay within the discant style, and it was the discant sections of Leonin's organum that Perotin rewrote. For many of Leonin's individual discant sections he created an alternative version, a substitute setting called a *clausula*.

The substitute clausula *Verita*(*tem*) of Perotin demonstrates the rhythmic refinements introduced by him (Illustration 5).

The clausula has as its text only the first three syllables of the word *veritatem*, corresponding to measures 25 through 36 of the composition of Leonin just examined. There are no difficulties in substituting the clausula for the corresponding section of Leonin's work, since the text is identical and the notes of the tenor reproduce the same fragment of the chant melody. At its end, the clausula rejoins the original version of Leonin on the syllable "tem," which would then be continued until the conclusion of the organum. Though the tones of the tenor have not been changed, its rhythmic pattern has been altered. Perotin relieves the monotony of the repeated pattern of three dotted quarter notes and a dotted quarter rest, by alternating it with a pattern of a dotted half note, dotted quarter note, and dotted quarter rest. Because of the difference in the rhythmic patterns, the tones of the chant are grouped in different phrases in the two versions. As a result one can scarcely perceive the identity of the two tenors: they sound like different melodies. The tenor of the clausula, furthermore, introduces a new feature, the repetition of the chant. The first twelve measures contain all the tones of the chant for the syllables "verita"; these are repeated in the last twelve measures.

ILLUSTRATION 5

[tem]

This double statement of the chant gives the composer a greater opportunity to unleash the propulsive forces inherent in modal rhythm.

In Leonin's discant style the regular coincidence of the rhythmic
patterns of the tenor and duplum repeatedly interrupted the continuity
of rhythmic movement. To avoid this somewhat halting motion, the
phrases of the duplum and the tenor are now made to overlap. While one
voice rests, the other continues, bridging the silence and producing a
dovetailing of the parts. By this device the rhythmic motion of the
clausula is continued without interruption from beginning to end. This
technique has been skillfully employed from measure five onward. A
more subtle use of the procedure appears in the second and fourth measures where the duplum fails only by a very brief pause to span the gap

created by the tenor rest. This clausula exemplifies the refinements that
Perotin introduced into the discant style of Leonin—refinements, it should
be noted, that are primarily rhythmic in nature.

In an age of intellectual ferment and expanding horizons, the creative
spirit could not for long be limited to the task of restoring and refurbish-
ing an older repertory. But before the old form of organum was abandoned, it was brought to a final brilliant climax. Completely new pieces
were composed by Perotin for the most solemn feasts of the church year
for three and even four parts. The greater complexity and grander proportions of the three- and four-voiced organa made them particularly
appropriate for feasts of special significance. Although the basic structure
of three- and four-part organa was essentially the same as that of the
older type, problems of harmony arose which had been absent in the
simple two-part compositions. This did not bring about a new harmonic
practice, however. Each part was brought individually into a harmonic
relationship with the tenor in the same manner as in an organum of only
two parts. Though on the first value of the rhythmic modes the perfect
intervals were employed almost exclusively, dissonant sounds often arose,
for one of the added melodies might be sounding a fourth above the
tenor and another the fifth, producing the dissonant interval of a second
between each other. On the second half of the modal foot, where dissonance had always been permitted, the degree of discordance measurably
increased, as two or three melodies moved freely against the tenor. Because the voices lie within approximately the same vocal range, they tend
to cross and recross as they proceed.

The two existing four-part organa of Perotin (only a fragment of
another has been preserved) are truly enormous compositions. The
Gradual *Sederunt*, for example, contains no less than 143 measures of
music for the initial word alone. Consequently the chant in the tenor,
which consists of only seven notes, is so extensively protracted that its
identity as a melody is virtually lost. The three-part organa must have
been preferred to the larger ones, for not only are more of them preserved but they also appear to have maintained a position in the repertory
for a longer time. Notwithstanding the great artistic merits of these
works the age of organum came to an end with the death of Perotin.
Thereafter, though the organa of Leonin and Perotin continued to be
performed until the end of the thirteenth century, almost no new ones
were composed.

Another category of musical composition, the *conductus*, had been
undergoing a somewhat similar development side by side with organum.
The conductus, a setting of a Latin poetic text, owes its origin to the

same creative impulse that produced the tropes and sequences. As its name implies, the conductus was presumably introduced into the liturgy at moments when the officiants were proceeding from one part of the church to another. Like the tropes and sequences, the conductus appears to have been related at its moment of origin to a pre-existing Gregorian chant. The tenors of the later polyphonic conductus are not, however, drawn from Gregorian melodies, but are freely composed. It has been discovered recently that in a few of these works the tenor occasionally quotes fragments of a chant, but this seems to have been an exceptional procedure. Though the relationship of the conductus to the liturgy is not revealed by musical associations, many of the texts are so clearly a poetic commentary upon the nature of certain feasts that they must have been intended for performances on a given day. Still others celebrate important events in history or refer to specific individuals. Thus the conductus functions both within and without the liturgy.

Without a pre-existent chant to serve as foundation in the tenor, the conductus was an original composition in all its parts. To be sure, the composer of organum imposed upon the chant its rhythmic design, but in the conductus the musician had to go one step further and create the melody of the tenor itself as well as its rhythm. Nevertheless, the method of composition remains the same, for the composer in making a conductus, we are told, must first invent a tenor "as beautiful as he can," and then add to it the duplum, the triplum (the third part) and the quadruplum (the fourth part) depending on how many vocal parts are employed. Though the conductus may use musical techniques characteristic of organum, it differs from organum in that its text is a Latin poem usually of several stanzas.

The impact of poetic form upon musical structure is a prominent feature of the music of the conductus. The successive strophes of the poem could be treated by the composer in two ways. First, he might simply repeat the music composed for the first stanza for each of the succeeding ones, a procedure described as strophic composition and generally used in hymns. Or the composer may choose to provide independent settings for each stanza. The term *through-composed* (from the German word *durchkomponiert*) is used to describe this method. Most of the time the text is sung simultaneously in all the parts in an essentially syllabic style. In some, but not all, conductus the composer adds *caudae* (literally tails or codas), extensive melismata, on certain of the syllables. Some of these features of the conductus are illustrated in the conductus *Salvatoris hodie* of Perotin reproduced in Illustration 6 (only the first four lines are given).

ILLUSTRATION 6

Triplum

Duplum

Tenor

Sal- va- to- ris ho- di e

San-guis pre- gu- sta-

tur in quo Sy- on fi- li- e

ILLUSTRATION 6 (*continued*)

Sto- la can- di- da-

tur.

Salvatoris hodie is a through-composed conductus consisting of three stanzas. The first two are set for three voices while the third employs only the tenor and duplum. The sense of the text suggests that *Salvatoris hodie* was composed for the Christmas season, and it is known that it was sung, at least in Beauvais, just after the Sequence in the Mass of the Circumcision Feast (New Year's Day). Though the trochaic rhythm of the poem may have suggested the use of the first rhythmic mode for this composition, it is surprising to discover that the rhythmic pattern of the music and the text almost never coincide. Normally the syllables are extended the length of the modal foot, transforming the text into a succession of spondees. Thus the meter of the poem is ignored in its syllabic declamation, but is taken up as the rhythmic mode of the composition as a whole.

The larger formal design of the poem, on the other hand, is scrupulously followed by the composer. Each line of the text is treated as an entity with caudae serving as pronounced marks of punctuation. The point at which the cauda is placed reveals the composer's regard for the meter of the poem. The first and third lines of the text contain seven syllables in trochaic meter and the music emphasizes the long at the end of the lines with a cauda on the final syllable. The second and fourth lines, however, have but six syllables with a feminine ending. In order to highlight the penultimate syllable (a long) the cauda is placed upon it rather than upon the final syllable. Thus the caudae not only serve to separate the lines of the strophe, but appear to be inserted with due regard for the meter of the poem.

The creation of the individual parts in successive order, a procedure inherent in organum in which the tenor was a pre-existent section of chant, is a fundamental characteristic of polyphonic music. It implies a primary concern on the part of the composer for the integrity of each part as a melody, while the superimposition of the parts one over the other producing the harmony is a matter of secondary importance. In other words, the composer's concern for the vertical relationship of the parts, the simultaneity of their sounds, is conditioned only by the necessity of producing consonant intervals at the beginning of each rhythmic part. Consequently, dissonant, and to our ears, harsh harmonies abound between stressed or cadential points. Measures twenty-eight through thirty-one dramatically illustrate this point; each part taken by itself is a perfectly satisfactory melodic phrase and at the beginning of each measure the harmony is consonant, yet between these points the voices rub abrasively against each other, producing striking dissonances.

In the syllabic sections of the example the discant style of composition prevails because of the perfectly coordinated declamation of the

text. In the caudae, on the other hand, melodic phrases frequently overlap, propelling the rhythmic motion ever forward. This procedure of
overlapping the phrases is given a new and peculiar form in measures
twenty-five and twenty-six. There the duplum and the triplum do, indeed, alternate, but now each sings a single note while the other rests,
resulting in a rapid hiccough-like effect. In mediaeval musical theory this
device, a rhythmic refinement within the discant style, is called a *hocket*.
This somewhat eccentric manner was apparently highly esteemed in the
thirteenth century, and a number of extended hockets were written as
independent compositions.

The conductus, as a category of musical composition, came to an
end near the middle of the thirteenth century, not because it was an
unfruitful field for further cultivation, but because it was supplanted by
a new type of composition, the *motet*, whose roots were more immediately nourished by the main stream of musical thought. Polyphony had
originated as a simultaneous trope of the chant, and reliance upon an
authoritative, pre-existent corpus of monodic music as the foundation
upon which new compositions were constructed was deeply imbedded in
the thought processes indigenous to the mediaeval mind. The conductus
with its original tenor set the composer adrift, as it were, with only his
native musical resources and the form of the poem to guide him. This
freedom of artistic inventiveness lay outside the characteristic mode of
mediaeval thinking and carried within itself risks and dangers that must
have left the musician somewhat uncomfortable.

Perotin's conductus, as well as his substitute clausulae and three-
and four-voiced organa, appear, in the light of subsequent history, as the
last stage in the exploration of the possibilities of long-established forms.
Perotin's music, brilliant in its exploitation of all the resources of polyphonic music, nevertheless remains conservatively within the framework
of a very old tradition. It would appear from this that the hitherto pro-
ductive process of troping had finally run its course. As far as musical
composition was concerned, for the moment it had. But for the poet this
was not so. Or, rather, as the poets turned to polyphonic music as a possible field for troping, they inadvertently revealed to the musician an
avenue of escape from his dilemma.

In order to understand how a poet's trope created a new field for
the musician we must return to the substitute clausula. In the organa
and substitute clausulae, when the composer troped the chant by adding
a melody of his own invention to be sung simultaneously with the chant,
it was always understood that the added parts sang the text of the chant
together with the tenor. But the substitute clausula, constructed over a
melismatic tenor and for this reason having very little text, presented an

open invitation for the poet to trope the words of the chant. Shortly after 1200 poets began to fit a different text to the added melody of substitute clausulae, a text which was, in fact, a trope of the chant text. The duplum was now both a musical and a textual trope of the chant. Since these new texts appeared in substitute clausulae, they were to be performed within the related organum and consequently in the liturgy. The duplum, provided with its own text, subsequently changed its name to *motetus*, from the French *mot*, word, and the troped substitute clausula became a *motet*. In this new area of literary activity the poet was simply taking advantage of an unexploited body of music created by the composer of polyphonic music—just as he had done when he created the sequence.

Once the idea of a troped text in the duplum was generally accepted, the relationship between the poet and the composer reversed itself. Instead of merely adding words to a pre-existent duplum, the poet now wrote texts for which the musician made a new composition designed to accommodate the metrical form of the poem. At first these poems continued to refer to the words or the subject matter of specific chants, and it was understood that the composer should set them to music by building his composition upon a melismatic fragment drawn from the indicated chant. Such motets could still be used as appropriate substitutes for a section of organum. Before long it was recognized that motets were, in fact, musical entities in themselves and could be performed quite apart from their context with an organum. When the motet was performed as an independent composition, the tenor was no longer sung, but was played on an instrument. This was because the tenor melody had only a few syllables from the text of the chant, and these had no meaning when divorced from the neighboring sections of chant.

The example in Illustration 7 shows the ambivalent function of the motet. (The triplum is a later addition to this composition and for the moment must be disregarded.)

The tenor encompasses the same portion of chant used in the substitute clausula, Illustration 5, which replaced the discant section of Leonin's organum *Propter veritatem*, Illustration 3. Therefore, insofar as the tenor is concerned, the motet is just another substitute clausula. But whether this composition may actually be inserted into the organum as a replacement of Leonin's discant section depends not only upon the tenor but upon the text of the motetus. The poem is in praise of Mary and, since Leonin's organum is a part of the Gradual for the Feast of the Assumption of the Blessed Virgin, the text of the motet is entirely appropriate to the liturgy of that feast. That the poet definitely had this Gradual in mind is revealed by the fact that the last word of his text is *veritate* and that on this word he departs from the rhyme scheme that

ILLUSTRATION 7

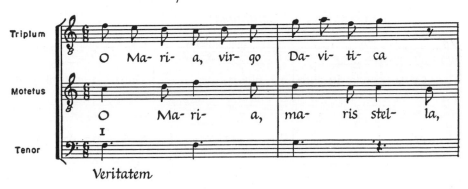

Triplum: O Ma- ri- a, vir- go Da- vi- ti- ca

Motetus: O Ma- ri- a, ma- ris stel- la,

Tenor: Veritatem

Triplum: Vir- gi- num flos, vi- tae spes u- ni- ca Vi- a ve- ni- ae

Motetus: Ple- na gra- ti- ae Ma- ter si- mul

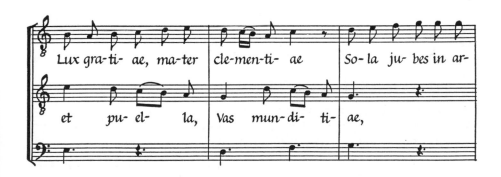

Triplum: Lux gra- ti- ae, ma- ter cle- men- ti- ae So- la ju- bes in ar-

Motetus: et pu- el- la, Vas mun- di- ti- ae,

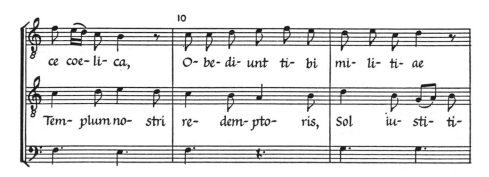

Triplum: ce coe- li- ca, O- be- di- unt ti- bi mi- li- ti- ae

Motetus: Tem- plum no- stri re- dem- pto- ris, Sol iu- sti- ti-

ILLUSTRATION 7 (*continued*)

ILLUSTRATION 7 (*continued*)

has prevailed throughout the poem. Though the motet may be inserted into Leonin's organum, this does not preclude its performance outside of the liturgy, for both the poem and its musical setting are complete in themselves.

In the motet the task of the composer is complicated by the fact that a pre-existent section of chant must be used for the tenor, while the length and formal structure of the motetus is established by the poem. Since the chant is essentially musical material with little text, it is more pliable in the composer's hands, while the poem possesses formal properties that had to be respected by the musician. Consequently the poem is the point of departure for the composer. The text of the motetus consists of 16 trochaic lines alternately of eight syllables and five syllables. Since the lines of five syllables all have the same rhyme (with the exception of the last), they divide the poem into eight members each containing thirteen syllables arranged in the first rhythmic mode, the equivalent of the trochee.

With the length and rhythm of the motetus established, the composer then had to lay out the pre-existent chant in the tenor to make it provide a suitable support for the motetus. First a rhythmic pattern had to be selected that would mesh with the first rhythmic mode of the motetus. Although either the first or sixth mode would fit with the rhythm of the motetus, the slower fifth mode was chosen as a rhythmic foundation for the more animated movement of the first mode above it. With the length of the motetus and the rhythmic patterns of both parts established the composer was ready to remold the melody of the chant to make it fit with the upper part. The original chant melody of sixteen notes, even while moving more slowly, was not long enough to match the length of the motetus. Some kind of repetition was necessary. As the Roman numerals in the example indicate, a threefold repetition in the tenor succeeds in stretching out the chant to a length commensurate with that of the motetus. But these repetitions are not exact. Moreover, the composer has occasionally duplicated a tone of the chant or dropped one of two repeated notes. The variations that occur represent the adjustments necessary in order to make the two parts equal in length. In the example in Illustration 8 the tenor has been set down schematically to show the variations made in successive repetitions. (The tenor melody should also be compared with the original fragment of chant present in Leonin's discant section given in Illustration 4.)

Although the length of the motetus and its rhythmic characteristics were determined by the structure of the text, its melodic contours are

ILLUSTRATION 8

conditioned by the tones of the chant in the tenor. In those passages where the tenor is exactly repeated (measures 13–16 and 25–28, also 21–24 and 29–32), the melody of the motetus is also repeated. Elsewhere the variations in the tenor made repetitions in the motetus impossible. Although these melodic repetitions provide additional details of formal order, they are subordinate to the essential structure which is erected upon elements of rhythmic order.

The triplum, which is a later addition to the composition, was conceived as a trope of the motetus. Even tropes were subject to troping! The complexities involved in the addition of the triplum suggest that the poet and musician were one and the same person, for the formal design of the poem seems to have been determined by musical considerations of a primarily rhythmic nature. By using the sixth mode in the triplum together with the fifth in the tenor and the first in the motetus, the composer achieved not only an inherently coordinated metrical scheme but stamped each part with a distinctive rhythmical character. Each moves in its own rhythmic framework, yet is perfectly compatible with each of the others. But the tenor and motetus establish almost too strict a formal order by the regularity of their periods. To superimpose another series of phrase lengths in the triplum with the same regularity of succession would produce monotony. Therefore, the structure of the poem in the triplum was arranged to offset the strictly repetitive scheme of rhythmic patterns in the motetus and tenor.

For the first two lines of text the phrases of the triplum neatly coincide with the regular patterns below. In measure five, however, a line of five syllables is introduced which causes the succeeding lines of ten syllables to be displaced by one measure. As a result, in measures six through nineteen the triplum consistently spans the pauses that mark off the rhythmic patterns of the motetus and tenor. In measures 20–23 the triplum is again interrupted in its regular progress by a single word, *quae*, standing alone and followed by four lines of five syllables. The normal ten-syllable lines then return, but to a new position in relation to the other parts. This time they anticipate by half a measure the regular patterns below with the result that all three parts reach the end together.

Within the theoretical limits of the rhythmic modes the greatest number of syllables a single foot might encompass was three. An expansion of this restriction, which ultimately led to an escape from the narrow confines of modal rhythm, is already apparent in the triplum. In measure 5 and also measures 20–23 four syllables are introduced in each foot instead of the normal three. At the moment these aberrations remain within the general framework of the sixth rhythmic mode. But once the door was opened, composers began to depart more and more extensively from the regularity of the modal rhythms until finally only vestiges of the old practice remained.

The addition of the triplum makes the motet's function as a substitute for the discant section of Leonin's organum doubtful. Although the text of the triplum was an appropriate trope, the introduction of a three-part composition within the framework of a two-part organum is problematical. Soon even the remotest possibility of using motets as substitute clausulae disappeared. Once the practice of singing motets as independent compositions began, it was no longer necessary to continue to trope liturgical texts. From this moment secular poems in both Latin and French were written to supply the demand for the increasingly popular motet. At times the motets are even polyglot with the motetus sung in Latin while the triplum carries a French text. But the musician was loath to divorce himself from the chant. Though he might choose any section of chant suitable for a motet tenor without regard to its position within the liturgy, he still held firmly to the stock of melodies the old repertory provided him. Thus the motet, born and nurtured in the church, became a secular category of the greatest importance for the next two centuries without breaking its vital contact with the chant. This strange new offspring of the organum typifies the intermixture of sacred and secular elements so characteristic of mediaeval life.

The expansion of the motet repertoire in the thirteenth century was so extensive that other forms of polyphonic music were neglected. The organum, though still performed, no longer attracted the attention of composers, while the activity of contemporary poets formerly directed toward the conductus was channeled into the motet. To an ever-increasing degree the motet became secular in its content, and the language of the poetry in the last half of the century was almost exclusively in the vernacular. After 1250 the restrictions of modal rhythm also gave way to a less schematically controlled rhythm. The practice of introducing two syllables in place of one, as in the triplum of Illustration 7, was extended to include from three to seven syllables in place of one.

This development may be seen in a motet composed by Pierre de la Croix at the end of the thirteenth century (Illustration 9).

The melody of the tenor is the concluding melisma of the Respond of the Gradual *Omnes de Saba venient*, for the Feast of Epiphany, January 6. Since this part of the chant is sung by the choir, not the soloist, it is obvious that the composer selected this fragment of chant not because it is a typical place for polyphony to occur but solely because of its musical properties. However, in the secular motet divorced from the liturgy there is no limitation upon the composer in his choice of chant melody for the tenor of his composition.

ILLUSTRATION 9

ILLUSTRATION 9 *(continued)*

Et je, qui li ai fait homma-ge, Pour li ser-vir tout mon

Car bonne

a- - ge, De loi- al cuer sans pen-ser tra- hi- son,

a- mour me fait de - si- rer

Chan-te- rai, Car de li tieng un si douz he- ri- ta-

La mieus

ge___ Que joi-e n'ai se de ce non: C'est la pen- sé-e

en- - se- gni- - e K'on puist en

ILLUSTRATION 9 (*continued*)

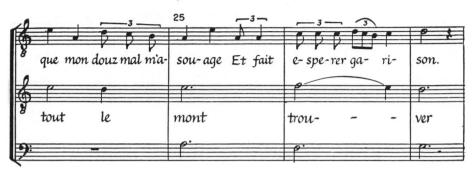

que mon douz mal m'a- sou- age Et fait e- spe- rer ga- ri- son.

tout le mont trou- - - ver

Ne pour quant seur moi puet cla- mer hau- sage A- mours, et

A li

moi tout mon vi- vant te- nir En sa pri- son.

ne doit on nule au- - tre com-

Ne ja pour ce ne pen- se- rai vers li mes- pri-

pa- - - rer.

ILLUSTRATION 9 (*continued*)

ILLUSTRATION 9 (*continued*)

Vestiges of the modal rhythms are still apparent in the tenor and motetus, although the note values used in the example obscure this fact. The tenor is laid out in the fifth mode, using for the first part of the motet the same pattern employed in the previous motet. The tenor melody is stated twice, the second time with the rests omitted. Without the rests the tenor becomes merely a succession of long values. To this extent a basic feature of modal rhythm has been cast aside. The motetus rather tenuously maintains the first rhythmic mode. In the second and third measures it is clearly present, at other times notes of shorter value intrude and obscure the characteristic pattern of the mode.

The triplum abandons the modal system almost completely. Only in measures 15, 30, 44, 46, 47, 50, 52, and 54 are the customary three syllables for each foot of the sixth mode present. Elsewhere, in place of one syllable two to seven are introduced. Obviously the pace of this triplum cannot be the same as that of one in the normal sixth mode. In relation to the former tempo of the sixth mode the triplum now moves more slowly because of the necessity of enunciating so many syllables. But with respect to the number of syllables to be sung, its pace has quickened. To accommodate the many notes of the triplum, the motetus and tenor move much more slowly than formerly and virtually lose their identity as modal patterns. By using the same scale of note values as that employed in Illustration 7 the first few measures of this motet would be written like those in Illustration 10.

It is immediately apparent to what extent smaller note values have been introduced and how much the pace of the composition departs from the characteristic pulse of modal rhythm. The new developments in rhythm, particularly in the triplum, produced a greater individuality of movement in the various parts. But the agitated movement of the triplum gave this part such prominence that the tenor and to some extent the motetus were reduced to a subordinate role as accompanying voices.

The rhythmic freedom of the music is a reflection of the metrical irregularity of the poetry. On the other hand, the recurrence of rhyming syllables is observed in the music, for they determine phrase lengths and mark the points of cadence. The triplum regularly alternates two rhyming syllables, *ge* and *on*, but only the latter coincides with the end of each musical phrase. The much shorter text of the motetus uses only one rhyme which consistently marks the end of each phrase in the music. Rhyme, to a large extent, has replaced meter as a governing factor in the relationship between music and poetry.

The dominant role of rhythm in the polyphonic music of the twelfth and thirteenth centuries is the most dramatic manifestation of the mediaeval concept of music as sounding number. If mathematical proportions

ILLUSTRATION 10

seemed to be a limiting factor as applied to harmony, they opened up vast new areas for the development of rhythm. By the coordination of the individual parts measured by proportionate numbers the voices in polyphonic music moved rationally in time. Without the regulation of movement for each part within a context of several voices, polyphony was doomed to remain in a state of primitive improvisation. For music is an art whose distinctive feature lies in the fact that it moves through time. Time had to be measured to be comprehended, and once brought under the order of quantitative measurement it became an element which could be manipulated and controlled. This was the major achievement of the composers of polyphony in the twelfth and thirteenth centuries.

V THE MIDDLE AGES

Part II. Of Time and the Temporal
1300-1400

THE CHRONICLE of the fourteenth century is a melancholy one. France and England became embroiled in a series of wars that dragged on into the middle of the next century. The French territory was ravaged time and again; for a period after 1420 even Paris was occupied by the invaders. Rebellions flared up in the two dominions whose kings were preoccupied with military maneuvers rather than the administration of their realms. Both countries suffered enormously from the drain on their economic resources. As if this were not misery enough, the bubonic plague crept into Italy in 1347. Within two years France, Spain, England, and Germany had experienced the horrors of the Black Death. Before the disease had run its course, as much as a third of the population of some countries had perished. A form of hysteria took possession of the people in these years. The hypnotic frenzy of the St. Vitus dance seized many villages, while bands of flagellants, chanting and scourging themselves, roamed the countryside.

Even the universal church was torn asunder. The French Pope, Clement V (1305–1314), and his successors never took up residence at Rome, but made Avignon in southern France the seat of the papacy. During their pontificates the church became the slave, willing or unwilling, of French interests and a pawn in the political maneuvers of the warring kingdoms. In the eyes of Christendom the removal to Avignon seemed an abdication of the papacy's claim to universal authority which derived from its occupancy of the seat of St. Peter's in Rome. Rightfully the pope should exercise his authority from the throne of St. Peter.

In 1377 Pope Gregory XI finally returned to Rome, but this did not improve the worsening situation of the church. When he died in the very next year, the college of cardinals under the pressure of a Roman mob elected an Italian pope. Within months the cardinals, most of whom were French, regretted their action and named another pope, Clement VII. Thus began the Great Schism during which the world was confronted with the spectacle of two popes, one in Rome, the other in Avignon, hurling anathema at each other and demanding the allegiance of all Christianity for themselves. The schism was not healed until 1417, when the Council of Constance deposed the claimants to the papal throne and elected Cardinal Colonna to be the head of a reunited church as Pope Martin V.

With these years of endless conflict and the decline of the authority of the church there came an inevitable secularization of culture. The spheres of sacred and secular thought, never too far apart in the Middle Ages, now intermingled even more freely. The mores of this society were those of the nobility who lived by the forms of courtly chivalry established as early as the beginning of the twelfth century. The basis of this code of conduct was the oath of loyalty binding lord and vassal together in a personal relationship. The greatest virtue of a knight was to be loyal and true, and the greatest vice to be false and disloyal. Another requisite of the chivalric character was bravery, for the primary obligation of the vassal was to render military service to his lord.

As conditions of life became more stable in the lordly chateaux, a certain elegance of deportment was demanded of their inhabitants. They must possess the art of well-speaking and the niceties of behavior which make social living tolerable. A series of conventions grew out of this way of life. One was the tournament in which the knight displayed his valor and military prowess in combat with his peers before a throng of spectators. Another was the ceremony in which the young squire was dubbed a knight after having been tested in the lists. Through this stylization of the mediaeval way of life the rude warrior of the past was transformed into a courtier.

The appearance of a social existence centering about the courts introduced a new relationship between the sexes. Hitherto women had been little more than chattels: their function had been to serve their master, to bear him children, and in the case of women of noble birth to act as pawns in political alliances through their marriages. Now another attitude towards women arose, reversing the traditional roles played by the sexes. The woman became the mistress and her suitor her humble servant. In courtly love the woman was a symbol, embodying in her physical beauty truth and perfection. In her grace of body and character there shone the order and proportion with which God had ordered the universe. One might love in her the truth and beauty of the world, just as one might aspire to that highest perfection which is God. Thus worthy of love, she demanded of her suitor an equal perfection of character, just as the love of God requires of us unblemished virtue and selfless endeavor.

Since this love was an ideal one, it mattered little whether the lady were married or not: the courtier was free to choose his own mistress. This etherealized amour was not, however, wholly divorced from the flesh. As it was hoped that the love of God would eventually culminate in union with Him, so the faithful lover longed for fruition in the arms of his beloved. The equivocal morality of this belief is revealed in the story of Lancelot and Queen Guinevere. Faithless to King Arthur in the betrayal of her marriage vows, Guinevere is nonetheless faithful to Lancelot and the ideals of courtly love in yielding herself to him.

An elaborate etiquette was devised to regulate the conduct of courtly love. The same conditions that prevailed in the relationship of lord and vassal were imposed upon that of the lady and her knight. The lover must swear eternal loyalty to his mistress; he must defend her fair name with the strength of his arms; and he must at all times display the politesse of the true courtier. A single misstep in the niceties of courtly etiquette was sufficient to banish him forever from his lady's graces. Growing ever more artificial, this code even led to the formation of courts of love where women of the highest birth debated the delicate problems that arose in the fulfillment of this ideal. What decision should be rendered in the case of the young man who, having been granted the hope of attaining the love of his lady only after swearing absolute obedience and vowing never in any way to mention her name, broke his oath one day by defending her reputation against the calumnies of some other knights? Was the lady right in denying her love to him because he had violated his promise by singing her praises in public? These were the matters that engaged the interest of wellborn women of the day, half in play and half in earnest.

The knights of these romances were supposed to possess the attributes of fair-seeming and fair-speaking. The demand for elegance in speech led them to the composition of poetry and music to beguile their loves. The tradition of these aristocratic poets, known as troubadours in the south of France and trouvères in the north, began with William IX, Duke of Aquitaine, whose works were composed between 1087 and 1127. His example was followed by scores of other nobles. Until well into the thirteenth century the ability to turn a polished verse was an essential accomplishment of the true courtier.

In subject matter the poetry of the troubadours ranges from the most delicate depiction of an idealized love to the grossest portrayal of the joys of sensual love. It is not a highly personal art, for it uses a conventionalized diction. The poet likens himself to a prisoner whose mistress holds the keys to release. He yearns for death to free him from the pangs of unrequited love and finds a new death in the ecstasy of love fulfilled. Certain themes appear many times with only slight modifications in words and ideas. Such is the *alba* or dawn-song in which the lovers or one who stands guard over their clandestine meeting reproach the day for coming to separate them. Not infrequently the poem is couched in the form of a debate, as in the *jeu parti* and the *tenso*.

However standardized the subject matter of the troubadour and trouvère lyrics might be, it was voiced in a multiplicity of verse forms too numerous to be recounted here. Only a few of them lived on to play an important part in the development of polyphonic music. Whether the troubadours also composed the music for their poetry is not quite clear. In some cases it appears that the poet was the author of the melody to which his poem was sung. At other times he probably relied upon a personal servant, a minstrel, to find the musical phrases suited to the words, or may even have adapted his poem to an existing melody.

As the chivalric tradition became ever more artificial, its forms and conventions were honored more than its substance. Gradually during the thirteenth century the troubadours and trouvères relinquished their art to their servants. The praises of courtly love were no longer sung by its aristocratic adherents but by professional minstrels. It is possible that the withdrawal of the nobleman from the field of poetic and musical activity was caused in part by the ever-widening influence of polyphony. Secular art could not remain forever aloof from this modern development, but the technical proficiency needed for polyphonic writing was more than a nobleman could be expected to acquire. He preferred instead to yield his muse to trained musicians.

Traces of the art of the troubadours began to appear in the French motets of the latter half of the thirteenth century. At first the composers of polyphonic music approached the literature of the courtly circles in an oblique manner. Lines and refrains borrowed from their lyrics were quoted by the anonymous authors of motet texts. Occasionally even musical refrains were inserted within the musical substance of the motet. Before the century had come to a close the complete verse forms of the troubadours had been assimilated by the composers of polyphonic music.

The first known composer of works in this genre was Adam de la Halle (c. 1230–c. 1288).

With the merging of the poetic art of the troubadours and the polyphonic music of the church there came a change in the status of the musician: the composer shifted his field of activity from the church to the court. One reason for this change was the growing weakness of the church in the fourteenth century. Divided against itself, it could no longer provide the artistic stimulation for the composer that it had in the past. Though the composer with but few exceptions was still a man who had taken religious vows, he now found an outlet for his creative talents in the service of some great prince rather than within the cloistered walls of the church. He had become a dependent of the court, a position which he retained until well into the eighteenth century.

The new status of the musician is brilliantly illustrated in the figure of Guillaume de Machaut. Born around 1300, Machaut entered the church in his youth. By 1333 he had been made a canon of Reims and the recipient of several benefices by Pope John XXII. The first part of his life, however, was spent in the service of the highest nobility. In 1323 he became secretary to John, the King of Bohemia and Duke of Luxembourg, and followed this restless warrior in his travels until his death at the battle of Crècy in 1346. Subsequently Machaut served John's daughter, the Duchess of Normandy, and was patronized by Charles King of Navarre, Jean Duke of Berry, and Charles the Fifth of France.

Cleric and courtier, Machaut also united in his person the accomplishments of the troubadour and the learned musician. He was both the greatest poet and the greatest musician of fourteenth-century France. In his verses he sings of courtly love and, more particularly, of his own love for a young lady named Peronne. A sense of pathos still shines through the conventional diction of the poetry in which the love of the elderly cleric and the adolescent girl is celebrated. As a musician, Machaut provided the polyphonic settings of his own poetry and also composed motets and a Mass which are among the most imposing musical structures of the century. The servant of God, servant of kings, servant of courtly love, Machaut is the embodiment of the ideals and manners of his century.

To speak of courtly love is to mention only one of the two streams whose confluence forms the main current of fourteenth-century music. The other is the tradition of music as a form of mathematical science. For all its acceptance of the formal elements of troubadour poetry, music subordinated itself neither to the rhythmic elements of verse nor to its content, but proudly maintained its own harmonious relationships as the constituent and determinant factors of its art. However, the dictum "Music is number related to sound" received a new interpretation in this period under the influence of Aristotelian philosophy. Earlier this statement had been taken to mean that the very substance of music was numerical proportion. Audible music was but one manifestation of the universal harmony of musica mundana, humana, and instrumentalis. Aristotle and his followers, however, maintained that the substance or material of music is properly only air in motion determined by specific mathematical relationships. They denied the music of the spheres and the music of the soul, for where in these is the air in motion that makes music?

Insofar as music is air, it is part of the natural world, which for Aristotle is the realm of that which comes into being and passes away. The world of change is one in which primal matter, amorphous and undifferentiated, is given existence by the imposition of forms upon it. That which was not becomes that which is and that which will pass away through the eternal process of form infusing matter. Nature is therefore the principle of motion and change, the measure of which is time. Though time is infinite, those portions of it in which a motion takes place may be measured by some arbitrary unit, be it the minute, the day, or the year.

Time, like motion and place, is a condition of all natural beings. Since music is sound, a form of air in motion that comes into being and passes away, time is one of its conditions. Music accordingly is a succession of tones capable of measurement. To put this statement another way: unless this succession of tones is measurable by some common unit, the relationship of one tone to another or the form of this motion will not be comprehensible to the human intellect. There must be a determinate temporal relationship between the tones. It is this consequence of Aristotelian science that influenced the musical thought of the fourteenth century. It is number as the measure of motion, number as musical rhythm, that becomes the primary interest of the composer.

The musicians took as a basis of rhythmic motion a unit called the *tempus* (time) which is nothing other than the short value or *brevis* of the older modal system. This arbitrary unit of duration may be used to measure values both larger and smaller than itself, just as the month may measure years or days. The tempus is divisible into smaller units, but the number of these divisions is limited by mediaeval conceptions of number. The number one is unity, indivisibility, and hence, perfection; two is difference; three is a new kind of perfection, because it includes both the number one and the number two. Subsequent numbers are but compounds of the first three. The fourteenth century therefore limited the division of the breve or tempus to two or three *semibreves* which are divisible in turn into either two or three smaller values called *semibreves minimae* (the smallest semibreves). When the breve is divided into three

semibreves, it is called perfect time (*tempus perfectum*). If divided into
only two, it is called imperfect time (*tempus imperfectum*). The accompanying diagram illustrates the subdivisions of the breve and gives
their modern equivalent in time signatures.

MUSICAL DIAGRAM

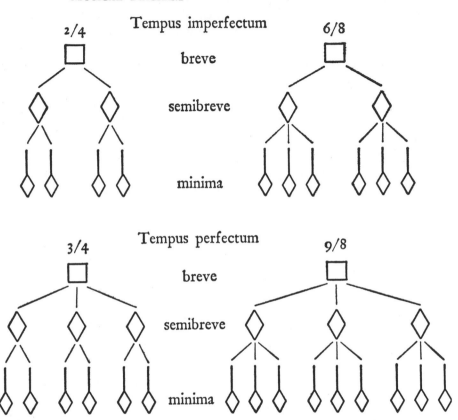

The codification of the four time signatures or prolations has long
been attributed to Philippe de Vitry, Bishop of Meaux (1291–1361).
Philippe, who was both poet and musician, presented the prolations in a
musical treatise called the *Ars nova* (The New Art). The title of this
work is now used frequently to designate the music of the entire fourteenth century.

The new conception of rhythm differs markedly from that of the
modal system. In the modal system the rhythmic patterns were predetermined entities. They were the result not of art, but of the properties
of number and proportion. To compose a measured composition was to
impose upon it *one* proportion, that of the reiterated modal pattern. In
the Ars nova the rhythmic values are no longer grouped in indivisible

metrical units, but may be arranged in any manner the composer desires. In this system the distinction between the first and second rhythmic modes no longer has meaning, for they both are but ways of arranging the subdivisions of the brevis. Syncopations, combinations of perfect and imperfect values such as three imperfect breves against two perfect ones, are now possible. The rhythmic progression is the product of art, not of nature. To quote a contemporary Italian musical theorist, Marchettus of Padua: "If someone should say that art imitates nature as much as possible, we should reply that this is true as regards fundamentals, but that nevertheless natural objects are disposed in art as they would never appear in nature. For art may combine a goat and a deer which are natural objects, creating a goat-deer. Such a thing is never to be found in the nature which art has as its fundament. It follows therefore that such an object is the product of art and not nature, albeit that art has taken it from natural things." Thus the composer, though dealing with natural elements, which in his case is sound, is free to impose any rhythmic form upon his material so long as it is rationally comprehensible through number.

The music of the fourteenth century is mainly secular in character, reflecting the changing milieu of the composer. Two types of music were cultivated, almost to the exclusion of all other forms of musical expression. Polyphonic settings of the lyrics of courtly love form by far the larger group, while the motet accounts for most of the remainder of the compositions of this period. Many of the motets, it is true, also sing of courtly love, but they borrow only the subject matter and not the poetic forms of the troubadours. Other motets usurp for themselves the themes formerly associated with the conductus, for their texts refer to contemporary events. They praise the virtuous and the mighty and censure the wicked; they mourn the death of a prince and celebrate the coronation of his successor. As the most grandly conceived musical structure of the epoch, the motet was particularly appropriate for the celebration of great political or religious occasions. As late as 1436, when the Duomo in Florence was dedicated with the monumental Renaissance dome of Brunelleschi still incomplete, the composer Guillaume Dufay could think of no greater tribute to pay this moment than to compose a four-part motet for it, his *Nuper rosarum flores*.

Like its predecessor of the thirteenth century, the motet continued to be a composition in which two or more texts were sung simultaneously in either Latin or French, and it also drew upon the Gregorian chant as a source for its tenor. Externally, the method of composing a motet remains the same, for the composer still proceeds by first imposing upon the Gregorian tenor a rhythmic order and then adding the upper parts in relation to it. But here the similarities cease, for the motet of the fourteenth century is no longer regulated by modal rhythm but is governed by the rhythmic system of the Ars nova. With the many rhythmic possibilities of this system at his disposal, the composer could order his composition with a freedom unknown to preceding generations. Freedom, however, for a man of the Middle Ages never meant license. Confronted with the numberless possibilities offered by the new rhythmic practice, Philippe de Vitry and his contemporaries devised a new means of controlling the creations of their artistic imagination, that of *isorhythm*.

The principle of isorhythm is one of the severest techniques ever used by the musician for the ordering of his work. It is applied above all to the tenors of compositions, though it may also appear in sections of the other melodic lines. In essence, isorhythm consists of the imposition of a rhythmic pattern upon the notes of the tenor. This pattern, unlike those of the rhythmic modes, is invented by the composer and it may be as long and as complex as he so desires. The use of isorhythm may be illustrated by one of Machaut's motets whose triplum begins with the words "De Bon Espoir" and the duplum or motetus with "Puisque la douce rousee." The tenor melody is derived from the melisma accompanying the word *speravi* in the Introit for the first Sunday after Pentecost. In modern chant books the melody appears as in Illustration 1.

ILLUSTRATION 1

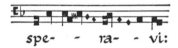

spe- - ra- - vi:

In his motet Machaut repeats this melody three times, as may be seen in Illustration 2, where the beginning of the melody in each of its occurrences is marked by a Roman numeral under the staff. (Machaut's melody varies slightly from that given in Illustration 1 above. An a is introduced between the second and third tones; and the fourth tone of the chant appears as a instead of b♭.)

The measures in Illustration 2 have been laid out to show their correlation. Each of the six lines of music contains one statement of the rhythmic pattern, which is called a *talea* (a cutting). As can be seen, the talea shows not the slightest trace of the patterns of modal rhythm. After three statements of the talea the value of each of its notes is cut in half, causing the pattern to move just twice as fast as formerly. Each statement of the talea can accommodate only twelve notes of the chant melody, which contains in all eighteen tones. Because of this disparity, the talea cuts across the melody in a quite arbitrary, though rational, way.

ILLUSTRATION 2

The second and fourth statements of the melody begin in the middle of the talea, and thus are given an entirely different physiognomy and sound than that of their first and third appearances.

Quite clearly Machaut is not the least bit interested in preserving the identity of the melody. For him it is only the raw material, the primal matter, which is to be given existence as part of a living artwork through the formative power of rhythm. He has taken something from nature, something given, and made of it a new being. Triumphing over nature, he has, in the words of Marchettus, created a "goat-deer."

Above this tenor, which is to be performed instrumentally, Machaut fashioned two melodies to accommodate the two texts he wrote for this work. These texts have clearly articulated poetic structures, and Machaut respects his handiwork by composing for them musical phrases whose lengths correspond to that of the individual lines of poetry. Several lines of the poems are sung during each repetition of the tenor talea, and these have been carefully adjusted to its length so that the end of the tenor pattern always coincides with the end of a musical phrase in the upper parts.

In some compositions the power of attraction of the isorhythmic pattern is so great that it casts its spell upon the other parts and over-throws the structure of the text. A striking example of this phenomenon is found in the Sanctus (Illustration 3) of Machaut's Mass, which is the earliest known polyphonic setting of the complete Ordinary. For the long texts of the Gloria and Credo Machaut made use of the note against note style typical of the conductus. But for the shorter texts of the Kyrie, Sanctus, Agnus Dei, and Ite missa est, he resorted to the isorhythmic principle developed in the motet.

The Sanctus, as well as all the other sections of the Mass, is written for four parts. It utilizes for its tenor, which is the next to the bottom voice, a Gregorian melody associated with this text. Not until after the exclamation *Sanctus* thrice repeated does the isorhythmic organization begin. Starting with measure 17 a talea eight measures long governs the tenor. It is repeated ten times before the movement comes to an end (only the first four statements are included in the example). Clearly there is no correlation between the talea and the form and meaning of the text. The first talea begins in the middle of the word *dominus* and concludes in the middle of the word *Sabaoth*. The next three taleae cut across the integral phrase *Pleni sunt celi et terra gloria tua*. In the remainder of the composition there exists the same disregard for the natural relationships of the words.

The force of the isorhythmic pattern is so compelling that the other melodies are drawn into its orbit. The lowest voice, called a *contratenor*, is also completely isorhythmic, having a talea that coincides in length with that of the tenor. In the two upper parts a sequence of rhythmic values four measures in length begins in the third measure of the tenor's talea. This sequence is repeated at exactly the same point in every talea of the composition. It is especially to be noted that this succession of values includes a hocket, which stands out in sharp contrast to the other portions of this work which are set in slower tones scarcely punctuated by rests. The sudden animation is somewhat startling to the auditor, but Machaut is not using this exotic device simply for the novelty of its effect. On the contrary, the hocket is fulfilling a most important function: it is serving as a structural device.

The form of this composition is created through the reiteration of a rhythmic pattern, but the fact that repetition is occurring is scarcely perceptible to the listener because of the length of the pattern. The flamboyance of the hocket, recurring at regular intervals in exactly the same form, focuses the attention of the listener upon it and makes him aware of the total structure of the composition. This practice is one indication of the extraordinary importance of rhythm in the music of the fourteenth century. In this Sanctus one can see that it is not melody or harmony that create form, but the rhythmic devices of talea and hocket.

In Machaut's motets musical form prevails over the poetic form. In

ILLUSTRATION 3

ILLUSTRATION 3 *(continued)*

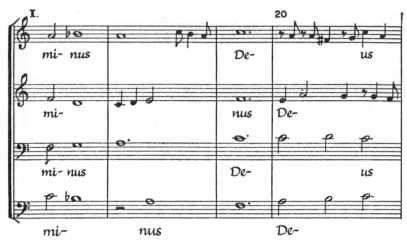

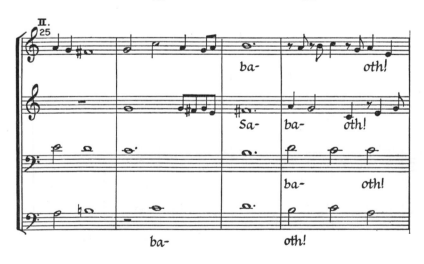

ILLUSTRATION 3 (*continued*)

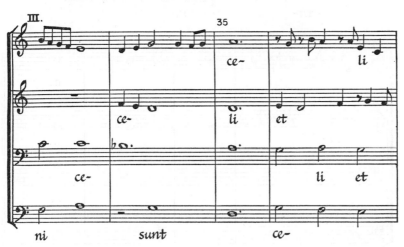

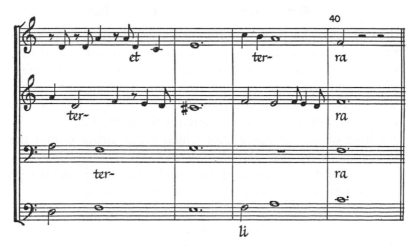

ILLUSTRATION 3 (*continued*)

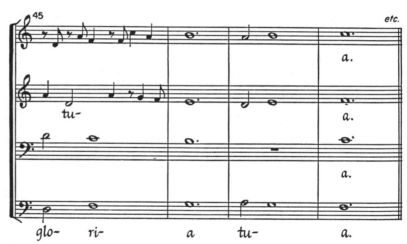

the settings of his poems written in forms inherited from the troubadours the reverse is true. These all have fixed and predetermined structures. For the composer the most important of the *formes fixes* are the *ballade*, the *virelai*, and the *rondeau*. The first two of these are strophic poems in which every stanza follows an identical scheme, but the rondeau normally has only one stanza. Characteristic of all three forms is the use of a refrain of one or more lines which recur either within the stanza or in successive stanzas.

A charming example of the rondeau is the following poem which was written in the earlier era of the troubadours.

1. *En ma dame ai mis mon cuer*
2. *Et mon penser.*
3. N'en partiroi a nul fuer,
4. *En ma dame ai mis mon cuer.*

5. Si m'ont sorpris si vair oeil
6. Riant et cler:
7. *En ma dame ai mis mon cuer*
8. *Et mon penser.*

Upon my lady I have fixed my heart and my mind. I shall not leave her for any reason, for *upon my lady I have fixed my heart.* I was so captivated by her hazel eyes, laughing and clear, that *upon my lady I have fixed my heart and my mind.*

The poem consists of only eight lines of which the first two form the refrain. The third line has the same number of syllables and the same rhyme as the first line of the refrain, which is repeated immediately after it. Lines five and six again agree in the number of syllables and in their rhyme with the two lines of the refrain, while the last two lines are a simple repetition of the refrain. The poet has skillfully fitted the lines together so that the reiteration of the refrain is not just a meaningless jingle but contributes to the meaning of the poem. Since all the lines have the same number of syllables and the same rhyme as the two members of the refrain, it is obvious that a musical setting of this poem would require only two phrases of melody, one for each line of the refrain. Each of the following lines would be sung to the phrase to which it corresponds in rhyme. In practice, the composer wrote down only the music of the refrain, leaving it to the performer to fit the lines of the poem to the appropriate phrase.

The music of this rondeau is simple to an extreme (Illustration 4).

ILLUSTRATION 4

The two phrases of the refrain are marked A and B in the score. In performance the two phrases are sung consecutively for the first two lines of the poem; then phrase A is sung twice to accommodate the third and fourth lines. For the last four lines the two phrases are sung one after the other two times. From the repetitions that occur in performance, a musical form results that may be diagrammed ABAAABAB. This is a form which, in opposition to that of the motet, is produced by melodic rather than rhythmic repetition. For all its clarity, this form is nevertheless not one which is born, like that of the motet, from purely musical factors. It comes into existence only as an incidental by-product of the text.

Machaut's rondeau *Rose, liz, printemps, verdure*, is a somewhat more complicated poem than the preceding one, for it has a refrain of three lines.

   1. *Rose, liz, printemps, verdure,*
   2. *Fleur, baume et tres douce odour,*
   3. *Belle, passes en doucour,*
   4. Et tous les biens de Nature
   5. Avez, dont je vous aour.
   6. *Rose, liz, printemps, verdure,*
   7. *Fleur, baume et tres douce odour.*
   8. Et quant toute creature
   9. Seurmonte vostre valour,
 10. Bien puis dire et par honnour:
 11. *Rose, liz, printemps, verdure,*
 12. *Fleur, baume et tres douce odour,*
 13. *Belle, passes en doucour.*

The rose, the lily, the Spring, the leaves, flower, tree, and sweetest scent, my beautiful, you surpass in sweetness, and all the best things of nature you possess, for which I adore you. *The rose, the lily, the Spring, the leaves, flower, tree, and sweetest scent.* How far your worth surpasses that of every creature I can well and truthfully say: *The rose, the lily, the Spring, the leaves, flower, tree, and sweetest scent, my beautiful, you surpass in sweetness.*

Despite the fact that the refrain consists of three lines, it is treated as if it had only two members, one of two lines and the other of one. If this poem is compared with the rondeau *En ma dame ai mis mon cuer*, it will be seen that lines 4 and 5 of Machaut's poem correspond to line 3 of the other. In other words, they are treated as a unit corresponding to the first member of the refrain, the two lines of which follow immediately in lines 6 and 7. The bipartite structure of the refrain is always adhered to in the rondeau, and Machaut's musical setting of this poem is no exception. In the example in Illustration 5 the two members of the refrain are marked off by a double bar, while the individual lines are designated A, B, and C.

The composition is set as an instrumentally accompanied solo song, and its mixture of vocal and instrumental timbres is characteristic of almost all the secular pieces of the fourteenth century. The instruments which are to perform the tenor, contratenor, and triplum are not specified. Any stringed or wind instrument having the appropriate range could be employed for these parts. It should be noted that the tenor and contratenor reveal no melodic idioms which could be associated with an instrument. On the contrary, they possess both the limited range and the

ILLUSTRATION 5

ILLUSTRATION 5 *(continued)*

ILLUSTRATION 5 *(continued)*

stepwise movement typical of vocal melody. In this rondeau, as in all secular songs, the tenor is not a pre-existent melody, but has been created by Machaut specifically for this piece. Both the tenor and contratenor function as a harmonic support of the facile melody of the voice or *cantus*, as this part is generally called. Their motion is consequently more subdued.

The concepts of melody and harmony in this composition are still remote from those which we readily understand. The melodic line of a Machaut song makes extensive use of melismata which break up the syllabic declamation of the text. To view these melismata as some kind of musical representation of the text or as an emphasis of certain words is wholly erroneous. That there is no such association can be seen in the fact that the melisma on the word *liz* is also sung to the insignificant definite article *les* of line 4. Machaut uses the melisma instead as a means of giving greater amplitude to the melody and as an opportunity to free the melody from the confines of a syllabically declaimed text. He also employs it to give the melody a cohesion that is quite independent of the text. Thus he uses a melisma in this rondeau to create a musical rhyme between the two members of the refrain, for the vocalization beginning in measure 20 is identical, except for its last three notes, with that beginning in measure 32. Machaut, the composer, has here introduced a musical correspondence, a formal element, that is not called for by the poem written by Machaut, the poet.

The harmony of Machaut's compositions is essentially mediaeval in its basic outlines—the perfect intervals are still regarded as the only pure consonances. Around these harmonies Machaut introduces anticipations and passing notes that are nevertheless oriented to the perfect intervals. These alterations succeed in enriching the mediaeval harmony in much the same way as nineteenth-century chord formations enrich the harmonic vocabulary of the eighteenth century.

One of the most striking and characteristic harmonies in the music of Machaut appears at the penultimate chord in important cadences. The tenor moves stepwise downward to its final tone; the voice part on the top moves in contrary motion stepwise to the octave above the tenor; while the contratenor approaches the fifth above the tenor on the final chord by a half step. This cadential progression may be observed at the end of the rondeau. The b in the voice part is the *leading tone* to its final (see Appendix, p. 460). The F♯ of the contratenor also functions as a leading tone to G. Such a cadence is called a double leading-tone cadence. (Although the penultimate note in the contratenor is not always raised by an accidental sign in the manuscripts, it is assumed that the performer supplied the sharp in order to avoid the tritone between his part and that of the cantus.)

The strong pull toward the final chord exerted by two voices moving upward by half steps against the downward stepwise motion of the lowest part produces an exceptional sense of finality as the tension is resolved in the last chord of the progression. With a cadential pattern of such power the composer had a tool with which he could emphasize points of division within a composition by purely harmonic means. Consequently, a way of marking off periods within a composition was available that was independent of rhythmic factors. With this device the structure of a composition could be articulated by something other than a repeated rhythmic pattern. In the secular songs with fixed poetic forms, the larger outlines of the form are determined by the poetic structure, but the smaller divisions are created through melodic phrases underlined by harmonic cadences.

The virelai differs from the rondeau in the fact that it has three stanzas. Each stanza has the same metrical scheme and begins and ends with a refrain. The form of each stanza consists of a refrain, followed by a couplet or two groups of lines identical in structure. These in turn are followed by a group of lines related to the refrain both in the number of syllables and in rhyme, and the stanza concludes with a repetition of the refrain. When all three stanzas are sung in succession, the concluding refrain of one stanza also serves as the introductory refrain of the next stanza. The first stanza of Machaut's *De tout sui si confortee* exemplifies the form of the virelai. (The Roman numerals mark the various sections of the stanza. I is the refrain; IIa and IIb are the couplet; III is the group of lines agreeing with the refrain; and IV is the repetition of the refrain.)

    I.   *De tout sui si confortee*
         Que jamais n'iert hostelee,

> Tristesse, n'esmay
> En mon cuer, aincois aray
> Lie et jolie pensee,
> Tant com je vivray.

IIa. Bien faire et avoir cuer gay,
      C'est tout; plus n'emporteray,
      Quant seray finee;

IIb. Dont lie et loyaulz seray
      Et le contraire feray
      De ma destinee,

III. Car lasse, desconfortee,
      Triste, dolente, esplouree
      Esté lonc temps ay.
      Mais je me conforteray
      Et celui qui tant m'agree
      Sur tous ameray.

IV.   *De tout sui si confortee,* etc.

I. I have been so comforted by all, that I should never have hatred, sadness, or dismay in my heart, therefore I shall have gay and beautiful thoughts as long as I shall live. IIa. To act correctly and to have a gay heart, that's enough; I can take nothing more with me, when I am dead. IIb. Therefore I shall be merry and loyal and I shall act contrary to my destiny. III. For I have been for a long time weary, disconsolate, sad, melancholy, and doleful. But I shall comfort myself, and I shall love above all the one who pleases me most. IV. I have been so comforted by all, etc.

Since all three stanzas of the poem have the same form, it is sufficient to provide a musical setting for only the first of them, leaving it to the singer to fit the remaining ones to the music. The melody conceived for the virelai will consist of two sections, one for the refrain (and the lines which rhyme with it) and one for the couplet. The second section is equipped with two endings, an indecisive one for the first part of the couplet and a more conclusive one for its second part. These two endings are called the *ouvert* (open ending) and *clos* (closed ending). Machaut's setting of this virelai typifies this musical form (Illustration 6).

Machaut has written this composition for only two parts, a voice and an instrument. In comparison to the rondeau previously discussed, the melody is extremely simple, having only one or two melismata of very moderate lengths. The syllabic declamation is typical of Machaut's virelais, most of which are not even polyphonic works but are written for one voice alone. Despite its simplicity, the melody has many finely wrought details. The tones of measures 3 and 4 are repeated again in measures 15 and 16; and the phrase of measures 6 through 11 is duplicated with only two variant notes in measures 17 through 22. The figure of

ILLUSTRATION 6

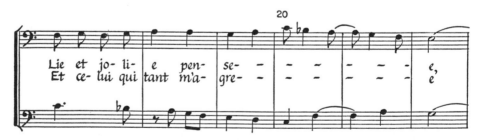

two pairs of descending notes which makes its first appearance in measure three, even though it is a cliché of the period, helps to give the melody cohesion as it recurs at various pitches throughout the piece.

Without doubt, the most important of the three secular forms cultivated by Machaut and his contemporaries was the ballade. Like the virelai, it is a poem of three stanzas of identical structure and rhyme. It

differs notably, however, from both the virelai and the rondeau in that its refrain occurs only once in each stanza, at the very end. For this reason one is not aware that a refrain exists, unless more than one stanza is performed. In the ballade the stanza begins with a couplet to which another couplet of like rhyme and the same number of syllables is appended.

Then comes a group of lines differing in rhyme and structure from the preceding couplets, and finally the refrain. Machaut's ballade *Je puis trop bien ma dame comparer*, which adapts classical allusions to the themes of courtly love, is an excellent example of this form. (Numbers Ia and Ib are the couplets, while II includes the final lines in which the refrain is italicized.)

> Ia.   Je puis trop bien ma dame comparer
>   A l'ymage que fist Pymalion.
> Ib.   D'yvoire fu, tant belle et si sans per
>   Que plus l'ama que Medee Jazon.
> II.   Li folz toudis la prioit,
>   Mais l'ymage riens ne li respondoit.
>   Einssi me fait celle qui mon cuer font,
>   *Qu'ades la pri et riens ne me respont.*

Ia. I can only too well compare my lady to the statue that Pygmalion made. Ib. It was of ivory, so incomparably beautiful that he loved it more than Jason loved Medea. II. The madman prayed to it continually, but the statue never replied to him. She who melts my heart does the same thing to me, *for I beseech her ever, and she answers me never.*

For the ballade the music is divided into two sections. One is for the first couplet and it is provided with ouvert and clos endings so that the second couplet may also be sung to it. The second section includes all of the remainder of the stanza (Illustration 7).

Like most of the later ballades of Machaut, this one is set for voice and two instruments. It happens to be a relatively short composition, but most of the ballades of Machaut are among the most extended of his secular works. The mediaeval predilection for the differentiation of the melodic lines is readily apparent in this setting. The tenor is distinguished by its long notes, the contratenor by a somewhat quicker motion, and the cantus by its rapid declamation and melismata. Once again Machaut uses internal correspondences to give the melody a coherence above and beyond that established by the form of the text. The opening melisma of the voice is repeated in measures 9 and 10 and returns once more in measure 29 where it is followed by a concluding phrase reminiscent of the melody of the clos ending.

The coherence of melody achieved by repetitions of melodic fragments does not affect the independence of the several voice parts. They remain unrelated melodically and are bound to each other only by harmonic and rhythmic co-ordination. But in the fourteenth century composers began to relate the parts occasionally by interchanging melodic fragments so that one voice seems to be imitating another. Rudimentary examples of this practice are to be found as early as the organa of Perotin,

ILLUSTRATION 7

but its potential as a means of making the total complex of voices into a melodically related whole had not been widely developed. A striking use of melodically related voices is to be found in the *round*, a composition in which one and the same melody is started by each of the singers at different points of time. A very familiar example of this would be *Row, row, row your boat*. The earliest known round is the famous *Sumer is icumen in* of the thirteenth century.

ILLUSTRATION 7 (*continued*)

ILLUSTRATION 7 (*continued*)

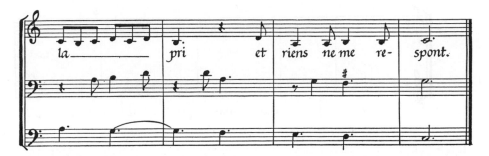

Somewhat similar to the round is the *chace* or *caccia* (chase), a form popular in the fourteenth century. One voice begins the melody a few beats after it has been initiated by another one, but the melody itself is not constructed so that at its end it is possible to begin it all over again and to repeat it ad infinitum, as in the round. It is instead a melody of considerable length, and one voice follows or chases the other to its very end without ever catching up to it. In such compositions the melody is notated only once, and the moment when the successive voices are to begin is usually indicated by written instructions. For this reason such a work is called a *canon* (law) because its performance is regulated or brought about by obeying the written prescription or canon.

The chace is usually a setting of a text which is associated with the hunt, and the effect of one voice chasing another is thoroughly appropriate to the subject matter. The text is often filled with onomatopoetic words and with the cries of the chase. The animation of these passages is captured by the composer by setting them as a hocket. The opening of an anonymous chace is given in the example in Illustration 8.

Here, with this complete identity of the parts, the integration of a polyphonic composition by melodic means has reached its highest possible level. But this solution was too radical and too schematic to enjoy more than limited use. Not until the fifteenth century did composers seriously begin to explore the uses of other, less rigid techniques of melodic imitation as a possible means of organizing their works.

The diversity of the musical techniques and forms cultivated by Machaut marks him as a composer of exceptional craftsmanship and genius. None of his French successors could match his many accomplishments. There are, it is true, many talented composers who come after him, but they concentrated their abilities almost exclusively upon the secular song, especially the ballade. Their works are remarkable for their rhythmic complexity. It appears that composers had become fascinated by the inherent possibilities of their system of notation, and wished to

ILLUSTRATION 8

exploit them to the utmost. In many of their compositions the task of co-ordinating the conflicting rhythmic configurations in the several voices is extraordinarily difficult. The preoccupation with rhythm that began in the twelfth century had at last been carried to its extreme limit. In the

ILLUSTRATION 8 *(continued)*

If I sing less than usual of the simple, modest maiden to whom I have given my heart, in winter because of the cold, it is because of my love for my beautiful falcons so good to fly by the river, etc. [Later, the text becomes very lively: "Huo, huo, houp! Hareu! il s'en va. Hau, hahau, hahau!"]

mannered artifice found in these works one discerns the end of an age.

Mediaeval polyphony was chiefly the product of French culture, and only one country, Italy, rose to challenge the supremacy of France. Suddenly, in the first half of the fourteenth century Italian composers appeared on the scene with an indigenous polyphonic art that eschewed the supremely rational isorhythmic motet in favor of polyphonic songs in which melody prevails over rhythmic considerations. The Italian songs use several of the fixed forms of the French, but give them different names. The fact that these forms have their points of contact is to be explained by the universality of mediaeval culture, which permitted a free exchange of literature and ideas. The earliest Italian songs were written for two parts, a florid vocal melody supported by a simpler melodic line in the lower instrumental part. Later in the century musical influences from France impinge upon the purely Italian concepts of polyphony. Isorhythm appears in a few compositions and some of the rhythmic complexities inherent in the French system of notation are introduced.

The three song forms employed by the Italians are the *madrigal, ballata,* and *caccia.* With the earliest composers the madrigal is the favored form, but in the latter part of the century the ballata takes precedence. The caccia always occupied a subordinate position to the other forms.

This Italian version of the French chace differs from it in that the composer provides an instrumental tenor as a support for two voices in canon. The Italians extended this lively form to include not only scenes of the hunt but outdoor life in general: the excitement of a fishing expedition, or the chatter of women washing clothes on the banks of a river. In terms of its poetic structure the caccia is not a fixed form as are the madrigal and ballata, although it is sometimes cast in the form of a madrigal.

The madrigal of the fourteenth century is in no way related to the madrigal that rose to such prominence in the sixteenth century. It is comparable to the French ballade, for it has two sections of music with the first repeated. Sometimes the first section is sung thrice followed by the second repeated. The second section, the *ritornello* or refrain, is usually differentiated from the first by a change in meter. The ballata, on the other hand, is related to the French virelai and has two sections, one for the refrain, and one for the couplets. *Gram piant' agli ochi* by Francesco Landini (c. 1330–1397), the greatest of the Italian composers, is a superb example of the ballata (Illustration 9).

ILLUSTRATION 9

ILLUSTRATION 9 (*continued*)

ILLUSTRATION 9 *(continued)*

1. *With eyes full of tears, with grave pains in the heart, with the soul over-whelmed, one dies.* 2. For this bitter, cruel separation I call to Death, but he will not hear me. 3. Against my will this life endures which makes me feel a thousand deaths. 4. And though I should live, I would not follow, did I not want to, my bright star and sweet love. 5. *With eyes full of tears, with grave pains in the heart, with the soul overwhelmed, one dies.*

Written as a vocal duet accompanied by an instrumental contratenor, this ballata contains many typical features of the Italian musical idiom of the fourteenth century. The melodies are extended by melismata, which seem to be applied less arbitrarily than those in the sophisticated melodies of Machaut. They occur regularly on the first syllable or the penultimate one of the individual lines. In between, the melody follows the text in a syllabic style. The stepwise motion and uncomplicated rhythms all contribute to make these melodies immediately appealing. A particularly striking cadential formula in the melody is found in measures 8–9 and again in measures 11–12. Instead of the more normal approach to the final tone of the phrase by rising to it through a half step or whole tone, the melody drops from the leading tone to the note below and then approaches the final from a third below it (see the last three notes of the phrases referred to). This cadence occurs so frequently in the music of Landini that his name has been given to it. This is something of a misnomer, however, for it is found just as often in the music of almost all the Italian and French composers of this period.

In listening to the Italian music of the fourteenth century one gains the impression that the composers were interested in the audible sounds of their music rather than its mathematical substructure. Problems of formal construction, the exploitation of rhythm as a manifestation of number, the effort to create independent parts through individualized texts and melodies: these characteristics of French art did not seem to have a wide appeal for the Italians. For them the ear rather than the intellect seems to be the final arbiter in their work. Because of this impression, it has been argued that the mellifluousness of the Italian music of the fourteenth century marks the beginning of the Renaissance, which in any case arrived in Italy earlier than elsewhere. It may be that the sweetness of Italian melody, like the "sweet new style" of Dante, does herald a new age, but it should not be forgotten that the new spirit made its appearance within forms and styles coined by the Middle Ages and accepted unquestioningly by the men of the fourteenth century.

VI THE RENAISSANCE

Part I. The Music of Humanism
1400-1520

AROUND 1400 the men of Italy became conscious of the fact that a vital new culture had emerged in their city-states. Wherever they looked they discerned a stirring of intellectual life, a reorientation of thought, that seemed to distinguish their own day from the preceding centuries. To these men the vigor of their own society and the flourishing state of the arts signalled the beginning of a new era. Their age seemed to be a rebirth of the intellectual vigor of Greece and Rome, a reawakening of the human spirit that had slumbered in darkness after the barbarian invasions had quenched the light of learning. Thus they spoke of their times as a renewal, a restoration, a rebirth or renaissance. By contrast, the centuries intervening between classical antiquity and their own day seemed a period of abysmal ignorance and intellectual decay. These were the Dark Ages, a featureless span of time between the past glories of Rome and the achievements of present-day society, so little esteemed that it was often referred to simply as the Medium Aevum: The Middle Ages.

The Renaissance began in the cities of Italy. The mediaeval towns had become busy commercial centers crowded with artisans producing goods for trade and objects of art to be bought by the new wealth. As the cities grew in importance, so did the power of the merchant princes. Imperceptibly authority passed from the hands of the landed aristocracy to a new aristocracy whose position derived from riches gained by personal talent and industry. This new ruling class quickly adopted the manners and customs of the older nobility. Intelligent and urbane, they cultivated the arts, filling their palaces with the conversation of learned men and with beautiful objects wrought by the greatest artists.

By their example these men revealed what could be achieved in this world by one's own efforts. Through the success of their activities they drew the attention of men away from the eternal heavens and focussed it in admiration upon man's present condition. No longer did temporal affairs and the products of man's hands seem vain and worthless when compared with the omnipotence of the divine; no longer did the body seem an ignoble prison preventing the soul from reaching its ultimate haven in God. Surely, they argued, the Maker had created man to function as man, and his attainments as a specifically human being should not be deemed unworthy. A new pride in the fact of their humanity stole into the hearts of men, a sense of the uniqueness of their position within the universe. Man had been placed in the very center of a universe created expressly for him, and had been given the power over his own destiny.

"At last the best of artisans ordained that the creature to whom He had been able to give nothing proper to himself should have joint possession of whatever had been peculiar to each of the different kinds of being," said Pico della Mirandola in his oration *On the Dignity of Man* (1486).

He therefore took man as a creature of indeterminate nature and, assigning him a place in the middle of the world, addressed him thus: "Neither a fixed abode nor a form that is thine alone nor any function peculiar to thyself have we given thee, Adam, to the end that according to thy longing and according to thy judgment thou mayest have and possess what abode, what form, & what functions thou thyself shalt desire. The nature of all other beings is limited & constrained within the bounds of laws prescribed by Us. Thou, constrained by no limits, in accordance with thine own free will, in whose hand We have placed thee, shalt ordain for thyself the limits of thy nature. We have set thee at the world's center that thou mayest from thence more easily observe whatever is in the world. We have made thee neither of heaven nor of earth, neither mortal nor immortal, so that with freedom of choice and with honor, as though the maker and molder of thyself, thou mayest fashion thyself in whatever shape thou shalt prefer. Thou shalt have the power, out of thy soul's judgment, to be reborn into the higher forms, which are divine." *

Newly conscious of their dignity, the men of the Renaissance felt more affinity for the civilization of ancient Greece and Rome than for the immediate past. Seeking to rediscover the spirit of Athens and of

* Tr. Elizabeth Livermore Forbes, *The Renaissance Philosophy of Man*, Chicago, 1948.

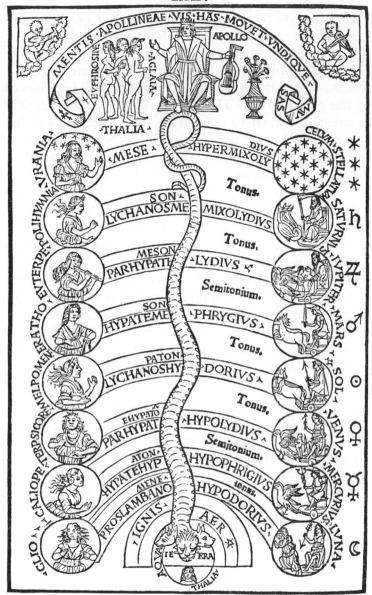

FRANCHINUS GAFFURIUS, *Practica musice*, 1496.

Apollo, god of music, rules the universe. Flanked by the three Graces, he rests his foot upon Time in the form of a serpent whose three heads represent Past, Present, and Future. Time links all the heavenly spheres, each of which is presided over by a Muse and bears the name of one of the notes of the Greek musical system as well as one of the modes. Between the spheres are intervals of whole tones and half tones creating a scale. (Chapter VI)

Rome, they turned to the long-forgotten literature of the Classical age. Monastery libraries were scoured for hidden manuscripts; agents were dispatched to Byzantium to procure copies of Greek writings; scholars were brought to Italy to translate the Greek authors and to impart their knowledge of this language to the men of the West; the remains of classical sculpture and architecture were exhumed and carefully examined. This feverish activity brought to light much of what we now possess of the dialogues of Plato, of Greek poetry and drama, and of Greek musical theory. The restoration of Platonic philosophy and the literature of antiquity, and the rediscovery of classical art complete the process of reassimilation of the classic past begun in the Carolingian Renaissance and continued in the reinstatement of Aristotle in the twelfth century.

From its inception the humanistic movement in Italy was inseparably united with literary studies. As early as the fourteenth century the traditional fields of grammar, rhetoric, and poetry were spoken of as the "studia humanitatis" or "studia humaniora," studies befitting a human being. At first the humanists were primarily concerned with the purification of the Latin tongue, endeavoring to recapture the pristine clarity of Ciceronian language. But Greek was also revived and many writers made use of this language so long unread and unheard in the West. The emphasis on classical languages was so pronounced that the development of the Italian vernacular as a literary medium was virtually halted for almost a century.

The humanists also rediscovered the highly developed literary theories of antiquity. The precepts of grammarians and rhetoricians, the aphorisms of Horace's *Poetic Art,* the ideal of the complete orator expounded by Quintilian, became their guides and models. From these sources they learned that language is a force which can direct and control the social and political activities of humanity, for it has the power to move the emotions. It is the key to the heart and, hence, to the motivations of men. Thus those who have mastered the arts of language are in a position to lead others. For the men of the Renaissance the orator, the man of words, best fulfilled this ideal of literature as an instrument of social and moral action. Well-versed in literature and broadly educated, he possessed the qualities most admired in this period. The exalted status accorded to literary studies had a profound effect upon all phases of artistic activity including, as we shall see, the art of music.

The center of humanism in the fifteenth century was the city of Florence. Under the aegis of the Medici, men of letters gathered there to translate and interpret the recently discovered works of the past. Painters, sculptors, and architects were summoned to embellish the city with works of art inspired by the remains of classical antiquity. A special impetus was given to the revival of Platonic philosophy when Cosimo dei Medici commissioned Marsilio Ficino (1433–1499) to translate the works of Plato from the original Greek. Ficino took up residence in a villa near Florence where he toiled at his task of translation and held meetings attended by a select group of humanists and noblemen. These assemblies in which the participants debated on matters of philosophy, art, and science were felt to be a revival of the Academy at Athens founded by Plato.

The members of the academy were very conscious of sharing in the restoration of an ideal of learning held by the school of Athens. "Our century," Ficino wrote to Paul Middleburg, "like a golden age, restored to light the liberal arts that were nearly extinct: grammar, poetry, rhetoric, painting, sculpture, architecture, music, the ancient performance of songs with the Orphic lyre. . . . And in you, oh Paul, it seems to have perfected astronomy. And in Florence it restored the Platonic doctrine from darkness to light." The Platonic Academy of Florence was soon imitated in other cities. In some of these institutions music was the primary concern. Subsequently some of these developed into concert organizations; others became official institutions for musical training; and several of them propounded theories that had immediate effects upon musical practice (see Chapter VIII).

In the above quotation Ficino pointed to the restoration of Platonic doctrine as the special contribution of Florence. He might well have said that this achievement was primarily his own. Not only had he translated the dialogues of Plato and mastered the doctrines of the neo-Platonists, he had written commentaries on them and, more importantly, had attempted a new synthesis of Platonism and Christianity. Although Ficino was not a truly creative philosopher, he nevertheless fashioned inherited elements of philosophy into a system differing markedly from that of mediaeval scholasticism. In it were contained ideas that had an important influence upon the arts of the Renaissance.

Borrowing from the doctrine of creation contained in the *Timaeus* and in the neo-Platonic commentaries upon it, Ficino postulated a universe created by the process of God thinking Himself. The Universe or Macrocosm is arranged in four successively less perfect realms. The highest of these hierarchic orders is the realm of pure ideas, the prototypes of all forms to be found in the lower zones. This is the Cosmic Mind, which is both stable and incorruptible. Below it comes the Cosmic Soul which is incorruptible but not stable, for it moves with a self-induced motion by means of which the pure ideas and intelligences are realized in the lower realms. The Cosmic Soul is identical with the heavenly spheres of the Ptolemaic universe. Each of the planets sheds a particular influence upon the world below it, determining the forms of the Realm of Nature. In this latter zone all is change and corruptibility, for here the ideas join with unstable matter to form the physical world. Below this lies the last of the four worlds, the Realm of Matter. This is Chaos, formless and lifeless, waiting to be born into the Realm of Nature through the life-giving touch of Idea. The whole Macrocosm is sustained through the force of divine Love. Radiating from on high, this love penetrates the lower worlds until it reaches Matter. Then the flow is reversed and love becomes an aspiration reaching ever higher until it attains the source from whence it came. Thus love animates and unites all things: like with like, form with matter, man with God.

Ficino constructs a parallel organism for Man or the Microcosm. As a physical being, man is part of the Realm of Nature, but he also possesses a human soul and a human mind. The soul is divided into a higher and lower soul, each containing particular faculties. The lower soul or Anima Secunda possesses the physiological faculties of growth, nourishment and propagation, the faculties of external perception or the five senses, and the faculty of imagination which creates coherent images from the manifold impressions of the senses. To the higher soul, the Anima Prima, belongs the faculty of Reason which utilizes the principles of logic to organize the images of the imagination. To it also belongs Mind or the Intellectus Humanus which corresponds to the Cosmic Mind. This faculty has the ability to grasp the truth intuitively. In a blinding and momentary flash of inspiration it is able to perceive the divine Idea in all its purity. Such moments of direct perception of eternal truth are rare indeed and its rapturous transports are accorded to few but poets, prophets, and seers. In this division of the soul, Reason stands between the Lower Soul and Mind, the highest faculty of all. It is uniquely human, for it is free and has the choice of directing man in the direction of his lower appetites or upwards to the eternal truth and beauty of God.

In this conception of the universe and of man's position within it, love, the link between Microcosm and Macrocosm and between the various realms, is of paramount importance. The nature of this love is examined by Ficino in his commentary on the *Symposium* of Plato. Love is first of all a desire, but it is to be distinguished from less worthy desires in that its object is divine goodness. God's perfect goodness, Ficino maintains, manifests itself in the universe in the form of beauty. The splendor of divine beauty is refracted through the various realms of the universe and comes to rest in the individual forms of the natural world where it is but a shadow or intimation of its former glory.

Thus love is a desire to possess beauty or the desire to take possession of goodness which reveals itself in beauty. Love may aspire to that universal beauty which resides in the Cosmic Mind or it may desire the individual incarnations of beauty that are perceptible to the senses. The latter kind of love is inferior to the former, but it is also a stepping stone to the higher form. It is permissible to enjoy earthly beauty only insofar as this love is the preparation for the higher love of God. We may fall in love with feminine beauty, but unless this leads us upward to the love of divine goodness our love is only a base desire of the flesh.

If love is the desire of beauty, how may we know what is beautiful? Ficino states that "Beauty is a certain grace, which is born principally of the correspondence and relationships of several things. This correspondence has three causes. Wherefore the grace which is in the soul is there by the relationship of several virtues; that which is in bodies arises from the concord of colors and lines. And furthermore that greatest grace which is in sounds is there through the consonance of several tones. Therefore Beauty has three causes: that is, through the soul, through bodies, and through tones. The beauty of the soul is known only by the Mind; that of bodies by the eyes; and that of tones is comprehended with nothing other than the ears." Beauty accordingly is something which can be perceived by only three of the human faculties, Mind, sight, and hearing. The Mind contemplates only the disembodied beauty of pure ideas, but sight and hearing are drawn to visible and audible objects of beauty. In his desire to possess the beautiful man may even be impelled to create forms in which beauty may reside. He may, in other words, introduce beauty in this world through the visual arts and through music.

The artist does not, however, *create* beauty: he only makes it possible for beauty to shine forth in his work by disposing his material so that beauty will flow into it and radiate from it. To attain this end the artist must establish relationships and correspondences between the parts of his artwork. He must, to phrase it differently, utilize the affinities—one might say the love—of like for like, the part for the whole. "The beauty of a body," writes Ficino, "is indubitably a certain fitness, liveliness, and grace that shine in the body through the influence (the flowing-in) of its Idea. This splendor will not descend into matter if the material has not been suitably prepared beforehand. And the preparation of the living body requires three things: order, measure, and species. Order means the distances of the parts; measure means the quantity of the parts; species means lines and colors. . . ." In the case of music "the order is the ascent from the low tone to its octave and the descent from the octave to the low tone (the scale or mode). The measure is the proper progression by means of thirds, fourths, and sixths, as well as by tones and semitones (intervals). The species is the resonance of a clear voice."

Ficino imposes an ideal upon art differing from that of the preceding age. Beauty can exist only where there is a congruity of parts, where no discordant element intrudes upon the balance and symmetry of the whole. The effect of the new Platonism is everywhere discernible. In architecture the facades of churches and palaces are framed of balanced elements with regular series of pilasters and columns, doors and windows of uniform structure, and with an exact correspondence between the two sides of the face of the building. This is an idealized arrangement of architectural elements, one which is imposed upon the surface of the building with only the slightest regard for the interior structure which it masks. The use of the dome, that most symmetrical of geometrical forms, is again one of the most characteristic features of the Renaissance pursuit of a beauty of balance and proportion.

The painter of the Renaissance, looking with a clear eye upon the world surrounding him, recorded the features and details of man and nature, but in his paintings he reassembled these objects in a harmonious relationship corresponding to an inner ideal of beauty. The figures are placed in perspective to give them a congruent relationship to the space in which they stand. They are arranged in symmetrical compositions of triangular or other regular shape. The relationships of the figures are established by supporting architectural details, by echoing colors and other such devices. The striving for a new unity based upon proportion and relationship is characteristic of the first century of the Renaissance and nowhere is it more in evidence than in the art of music.

Paradoxically the men who established the musical style of the Renaissance were not Italians, but men of the North. From the beginning of the fifteenth until well into the sixteenth century a small area comprising the northernmost part of France and the adjacent lowlands, which now form modern Belgium and Holland, poured forth a seemingly endless flow of singers and composers of genius. They were eagerly sought after by all the courts of Europe and at the height of their sway around 1500 almost every major chapel contained a majority of Franco-Flemish musicians. Italy was no exception to this. But while she succumbed to the spell of the northerners, she in turn captivated them with the beauty and magnificence of her courts and imbued them with the humanistic spirit of her Renaissance.

The half century from the death of Machaut until the emergence of Guillaume Dufay (*c.* 1400–1474) as the towering figure of the first half of the fifteenth century was truly a period of cross currents and experimentation. During this era the English, particularly John Dunstable (*c.* 1380–90 to 1453), seem to have exerted an important influence on the music of the continent. Since far back in the Middle Ages the English appear to have had a proclivity for full, rich sounds and pleasant harmonies. These were introduced to the continent around the turn of the century through musicians such as Dunstable who spent much of his life in France in the employ of the Duke of Bedford who at one time ruled Paris. The sweet sound characteristic of English music was described by a contemporary French poet, Martin le Franc, as "la contenance Angloise." The influence of "the English guise" upon Dufay and his contemporary Gilles Binchois (c. 1400–1460) is mentioned by him in his long poem *Le Champion des dames* (1441–1442):

Car ilz ont nouvelle pratique	For these a newer way have found,
De faire frisque concordance	In music high and music low,
En haulte et en basse musique,	Of making pleasant concord sound—
En fainte, en pause, et en muance,	In "feigning," rests, *mutatio*.
Et ont prins de la contenance	The English guise they wear with grace,
Angloise et ensuy Dunstable	They follow Dunstable aright,
Pour quoy merveilleuse plaisance	And thereby have they learned apace
Rend leur chant joyeux et notable.	To make their music gay and bright.*

The sonority of English music was created by a harmony consisting of a preponderance of thirds and sixths mixed with a lesser number of the perfect intervals, fourth, fifth, and octave. This ratio of imperfect to perfect intervals is, of course, just the opposite of that found in French music. The predominance of perfect intervals in French music had been justified by the mediaeval belief in music as sounding number: they were chosen because of their mathematical perfection. No justification could be advanced for a harmony based on imperfect intervals other than a judgment made by the senses: it pleased the ear. It is no accident that this breakthrough from mediaeval concepts of harmony occurred at the moment in history when man no longer disdained the world of sense perceptions.

Dufay, whose early career was spent in northern Italy and who was later a member of the papal choir at Rome, codified the English use of thirds and sixths within the central tradition of Western music. Hoping to reconcile the English harmonies with continental practices, he devised a type of musical setting called *fauxbourdon* (false bass) sometime around 1430. Just as mediaeval harmony had begun as a form of improvised singing, so too this new harmonic practice first appears as a partially improvised form. Departing from mediaeval tradition, Dufay in his earliest examples of fauxbourdon placed the pre-existing melody in the top voice, below which he wrote a supporting melody. This bottom part begins on its first note an octave below the upper part and returns to the octave position in relation to the melody above from

* Text and translation from Reese, *Music in the Renaissance*, W. W. Norton & Company. 1954, p. 13.

time to time, especially at the cadential points of the melody. Between these octaves the lower voice moves in parallel sixths with the upper part.

To these two voices a third part is improvised according to a set system: it begins a fourth below the upper melody and consistently maintains that interval throughout. Although it is improvised as a fourth below the melody, this at the same time places it a third above the bottom voice which is moving in sixths with the melody. Consequently a succession of sonorous chords built of a third and a sixth is created in a

ILLUSTRATION I

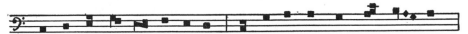

Chri-ste red-em-ptor omni-um   ex pa-tre pa- tris u- ni- ce

so- lus an- te   princi- pi- um   na- tus in- ef- fa- bi-li- ter.

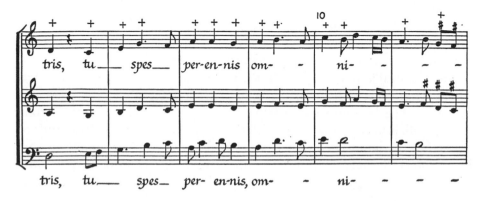

ILLUSTRATION I (*continued*)

piece of fauxbourdon. Dufay set a number of hymns in this style, including *Christe redemptor omnium* (Illustration 1).

In this example the first stanza of the hymn is given in Gregorian
notation along with the polyphonic setting of the second stanza, for in
practice only alternate stanzas of the hymns were sung in polyphony.
Dufay has "modernized" the chant in his setting by transforming its unmeasured notes into a flow of rhythmic values typical of his day. He has
also added a few tones to the melody, most of which ornament the
Gregorian hymn with a cadential formula, the Landini cadence, which
was so popular at this time (see Chapter V, p. 141). Though the richness
of the 'English' harmonies prevails throughout, Dufay still pays allegiance
to the Middle Ages by utilizing only perfect intervals at the principal
cadences. The bottom part written by Dufay occasionally escapes from
rigid parallelism with the hymn melody by melodic and rhythmic differences, but the improvised middle voice is fettered from beginning to end
by its intervallic relationship to the upper part. A technique such as this,
which depends upon the parallelism and partial improvisation of the

voices, soon proved to be too confining for the artist's imagination and he devised ways to employ these new sonorities without limiting himself to the strict procedure of fauxbourdon.

The development of new harmonic practices did not immediately erase all features of mediaeval music. In fact it took place within categories of composition inherited from the past. Dufay continued to write isorhythmic motets until the middle of the century, but after that time this archaic form rapidly disappeared from the musical scene. He also cultivated the secular song forms of the fourteenth century, though he and his contemporaries preferred the rondeau to the ballade which had been the favorite of their predecessors. The subject matter of their chansons remained much the same; the joy and melancholy of love, Maying songs, and occasionally poems in praise of good wine. But despite their outward resemblance to the songs of the immediate past, the compositions of Dufay and his generation unmistakably breathe the spirit of the Renaissance, in their harmony, in their melody, and in their rhythm.

In these chansons the fantastically intricate rhythmic devices frequently employed by French composers of the end of the fourteenth century are replaced by simpler configurations, no more complicated than the ear can readily grasp. It is the capacity of the ear, not the abstract concepts of the intellect, that determines the disposition of the sounding rhythm. Dufay purged his songs of rhythmic complications except for the easily comprehended ambiguity of 6/8 metre alternating with 3/4 metre. By shifting the meaning of 3/4 time (three groups of two eighth notes) to 6/8 time (two groups of three eighth notes) the rhythmic movement becomes subtly flexible without disturbing the steady pulse of the eighth-note values. An example of this so-called *hemiola* rhythm is to be found in the phrase (Illustration 2) taken from Dufay's ballade *Mon chier amy*, where the top part switches to a pattern characteristic of 6/8 time in the last two measures before the cadence.

ILLUSTRATION 2

ILLUSTRATION 2 (*continued*)

This ballade was written for two voices and an instrument. Unlike the instrumental parts of the Middle Ages, this one does not function as the basis of the harmony; it serves instead only as an enrichment of the harmonic fabric woven by the two vocal parts. If it were removed, the two outer parts would still form a completely satisfactory harmony, a harmony, furthermore, that consists primarily of thirds and sixths. An examination of this example reveals how the chords produced by the fauxbourdon technique have been incorporated into the harmonic texture without resorting to a strictly schematic arrangement of the parts. In the bracketed section, the tenor moves in sixths with the cantus even though the movement is not exactly coordinated. In the first of these measures, the instrumental contratenor, despite its syncopations, follows the upper melody at the interval of a fourth, just as in an improvised fauxbourdon, but in the next measure moves more independently to strengthen the drive to the final cadence.

The fact that *Mon chier amy* has been created for two voices with a supplementary, one might even say optional, instrumental part is symptomatic of the new artistic goals of the fifteenth century. The mediaeval musician had emphasized the different elements of his musical structure by opposing the instrumental tones of the tenor to the sound of the human voice singing the melody. Dufay, on the contrary, is striving toward a greater unity within his work by assigning the most important structural elements, the tenor and the cantus, to two parts of similar rather than dissimilar timbre. The instrumental contratenor is in reality an extraneous part, a vestigial remainder of the mediaeval ideal of sound.

In some of his later works Dufay began to strengthen the relationship between the parts by the occasional use of melodic imitation. This is discernible in his rondeau *Adieu m'amour* (Illustration 3).

ILLUSTRATION 3

ILLUSTRATION 3 *(continued)*

Adieu m'amour! adieu ma joye!
Adieu le solas que j'avoye!
Adieu ma leale maistresse!
Le dire adieu tant fort me blesse,
Qu'il me semble que mourir doye.
De desplaisir souvent lermoye.
Il n'est reconfort que je voie,
Quant vous eslongue, ma princesse.

Adieu m'amour! Adieu ma joye!
Adieu le solas que j'avoye!
Adieu ma leale maistresse!
Je prie a dieu qu'il conuoie
Et doient que briefment vous revoie,
Mon bien, m'amour et ma deesse;
Car lors tout ennuy me delesse,
Et apres payne joie aroie.
Adieu m'amour, etc.

Farewell my love! My joy, good-by!
Farewell the solace that once had I!
Farewell my faithful mistress!
To say farewell gives such distress
Methinks that I shall die.
For grief oft times I cry.
There is no comfort that I can spy,
When you depart, my princess.
Farewell my love! My joy, good-by!
Farewell the solace that once had I!
Farewell my faithful mistress!
I pray to God, may he hear me sigh,
And grant that soon I may again descry
My boon, my love, my goddess;
For then all trouble from me will regress,
And after grief joy will be nigh.
Farewell my love! My joy, good-by!, etc.

In measures 13 and 14 the tenor imitates the melody begun by the cantus two notes earlier. In measure 17 even the instrumental contratenor is briefly introduced into the imitative play as it states a phrase of four notes imitated immediately by the tenor and then the cantus. Again in measure 22 the tenor quotes the first three notes of the phrase just initiated by the cantus. Though polyphonic imitation is used by Dufay in this composition in only a tentative manner, the intention behind it is clear: to link the parts through melodic identity and thereby to create a greater degree of unity in his artwork. When each part in a polyphonic complex maintains complete melodic independence, as in the music of the Middle Ages, the listener normally recognizes one part as the bearer of the principal melody and relegates the others to the subordinate role of supporting parts. By means of an imitative procedure, as in the example above, the voices acquire equal importance. The listener, made aware of the identity of the melodies in each part, must accord them equal attention. A new grace has been added to the work of art, the beauty arising from the affinity and correspondence of like to like.

Among Dufay's many contributions to the development of the new musical language of the Renaissance one of the most important is his treatment of the Ordinary of the Mass. During the early years of the fifteenth century the Ordinary had increasingly engaged the attention of composers. In contrast to the ever-changing texts of the Proper, the texts of the Ordinary remain constant throughout the church year. This undoubtedly attracted composers to the task of making polyphonic settings for them, because of the much more frequent use that could be made of their compositions. In the late fourteenth and early fifteenth centuries musicians began to compose movements of the Ordinary in pairs. The usual pairings were the Gloria and Credo or the Sanctus and Agnus Dei. This tendency ultimately led to the composition of the Ordinary as a whole, consisting of the Kyrie, Gloria, Credo, Sanctus, and Agnus Dei.

There is no inherent relationship between the chants of the Ordinary. They are separated from one another within the liturgy and each serves a different function in the service. Each, furthermore, has its own melodies. It is surprising, then, to discover that around 1400 composers began to link the movements of the Mass by quoting the same melodic material at the beginning of each one of them. In using such initial melodic phrases or *head-motifs*, the artist establishes a relationship between the individual parts of the Ordinary that cannot be explained or justified on liturgical grounds but only on artistic grounds. There can be no more striking demonstration of the growing importance of the artist and the increasing pride in the works of man than this. The artist imposes his signature on each of the movements in the form of a head-motif and at the same time establishes a unity in his Mass that answers no liturgical but only an artistic need.

The use of a head-motif was a somewhat limited means of creating a unified Mass cycle and composers, among them Dufay, soon relinquished this device in favor of an even more radical one: the use of *one* melody as a *cantus firmus* or subject for *all* the movements. In this case the composer departs even more widely from the liturgy, for he strips the texts of the Ordinary of their ordained melodies and substitutes one of his own choosing. Only artistic judgment determines his choice. He may select a chant melody or even a secular tune drawn from the repertory of polyphonic music as well as from monodic works. Through the reiteration of the cantus firmus in all the movements the composer creates a cohesive artwork from a group of heterogeneous texts which in themselves neither possess nor require such unity.

When all the movements of a Mass cycle are based upon one pre-existing melody, the Mass is generally known by the name of its cantus firmus. Dufay's Mass *Se la face ay pale* is so designated because its cantus firmus is the melody of the tenor part taken from his own chanson of the same name. Like all of Dufay's cantus firmus Masses, this one is written for four voices. As in Machaut's Mass, the cantus firmus or tenor is placed in the next to bottom voice. Below it is the *contratenor bassus,* which we call today simply the bass voice. Above it is the *contratenor altus* (alto) and higher still, the *cantus* or soprano. The cantus firmus, occupying the same position in all the movements of the Mass, does not sing the words of the chanson but has the chant text fitted to it.

The choice of four voices, instead of a mixture of voices and instruments, may seem to us at first just an insignificant detail. But when compared with the means of performance favored by the past age, it becomes apparent that Dufay's setting represents a major shift in musical sensibilities. Instead of a combination of disparate sounds, we find here only the human voice in its various qualities, high and low. An ideal of homogeneous sound has replaced the heterogeneity of the Middle Ages.

This sound has also been enriched by the addition of a fourth voice to the three-part texture that had prevailed in the past. Even more significantly, it has been enriched not just by the addition of another part but also by an increase in the number of performers, for this composition is intended for choral performance. It is at this moment in history that a choral instead of soloistic rendition of polyphonic works first makes its appearance. It came in response not only to the Renaissance desire for sensual effects but also to its search for a unity born of relation and identity. The change to a vocal conception of polyphony did not by any means exclude the use of instruments. They continued to be employed, but now only as a reinforcement of the sound by duplicating the individual melodic lines.

The melody upon which Dufay based his Mass *Se la face ay pale* is given in Illustration 4. It has been divided into three phrases, A, B, and C,

ILLUSTRATION 4

ILLUSTRATION 4 (*continued*)

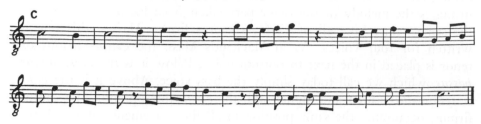

which correspond to the division of the melody made by Dufay in his use of it as a cantus firmus. Since the texts of the chants vary greatly in length, he was compelled to extend the melody in various ways. In general, it is written in longer note values than those of the other voices. In the Kyrie he used phrases A and B for the first Kyrie, omitted the cantus firmus entirely for the Christe section, and returned to phrase C for the final Kyrie. In both the Gloria and Credo he repeated the entire cantus firmus three times in order to accommodate their extensive texts, but changed the value of the notes in the successive repetitions. It appears first in 9/4 time, then in 3/2 time, and finally in 3/4. The Sanctus, divided into five subsections, utilizes the melody only once, but interposes a section of music without cantus firmus between each of its three phrases. The Agnus Dei has been handled in the same manner as the Kyrie, and its final section based upon phrase C is given in Illustration 5.

The cantus firmus stands out in bold relief from the surrounding polyphonic voices because of its longer note values. Its deliberate motion makes it readily perceptible so that its function as an integrative device is maintained unambiguously throughout the Mass. But the added parts have no melodic relationship to the tenor and only occasionally in the individual movements do they briefly imitate one another. For this reason the four melodies still move with the freedom characteristic of mediaeval polyphony. Nevertheless the richness of the harmonies they form and their vocal quality unequivocally distinguishes the combination of these lines from that of the preceding age.

The increasing preoccupation with settings of the Ordinary of the Mass was accompanied by a renewal of interest in the sacred motet. The motet had lived in the fourteenth century as a secular or ceremonial form, but in the fifteenth century it reverted to the language of its earliest stage and became once again a setting of a Latin text drawn from the Proper or of devotional character. Texts in praise of the Virgin were especially popular. In most of his motets Dufay employs the liturgical melody associated with the text, but frequently he sets it as if it were a secular melody. In his motet on the Marian antiphon *Alma Redemptoris*

ILLUSTRATION 5

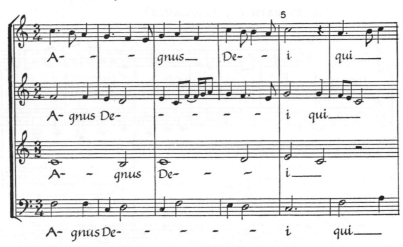

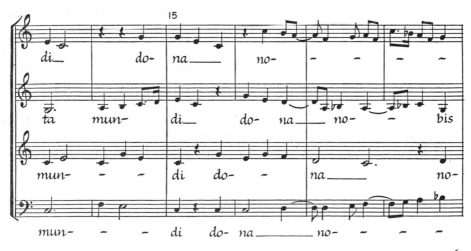

ILLUSTRATION 5 (*continued*)

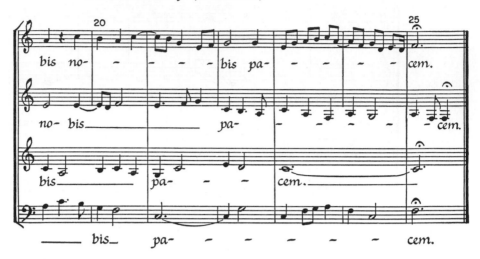

Mater, for example, he places the chant in the top part and supports it with two melodies probably intended for instruments. The chant melody has been altered by the introduction of melismata and rhythmic figures in the same manner as that employed in the hymn *Christe redemptor omnium* (Illustration 1), though in a much more elaborate fashion. In only a few of his latest motets did Dufay relinquish this secular style in favor of the newer idiom of his Masses. His successors, however, raised the motet to a position of importance equalling that of the Mass.

The younger contemporaries of Dufay continued to explore the new horizons of religious polyphony. In their hands the now standard texture of four voices was increasingly clarified. Dufay's compositions had had a somewhat limited tonal range, and for this reason the individual lines tend to cross and re-cross each other, blurring their outlines, as can be seen in the tenor and alto voices of Illustration 5. To overcome this, his followers extended the total range of musical sound, thereby providing space enough for each voice to move in an orbit belonging only to itself. This also permitted a more extensive and more articulate use of melodic imitation between the parts. At the same time the somewhat obtrusive use of a cantus firmus in long notes was overcome, first by giving it a rhythmic motion commensurate with the other voices, and finally by using its material for themes imitated by all the other parts.

These developments were brought to a climax in the music of Josquin des Prez (*ca.* 1440–1521). Born in the northern region of France bordering on Belgium, he came early to Italy where he was employed in Milan, Rome, and Ferrara. He may also have been for brief periods in Modena and Florence. Shortly after the turn of the century he became *maître de chapelle* to Louis XII of France, remaining in his service until the death of the king in 1515. In his final years Josquin returned to the region of his birth, where he died in 1521.

In the music of Josquin the aspirations of the Renaissance reached their fulfillment. By a masterly synthesis of all the trends of the fifteenth century, he created a musical style which became the basis for all subsequent developments in the music of the sixteenth century. His compositions may be said to represent the classical moment in the music of the Renaissance, the moment when style and idea have been brought into perfect equilibrium. Josquin was acknowledged everywhere as the greatest musician of his time, the spokesman of his age. And he was compared to that other Titan of the Renaissance, Michelangelo. "Josquin may be said to have been, in music, a prodigy of nature, as our Michelangelo Buonarotti has been in architecture, painting, and sculpture; for, as there has not thus far been anybody who in his compositions approaches Josquin, so Michelangelo, among all those who have been active in these his arts, is still alone and without a peer; both one and the other have opened the eyes of all those who delight in these arts or are to delight in them in the future." * So wrote Cosimo Bartoli in 1567.

Josquin's achievement was to weld the musical advances of his predecessors into a perfectly integrated style, one in which the voices of a polyphonic composition are completely related through the systematic use of imitation. This technique he fused with a melodic idiom in which the music is wedded to the text through an identity of rhythm and phrasing. Here the literary humanist and the musical humanist become as one. Josquin used this style as a universal means of expression, applying it to every category of composition, sacred and secular. It appears in full clarity in the excerpt (Illustration 6) from his chanson *Incessament.*

The direct relationship of all five voices leaps to the eye in the very first measures. Each part begins with the same melodic pattern, even though at different pitches. It would be impossible to say from observing only these opening measures which voice is the dominant one, for all sing the words and all have the same melody. Closer examination of the piece will reveal, however, that Josquin has built it upon the tenor melody, which may be of his own invention but more probably is a pre-existing song. In its original form the melody must have appeared somewhat as it does in Illustration 7.

The repetitions in the melody have been occasioned by the form of the poem. The first two lines have the same number of syllables and the same rhyme, so the melodic phrase of line 1 (measures 1 through 9) has

* Reese, *Music in the Renaissance*, p. 259–60.

ILLUSTRATION 6

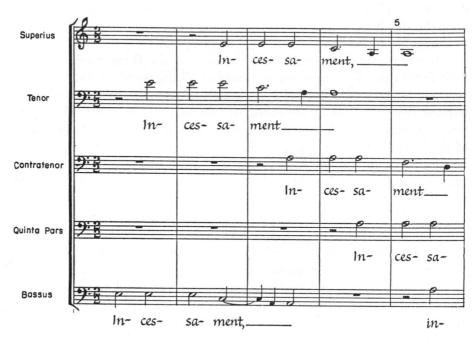

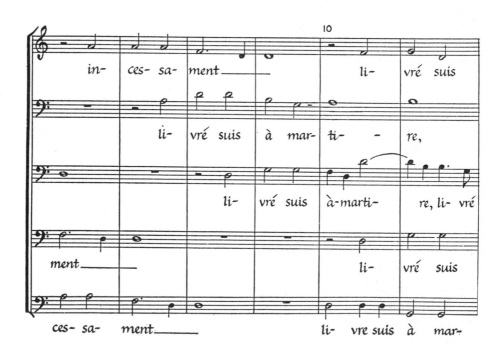

ILLUSTRATION 6 (*continued*)

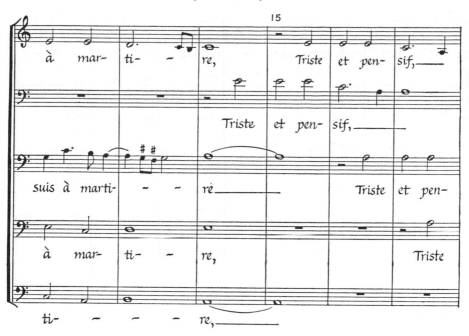

ILLUSTRATION 6 (*continued*)

ILLUSTRATION 7

In- ces- sa- ment_____ li- vré suis à mar-
ti- re, Triste et pen- sif,_____ tou- siours mon
mal em- pi- re Ain- si do- lent me con-duit des-
- plai- sir, Cel- le qui peult, ne me veult se- - cou-
rir: Mon mal-heur est de tous aul- tres le pi-
re, de tous aul- tres le pi- - re, le pi- re.

Ceaselessly I yield myself to martyrdom; sad and pensive, my woe grows ever worse; thus lamenting, grief accompanies me. She who could succor me will not do so: my misfortune is worse than all others.

been repeated for line 2 (measures 10 through 18). For the same reason the melody of line 3 (measures 19 through 25) is used again for line 4 (measures 26 through 32). The final line of the poem is stated twice, each time to a different musical phrase. If this song were being set in polyphony by an earlier composer, he would have composed only lines 1, 3, and 5, leaving it to the performer to fit lines 2 and 4 to their corresponding phrases. That Josquin has not done so is no accident. Though he does respect the principle of repetition, he has been compelled to write out the entire composition because in imitative polyphony the parts do not coincide. They do not come to a simultaneous cadence which could be used as the termination of a period to be repeated.

In his setting of *Incessament* Josquin has used both strict and free forms of imitation. The *Quinta Pars* is derived from the tenor melody by a canon and duplicates every note of the tenor at the interval of a fifth below the original. The other parts are not so restricted. Though the opening phrase of the tenor is imitated exactly by all voices, the next one *livré suis à martire* is duplicated only by the contratenor and even he departs from the original after the first three notes. In measures 27 through 32 the descending line of *Ainsi dolent* is reproduced only by the *Superius*, again with some modifications of it.

One might argue with some justification that such freedom in the treatment of the individual voices is a denial of the principle of imitation. But imitation is governed by more than melodic repetition, it is regulated by the text as well. One can easily see that Josquin's composition is constructed of a number of individual sections in each of which only one fragment of the text appears. In the first seven measures only the word *Incessament* is sung. Here the text has been identified with a specific musical phrase. As each voice enters one instantly perceives its textual and musical relationship to the other voices. In measure 7 a new phrase makes its appearance in the tenor. Though the musical material of this phrase is imitated by only the Contratenor and the Quinta Pars, the relationship of the other two voices is still apparent through their repetition of the same text in more or less the same rhythmic values. Furthermore the fact that each voice enters after a period of rest calls attention to its appearance and in so doing stresses both its individuality and its musical or textual relationship to the others.

The importance of the text in the concept of musical imitation cannot be overemphasized. It is the line or the phrase of text which determines the length and usually the rhythm of the musical phrase. It establishes what might be called the subject to be imitated in every section. In addition it conditions the very style of the melody. It can be seen in this composition that the extended melismata which appeared with such frequency in the music of the past have virtually disappeared. We find instead phrases that are relatively short and that utilize a syllabic declamation in order not to violate the text.

Besides creating the themes of each section of the composition, the text also determines the total structure of the work: there will be as many sections, each built upon one theme, as there are phrases in the text. As a result, the musical form produced by polyphonic imitation is an open one. No musical repetitions take place between the individual sections unless the text itself suggests it, as in the chanson *Incessament*. The continuity of a composition therefore depends not upon musical, but upon textual factors. Nevertheless the composition is given musical coherence by the use of a single technique, that of polyphonic imitation. It creates a uniform texture, and overcomes the sectionalism of the form created by the text through its method of overlapping and dovetailing the individual sections. (Note how the phrase *livré suis à martire* is begun before the preceding section has come to an end.)

In his cantus firmus Masses Josquin naturally has to apply the technique of polyphonic imitation in a somewhat different manner than in his chansons. The fact that movements with texts of varying lengths must be built upon one pre-existent melody means that the cantus firmus cannot determine the structure of the composition as directly as it does in secular songs. It must itself be shaped and modified by the composer to serve his purposes. In his desire to create a completely integrated work of art, Josquin no longer isolates the cantus firmus from the other voices by setting it in notes of long duration, as Dufay had done in his Mass *Se la face ay pale.* The melodic motion of the cantus firmus is now indistinguishable from that of the other parts, and its phrases, imitated by all the voices, pervade the entire composition.

One of the finest examples of Josquin's Masses is his *Missa Pange lingua,* based upon a Vesper Hymn for the Feast of Corpus Christi. In this Mass the melody of the hymn *Pange lingua* never appears in its original form, nor are its phrases ever presented continuously. Josquin uses it instead as a fund of melodic ideas from which he extracts a phrase that he recasts in his own melodic style to serve as a subject for imitation by the other voices. The first Kyrie is characteristic of this treatment which is maintained throughout the Mass. In this section (Illustration 8)

ILLUSTRATION 8

ILLUSTRATION 8 (*continued*)

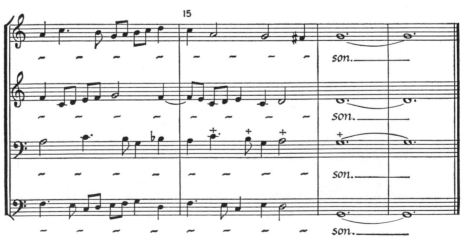

only the first two phrases of the hymn appear; the remaining phrases are drawn upon for the Christe eleison and the final Kyrie.

The asterisks over the notes in the tenor part identify the chant melody. At the beginning Josquin follows the chant strictly until he arrives at the penultimate note of the first phrase. Between the repeated c's at the end of the phrase in the chant he introduces a melisma that carries the voice in a soaring line up to e before gently settling down to the final c. The bass, in a freely imitative line, enters a fifth below the tenor, forming a duet with it that ends only after the soprano and alto have entered with the same material. Thus the opening phrase of the chant is treated in successive duets, neatly joined by the overlapping of the voices. This pairing of the voices, called a *bicinium,* is one of the hallmarks of Josquin's style.

The second phrase is introduced in the ninth measure by the bass, followed by the tenor and soprano in successively higher octaves. Again Josquin follows the hymn melody quite closely for the first five notes, after which he introduces a long melisma terminated in the tenor by the cadential notes of the chant. These extended melismata differ greatly from those of earlier eras which give the impression of being spontaneous, almost improvisatory, effusions. Josquin's are controlled by repetitions of phrases and by correspondence between the different parts. The opening notes of the bass melisma in measure 13 are repeated immediately in the next measure. This figure is also imitated within the soprano's melisma in measure 14 and its five ascending notes are echoed by the alto in the same measure. In this integration of the formerly free melisma one again discerns Josquin's striving to achieve an ideally unified work of art.

In this Kyrie eleison, which is divided into two sections, each dominated by a phrase from the hymn, Josquin creates a composition of increasing emotional intensity. Beginning tranquilly, the lower voices are gradually animated by the faster moving melisma until they reach a point of climax on the high e of the tenor. The repetition of this duet in the upper octave by the soprano and alto raises the level of intensity once again. The entrance of the bass in measure 9 and its imitation in rising octaves by the tenor and soprano bring the full sound of the choir into play. The emotional peak reached at this moment is sustained until the final cadence in the convoluted lines of the long melismata.

During Josquin's lifetime composers were turning with increasing frequency to the motet as a vehicle for their most imaginative musical ideas. In the Latin texts drawn from the Proper and the Bible they found an array of subject matter more appealing and varied than that of the Ordinary of the Mass where the text remains ever the same. The emergence of the motet as a favored form for the expression of religious senti-

ILLUSTRATION 9

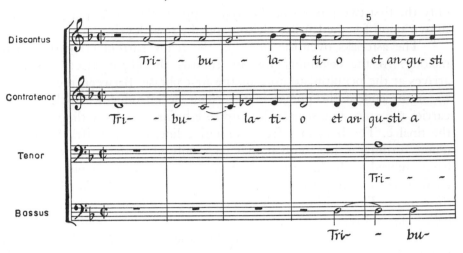

ments is indicative of the growing importance of the text as the point of departure for musical invention. Many motets, it is true, were still based upon liturgical melodies, in which case the text itself could not influence the composer's setting too greatly. But side by side with these more traditional compositions are motets whose texts are either taken from the liturgy without their accompanying chants or are chosen directly from the Bible, especially the Psalms. Such a motet is Josquin's *Tribulatio et angustia invenerunt me* (Illustration 9) based upon the Biblical text: "Trouble and heaviness have taken hold upon me: yet is my delight in Thy commandments. I have found trouble and heaviness and I have called upon the name of the Lord."

Josquin has divided the first phrase of the text into two parts, each of which is made the subject of imitation. The contrast between the melodic idea conceived for the words *Tribulatio et angustia* and that for *invenerunt me* is most striking. The long note values and the restricted range of the first melody with its many repeated notes captures the sense of the words "trouble and heaviness," while the animation of the next melodic phrase portrays the motion implied in the words "have taken hold upon me." The hold or *fermata* on the final note of this section deliberately separates this portion of the composition from the next to intensify the antithesis between the sorrow of the one and the delight of the other. In this motet we discover the final, logical development of musical humanism: word and tone are so closely united that verbal meaning has become musical imagery. Music now seeks to interpret the text.

During this period an event of far-reaching influence opened up new possibilities for the dissemination of musical culture. In 1501 Ottaviano de' Petrucci published the first collection of polyphonic compositions printed with movable type. Henceforth, manuscript copies were no longer to be the only means of disseminating music. The more modest cost of printed music was instrumental in bringing music to the homes of people for whom a manuscript copy was prohibitively expensive. Eventually this was to lead to the transference of musical culture to the middle classes, but in the sixteenth century music was still the property of the elite—the humanists, the clergy, the nobility and merchant princes.

VII THE RENAISSANCE

Part II. Mannerism
1520-1600

"I ACKNOWLEDGE two masters, Christ and literature." With
these bold words the humanist Ermolao Barbaro (1480) epitomized the
transcendent status of literary studies in the Renaissance. From the beginning the humanistic preoccupation with linguistics had been intimately
associated with the problems of human society. Language, as the means
whereby men communicate with and influence one another, was seen
to be a key to the problems of human knowledge and conduct. Through
language, through grammar and rhetoric, which are the product of the
human spirit and belong to man alone, the humanists sought to justify and
explain the moral and spiritual behavior of mankind.

Thus the kingdom of letters began to encroach upon areas of knowledge which had once been the exclusive property of philosophy. Forced
to yield before the onslaught of a horde of literary humanists, traditional
Aristotelian philosophy withdrew to the outer fringes of the scholarly
world where it contented itself with tedious disputations and the splitting
of dialectical hairs. The grammarian and rhetorician now installed themselves upon the thrones of the philosophers. In the pride of newly won
authority, the Florentine humanist Angelo Poliziano, author of books in
medicine, ethics and philosophy, could state: "I do not claim the title
of philosopher, but demand no other name for myself than that of
grammarian."

The world that the humanist claimed for himself is not the realm of the absolute, as it was for the mediaeval philosopher, but the domain of human activity. Where the aim of the Aristotelians had been to attain knowledge of eternal verities through the use of dialectics, the humanists sought to establish the relative truths of human affairs from models of behavior provided by literature. The arts of language are to be used to effect specific results: the poet and orator with all the means at their disposal are to persuade and move men to proper actions, leading them to virtue and away from evil. The rhetoric of the poet and orator, not the frigid argumentation of the logician, is the moving force in society, stirring the hearts of men and persuading them to right conduct. "Hail to thee, Oh Poetry! fertile mother of every doctrine!" wrote Giovanni Pontano. "You have come with the immortality of your authors to succor humanity condemned to die. You have drawn men out from caves and forests. Through you we have knowledge, through you we have before our eyes the things of the past; through you we understand God, through you we have religion and its ritual."

Poetry and philosophy, rhetoric and humanity: these are all for the humanist one and the same thing. The danger inherent in such a view is that the value of literature may be exaggerated and that literary studies may become an end in themselves. Problems of literary style may come to outweigh all other considerations. Just such an overemphasis began to manifest itself in the latter part of the fifteenth century and in the early years of the sixteenth. Arguments arose about which language was the most perfect, Latin, Greek, or the vernacular. Should Ciceronian Latin be taken as an idealized model to be imitated slavishly or should it only serve as a point of departure for a contemporary, living language?

In the case of the Italian vernacular the problem of literary style was settled for the sixteenth century by canonizing the poetic idiom of Petrarch. Not only the poetic forms and the turns of speech of Petrarch, even his subject matter was adopted by the poets of this new era. They sing of sighing lovers in language encrusted with metaphor and glittering with paradox. An enamored youth, losing his soul in the raptures of love, exclaims:

> The white and winsome swan
> While singing dies, and I,
> Complaining, near the end of my existence.
> Strange and different fates,
> That he should die disconsolate
> And I should die in bliss!
> Death that e'en in dying
> Filleth me with joy replete and with desiring.

> If no other pain I feel in dying,
> A thousand times a day I gladly would expire.

These are not the accents of true emotion, but the polished conceits of the litterateur. In this poem of Alfonso d'Avalos, which when set to music by Jacques Arcadelt became the most famous madrigal of the sixteenth century, it is style and manner which is of paramount importance. Love's passion is transmuted into rhetoric.

Into this world where a problem of correct literary usage could touch off a war of polemics there was introduced at the very end of the fifteenth century a book destined to dominate artistic theory for nearly three centuries. In 1498 Giorgio Valla published a Latin translation of the *Poetics* of Aristotle, a work which had been unknown to the Middle Ages. In a society intensely preoccupied with art and its relationship to life, the *Poetics* was received as if it were divine revelation; for this treatise, though incomplete, presents a consistent theory of art which may be integrated with the whole philosophical system of Aristotle.

One should not assume from the title of this work that Aristotle is here concerned only with poetry. Though his discussion is centered around dramatic and epic poetry, his use of the term "poetics" has a much broader connotation. For Aristotle all knowledge is divided into three branches: theoretical, practical, and poetic. The first deals with speculative thought, the investigation and contemplation of the eternal laws of the universe, while the second is devoted to the realization of these laws by man in his activities as a member of society. Poetics on the other hand is that branch of knowledge concerned with man the creator, and its name means literally the art of "making." The wheelwright, the architect, and the dramatist are all in a sense "makers," since all are engaged in applying certain types of knowledge in order to create some material object.

Some of these arts are utilitarian, while others serve no such practical end. The latter are what we call the fine arts, and it is for the men who work in these fields, the dramatist, the musician, the choreographer, that the title of poet, "maker," is reserved. Though these arts may differ in substance, they are related by common principles. For this reason the doctrine expounded by Aristotle primarily in terms of poetry is applicable to the other arts as well.

The central tenet of the *Poetics* is that art imitates nature. Aristotle maintains that imitation is a basic element of human nature and that imitative art is therefore one of the most natural forms of expression in man. "The instinct of imitation is implanted in man from childhood, one difference between him and other animals being that he is the most imitative of living creatures, and through imitation learns his earliest lessons; and no less universal is the pleasure felt in things imitated. . . . Objects which in themselves we view with pain, we delight to contemplate when reproduced with minute fidelity: such as the forms of the most ignoble animals and of dead bodies. The cause of this again is, that to learn gives the liveliest pleasure. . . . Thus the reason why men enjoy seeing a likeness is, that in contemplating it they find themselves learning or inferring, and saying perhaps, "Ah, that is he." For if you happen not to have seen the original, the pleasure will be due not to the imitation as such, but to the execution, the colouring, or some such other cause." *

When Aristotle says that art imitates nature, he does not mean that art copies natural objects such as scenery. Nature for Aristotle is in this case specifically the world of man. "The objects of imitation," he states, "are men in action," the moral character of the soul revealing itself in terms of specific events. "Tragedy is the imitation of an action; and an action implies personal agents, who necessarily possess certain distinctive qualities both of character and thought; for it is by these that we qualify actions themselves, and these—thought and character—are the two natural causes from which actions spring, and on actions again all success or failure depends." What art imitates are states of the soul, either permanent characteristics such as courage and magnanimity or transient emotions such as pity and anger. In thus depicting emotional states through events the poet arouses in his audience reciprocal emotions which are pleasing and at the same time instructive and edifying.

The world of nature of which Aristotle speaks is not static, but full of motion and action. It is a world in which everything is the product of form realizing itself in matter. Since this is a dynamic process constantly renewing itself, those arts which are able to represent the flux and motion of things coming into being are more to be esteemed than those which can only represent a single, fixed moment of an action. Painting and sculpture can portray the outward appearance of an emotional state, but it is an emotion forever frozen in time. Poetry, music, and the dance, however, are by their very nature arts in which motion is an essential element. Thus they are able to imitate an action from its inception to its completion.

In the arts of motion

the imitation is produced by rhythm, language, or 'harmony' [melody], either singly or combined. Thus in the music of the flute and of the lyre 'harmony' and rhythm alone are employed; also in other arts, such as that of the shepherd's pipe, which are essentially similar to these. In dancing, rhythm alone is used without 'harmony'; for even dancing imitates character, emotion and action, by rhythmical movement. There is another art which

* This and the following quotations are from S. H. Butcher's translation of the *Poetics*.

imitates by means of language alone, and that either in prose or verse—which verse, again, may either combine different metres or consist of but one kind. . . . There are, again, some arts which employ all the means above mentioned, —namely, rhythm, tune, and metre. Such are Dithyrambic and Nomic poetry, and also Tragedy and Comedy; but between them the difference is, that in the first two cases these means are all employed in combination, in the latter, now one means is employed, now another.

If art imitates nature, the task of the artist is to abstract the form from an action of man and to impose this form upon the particular material of his art. The poet orders his words to conform to the event that he has chosen to imitate, and the musician orders his melody and rhythm for the same purpose. In such a theory the value of the artwork lies not in the subject matter being imitated but rather in the appropriateness of the manner of imitation. It is therefore on questions of style that the artwork is to be judged. Through style the artist will make the meaning of his subject matter apparent to his audience; through style he may ennoble or demean the actions of his narrative; through style he will depict and arouse the appropriate emotions and sentiments.

To imitate successfully the artist must utilize all the resources of his art, choosing whatever is appropriate to the subject at hand. In the *Art of Rhetoric* (III, vii) Aristotle states that

propriety of style will be obtained by the expression of emotion and character, and by proportion to the subject matter. Style is proportionate to the subject matter when neither weighty matters are treated offhand, nor trifling matters with dignity, and no embellishment is attached to an ordinary word; otherwise there is an appearance of comedy. . . . Style expresses emotion, when a man speaks with anger of wanton outrage; with indignation and reserve, even in mentioning them, of things foul or impious; with admiration of things praiseworthy; with lowliness of things pitiable; and so in all other cases. Appropriate style also makes the fact appear credible; for the mind of the hearer is imposed upon under the impression that the speaker is speaking the truth, because, in such circumstances, his feelings are the same, so that he thinks (even if it is not the case as the speaker puts it) that things are as he represents them. . . .*

The influence of Aristotle's theories began to make itself felt in all fields of artistic endeavor in the third decade of the sixteenth century. This intrusion of Aristotelian dogma precipitated an artistic crisis. The problem confronting the artist of the sixteenth century was to reconcile the precepts of Aristotle with the idealized art that had emerged from Florentine Platonism: to imitate man in action while preserving the formal unity and symmetry of the Platonic Idea. In the paintings of this

* tr. J. H. Freese. *The Loeb Classical Library.*

new generation, the figures turn and twist as if caught in the middle of some action that will be completed as soon as we take our eyes from them. The tension and sense of motion in their gestures are at variance with the formal scheme in which they have been disposed. Where the figures of a Raphael seem forever at peace within their pyramidal and spherical arrangements, the formal structures of the mannerist painters seem as impermanent as the gesticulations of the figures of which they are composed. The eye is attracted everywhere by flickering motions of hands and limbs and arrested by countenances frozen in the distorted grimaces of emotion. These paintings, in comparison with those of the preceding generations, are richly ornamental, crowded with figures and adorned with the rhetoric of gesture.

A similar transformation is to be discerned in the music of the sixteenth century. Perhaps the best formulation of the new attitude is to be found in the *Istituzioni armoniche* published in 1558 by the theorist Gioseffe Zarlino. In agreement with classical authority, he maintains that the function of the poet and musician are one and the same. "The proper aim of the musician, like that of the poet, is to please and delight with singing or instrumental music according to the rules of musical art." The pleasure that we derive from music must not, however, be superficial or unworthy. It must be used to inculcate good habits and virtuous character. "The proper office of music is to delight; and we must use it not dishonestly, but honestly."

Since music is an imitative art, the musician, like the poet, must first choose a subject to be imitated. "Just as the builder, in all his operations, looks always toward the end and founds his work upon some matter which he calls the subject, so the musician in his operations, looking toward the end which prompts him to work, discovers the matter or subject upon which he founds his composition. Thus he perfects his work in conformity with his chosen end. Or again, just as the poet, prompted by such an end to improve or to delight . . . , takes as the subject of his poem some history or fable, discovered by himself or borrowed from others, which he adorns and polishes with various manners, as he may prefer, leaving out nothing that might be fit or worthy to delight the minds of his hearers, in such a way that he takes on something of the magnificent and marvelous; so the musician, apart from being prompted by the same end to improve or to delight the minds of his listeners with harmonious accents, takes the subject and founds upon it his composition, which he adorns with various modulations and various harmonies in such a way that he offers welcome pleasure to his hearers." *

While Zarlino accepts without reservation the Aristotelian thesis

* Oliver Strunk, *Source Readings in Music History*, p. 229.

that art is a process of imitation and adornment of a chosen subject, he
carries this theory beyond the limits imposed by Aristotle. Where the
philosopher had limited the subject matter to men in action, the musician
broadens it to include purely musical material. Rationalizing existing musical techniques, Zarlino transforms all of them into modes of imitation.
According to Zarlino, counterpoint, in which one part is derived from
another because of its harmonic relationships to it, and successive imitation, in which all the voices state the given subject, are forms of
imitation.

Beginning with the first, then I say that, in every musical composition,
what we call the subject is that part from which the composer derives the
invention to make the other parts of the work, however many they may be.
Such a subject may take many forms, as the composer may prefer and in
accordance with the loftiness of his imagination: it may be his own invention,
that is, it may be that he has discovered it of himself; again, it may be that
he has borrowed it from the works of others, adapting it to his work and
adorning it with various parts and various modulations. And such a subject
may be of several kinds: it may be a tenor or some other part of any composition you please, whether of plainsong or of figured music; again, it may
be two or more parts of which one follows another in consequence or in
some other way, for the various forms of such subjects are innumerable.
When the composer has discovered his subject, he will write the other
parts in the way which we shall see later on. When this is done, our practical
musicians call the manner of composing "making counterpoint."
But when the composer has not first discovered his subject, that part
which he first puts into execution or with which he begins his work, whatever it may be or however it may begin, whether high, low, or intermediate,
will always be the subject to which he will then adapt the other parts in
consequence or in some other way, as he prefers, adapting the harmony to
the words as the matter they contain demands. And when the composer goes
on to derive the subject from the parts of the work, that is, when he derives
one part from another and goes on to write the work all at once, as we shall
see elsewhere, that small part which he derives without the others and upon
which he then composes the parts of his composition will always be called
the subject.

By reinterpreting the musical practices of the past in the light of
Aristotle, Zarlino sanctified and safeguarded them for his own time.
Nevertheless the position of these old techniques was not secure, for the
doctrine of imitation imposed still other demands upon music, demands
which were soon to undermine and then destroy the centuries old polyphonic tradition. If music was to be a truly imitative art, it must imitate
men in action; it must, in other words, endeavor to imitate the text which
embodies the emotions and actions of men. Musical equivalents must be

found for the meanings of the words; melodic progressions, rhythmic motions, and harmonies must all conform to the text.

In his treatise Zarlino described the numerous means which practicing composers had devised to express the content of their text. In melodies grief, sadness and other "feminine" emotions were to be depicted through small melodic intervals, while larger intervals would be chosen to represent harshness, anger, and other "masculine" emotions. The melodic line would also be colored by the use of accidentals for grief and languishing. Slow and fast notes would be chosen to represent sorrowful and happy emotions. At the same time the rhythmic progression must be made to conform to the metrical rhythm of the text, matching long notes with accented syllables and shorter notes with unaccented ones. The harmonies too must be obedient to the text: minor intervals were to be applied to words of grief, while major intervals were equated with the more aggressive emotions. For bitter, harsh words it was fitting to introduce dissonances and harmonic clashes.

A vocabulary of imitative musical devices was created in this manner, a vocabulary rooted in metaphor and onomatopoeia. For such words as hill, climb, and heaven the melody must ascend; similarly it must descend for such words as valley and hell. Laughter was transformed into a passage of rapid, purling notes, and sighs became rests interpolated within the melodic phrase. Composers even resorted to what has been called "eye-music," sharping a note when the text refers to a pointed arrow or introducing two blackened notes into a passage written in white notes because the text is describing a pair of black eyes. There is scarcely an aspect of the text which did not determine in some way the musical setting chosen for it. Even punctuation was brought to bear upon the musical structure, and cadences were formed when the sense of the words was closed by a comma or period.

In this theory it is assumed that music moves the emotions through the imitation of the text. The desire to create an emotional response was whetted by the testimony of classical literature that ancient Greek music could modify the souls of men, heal the sick, tame wild beasts, and even move the rocks and trees. If music's power was such in ancient times, why was its efficacy no longer the same? One theory was that music had lost its ability to achieve such results because it had neglected the words. Had not Plato said in the *Republic* that music and rhythm must follow speech? Therefore if music is made subservient to the text, its power to stir the emotions will be restored.

Another theory held that modern music used only diatonic scales, whereas Greek music had also employed the chromatic and enharmonic genera. If modern music was to achieve its ends, then it must revive these other scales. The most ardent advocate of this theory was Nicolo Vicentino (1511–1572). He composed madrigals employing chromatic and enharmonic intervals, constructed instruments capable of performing these finely gradated tones, and wrote theoretical works explaining and defending his practices. Vicentino, it goes without saying, failed in his attempt to rehabilitate these long-forgotten scales, but his theories had some effect upon later composers. Many musicians used chromaticism in their works, and in so doing they introduced an element contributing to the downfall of the old modal system.

The musical theories introduced in the sixteenth century are a notable departure from those of the past. Music, in accepting its literary yoke, had abdicated its lofty position within the quadrivium. It is now the servant of poetry, and the laws which govern it are no longer drawn from its own nature but are derived from another tradition. Though the composer of the sixteenth century still clings to imitative polyphony as his medium of expression, slow and rapid passages, polyphony and homophony are now juxtaposed in a logic derived not from music but from the text. Each significant word evokes a musical image which passes hastily from voice to voice, creating a nervous, brilliant mosaic of short, graphic motifs. The composer does not strive to attain a uniform musical texture or to create a single emotional atmosphere. He chooses instead to reveal his subject and to create his effects through musical rhetoric. Piling musical figure upon figure, he sways his audience as an orator would, by technical brilliance and luxuriant imagery. This is indeed a "mannered" music.

The role that Josquin played in preparing the ground for this reorientation of musical art has already been observed in his motets. But it was not within the motet that succeeding generations of composers worked out the new style. In that category of composition Josquin's successors preferred to maintain the more conservative, traditional approach to musical composition. Similarly, the French chanson was already too steeped in its own tradition to allow the full development of new musical ideals. It is an axiom of art that new ideas are usually worked out in forms least encumbered by convention. So it came about that the vehicle chosen for the expression of the new aesthetic aims of the sixteenth century was not one of the forms assiduously cultivated by the northerners, but the Italian madrigal.

Italian music had languished in the fifteenth century when the northern musicians made their conquest of the courts and chapels of Italy. Their magnificent compositions for the ceremonial of the church and their elaborate French chansons for courtly entertainment supplanted the music of native composers. Not until the end of the century did

Italian creative activity begin to reassert itself in songs written in the vernacular. These *frottole*, for all their simplicity, rapidly acquired great popularity at the courts of Verona, Padua, Venice, and, especially, Mantua where they were cultivated under the patronage of Isabella d'Este. One may even say that it is the very fact of their simplicity that accounts for their extraordinary vogue. In these unpretentious songs the highly so-phisticated courtiers discovered the novelty of naïveté, however artificial it might be, just as Marie Antoinette and her maids-in-waiting were to find pleasure in playing milk-maid amidst the splendors of Versailles. So much did these Italian songs appeal to the courtiers that even northerners such as Josquin des Prez occasionally composed them, and no less than eleven books of frottole were published by Petrucci between 1504 and 1514.

The two leading composers of this new category were Bartolomeo Tromboncino and Marco Cara. They composed their frottole to various poetic forms such as the *strambotto, capitolo, oda,* and *frottola.* The latter consists of stanzas of six or eight lines and a refrain (*ripresa*) of four lines which is customarily sung before and after each stanza. The refrain and stanza are each provided with a musical setting in which the melodic phrases are fitted to the lines of the poem in a syllabic style. Fre-quently rhyming lines are sung to the same musical phrase. The music was written for four-part singing in a basically homophonic style, but a favorite method of performing them was by solo voice with the re-maining parts played by a lute or by three instruments.

Marco Cara's *O mia cieca e dura sorte* (Illustration 1) is a repre-sentative example of the hundreds of frottole found in manuscripts and prints. Conventional in phraseology and of slender literary merit, its verses were obviously created only to be set to music.

ILLUSTRATION I

ILLUSTRATION 1 (*continued*)

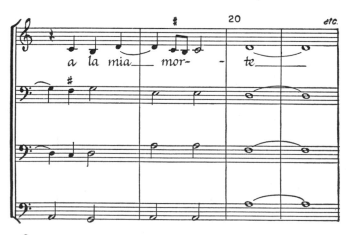

O my blind and cruel fate by grief ever nourished, O misery of my life, sad herald of my death.

In these twenty measures, which contain only the ripresa, the melodic interest is centered in the upper part. With its narrow range and many repeated tones, the melody is immediately appealing. Cara, though he is working here in miniature, is not sparing of detail. He employs the melodic phrase of the second line for the third one as well because of their rhyme, but takes care to vary it by repeating it at a lower pitch. To give a greater sense of finality to the end of the refrain he repeats the second half of the fourth line, again at a lower pitch. He also uses this final phrase (measures 18 through 20) to underline the corresponding rhyme of lines 1 and 4 in a subtle way, for the melody of the soprano is the same as that of the alto at the end of line 1 (measures 2 through 4). He even makes a witty allusion to the difference between his art and that of the learned northerners by introducing a facile snatch of imitation between the lower parts in measures 16 and 17. This is truly an ultra-sophisticated art.

The limited scope of the frottola could not satisfy composers nor their audiences for long, accustomed as they were to the musical riches of the polyphonic style. With increasing frequency the imitative techniques of northern polyphony began to appear in the frottola settings. At the same time the growing interest in music composed to Italian poetry brought with it a search for literary materials of greater distinction than the frottola verses—a search which soon led to the great poets of the past, to Petrarch in particular. The variety of language and of form found in his *canzone* inspired imitations by contemporary poets. Mistakenly called madrigals, these verses are distinguished by the freedom of their structures built of irregularly recurring lines of seven and eleven syllables and shifting rhyme schemes. For these poems the schematic repetitions of the frottolists no longer sufficed, and the musical setting of the madrigal took on the open form of the motet.

Madrigalesque compositions began to appear in the later collections of frottole, but it was not until 1530 that the first volume of madrigals was published. The artistic merit of the madrigal had by this time engaged the interest of the northern composers, and the leading practitioners of the new genre were the Frenchman Philippe Verdelot († *c.* 1540) and the Netherlanders Adrian Willaert (*c.* 1480–1490 to 1562) and Jacques Arcadelt (*c.* 1505–after 1562). Only one Italian stood by their side, Costanzo Festa (*c.* 1480–1545). Arcadelt's madrigal *Il bianco e dolce cigno* (Illustration 2), published in 1539, is one of the most polished of these early works. (A translation of the text appears on p. 175.)

The simplicity of its four-part setting provides a graceful and trans-

ILLUSTRATION 2

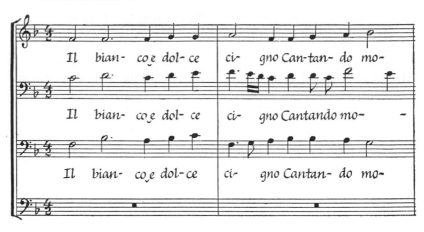

parent frame for this typical text. The syllabic declamation, the frequent appearance of repeated notes, the regard for the prosody of the verse, and the reliance upon a chordal or homophonic texture are features that re-call the earlier frottola. But other details are characteristic of the con-temporary motet: the creation of new melodic ideas for each phrase or clause of the poem, the slight overlapping of the parts which provides a virtually uninterrupted flow from beginning to end, and the introduction of imitative polyphony for the final line of the poem.

From the outset Arcadelt reveals his concern for the meaning of the text rather than its outward form by composing his musical sections in conformity with the oratorical structure rather than the rhyme scheme of the poem. This is particularly apparent in the cantus melody. It sings the first three lines of the poem in three phrases marked off by the rests in measures 3 and 4. But these phrases do not coincide with the metrical divisions of the poem, as one would expect. They follow instead the sense of the words. The first rest separates the description of the swan from the depiction of the plight of the singer. The second rest in-tensifies the effect of the word *piangendo* (complaining or weeping) and suggests a sob or a sigh. The most important words in the first phrase (*cigno* and *more*) are stressed by half-note values and by making their accented syllables coincide with the highest notes of the melody. The completion of the sense of the first phrase is delicately indicated on the word *more* by a full musical cadence.

In the next phrase the composer imitates the plaintive nature of the words in several ways. Significantly, he has reserved the entrance of the bass part until this moment, so that the grave tones of this lowest voice may re-enforce the sombreness of the words. As we have already seen, Arcadelt detaches the words *ed io piangendo* from the balance of the phrase by a brief rest in the cantus part. In addition, on the word *piangendo* an E♭, foreign to the mode of the piece, is introduced into the harmony. Arcadelt equates the lowering of this tone with depression and grief. The remaining words, "near the end of my existence," are inter-preted appropriately by the descending line of the cantus, equating its falling tones with the failing of vital powers as the end of life approaches.

The last two lines of the poem are two clauses of a single sentence, but the words *di mille mort' il dì* offer an occasion for imitative treat-ment. The homophonic texture disintegrates suddenly with the ap-pearance of a new phrase in the alto part, as the other voices are con-cluding the previous section. It consists of a leap of a fourth followed by five descending tones. Immediately each voice imitates the alto in rapid succession, overlapping one another, as if to illustrate in musical terms the multiplicity of a thousand deaths. Here Arcadelt demonstrates one of the many ways that the technique of imitative polyphony may be used as an interpretative device.

The prevailing homophony of the early madrigals, such as this one of Arcadelt, was soon supplanted by a completely imitative style. By the middle of the century five-part writing had become the favorite medium for composing madrigals. The presence of an additional voice enriches the harmony and also provides the composer with a means of constantly varying the texture. It permits him to compose passages for various combinations of three voices alone, to alternate groups of two and three voices at contrasting pitches, or to oppose passages of transparent contrapuntal imitation with the denser sonority of homophonic writing. Additional means of imitating verbal ideas in music were continually discovered, and the desire to represent each word of a poem in each voice-part led to an expansion of the madrigal to proportions considerably larger than those of the earliest ones.

The full-blown style of the madrigal for five voices is revealed in *Scaldava il sol* by Luca Marenzio (1553–1599). One of the most outstanding of the Italian composers who began in the second half of the century to replace the northerners who had dominated the musical scene for so long, Marenzio chose for his madrigals poems replete with imagery which could be mirrored in the music. His *Scaldava il sol* (Illustration 3), published in 1582, is based on a poem by Luigi Alamanni that conjures up the intense heat of midday in the Roman Campagna by means of an abundance of picturesque details.

The text with its archaic metaphors is printed here together with a translation that preserves the order and literal meaning of the words as closely as possible, in order that the reader may better discern the relationship of the music to the text.

SCALDAVA   IL   SOL DI MEZO GIORNO   L'ARCO
Warming was the sun of   midday   the arc

NEL   DORSO   DEL   LEON SUO ALBERGO   CARO.
In the back of the Lion, its mansion beloved.

SOTTO'L   BOSCHETTO PIU   DI FRONDI CARCO
Under the bushes   with leaves heavy-laden

DORMIA'L   PASTOR   CON LE SUE GREGGI   A PARO;
Slumbered the shepherd with   his flock   at his side;

GIACEVA   IL   VILLANEL   DE L'OPERA   SCARCO,
There lay the farmer boy from   work   released,

VIE-PIU   DI   POSA CHE DI   SPIGHE   AVARO;
Far more for repose than for ripened corn greedy;

ILLUSTRATION 3

ILLUSTRATION 3 (*continued*)

ILLUSTRATION 3 (continued)

ILLUSTRATION 3 *(continued)*

ILLUSTRATION 3 *(continued)*

GL'AUGEI   LE FERE   OGN'HUOM S'ASCONDE E   TACE;
The birds, the beasts,   all men disappear   and are still;

SOL   LA CICALA NON SI   SENTE IN PACE.
Alone, the cicada does not   feel at peace.

Marenzio approaches the text not as an orator, but as a rhetorician. Each word of the text, regardless of its grammatical context, is translated, if possible, into a musical metaphor. In the first line of the text he separates the word "sun" from its modifying phrase "of midday," and paints in the Quinto part the sun at its zenith by a melodic line which terminates at its highest point on the word *sol*. In the same manner he isolates *l'arco* from *Nel dorso del Leon*, giving to this one word a melismatic figure which literally describes an arc in its notation. Similarly, he distinguishes the phrase "with leaves heavy-laden" from the noun which it modifies, by giving it a distinctive, rapid declamation, which suggests in its motion the rustling of the myriad leaves.

Thus far in his composition Marenzio has utilized only the medium of imitative polyphony. Each group of words, or even a single word, is given a musical phrase imitated by most of the voices. It is a sophisticated form of musical imitation, full of licenses. The rising line of the first musical subject also appears in reverse motion, as in the first entrances of the tenor and the top voice. The subject of *di mezo giorno* is distinguishable in the different voices only by the three rising notes of its second, third, and fourth syllables. If the subject is a graphic one, such as *l'arco*, it will be imitated and repeated many times. Otherwise, it is passed over quickly, as in the phrase *di mezo giorno*.

Suddenly in measure 22, the imitation between the voices is brought to a halt by the image of the slumbering shepherd. His repose is depicted in the single, droning chord of the next few measures. The homophony of this passage is carried on for the next words "with his flocks at his side," but with a different image in mind. The simultaneity of the voices stands for the proximity, the "togetherness" of the pastor and his sheep. Just as suddenly, imitative polyphony and rapid motion return on the word *villanel*, where Marenzio makes a pun on two meanings of the word. *Villanel*, a shortened form of *villanello*, means country boy, but it is also the name of a currently popular, light-hearted type of vocal music notable for its use of parallel motion. The animation of this passage immediately passes into relatively sedate homophony to indicate the inactivity of the farmer lad.

The remainder of the poetic text is interpreted by Marenzio with the same attention to detail. One of his most novel inventions appears in measures 50–53. Ignoring the fact that the words *tace* and *sol* belong to different grammatical constructions, he unites them in a striking musical image. Too sophisticated an artist to interpret the words "are still" with the obvious device of a rest, he gradually, but with extreme rapidity, reduces the number of voices, leaving only one to sing in solitude the word "alone."

Brilliant as this madrigal is, its preoccupation with the graphic translation of verbal meaning into the medium of five voices has gone far towards destroying the original musical basis of the classical vocal style of the Renaissance. The composer is concerned only secondarily with the maintenance of musical equality and melodic independence among the voice parts, or with the musical coherence of the work as a whole. Each section is based upon a "point of imitation," but this concept of imitation is focused upon the text, and its musical projection depends upon the manner in which each composer manipulates the musical devices of madrigalesque rhetoric. Picturesque verbal details are often elaborated at the expense of the whole meaning of the text. At the same time the composer's display of his skill in this respect not infrequently obscures the audibility of the text itself by the simultaneous enunciation of different syllables.

By the last quarter of the century the vogue for the madrigal had spread throughout Europe. Copies were printed in one edition after another by publishers in the north as well as in Italy. Imported into England in their original language, they were soon circulated in translation, inspiring one English composer after another to try his hand at composing madrigals to original English verse. Around the turn of the century hundreds of English madrigals appeared in collections and anthologies, such as the *Triumphs of Oriana* (1601), to grace the closing years of the reign of Elizabeth the First.

At the end of the sixteenth century madrigal composers began to turn away from the pastoral world of Arcadia and its artificial emotions to expend their imaginative musical ideas upon poems of a more subjective character. In their works exuberant playfulness gives way to the poignant and pathetic. In order to express the contrast and intensity of feelings within a single madrigal the range of melodic figures and harmonic progessions was extended to lengths previously unheard of. The madrigal becomes a succession of astonishing rhetorical effects whose organic musical relationship is scarcely perceptible.

The masters of this last phase of the polyphonic madrigal are Claudio Monteverdi (1567–1643) and Carlo Gesualdo, Prince of Venosa (1560–1613). The former perceived the possibility of transforming the madrigal to conform to the new ideals of the Baroque era, and his work must therefore be described in the following chapter. Gesualdo, however, never departed from the framework of the sixteenth-century madrigal. A man of violent, even pathological emotions, Gesualdo found in the exploitation of chromatic harmonies a means of making the madrigal a vehicle for feelings of the utmost intensity. Gesualdo's madrigals were published in seven volumes between 1594 and 1626. In the earlier collections most of the poems are still conventional, but for the later volumes he chooses lyrics that express in concentrated form the anguish of the forsaken lover. The prevailing subjectivity of such poems is palpable in *Io pur respiro in così gran dolore:*

> I still breathe in such great pain,
> And you still live, O pitiless heart?
> Alas, no longer is there hope
> Of seeing again our beloved!
> O death, lend assistance:
> Kill this life;
> Mercifully wound me, and with a single stroke
> Put an end to my life and to my suffering.

The extreme mannerism of Gesualdo's treatment of this text is audible in the opening measures of his madrigal (Illustration 4). For Gesualdo each detail of the text demands a distinctive musical expression. The first two lines of the poem pivot upon the antithesis between the poet's pain and the living, pitiless heart. But Gesualdo finds still another antithesis in the opening line: the contrasting motions of breathing and suffering. The madrigal begins accordingly with the syllabic motif of the cantus, deliberately severed by a rest, in imitation of a breath, between

ILLUSTRATION 4

ILLUSTRATION 4 (*continued*)

the first two syllables of *respiro*. This motif is imitated in close succession by each of the voices until its short-lived energy is dissipated, leaving the tenor, alone, to introduce the next phrase. Startlingly different in character, this rises haltingly in a series of chromatically altered tones. With the successive repetitions of this phrase, the harmonic tensions generated by its chromatic progression reach a deliberately dissonant climax on the word *dolore* in measures 13 and 14. The cantus reaches its highest point on F♯, forming a strident major seventh with the persistent G of the bass, and ends irresolutely a moment later on the only slightly less dissonant F♮, forming a minor seventh with the bass.

The linking of clashing images, producing a mood of nervous intensity, is continued throughout the madrigal. Before the mournful,

ILLUSTRATION 4 (*continued*)

drawn-out harmonies of the second musical section have been resolved, Gesualdo moves to a brief motif of eighth and quarter notes (*e tu pur vivi*). The rest after *tu* (you) throws an emphasis upon it, singling it out as dramatically as if an accusing finger were suddenly thrust forward. Though the voices seem to tumble over each other in their haste, the musical flow is unbroken because of their overlapping entrances. Without warning, this activity is suddenly broken off in measure 19 by total silence. Then an anguished cry is heard, made even more wracking by the following chord which is totally unrelated to it harmonically. In this distorted and distraught imagery of Gesualdo the polyphonic madrigal of the sixteenth century reaches its end. Such emotions had taxed the musical vocabulary of the Renaissance to the utmost: a new language, and with it a new era, had to come into being.

While the madrigal was being brought to such extremes of expression, other categories of music were not being neglected. Though some composers, fascinated by the infinite variety offered by the madrigal, concentrated almost entirely upon this one aspect of music, the majority of creative musicians continued to devote their energies to the forms brought to a peak of development by the generation of Josquin: the polyphonic chanson, the motet, and the cyclic Mass. The secular songs to French, German, or English texts increasingly took on the guise of the madrigal, but the motet and Mass were less influenced by it.

The primary cause of the more conservative spirit of religious music is to be found in the various movements of religious reform which came to a climax early in the sixteenth century with the Reformation of Luther and shortly thereafter with the Catholic Counter Reformation. The growing awareness of contemporary abuses and malpractices within the church was inevitably accompanied by a desire to recapture the purity and simplicity of earlier forms of Christianity. To many the manner in which the polyphonic style obscured a clear pronunciation of the text by its vocal artifice was as objectionable as the use of secular melodies for the cantus firmus of a Mass. "We have introduced an artificial and theatrical music into the church, a bawling and agitation of various voices such as I believe had never been heard in the theatres of the Greeks and Romans," wrote Erasmus. "Amorous and lascivious melodies are heard such as elsewhere accompany only the dances of courtesans and clowns."

In answer to such objections some of the Protestant sects removed part-singing from their services entirely. Others, such as the Calvinists, confined part-music to radically simple chordal settings of the Psalms. Martin Luther, on the other hand, welcomed polyphonic music but was vitally concerned that the words of the liturgy should not be obscured. He provided German verse translations for the texts of the Ordinary and also for certain parts of the Proper, laying the foundation for a vast new repertory of hymns or chorales, as they more often are called. Luther sanctioned the continued use of Latin for the Lutheran liturgy in communities that desired it, which meant that much of the polyphonic music written for the Catholic church could still be used.

The question of what constituted true religious music was one of the issues debated at the Council called by the Roman Catholic church to institute reforms within its house. Prominent upon the agenda of the Council which assembled in Trent for the first time in 1545, and sporadically thereafter for nearly twenty years, were abuses in the liturgy. Chief among these was the unlimited use of the Sequence whose numbers had multiplied enormously since the tenth century. The Council of Trent excluded all but four of them from the liturgy: *Victimae paschali laudes, Veni Sancte Spiritus, Lauda Sion* and *Dies irae.* It also authorized the modernization of the melodies of Gregorian chant in accordance with contemporary principles of Latin accentuation.

The virtues and the vices of polyphonic music were argued vigorously by both ecclesiastics and lay deputies, for a number of the most ardent reformers were eager that it be forbidden in the liturgy. They objected to the obscuring of the text by the overlapping of the voice parts, to the multiplicity of performers, both vocal and instrumental, and to the use of profane melodies as cantus firmi. The final decision of the Council came only in the form of a recommendation that "in the case of those Masses which are celebrated with singing and with organ, let nothing profane be intermingled, but only hymns and divine praises. The whole plan of singing in musical modes should be constituted not to give empty pleasure to the ear, but in such a way that the words may be clearly understood by all, and thus the hearts of the listeners be drawn to the desire of heavenly harmonies, in the contemplation of the joys of the blessed." *

The means by which these lofty objectives were to be attained were not spelled out by the Council of Trent, nor by the special commission which met in Rome in 1564–65 to consider the role of music. The enforcement of these aims was largely left to the inclination of individual princes and primates of the church. In some cases secular melodies continued to function as the cantus firmi of Masses. In others, composers continued to use them but concealed the identity of the melodies by designating their Masses as "sine nomine" (without name). Composers also wrote Masses on melodies derived from the chant, or fabricated from the tones of the scale. More frequently, however, the cantus firmus in any form was given up in favor of a technique which had already made its appearance in the work of Josquin and his generation: the paraphrasing of an existing polyphonic work, creating what is called a *parody Mass.*

For such a Mass the composer may choose a motet, a chanson, or even a madrigal. The composer is guided in his choice primarily by the artistic qualities of the original composition, though he adapts and modifies his model unhesitatingly to serve his own purposes. Through the exercise of his craftsmanship he expands upon the original work, creating a composition equalling or even surpassing the dimensions of the cantus firmus Mass. Though the parody Mass is not unlike the cantus firmus Mass in the fact that it uses pre-existent material, it is clearly the product

* Reese, *Music in the Renaissance,* p. 449.

of men who have mastered all the intricacies of polyphonic writing and for whom the display of a polished style has become in itself the highest goal.

Among the many composers who devoted their highest talents to writing polyphonic music for the traditional liturgy, few could match the Italian Pierluigi da Palestrina (1524–1594) or the Netherlander whose name was Italianized as Orlando di Lasso (1532–1594). Strongly influenced by the spirit of piety and devotion called for by the Council of Trent in its definition of the goal of sacred music, Palestrina devoted his prodigious talents almost exclusively to the composition of music for the church. Working entirely in Rome, his hundreds of motets and Masses were intended for the use of its principal churches, especially the Sistine Chapel. Deeply concerned over the fate of sacred music, Palestrina was one of the men who submitted polyphonic compositions to the Council to vindicate the suitability of this style for liturgical use. The combination of religious idealism and stylistic consistency in his works is reflected in those of a number of other Roman composers, who form the so-called Palestrina or Roman school. Their compositions in the "a cappella" style (literally the chapel style, but implying the use of only voices) are still advocated by the Roman church as models for the composition of liturgical music.

To Palestrina the texts of the Ordinary of the Mass are the embodiment of religious doctrine and spiritual truths. His respect for these texts and for the Bible and other liturgical texts is such that he never resorts to the kind of word-painting which gives the contemporary madrigal its vivid intensity of expression. The majority of his many parody Masses are based upon motets rather than chansons or madrigals. His expansion of the materials from earlier compositions is carried out with scrupulous care for the correct accentuation of the texts to which they must be adapted. When he increases the sonority to five, six, or even seven voice parts, or when he creates sections of complex imitative counterpoint, he is careful to avoid the simultaneous enunciation of different words. By combining syllabic and melismatic melodies, he is able to present in full clarity a complete phrase of text in one or two synchronized voice-parts, while the remaining voices are prolonging the vowel sound of a single syllable through a series of melismatic undulations. Such passages alternate with homophonic sections, where the text stands out in particularly bold relief because of the simultaneous declamation of all the voices.

Orlando di Lasso is in many ways the antithesis of Palestrina. While the latter epitomizes the ascendant spiritualism of the church, Lasso represents the turbulence of his age. Palestrina worked entirely in Italy, but Lasso traveled widely throughout Europe, summoned by rulers who admired his works. Born in Belgium he spent more than a decade of his youth and early manhood in Italy before returning to the North, first to Antwerp and then to Munich where he spent the last thirty-six years of his life in the service of the Dukes of Bavaria.

A most prolific writer, Lasso set his hand to every existing category of music, producing quantities of French chansons, Italian madrigals, and German secular songs. He composed numerous Masses and settings of other liturgical texts such as the Gospel account of the Passion, hymns, and the Magnificat. After 1557 he devoted his efforts primarily to the composition of motets for the liturgy and for civil ceremonies. In his lifetime Lasso's fame, earned by his unexcelled mastery of every form of writing, far surpassed that of Palestrina whose subsequent prestige is largely the result of the church's stamp of approval upon his works.

Lasso's compositions reflect the current trend to musical depiction of the text. Possessing complete mastery of the techniques of the early sixteenth century, he moulded them boldly and sensitively to the demands of each text, whether he was writing for a small number of voices or for eight or ten parts divided into two choirs. So successful was he, his German successors regarded his works as a lexicon of musical rhetoric. Typical of his motets is *Super flumina Babylonis* (Illustration 5), a setting of the Offertory for the twentieth Sunday after Pentecost which uses the first verse of Psalm 137: "By the rivers of Babylon, there we sat down: yea, we wept, when we remembered Zion."

Abandoning the original melody of the chant, Lasso divides the short text into four sections in order that the meaning of each idea may be amply illustrated in musical terms. The words *Super flumina Babylonis* are set to an extensive phrase initiated by the tenor. Though the naturally accented syllables *Su*-per and Baby-*lo*-nis are stressed by longer time values and higher pitches, the shape of the phrases is governed by other considerations than that of correct prosody. It is the image of the waters that has evoked the undulating melisma on the last syllable of *flumina* and the analogous rise and fall on *Babylonis*. As the voices enter in succession they imitate the first part of this subject strictly for a period of seventeen measures. In the seventeenth measure the cantus without a pause begins the next phrase *illic sedimus*, the other three voices catching up one beat later at the beginning of the next measure. The static melody and repeated chords of this section are obvious transliterations of the text. This phrase is repeated at measure 20 but now the lower three voices proceed directly onward to *et flevimus*. The descent of the cantus beginning in measure 22, paralleled by alto and tenor, progresses over the suspended tones of the bass to an expressive modulation symbolic of grief at the very end of the phrase.

ILLUSTRATION 5

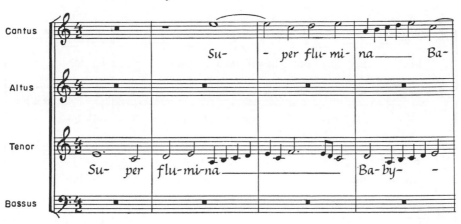

ILLUSTRATION 5 (*continued*)

ILLUSTRATION 5 (*continued*)

ILLUSTRATION 5 (*continued*)

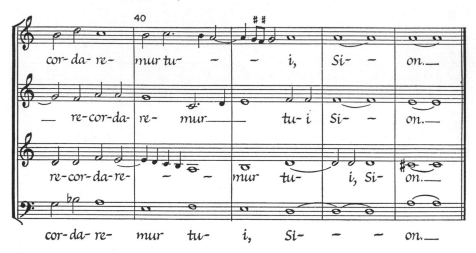

In order to intensify the meaning of *recordaremur* (we remembered) Lasso causes the B♭ of the bass phrase (measures 34–35), which is imitating the previous entrances of cantus and alto, to clash with the B♮ quitted by the cantus just half a beat earlier. The close proximity of these opposing tones is a device called a *cross-relation*. It was used extensively by men of Lasso's generation to create intensity of feeling. Lasso emphasizes its expressive impact once again by repeating this concluding section of the motet.

Lasso's many motets for double choir reflect a technique most brilliantly developed in the later decades of the century by composers working in Venice. This city-state at the height of its power in the sixteenth century became the center of the most progressive developments in music as well as painting. In the private life of the aristocracy the madrigals and other contemporary forms of secular music published by the great Venetian printers were a constant source of pleasure. Music also played a conspicuous part in the observance of the major religious feast days which were celebrated by the municipality with ceremonies of unparalleled magnificence.

St. Mark's Cathedral with its many galleries separated from each other by unusually ample space was an especially favorable site for the performance of polychoral music. Adrian Willaert, who directed the music of the Cathedral between 1527 and 1562, exploited this architectural feature in his settings of Psalms for two separate choirs. During the last third of the century the use of *cori spezzati* (separated choirs) was extended and elaborated by Andrea Gabrieli (c. 1520–1586) and his nephew Giovanni Gabrieli (1557–1612) to include choirs of instruments as well as voices in various numbers and combinations. In Giovanni Gabrieli's later publications the number of parts is increased in some instances to as many as sixteen, divided into four separate groups.

Such music is created not just for its antiphonal effect, but to exploit contrast as a musical device. In the past, contrasts in sonorities had been limited to such features as the alternation of passages of imitative counterpoint and sections of homophony. Josquin and his Roman successors had also woven their music with duets or trios, which in longer works such as Masses were often maintained alone for large portions of the composition. But the contrast between these sections with the full-voiced passages surrounding them is minimal. With Gabrieli contrast becomes the primary objective, and it is achieved by a number of methods which are strongly opposed to the musical principles cultivated by the Roman school.

To Gabrieli the strongest elements of contrast are those of pitch and color. Choirs composed of predominantly high or low voices are basic factors of his polychoral style, since they emphasize the difference between the clear, penetrating qualities of boys' treble voices and the opaque, full-bodied tones of men. In his use of instruments Gabrieli also departs from the normal practices of the sixteenth century. Instruments had often been used in the performance of polyphonic music to double the voices or even as substitutes for one or more of the vocal parts. They were employed, however, only to add greater volume to the sound, and the choice of instruments was apparently dictated simply by what instruments were available. Gabrieli almost always provides definite directions for the instrumental scoring he desires. Whether duplicating the voice parts or replacing some of them, instruments such as viols and organ complement the thin, clear sounds of the upper choir, while the mellow tones of *cornetti* (wooden wind instruments) and trombones are reserved for the lower choir. Thus even when the same music is performed by the different choirs, it will sound differently because of the dissimilar colors. When, after an antiphonal passage, the different bodies are joined in a passage for all, a *tutti*, a further element of contrast appears—that of dynamic volume.

To be successful, these methods of achieving contrast require a comparatively rapid alternation between the single or combined choirs. Accordingly Gabrieli composes brief syllabic phrases for each textual idea, phrases which are not designed to be extended horizontally by the techniques of imitative counterpoint but to be supported by vertical harmonies. Though the voices often maintain a degree of melodic independence, crossing each other from time to time, their motion is in fact controlled by the chordal progressions. Because these homophonic sections

ILLUSTRATION 6

ILLUSTRATION 6 (*continued*)

differ in length, the exchanges between the choirs do not occur at regular intervals. Gabrieli employs a variety of rhythms and tempi to accord with the various connotations of the text, with the result that a section in slow duple rhythm may be abruptly succeeded by the dance-like motion of rapid, triple time.

Gabrieli's *O magnum mysterium,* a setting of the fourth Responsory at Matins on Christmas Day, was published in 1587. The character of the text with its mystical opening and its conclusion of jubilant alleluias seems highly appropriate for a style based upon contrasting effects: "O great mystery and wonderful sacrament, that all creatures could gaze upon God, lying in the manger, Blessed Virgin, whose womb was worthy of carrying the Lord Christ, Alleluia."

The most striking feature of the opening of this motet is the constant use of cross-relations between B♭ and B♮. The first B♭ of the alto is contradicted almost immediately by the B♮ of the cantus. At the end of the first phrase the B♮ of the cantus is succeeded with no preparation by the B♭ of the second chorus. The strangeness of this harmonic effect is intended to convey the marvel and mystery of the Incarnation. After a rhetorical pause (measure 9), the choirs, joined now in a sumptuous texture of eight parts, repeat the opening section.

The balance of the text is divided into its smallest components of meaning, each represented by a characteristic melody and harmony. At times the choirs alternate in vertical blocks of sound; at others, the eight voices enter successively, as if in polyphonic imitation, producing a contrast of color and texture. At measure 45 (see Illustration 7), to express the jubilant feeling of the concluding alleluia, the composer commences the final section with materials sharply differentiated from the rest of the motet.

He abruptly alters the tempo by making the fundamental beat, a dotted half note, equal in time to the half note of the previous section, thereby accelerating the tempo. He also introduces a dance-like rhythm in which the off-beat stresses produce a strong sense of syncopation within each three-measure phrase. The two choirs are rapidly alternated, and the section is brought to a climax at measure 64 from which point the final cadence is drawn out slowly over four measures. The effectiveness of this cadence is the result of the shift in tempo and note values to produce a carefully contrived *ritardando* (slowing down), emphasizing the opulent sonorities of the eight parts extended over a range of two octaves and a half.

ILLUSTRATION 7

ILLUSTRATION 7 (*continued*)

The rhythmic vitality of the alleluia section is evidence of the gulf between the style of the Venetian, Gabrieli, and the conservative orientation of the composers of the Roman school. To express the content of the liturgical text, Gabrieli dispenses with the principal features of the traditional style of polyphony or gives them subordinate functions. In their place appear successions of chords in a rich many-voiced fabric, many of whose patterns foreshadow the harmonic procedures of the music of subsequent centuries.

VIII THE BAROQUE

Part I. The Accents of Passion
1600-1660

And new philosophy calls all in doubt,
The Element of fire is quite put out;
The Sun is lost, and th' earth, and no man's wit
Can well direct him where to looke for it.
And freely men confesse that this world's spent,
When in the Planets, and the Firmament
They seeke so many new; then see that this
Is crumbled out againe to his Atomies.
'Tis all in peeces, all cohaerence gone;
All just supply, and all relation. . . .

We thinke the heavens enjoy their Sphericall,
Their round proportions embracing all.
But yet their various and perplexed course,
Observ'd in divers ages, doth enforce
Men to finde out so many Eccentrique parts,
Such divers downe-right lines, such overthwarts,
As disproportion that pure forme: It teares
The Firmament in eight and forty sheires,
And in these Constellations then arise
New starres, and old doe vanish from our eyes:
As though heav'n suffered earthquakes, peace or war.

DONNE, *The First Anniversary*, 1611

IN THIS POEM John Donne has recorded the scientific discoveries which were destroying the universe that men had known. For hundreds of years man had believed in a world scheme substantially that of Ptolemy (second century A.D.) which had become the official view of Christian theology. It was a geocentric system. Around the immobile earth revolved the spheres of the four elements and the planets. Beyond the planets lay the sphere of the fixed stars, the Primum Mobile, and finally the Pure Empyrean where God the Unmoved Mover dwells. The motion of the spheres was imparted to them by the Primum Mobile, the sphere of first motion, which began its revolution through the attraction of the desirability of God. It was also generally accepted that the distances between the planets corresponded to the ratios which govern musical intervals. This was a universe framed for man whose habitation stood at its very center. It was a universe created with an end in view, the relationship of man to God and of God to man. For this reason men had endeavored to explain the phenomena of existence by searching for final causes or purposes. They did not ask *how* things acted but *why* they acted as they did.

The complacency with which men regarded their universe was first shaken by Nicolaus Copernicus (1473–1543). A Platonist convinced that numbers and proportions underlay the universe, Copernicus learned through his studies that the ancients had disagreed about the precise nature of astronomical relations. Thus he was led to re-examine the motions of the universe. He found that by assuming that the earth, instead of being stationary, actually revolved around the sun he could explain the motions of the planets with a system of only two cycles instead of the three postulated previously. Now it is an axiom of mathematics that the simplest hypothesis which will explain a given set of facts is to be preferred to a more complex one. Accordingly Copernicus felt justified in assuming that he had given a truer picture of the mathematical nature of the world.

For many years the literally world-shaking theory of Copernicus was held to be only a mathematical theorem. It was quite possible for men of the sixteenth century to accept this theorem without believing that it applied to physical nature. But here and there some were kindled by its implications to investigate the heavens anew. In 1572 Tycho Brahe discovered Nova Cassiopeia and in 1606 Johannes Kepler published an account of his discovery of a new star in the constellation of Serpentarius. Thus the idea of a fixed and unchangeable heaven could no longer be maintained, for new bodies were to be seen in it. In 1600 William Gilbert issued his *De magnete* in which he advanced the idea that the motion of the earth was the product of the earth's own magnetism. Erroneous as this premise might be, Gilbert cast doubt upon the sphere of the Primum Mobile as the first cause of all motion. In 1609 Kepler again contributed to the intellectual ferment by publishing his *De motibus Stellae Martis* (*Concerning the Motions of Mars*). By proving that the planets revolved not in perfect circles but in ellipses, he destroyed forever the perfect spheres of Ptolemy.

Finally in 1610 came incontrovertible evidence that the Copernican picture of the universe must be the true one. In that year Galileo published "The Astronomical Messenger. Containing and setting forth observations lately made with the aid of a newly invented Telescope respecting the Moon's surface, the Milky Way, Nebulous Stars, an innumerable multitude of Fixed Stars, and also respecting Four Planets never before seen, which have been named the Cosmion Stars." With the aid of the telescope it was plain for all to see that the universe was a vast complex of bodies, infinitely more involved than had ever been dreamed of. The safe, snugly enclosed world of the past had suddenly crumbled away, exposing man to an unfamiliar sky.

It is noteworthy that the men who discovered the new universe were with but few exceptions avowed Platonists. Imbued with the idea of a world constituted of numbers, they had inadvertently opened the door to modern science with the key of mathematics. For these men the universe was rationally organized by harmonious proportions. Therefore they constructed musical cosmogonies, a fact clearly revealed by the titles of their major works. Kepler's largest opus is called *Harmonices Mundi* (*The Harmonies of the World*, 1619). After this came Robert Fludd's *Monochordum Mundi Symphoniacum* (*The Harmonious Monochord of the World*, 1622) and Marin Mersenne's *L'Harmonie Universelle* (1636–1637). It is one of the paradoxes of history that the beginning of the modern scientific age is in many ways the result of the humanistic revival of the 'unscientific' and idealistic philosophy of Plato and the musical speculations of the ancients.

Though the new world was born in the matrix of the Renaissance, it brought with it from the beginning ideas which were to separate it from its parent. The discoveries made by mathematical speculation and corroborated by such scientific tools as the telescope undermined the premises of Aristotelian science which had its ultimate basis in the evidence of the senses. The world did revolve—all evidence of the senses to the contrary—and the telescope proved that the naked eye gave but an imperfect picture of the starry heavens. Hence it was concluded that the path to truth must lie in mathematical demonstration, an abstraction known only to the intellect. The world of reality is not to be discovered in the surface qualities of things as perceived by the senses, but in the quantitative or numerical characteristics of objects. According to Kepler "nothing can be known completely except quantities or by quantities. And so it happens that the conclusions of mathematics are most certain and indubitable. . . . Just as the eye was made to see colours, and the ear to hear sounds, so the human mind was made to understand, not whatever you please, but quantity." * In the new science the universe is to be viewed as measurable quantity (bodies) in measurable motion within measurable time.

The man of the seventeenth century was called upon to reject all his former notions of the universe and to abandon a cosmological scheme which not only had determined how he interpreted nature but had also sustained his religious beliefs. This blow but added to the shock felt earlier when Martin Luther's protest against the abuses prevalent in the Catholic church culminated in a revolt against the church. Led by Luther, Zwingli, and Calvin, the Protestant faith after many tribulations gained a permanent and even official place in the countries of northern Europe. Thus in the first half of the sixteenth century the universal church which had united all men since the fall of Rome was torn asunder. But the Catholic church was not slow in attacking the Protestant heresy and the abuses within its own house which had led to the revolt. Through a series of reforms promulgated by the papacy and the Council of Trent (1545–1563), the Church was purged of malpractices and its doctrine was reaffirmed. At the same time the heretical faith was combatted on every side with such instruments as the Inquisition and the Index of banned books.

The period of the Protestant Reformation and the Catholic Counter Reformation was a time when every man was compelled to examine his conscience and to make agonizing decisions about his religious beliefs. The tensions of this age created an atmosphere of heightened emotion that was reflected in the arts. In its fight to save men's souls the Roman church in the seventeenth century frankly appealed to their emotions and senses to hold them in the fold of the true faith. In the interiors of churches the eye was led from painted tableaux of Biblical histories to sculptured saints in ecstasy and on upward to the ceiling of the dome where angels seemed to float among the clouds in endless spirals ascending to a sunburst of glory in the highest heaven. Architecture, sculpture, and painting became as one, mingling to give an overwhelming sense of the immediacy of the religious experience.

The Protestant churches tended to frown upon or, as in the case of those of Calvinistic persuasion, to condemn this outward show. They emphasized instead such expressions of the community of religion as the

* Edwin Arthur Burtt, *The Metaphysical Foundations of Modern Physical Science*, p. 68.

congregational singing of hymns, more commonly called chorales, and the pastoral sermon. In the latter they shared a belief in common with their Catholic opponents, for it was universally accepted that eloquence was the most effective means to persuade men and to lead them into the paths of truth. The emotions of men can be stirred through figurative language. They may be swayed to actions and beliefs contrary even to their own will. Thus richness of language and the emotional inflections and gestures of the speaker were deemed valuable and even mandatory aids to move men, and in moving to persuade them.

The emotionalism of this period was not simply an official attitude nor one of expediency. It was also a personal one. Confronted by the doubts raised by religious dissension and the import of the new science, many men turned to the subjective experience of their soul to find a confirmation of their beliefs that neither the dogmatic proclamations of the church nor the demonstrations of science could offer them. A strong current of mysticism runs through this period. Many followed programs of religious exercises and devotions with the aim of attaining a state of religious ecstasy and a sense of direct communion with the divine. Such experiences gave birth to a form of literary expression laden with imagery and involuted meaning. This is the "dark" style of the Metaphysical poets, a style made rich with overtones in an attempt to recapture the reality of the poets' mystic experience.

The concatenation of scientific discoveries and religious upheaval produced around 1600 a change in the outlook of the world. Doubts and uncertainties were to be found on every side. New horizons were opening everywhere, challenging men to explore them. Old ways of thought had to be abandoned or modified to meet the altered conditions. As it happened, most men in the first half of the seventeenth century chose the second of the alternatives. Just as a scientist such as Kepler tried to fit his new conception of the heavens within the ancient musical cosmogony, so painters, architects, and poets poured their new emotionalism into molds inherited from the humanistic Renaissance. The painter, while filling his canvasses with motions and tensions foreign to the art of the High Renaissance, still depicted themes drawn from Greek and Roman mythology and still garbed his figures in classic togas or depicted them in classic nudity. The architect, while creating buildings that overwhelm the spectator with their monumentality or ornateness, still worked with architectural elements borrowed from the classic past. The poet and musician, too, still adhered to humanistic ideas cultivated during the fifteenth and sixteenth centuries. The new art of the seventeenth century represents not so much a rejection of the Renaissance as it does a transformation of its elements into a swelling, emotional style that later generations were to call contemptuously "baroque," meaning extravagant and in bad taste. Today this once pejorative term is used in a positive sense to characterize that cultural period which begins in the late sixteenth century and extends to the middle of the seventeenth, and even in many cases into the middle of the eighteenth century.

At the beginning of the seventeenth century musicians created a musical style that was a radical departure from that of the Renaissance. Their innovations transpired, however, within the framework of ideas inherited from the humanists. During the preceding century, as we have seen (Chapter VII, p. 176), the domain of creative activity had become separated from the areas of theoretical and practical knowledge. Aristotle's conception of "poetics" was taken up by musicians and translated into a doctrine of musical creation known as *Musica poetica*. At first this term meant little more than how to use the basic elements of music when composing. It explained such purely technical matters as musical notation, intervals, the resolution of dissonances, and the various methods of combining melodies, either note against note or in more florid forms of counterpoint. Gradually, as the act of musical creation became increasingly concerned with the problem of translating textual matters into musical terms, Musica poetica borrowed more and more of its precepts from the literary disciplines.

Since music, poetry, and oratory shared the same goal, namely to move the emotions, it was assumed that music should achieve this end with means analogous to those employed in the literary arts. If the affective power of poetry and oratory was the result of rhetorical devices, did it not follow that music must have equivalent figures, a rhetoric of its own? Accordingly the musicians and theorists began to analyze and formulate the musical techniques of their day in terms of rhetoric. How widespread this conception of musical rhetoric came to be may be illustrated by a statement in the *Sylva Sylvarum* (1627) of Francis Bacon, that ardent exponent of the empirical approach to science. In this work, presenting hundreds of experiments to be performed in all fields of knowledge, he prefaced the section dealing with experiments to be undertaken in music with the flat pronouncement: "There be in Musick certain figures or Tropes, almost agreeing with the Figures of Rhetorick."

One of the most complete presentations of musical figures is to be found in the writings of Joachim Burmeister (*c.* 1566–1629). According to him a musical figure is "a musical movement in harmony as well as in melody circumscribed within a specific period which begins and ends with a cadence; and which differs from the principle of simple composition and assumes a more ornate appearance." It is therefore a particular handling of the musical material within the individual phrase. Burmeister distinguishes numerous figures of melody and of harmony. There is, for example, *hypallage* which in rhetoric is the substitution of one name for another, as Ceres for grain. In music this figure is the polyphonic device of imitating the theme or subject in inversion. *Noema*, to cite another instance, means in rhetoric a pregnant sentence or statement that signifies something beyond the literal words involved. The musical noema is a homophonic passage which attains its emphasis by the sudden simplicity of chordal harmonies coming after the intricate movements of imitative polyphony. Or again there is *hypotyposis*, the use of vivid language which so represents facts that they appeal to the eye rather than the ear. (Quintilian gives as an example: "He came into the forum on fire with criminal madness; his eyes blazed and cruelty was written in every feature of his countenance.") According to Burmeister the musical equivalent is "that ornament by which the meaning of the text is so reflected that those things which are in the text and do not have life and spirit seem to be provided with life," as when the music breaks into a fast triple time to express joy or other such lively emotion.

By the end of the sixteenth century the doctrine of Musica poetica had come to mean the art of composing according to rhetorical precepts. Though the musical figures were not new devices for the most part, this does not detract from their importance. First of all they are of immediate practical use, for they provide a convenient tool whereby individual musical techniques can be analyzed and taught. Secondly, they are illustrative of the artistic trend of the music of the sixteenth and seventeenth centuries, revealing the deliberate attempt to reconcile musical expression with the aims of the literary arts. If music must move the emotions, the composer must find a means to this end equivalent to the rhetoric of poets and orators. He must find the musical correspondence to the text which he is setting. The aims of the musicians of the seventeenth century are set forth succinctly in the statement of Joannes Ban, the Archbishop of Harlem and intimate friend of René Descartes, that "in the invention and constitution of melody lies the whole substance of music; so that the tones are to be adapted to the quantities of the words and syllables, and to their meaning and sense, so that the music will have the force and will approach the function of the orator: to teach, and in teaching, to delight and to move."

The dictum that the function of music is to delight and to move the affections was generally accepted by the men of the seventeenth century. But in the emotional atmosphere of that era the emphasis was placed increasingly upon the latter function. One solution to the problem of how to move the emotions was to create a musical rhetoric. An even more radical solution was offered by a group of men in Florence. There in the latter years of the sixteenth century, the Camerata, one of the typical informal academies of the Renaissance, met in the home of Count Giovanni de' Bardi. Like true humanists these men indulged in studies related to universal knowledge, but their special interest lay in the field of music. They all knew the ancient legends of music's marvelous power over nature and the emotions, and they could not but wonder at the inability of modern music to recreate the same effects. Under the guidance of Vincenzo Galilei, the father of the great astronomer, they inquired into the nature of ancient Greek music and sought to put their discoveries to use in modern music.

According to Galilei, whose conclusions appeared in his treatise *Dialogo della musica antica et della moderna* (1582), the greatest difference between ancient and modern music lay in the fact that the music of the Greeks was monodic while the music of his day was polyphonic. The Greeks therefore had created their powerful music with the force of melody alone. Since modern music was founded upon the combination of two or more different melodies it was deprived of any potency through the confusion of so many melodies. Moreover, the music of the Greeks was designed to be an immediate and inseparable expression of the text. It was not chained by modern music's arbitrary rules governing the proper use of harmonic consonance and dissonance. If the intimate union of words and melody is to make itself felt upon the auditor, Galilei concludes, the ridiculous confusion of melodies and different words that reigns in contemporary practice must be abandoned. Music must turn its back on modern usages and revert to monody.

If the music of the ancients was a single melody framed to portray and intensify the words, the next question is how the musicians of old accomplished this. Galilei's answer is that they endeavored to imitate *the manner of the person speaking*. The musician "first considered very diligently the character of the person speaking: his age, his sex, with whom he was speaking, and the effect he sought to produce by this means; and these conceptions, previously clothed by the poet in chosen words suited to such a need, the musician then expressed in the tone and with the accents and gestures, the quantity and quality of sound, and the rhythm appropriate to that action and to such a person." * In other words, music must not imitate the meaning of the individual words and conceits as the madrigalists had done; it should attempt to reproduce the inflections of speech, to capture the accents of passion.

Buttressed by the theory of Galilei, the men of the Camerata resolved to recreate the drama of the ancients which they knew had been tragedy allied with music. The results of their experiment are well known:

* Strunk, *Source Readings in Music History*, p. 319.

their drama turned out to be the beginnings of opera, and their monody completely transformed the nature of music in the first decades of the seventeenth century. Opera and monody were to become the hallmarks of the musical Baroque, but it is well to remember that they are the fruit of seeds sown by Renaissance humanism.

Music was already used extensively in theatrical performances during the sixteenth century. In these productions the function of music was largely decorative, and generally took the form of madrigals and dances performed between the scenes of spoken drama. To unite poetry with music continuously throughout a drama the musicians of the Camerata created a style of musical recitation, a *stile recitativo*, drawing upon evidence contained in antique sources and their own experimentation. Though the new *dramma in musica* was founded on this innovation, it continued to make use of the earlier musical and poetic features of the Renaissance drama.

The poetry of the earliest Baroque opera belongs to a type of drama cultivated at Renaissance courts called the pastorale. Though not countenanced by Aristotle, it was one of the sixteenth century's efforts to revive the theatre of the ancients. The pastorale was a lyrical poem describing the amorous passions and adventures of nymphs and shepherds in an imaginary Arcadia populated by the gods and goddesses of Greek mythology. From this material was drawn the story of Orpheus and Euridice, the subject of the first operas. Sixteenth-century performances of the pastorale had been the occasion for lavish productions. The stage was animated by large numbers of singers and dancers, and decorated by splendidly painted scenery, not the least of whose attractions were astonishing transformations accomplished by stage machinery. The earliest opera was molded by the tradition of the pastorale and by the taste for spectacular visual effects. Although these elements continued to appeal to the audiences of the early seventeenth century, it was the eloquence and power with which the newly-created theatrical style of music expressed the human passions that accounts for the success of the new art form.

The history of opera begins with *Euridice*, for this is the first of the Florentine experiments to have survived. Written by Ottavio Rinuccini, the leading poet of the Camerata, and set to music by Giacomo Peri, one of its principal musicians, it was performed in 1600 as the climax of festivities celebrating the wedding of Maria de' Medici, daughter of the Grand Duke of Tuscany, and Henry IV of France. *Euridice*, in effect, supplanted the theatrical entertainments in vogue at the Italian courts. It was regarded as an artistic achievement so exceptional that it was worthy of this momentous political and dynastic occasion, and it presented an example for other princely patrons to emulate. The next decisive stage in the development of Baroque opera occurred under the aegis of Vincenzo Gonzaga, Duke of Mantua, whose enthusiasm for the arts was matched by his resources. He sponsored the famous performances of Claudio Monteverdi's *Orfeo* (1607) and *Arianna* (1608) which were notable for their sumptuous presentations as well as the eloquence of their music. During the next two decades opera made its debut in many of the courts of northern Italy, in Venice, and in Rome. Through the agency of Italian composers it even became established in the Catholic cities of southern Germany, particularly in Vienna, the capital of the Empire. In Paris Italian opera was accepted more slowly, becoming known only through occasional performances by Italian artists during the first half of the century.

The early operas were written for special, non-recurrent occasions. Not until 1637 was the first public opera theatre opened in Venice. It was followed within a few years by a second and a third and then by dozens of theatres. The demand for a constant supply of operatic works for these and other stages provided a vital stimulus to poets and musicians alike. Both music and drama were shaped by the taste of audiences consisting not only of Venetian patricians and aristocratic tourists but also of humbler elements of the city's population. Pastoral subject matter rapidly gave way to dramatic episodes drawn from history. In these the passions motivating the protagonists produce a series of conflicts and crises. The increasing emphasis upon the passions afforded ample opportunities for musical expression, challenging the abilities of singers to convey by vocal force and agility the heightened accents of passion. The stylized voices of *castrati*, unsurpassable in power and flexibility, began to dominate the operatic stage in feminine as well as masculine roles.

None of the secular vocal forms cultivated in the late sixteenth century were unaffected by the new theatrical music of the passions. The composers closest to the art of the Florentines soon turned to the writing of solo monodies. In these the flow of the vocal line is governed by the inflection of the words and by the grammatical structure of the text. The through-composed madrigal with its characteristic texture of five voices rapidly disappeared, or was drastically modified and transformed to express the passions of the text in the most direct fashion. It evolved into a new category of music, the chamber *cantata*, which maintained the same artistic values as the opera, but expresses them more intimately. The cantata uses the simplest means, often just a soloist with an accompanying instrument. Though performed without stage costumes or action, it presupposes a theatrical conception of music as a means of moving the passions of its auditors. It is music to be listened to, a performance to be witnessed, rather than music in which to participate as was the madrigal of the sixteenth century. An invisible proscenium has appeared in the salon.

The basic musical idiom of the Renaissance had been formulated in religious music and then carried over into secular forms. In the new epoch, sacred music loses its leadership in the establishment of stylistic principles. The motet as a generic term covering musical settings of liturgical or religious texts survives in name only, as the characteristics of the dramatic madrigal and the solo cantata are impressed upon it. But the secularization of Catholic and Protestant liturgical music was by no means universal. Claudio Monteverdi, the foremost composer of the first half of the seventeenth century, defends his new melodic and harmonic procedures occasioned by the text, as having been written according to the tenets of the "secunda prattica" (second or modern practice). This term presupposes a "prima prattica," namely the polyphonic choral style of the Flemish and Italian composers of sacred music during the sixteenth century. The Council of Trent had placed its stamp of approval upon the polyphony of Palestrina and contemporary Roman artists and this idiom was maintained with the revival of spiritual fervor that accompanied the Italian Counter Reformation. Already known as the "stile antico" (the old style) by 1610, it nevertheless continued to be practiced throughout the seventeenth and eighteenth centuries, especially in the Sistine Chapel in Rome. Employed particularly for the Mass, its dignity and restraint are in marked contrast to the excited intensity of the new style.

The application of the new theatrical style to the expression of religious affections led to the creation of a new form—the sacred *Oratorio*. One of the most devout of the new religious orders founded in the spiritual revival of the sixteenth century, the Congregazione dell'Oratorio, is largely responsible for its name. From their inception in 1564, the Oratorians established ceremonies apart from the regular liturgy stressing the importance of prayer, meditation, preaching and music. Performed in halls or buildings called Oratories, the music of these services consisted primarily of devotional songs. The dialogue form of many of these so-called "laude" lead to their performance by different groups of singers, and ultimately to simple forms of dramatic performance. By the opening of the seventeenth century, elaborate "Sacre Rappresentazioni" (Sacred plays), such as the allegorical *Drama of the Body and the Soul*, 1600, were being composed in the new dramatic musical style. The Jesuits were prompt to recognize the powers of the new music just as they were the first to adopt the Baroque style of painting and sculpture to decorate their churches for the purpose of exciting religious passions. It was the musical director of the Jesuit's German College in Rome, Giacomo Carissimi (1605–1674) who first drew these religious and musical elements together into compositions of extensive proportions. Carissimi's "Sacred Histories" were musical settings of narrative texts of the Old Testament in the dramatic recitative style, performed at special Lenten services held in the Oratorio del Crocifisso.

Many of the basic features of the all-pervasive new musical style are to be found in the *Nuove Musiche* (New Pieces of Music) published in 1601 by Giulio Caccini, a member of the Florentine Camerata. *Dovrò dunque morire?* (literally: Must I then die?) (Illustration 1) is a characteristic example of what Caccini calls a madrigal for solo voice and lute as opposed to other solo songs in the collection called arias which are strophic songs. All of the pieces in the collection are written as accompanied monodies (monody being the term preferred by the humanists for solo song). Caccini states in his preface that the radically new style of these songs was created in order that the words might have the maximum effect upon the auditor, something that was impossible in polyphonic compositions. "Unless the words were understood, they could not move the understanding. I have endeavored in those my late compositions to bring in a kind of music by which men might, as it were, talk in harmony, using in that kind of singing, as I have said at other times, a certain noble neglect of the song, passing now and then through certain dissonances, holding the bass note firm except when I did not wish to observe the common practice, and playing the inner voices on an instrument for the expression of some passion, these being of no use for any other purpose."

In this monody the passionate declamation of the text is immediately apparent. One needs only to observe the intensity of expression of the first phrase to sense the new dramatic feeling of the century. Caccini respects the accentuation of the text by placing the longest notes upon the natural stress of the third and sixth syllables, but he captures the emotional inflection of the line by creating a melodic phrase that rises to the word "then," thus giving it an accent of protest before falling to the word "morire" where a rising tone on the last syllable imitates the inflection of a question. There is a notable tendency to begin each melodic phrase on a high note from which the melodic line gradually descends as if the breath were gradually expending itself after the first violent exclamation.

The same careful attention to passionate declamation is to be seen in the nineteenth and twentieth measures where the exclamatory "O" is given greater force by repetition on a higher pitch. Caccini in general does not allow the *coloraturas* or ornamentations of the vocal line to obscure the meaning of the text, but confines them to the end of a phrase which is repeated (*O miseria inaudita*). Although there is no indication of this in the score, Caccini expects the singer to add emotional life to the melody by means of such devices as swelling or diminishing the voice at suitable moments. Thus musical dynamics, placed in the service of the

ILLUSTRATION I

ILLUSTRATION I (*continued*)

ILLUSTRATION I (*continued*)

expression of the passions, begin to assume an important role in musical performance almost for the first time.

To accompany the voice the composer has provided a single bass line from which the accompanist, be he a lutenist or a keyboard player, is to improvise harmonies, adding appropriate tones between the bass note and the melodic note. Below the bass line certain numbers and signs of accidentals are to be seen. Where no figures appear, the harmony to be supplied is that of the triad built upon the bass note, as in the first and third notes. At times the tones of the bass line are to be construed simply as passing notes implying no change in harmony, as in the fourth and fifth notes. Where accidental signs and numbers appear, the composer wishes a specific chord to be used. The flat sign indicates a minor triad, and the sharp a major triad. The numbers signify a particular interval above the bass note, as in the third measure where the sixth together with a sharp specify the use of C♯ which is the major sixth above the E of the bass. (Caccini's indications have not always been faithfully followed in this seventeenth-century transcription of his madrigal by Robert Dowland.)

This notational procedure, the so-called *basso continuo*, thorough bass or figured bass, is one of the most distinctive features of the new musical style. Within a few short decades of its first appearance it had become so indispensable that the era from 1600 to 1750 has been called with ample justification the "Age of Thorough Bass." Although it was originally designed to throw the dramatic vocal line into prominence by reducing the harmonies to an unobtrusive, non-vocal support, this practice soon spread to instrumental music as well.

The thorough bass, far from being merely a convenient system of notational shorthand or a practical solution to the needs of an accompaniment, must be regarded as a new and basic principle of style: the *stile concertato* or concerted style. This word is derived from the Italian word *concertare*, meaning to vie with or to contend with, and it implies a contrast or opposition of forces. In the new accompanied monody such contrast is an inherent element. There is first of all the contrast in function between the two parts. To the voice is allotted the role of the bearer of the melody, while the instrumental part functions as the provider of harmonic sounds. There is furthermore an implicit contrast between the vocal melody and the line given to the instrumentalist. Unlike the individual lines of sixteenth-century polyphony which were linked thematically through imitation, these two lines are totally distinct one from another.

During the seventeenth century the dissimilarity of the two parts was gradually heightened by allocating ever more individual and characteristic melodic phrases to the continuo. In addition to these factors, we find also the contrast of timbre and texture; vocal sound opposed to instrumental sound, the single melodic line of the voice opposed to the harmonic texture of the instrument. Such contrasts and oppositions are, of course, a complete denial of the Renaissance striving for unity which had led to a style stressing homogeneity of sound and the closest relationship of the individual parts through imitation. This element of contrast, which appealed instinctively to the sensibilities of the new age, was to be given the widest and most varied application in the century and a half after its first appearance. The permutations of the stile concertato in terms of the contrast and opposition of voice and instrument, of solo and ensemble, of pitch, timbre, and dynamics, are among the most striking phenomena of Baroque music.

Caccini's monodies are his interpretation of the theories of affective music propounded by the members of the Florentine Camerata. A more extended application of their theories is found in the opera *Euridice* of 1600, which was written mainly by Jacopo Peri, though Caccini also contributed some of the music. In this version of the Orpheus legend (the very choice of subject matter is a clear indication of the Camerata's preoccupation with the problem of music's power to move the passions), the poetic monologues or dialogues of the principal characters are set in *stile recitativo*, a form of musical declamation supported by the basso continuo. The vocal line obeys only the laws of speech, deriving its rhythmic values from the accents of the text, and its melodic motion from the higher or lower pitches of impassioned speech. In the recitative, elements of purely musical form and order are entirely subordinated to the sense and the structure of the poetry. But when choruses, dances, and songs occur within the drama, they are cast in existing simple musical forms.

The Florentine ideal of music as a form of animated speech is profoundly modified in Monteverdi's first opera, *Orfeo*. Like the Florentine opera and the earlier pastorales, *Orfeo* commences with a prologue addressed directly to the audience. The poetic text sung by the allegorical figure, Musica, extols, appropriately, the power of music to move the passions. As though in answer to this challenge, Monteverdi composes a vocal line which, while closely adhering to the text, possesses a lyrical, melodious quality. Without taking on the symmetrical order of formal song, this development of the recitative style elevates and intensifies the verbal passions. Since it partakes more of melody than of simple declamation it is described as the *arioso* style.

Monteverdi's realization of the powers of music is vividly demonstrated throughout this opera, but achieves its greatest distinction in the climactic scene which concludes the fourth act. In the action leading up to this scene Orfeo has followed the shade of Euridice, struck down by the jealousy of the gods, to the underworld; he has overcome by the power of his musical and poetic eloquence Carone, the guardian of the river Styx, and has gained the right to restore Euridice to life from Pluto and Proserpine, the rulers of Hades. The success of this mission is bound to the condition that he must not look back at Euridice as she follows him until they have reached the upper world. The scene commences with the announcement of permission for their departure. As they proceed on their way, Orfeo, jubilant at first, is soon alarmed by mysterious noises. He turns in apprehension, causing his beloved to sink again into death, and is left desolate and despairing.

The scene presents in rapid succession the antithetical emotions of supreme joy, agitation, fear, dismay and, finally, despair. The first of these is embodied by the poet in three short stanzas, whose formal coherence and balance are framed by Monteverdi with a short instrumental refrain or *ritornello* for two violin parts in parallel thirds before the first stanza and again after the first and second. The formal unity produced by this threefold repetition of the ritornello is supplemented in the vocal sections by the regular rhythmic motion of the figured bass part, which is maintained identically for each of the stanzas. The repetitions of the continuo melody, by assuring the unity of this piece, allow the vocal melody to follow in freedom the different words in each stanza. The six sections of this musical form are further united by a harmonic orientation to G major, emphasized by the similar cadences which conclude each of the sections (Illustration 2).

As Orfeo's happiness gives way to more disturbed feelings, Monteverdi abandons stable harmony and form for the sensitive pliability of the recitative style. He shapes the contours of the vocal phrases to conform to the emotional stress of the text, leading them in the irregular, formless progressions of increasingly agitated speech. At Euridice's exclama-

ILLUSTRATION 2

ILLUSTRATION 2 *(continued)*

Qual ho-nor— di te sia degno mia cetra omni- po-

tente, S'hai nel tar-ta-reo re-'gno piegar po-tu-to o-gni in-du-

ra- ta men- te. Ritornello

Luogo a- vrai— fra le più bel- le i-ma-gi-ni ce-

ILLUSTRATION 2 (*continued*)

tion: "Ah sight that is too sweet and too bitter" (Illustration 3) the continuo harmony and the succession of tones of the voice part match the intensity of passion contained in the words. Pain is equated with the dissonance which appears on the opening expletive and on the word "amara." The bitter pain of "troppo dolce" is expressed by the chromatic progression of two totally unrelated chords, C minor and E major. Orfeo's final lament, which is the scene's climactic point of tension, applies all of these devices with the greatest intensity. The progression of the basso continuo part is so contrived that harsh dissonances with the voice part coincide with emotional stresses as points of maximum tension. This is apparent in the very first measure where the voice leaps to an F which clashes

ILLUSTRATION 3

with the chord derived from the C♯ of the continuo. The despairing quality of the phrase "Dove te'n vai, mia vita?" (Where are you going, my life?) (Illustration 4) is emphasized by the jagged shape of the voice part and the musical punctuation, while the dread words: "Qual occulto poter di questi orrori di questi amati orrori" (what occult power of these horrors, of these beloved horrors) is expressed through monotonous repetitions of notes and stationary harmony.

The success of such intensely dramatic expression posed a challenge

ILLUSTRATION 4

to the favorite form of sixteenth-century music, the madrigal. For many composers it meant that the texture and integrated relationships of the voice parts of the older madrigal must be rejected immediately in favor of the new recitative style. Monteverdi pursued a different path. In the course of the years 1587 to 1638 he published eight volumes of madrigals which illustrate in fascinating succession the progressive modification and transformation of the musical values of the sixteenth-century madrigal by the new aesthetic requirements and the stile concertato.

Ostensibly the madrigals of the first volume of 1587 conform in style to the principles of the end of the sixteenth century. The five-voiced texture, combining richness of sonority with polyphonic activity, and the use of conventionalized musical figures to illustrate the meanings of individual words are all to be found in this collection. But in madrigals such as *Ecco mormorar l'onde*, the five-voiced texture is frequently broken up into smaller groups consisting of three voices opposed in pitch or in sonority. In these trio passages melodic activity is predominantly in the upper parts above a less active lower part which outlines the harmonic progressions in a fashion suggesting the procedures of accompanied monody.

Between 1587 and 1614, when his sixth book of madrigals appeared, Monteverdi invented ever new solutions to the absorbing problem of expressing the passions contained in each poem, still within the medium of five voices. All vestiges of the "old" madrigal disappear in the subsequent volumes. They are now written for solo voices, or for two or three related and similarly pitched voices. At times the fabric is expanded to more ample combinations, but is always supported by the instrumental basso continuo. These works reveal the full exploitation of the possibilities of the concertato style. The sudden unforeseen harmonic modulations, the dynamic opposition of loud and soft sections, the renewed use of the stereotyped illustrative figures of the older madrigalists—all are the consequences of the emotional extremes and dramatic nature of the texts chosen by Monteverdi. A large number were written by Giambattista Marino, whose fondness for rhetorical inversions and antithesis created texts replete with contrasts. A single passion may underly an entire poem or at least a portion of it, against which a variety of intense, if subordinate, feelings may be expressed. Recognition of this fact by Monteverdi and his contemporaries led to various ways of representing in their music both the basic affection and the contrasting ideas. One solution entrusted the representation of the principal emotion to the instrumental continuo by arranging its motion in an undeviating or "obstinate" rhythmic pattern. This solution, already exemplified in brief in the joyous song of Orfeo in Act IV, takes the form of the so-called *basso ostinato* in a number of Monteverdi's later works. An example of the greatest beauty is the *Lamento della Ninfa* (Lament of the Nymph) published in the eighth book of madrigals.

This "madrigal in representative style," as Monteverdi designates it, is essentially a brief, dramatic scene; its poetic ingredients are in essence those of a chamber cantata. It consists of three parts, the first of which is expository, establishing the dramatic situation, while the last presents a moral conclusion. The central section is pure drama, an eloquent and highly emotional lament by the nymph for her faithless lover. The composer frames this section by setting the introduction and conclusion in choral style for a trio of male voices and the basso continuo. The monologue of the nymph is constructed upon a basso ostinato figure of four descending notes, symbolizing in its falling line and its monotonous repetition the prevailing emotion of dejected grief (Illustration 5).

ILLUSTRATION 5

The insistent repetitions of the continuo contrast sharply with the stanzas of the nymph which are composed with the melodic freedom and psychological sensitivity of the arioso style. The melodic phrases are shaped to conform to the ebb and flow of feeling without any correspondence to the regular phraseology of the bass line. To add to the moving quality of this brilliant example of the concertato style Monteverdi introduces from time to time interjected comments by the three male voices. In this madrigal every element of musical style is made subservient to emotional expressiveness. By allocating the narrative elements of the text to the male voices, by the use of a symbolic figure of grief in the continuo, and by creating a sense of the physical isolation of the nymph through the introduction of the three male voices as commentators or witnesses to her torment, Monteverdi has created a moving, living image of distraught sorrow. At the same time he has managed to impart a musical unity to the largest part of the madrigal through the repeated phrase of the basso ostinato.

The importance Monteverdi assigns to the expression of all the human passions carried with it the postulate that "contrasts more than anything else move our souls." It also led him to the conclusion that among the principle affections of the soul no composer had yet found a means of expressing wrath or indignation. He found his solution to the problem of representing these emotions in his reading of classic literature where he learned that for the presentation of agitation or of wrath the classical poets had employed the rapid pyrrhic meter of two short syllables, while they had utilized the slow spondaic meter of two long ones for the opposite emotions. Taking the whole note as the equivalent of one spondaic beat, Monteverdi divided it into sixteen equal parts or sixteenth notes. Foreseeing that the rapid pace of these notes, which he assumed were an approximation of the pyrrhic meter, might make them unsuitable for the vocal rendition of the text, he applied them in his first experiment to the instrumental accompaniment of his setting of Tasso's *Combattimento di Tancredi e Clorinda*, first performed in 1624.

This rapid reiteration of the same notes as a regular metric pattern which Monteverdi calls the "stile concitato," the excited style, is the antecedent of the agitated tremolo. At times he adds interest to this rhythmic motion by varying it with groups of dotted eighths and sixteenth notes. As worked out in the "bellicose" madrigals published in Book VIII (1638), these distinctive meters take on great importance as a means of establishing formal unity within a composition. For apart from their representational qualities, such easily perceived rhythmic patterns give a sense of cohesion and homogeneity to the section of the composition in which they are employed.

Monteverdi's later madrigals abound with various techniques of the concertato style designed to express in musical terms the accents of passion contained in the text. They profoundly shaped the course of Baroque music because of the exceptional artistry with which he employed them. With their dramatic presuppositions and connotations, they provide an artistic bridge to the new category of the cantata, which crystallized as a form of chamber music by the fourth decade of the century. The leading artists in the development of the chamber cantata were Luigi Rossi (1598–1653) and Giacomo Carissimi (1605–1674).

The cantata is clearly the product of a collaboration between musicians and writers of sophisticated, polished verse to please connoisseurs of the arts. Defined by a contemporary critic as a "Dialogue without stage," the slender dramatic situation in the early cantata, is often "acted" by a single person. In Rossi's cantata, *Del Silentio*, the text is an extended monologue on the passion of love. The composer divides the text into musical sections differentiated by their contrasting vocal styles of recitative and aria. The difference between the two styles is in this case partially obscured by the smooth, sustained vocal phraseology which emphasizes stepwise and consonant melodic intervals. Rhetorical values, accents and inflections of the text control the melodic progression and design, but they are integrated with the ideal of extended melodic periods, producing a result which later became known with justice as the *bel canto* (beautiful singing) style.

The sixth section of this cantata, as well as the fifth and the ninth, is composed as a closed form or aria (Illustration 6). The unity of the musical form is achieved by the predominant use of triple meter and by the fact that the tonality in which it begins is confirmed in the final

ILLUSTRATION 6

ILLUSTRATION 6 (*continued*)

Se co-si,   lu- ci mie bel- le,   Mi commanda- no   le___

stel-   le, Mi_com- man- da-   no   le_____   stel-   le?

cadence. The vocal part has many correspondences in its phrases that are not called for by the text but are introduced to create a coherent melody. The melodic fragment of measure three is repeated in measure four and again, slightly modified, in measure five. The rhythmic pattern of measure six is echoed in measure seven. In measures ten through twelve the melodic and rhythmic configuration of "Mi commandano" is used again to complete the phrase ("le stelle"), and then this sequence is reiterated to conclude the aria. The cohesion of such a melody distinguishes it from the amorphous flow of recitative. The distinction between aria and recitative was to be drawn with even greater clarity by succeeding composers.

The influence of the new secular forms and styles quickly spread to sacred music. The dichotomy between the new idiom and traditional practice is reflected in the collection of sacred music published by Monteverdi in 1610. This volume contains a Mass and settings of the liturgy of the Vespers of the Blessed Virgin Mary. Paraphrasing the motet *In illo tempore* of the early sixteenth-century composer Nicholas Gombert, the Mass is a masterly example of the contrapuntal techniques of the stile antico. In striking contrast are the settings of the texts of the Office, which are written in various forms of the concertato style.

For the Psalms, hymns, and Magnificat Monteverdi maintains a close association with the liturgy by using the Gregorian tones as cantus firmi. But he contrasts the Gregorian melodies with different combinations of groups of solo voices and instruments above a basso continuo. The second of the two settings of the Magnificat is particularly notable in this respect. Each of the verses of the text, in spite of their monotonous, unchanging cantus firmus, is given an imaginatively varied treatment. For the more subjective and emotional antiphon texts Monteverdi relinquishes the use of a cantus firmus altogether. He translates them in subtle, plastic forms of the arioso style for one, two, or three solo voices and basso continuo.

The conflicting styles of the Mass and the music for Vespers in this one volume is symptomatic of the growing cleavage between sacred and secular music. Earlier centuries had employed one basic idiom for sacred and secular music alike. But since the beginning of the seventeenth century it has been assumed that the styles of sacred and secular music must be carefully distinguished. This has frequently posed a problem for the composer who feels compelled to write for the church in a musical language that is no longer a living, immediate expression of his own time.

The stylistic dichotomy exemplified in this collection is further illustrated in the work of the leading Roman composer of religious music in the middle years of the century, Giacomo Carissimi. His Masses are written in the older polyphonic style, but his motets use a solo voice or small solo groups and continuo. In his settings of texts for private meditation and devotion and, above all, in the new category of the oratorio, for which he is most celebrated, Carissimi wholeheartedly adopts the theatrical recitative and arioso. The subjects of the oratorios are almost invariably accounts of martyrdom drawn from the Old Testament. Their texts are based upon the Vulgate with skillful poetic interpolations or paraphrases by an unknown colleague of Carissimi. The narrative form of the original subject matter is maintained, but the narration itself (as opposed to the words spoken directly by the participants in the drama) is given to the part of the *Testo* (literally authority or witness). It is presented musically in unadorned stile recitativo for solo voice or chorus. Carissimi's greatest musical eloquence was reserved for the climactic scenes in which the passions of martyrdom, suffering, and lamentation predominate. The oratorios *Jephthe* and *Jonas* were justifiably considered by contemporary audiences to be the most moving examples of Carissimi's art. In the lament of Jonas, *Justus es Domine*, the composer portrays the pathetic emotions of the text in the expressive contours and harmonic dissonances of the arioso style. At the same time he skillfully provides a sense of formal symmetry by repeating the penitential refrain (*Placare, Domine, ignosce, Domine et miserere*) at the end of each of the three sections of the text (Illustration 7).

The various means developed in Italy to attain the ideal of an oratorical music conflicted dramatically with existing artistic procedures, and gained acceptance elsewhere in Europe more slowly. A major factor in the dissemination of the new music was the thriving publishing industry which was particularly active in Venice and in the cities of the Low Countries. A second and more powerful means were the musicians themselves whom Italy produced in ever increasing numbers for the next two centuries. Rated as "exotic foreigners" in France and England, where existing musical traditions were strong and well defined, they nonetheless acquired leading positions for themselves and their art at the principal European courts. Ultimately they were followed and imitated by native musicians. Still another means by which the new Italian music gained enthusiastic support was through the observations and personal

ILLUSTRATION 7

ILLUSTRATION 7 (*continued*)

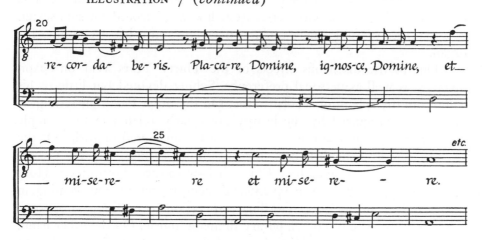

re- cor- da- be- ris. Pla-ca-re, Domine, ig-nos-ce, Domine, et

mi-se-re- re et mi-se- re- re.

experiences of visitors from the north. Many of these Frenchmen, Englishmen, and Germans wrote enthusiastic accounts of the sumptuous
performances in theatre and church. Particularly impressed by the powerful emotional effect of the vocal style they urged the adoption of the
art of the Italians in their own milieu.

One of the first to introduce the new art to his country was the
German composer, Heinrich Schütz (1585–1672). A devout Lutheran of
exceptional intellectual capacities, Schütz as a young man was dissuaded
from the pursuit of the legal profession by his patron, Prince Moritz of
Hesse-Cassel. Sent to Venice in 1609, Schütz remained there for three
years studying and absorbing the art of the Venetians, particularly that
of Giovanni Gabrieli. Six years later he undertook the duties of director
of music to the Elector of Saxony at Dresden, a post that he retained
until his death in 1672. In 1628, as a mature artist, he made a second
visit to Venice in order to study the newer music of Monteverdi and his
younger followers.

The results of Schütz's Italian sojourns are embodied in his deeply
expressive music for the Lutheran church. To use music as a means of
interpreting the Biblical Word became his central goal. Schütz's ability
to translate the text into musical oratory is demonstrated in such collections as the *Psalms of David* (1619) written in the expansive concertato
style of Gabrieli. It is also manifested in the *Kleine geistliche Konzerte*
(1636–39) containing accompanied monodies and works for small solo
ensembles, of which the first composition is revealingly headed "in stile
oratorio" (in the oratorical manner). In subsequent works both methods
of composing are superbly integrated, particularly in Part III of the
Symphoniae Sacrae (1650). An impressive example of this synthesis is

his setting for the text of the conversion of St. Paul taken from the Acts of the Apostles, "Saul, why persecutest thou me," scored for solo sextet, two choruses of four voices each, two violins and a basso continuo for organ.

Due to the disastrous effects of the Thirty Years War on Saxon finances, as well as personal preference, Schütz devoted but little of his abilities to the sphere of secular music. On the other hand, his setting of Gospel texts required by the liturgy are clearly related in their ample proportions and dramatic intensity to the Italian sacred oratorio. Of the six works written in this form, the last three, settings of three Gospel accounts of the Passion of Jesus Christ, belong to special liturgies of Holy Week. They are unique in seventeenth-century music, representing in their simple austerity an extraordinary reversion to tradition as opposed to the flamboyance of contemporary dramatic music. On the other hand, in *The Christmas Story* (*Historia von der Geburt Jesu Christi*) of 1664 Schütz reveals complete mastery of the theatrical style while maintaining a quality of simplicity and naïveté in accordance with the nature of the subject.

In the *Christmas Story* the narration is told in recitative. The words of the various personages in the drama are set apart as "dramatic intermedia." Written for solo or ensemble according to the dictates of the text, they are provided with different instrumental accompaniments defining by their distinctive sonorities the affective content of each intermedium. Thus the pastoral recorders accompany the shepherds, the regal trumpets, King Herod. The relationship of these instrumental parts to the musical fabric differs from that which is typical of their concertato role in the earlier part of the century. Instead of opposing the vocal part and the continuo with independent musical material, the instruments cooperate with the voice parts in what may be defined as the "concertante" style. In the first intermedium, for example, the melodic material of the vocal and instrumental parts is directly related by polyphonic imitation or, less directly, by analogous musical ideas (Illustration 8). Such a use of obbligato concertante instruments becomes increasingly frequent in the middle of the seventeenth century as a means of enriching the musical texture of arias in operas and cantatas.

The growing role of instruments in the new concertato style was accompanied by a heightened interest in their affective qualities and, consequently, by a keener sense of their idiomatic potentialities. Nevertheless the status of instrumental music in the first half of the seventeenth century remained subordinate to that of vocal categories. In this period the organ rapidly developed in size, complexity and variety of sonorities, especially in northern Europe. But its paramount function still continued

ILLUSTRATION 8

to be its participation in the musical liturgies of Catholic and Protestant churches. Of the instrumental forms cultivated by organists, the *canzona*, modelled upon the polyphonic style of the sixteenth-century motet, and the *toccata*, which exploits to some extent the characteristic rapid running figures of which keyboard instruments are capable, were still the most important. But because of the increasing interest in the expression of contrasting affections, the sections normally comprised in organ canzonas and toccatas became increasingly differentiated in their dynamics, texture and style. Still another tendency, namely to construct an entire composition upon a single melodic subject, is exemplified by the *ricercar*.

As opposed to the organ, whose musical style and forms continued to be conditioned by its ecclesiastical milieu, progressive tendencies began to appear in secular music composed for the harpsichord and the violin. The former gradually superseded the lute as a continuo instrument and as a favored solo instrument. Composers writing for the harpsichord made use of idiomatic characteristics of various contemporary styles, such as imitative polyphony and, more importantly, the decorative melodic embroideries and quasi-polyphonic texture of lute music. One of the primary uses of the lute had been the playing of dances, either as an instrumental accompaniment to the voice or by itself. The expressiveness with which an accomplished lutenist was capable of playing was such that the *allemandes*, *courantes* and other dance forms had acquired an artistic status by the beginning of the seventeenth century far above their original social and utilitarian function. These dances were characterized by a form consisting of two more or less equal sections, each of which was usually repeated, and by certain stereotyped rhythmic patterns dictated by the dance steps which such music originally accompanied. Within this form writers for the harpsichord developed an increasingly eloquent keyboard style, which combined the characteristics of the older lute techniques and the affective phraseology of the new vocal style.

One of the more important composers in the development of harpsichord music was Johann Jacob Froberger (1616–1667). Among other things he made a practice of grouping a number of these dances together after the fashion of the French lutenists to form a *partita* or *suite*. The individual dances of such a partita are related through the use of the same key. Frequently a single melody is used throughout so that each piece is melodically and rhythmically a variation upon the first dance, usually a slow allemande. The form and style of such an allemande are exemplified by the famous *Lamento sopra la dolorosa perdita della Real Maestà Ferdinand IV*, which also reveals how instrumental music was beginning to portray affections through the use of stylistic features borrowed from vocal music.

1. GREEK VASE OF THE FIFTH CENTURY B.C.

Copenhagen, Nat. Mus., Antikensammlung Inv. 13817. The Greek poet
Phrynichos (5th c. B.C.) sings his verses at a festival of Dionysius in the agora
of Athens. He leads the four members of the chorus in the performance of a
dithyramb, while the instrumentalist accompanies the singers with an aulos
(an oboe with two pipes). (Chapter I)

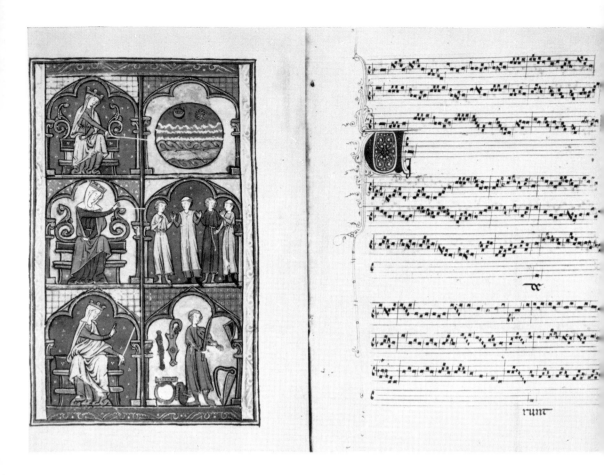

2. THE ANTIPHONARY OF PIERO DEI MEDICI.

Florence, Biblioteca Medicea-Laurenziana, pluteus 29.1. On the left hand page
of this thirteenth century manuscript musica mundana points to the chaotic
elements which she rules; below her musica humana links four men in amity,
while musica instrumentalis raises an admonitory finger to the fiddle player.
At the feet of the instrumentalist appear a harp, a bagpipe, and a monochord
marked with numbers to measure off musical intervals. The music on the right
is the opening of Perotin's setting of the Christmas Gradual *Viderunt omnes*.
(Chapter IV)

3. *Encomium musices,* CA. 1590.

On the left and on the far right, groups of singers and instrumentalists stand before large choir books during the celebration of Mass. The separation of the two groups suggests a performance in the manner of the Venetian *cori spezzati.* (Chapter VII)

4. *Il S. Alessio, Dramma musicale,* 1634.

The opera Sant' Alessio was first performed at the opening of the private
theater of the Barberini palace in Rome in 1632. The music was by Stefano
Landi, the libretto by Monsignor Rospigliosi (later Pope Clement IX), and
the stage sets and machines by Gian Lorenzo Bernini. In this scene Saint Alexis
is revealed in heaven surrounded by angels making music, while Religion and
the eight Virtues stand below. (Chapter VIII)

5. GIUSEPPE GALLI-BIBIENA, VIEW OF THE PROSCENIUM AT THE THEATRICAL
FESTIVAL ENTITLED *Angelica Vincitrice di Alcina.*

This opera was staged outdoors in Vienna in 1716 to celebrate the birth of a
son to the Emperor Charles VI. The music was by the court composer Johann
Fux and the settings by Ferdinando and Giuseppe Galli-Bibiena. (Chapter IX)

6. JOSEF KRIEHUBER, *Une Matinée chez Liszt.*

Liszt improvises for his friends, Josef Kriehuber, Hector Berlioz, Karl Czerny, and Heinrich Ernst. (Chapter XI)

7. JOSEPH HOFFMANN, SETTING FOR ACT II OF *Siegfried*, 1876.

Siegfried, hero of the third opera of Wagner's *Ring of the Nibelungen*, slays the dragon Fafner, possessor of the Rhinegold. (Chapter XII)

8. PABLO PICASSO, *Musiciens aux masques*, 1921.

(Chapter XIII)

The literature of music composed for the recently developed instruments of the violin family grew rapidly in the seventeenth century. Thanks to the craft of their north Italian makers, which reached perfection during this century, the ability of these instruments to realize in an idealized manner the passionate accents and melodic inflections of the singing voice attracted the creative talents of many Italian composers. Of the various types of music written for them the most important, because of its later evolution, is the Sonata. The word *sonata* as applied to many compositions of this period does not connote any particular form. It means merely a "piece to be sounded" as opposed to the cantata, a "piece to be sung." By the end of the sixteenth century the title *canzon da sonar*, meaning a canzona to be sounded by instruments, began to be replaced by the shorter term, sonata, in the works of many composers. At the same time the polyphonic style resembling that of the chanson (for which the word "canzon" is the equivalent) began to yield to the soloistic texture of the concertato madrigal, employing one, two, or three solo instruments supported by a continuo. Giovanni Battista Fontana (d. 1630) was one of the early seventeenth century composers to write a number of such sonatas before 1630, while Tarquinio Merula (*fl.* 1615–1652) developed this category further, though still retaining the generic title *Canzoni da suonare* for his works. A comparison of two works published in the *Historical Anthology of Music* * (nos. 198 and 210) will reveal both common and contrasting features. Fontana's sonata consists of a number of short musical sections in contrasting styles and metres which commence either upon or immediately after a full cadence; the solo violin melody within each of these sections is spun out in long curves, broken up occasionally by rapid figurations; the continuo part which has both melodic and rhythmic interest participates from time to time in the melodic material of the violin by points of imitation. Merula's *Canzon detta la Visconta*, less extensive in span, is written for two violins and continuo in the trio texture so much favored by Monteverdi. This was to become subsequently one of the principal characteristics of the well-defined sonata in the later seventeenth and early eighteenth centuries. In Merula's canzon the number of contrasting sections is reduced, the melodic motives are more sharply defined and more rigorously spun out, and the two violins function as a pair operating in concertato fashion in opposition to the continuo which for the most part carries on an independent existence.

The development of the affective and technical idiom of these instruments is a significant aspect of music in the first half of the seventeenth century. Nevertheless instrumental music still remains a form of

* Vol. II, Ed. Davison and Apel.

expression subordinate to the passionate oratory of the contemporary opera. As the musical language of the new style became meaningful in itself, even apart from the words from which it was derived, instrumental music began to borrow its imagery for its own expressive uses. In this way instrumental music after 1650 gained an increasingly prominent role in the musical life of the Baroque, which demanded above all else that art should "teach and delight and move the passions."

IX THE BAROQUE

Part II. The Musical Enlightenment 1660-1750

IN THE EARLY SEVENTEENTH CENTURY the old world order had been shaken to its foundations by the discoveries of the new science. Even the most self-evident conclusions of philosophy and theology had been called into question. To accept the facts of the new astronomy and the possibility of myriad worlds beyond our own meant to doubt Christian beliefs about the creation of the world and man's position as the chosen creature of God. The startling vision that men had glimpsed of heavens reaching into unknown space demanded a new explanation of the nature of the universe and the role of man.

The foundations of a new philosophy answering the needs of the age were laid by René Descartes when he published in 1637 his epoch-making *Discourse on the Method of Rightly Conducting the Reason, and Seeking Truth in the Sciences*. In this work Descartes recounts how he had arrived at his new conclusions. Troubled by the uncertainty of existing knowledge, he resolved to doubt everything he knew.

I supposed that all the objects that had ever entered into my mind when awake had in them no more truth than the illusions of dreams. But immediately upon this I observed that, whilst I thus wished to think that all was false, it was absolutely necessary that I who thus thought, should be somewhat; and as I observed that this truth, *I think, hence I am* (*cogito, ergo sum*), was so

247

certain and of such evidence, that no grounds of doubt, however extravagant, could be alleged by the Sceptics capable of shaking it, I concluded that I might, without scruple, accept it as the first principle of the Philosophy of which I was in search.*

Examining this principle, Descartes came to the further conclusion that the "I" was a "substance whose essence consists only in thinking, and which, that it may exist, has need of no place, nor is dependent on any material thing; so that "I," that is to say, the mind by which I am what I am, is wholly distinct from the body."

Granted this first principle, how is one to proceed to other truths? Descartes returns to his original premise to see what exists in it that leads him to accept it as a truth. "And as I observed that in the words *I think, hence I am*, there is nothing at all which gives me assurance of their truth beyond this, that I see *very clearly* that in order to think it is necessary to exist, I concluded that I might take, as a general principle, that all the things which we very clearly and distinctly conceive are true, only observing, however, that there is some difficulty in rightly determining the objects which we distinctly conceive." The criterion of a truth is first of all that it must be an ultimate conception, which the mind perceives intuitively with clarity and distinctness. If an idea remains hazy and obscure—even if only in part—it cannot be accepted as a valid truth. If the idea is a compound of ideas, it is not an ultimate truth in itself, but must be reduced to its simple irreducible components.

It is the faculty of reason which perceives truth and not the "imagination" which depends upon sense perception. "It is not a dictate of Reason that what we thus see or imagine is in reality existent; but it plainly tells us that all our ideas or notions contain in them some truth; for otherwise it could not be that God, who is wholly perfect and veracious, should have placed them in us." As the starting point for his philosophical system Descartes has postulated the existence of the soul, an immaterial substance which thinks and which operates through reason, the key to ultimate truths. With this assertion of the primacy of reason begins that period in history when reason is exalted above all else. The men of the late seventeenth century and of the first half of the eighteenth century themselves spoke of their time as the Era of Enlightenment or the Age of Reason.

Having thus deduced the nature of the soul, Descartes had to formulate a conception of the physical world. He states that the knowledge of the material world brought to us by our senses is at best only an amalgam of ideas, some clear, some confused and indistinct. But one idea remains

* This and the following passages from the *Discourse* are taken from the translation of Veitch.

always clear and distinct: anything material must always have extension. A piece of wax may assume many different shapes, and may even be in a liquid state, but the one constant that remains throughout all these manifestations is its extensibility. At the same time this object, which occupies space, has the capabiliy of being moved and thus of occupying different places at different times. Consequently the distinguishing features of the material world are extension and motion. All phenomena of the physical world can be explained in terms of these two factors. They are accountable to two sets of mathematical laws, those of extension (geometry) and those of motion (mechanics). No matter how complex the physical phenomenon may be, Descartes is certain that it can be reduced ultimately to its component parts, each of which will be a clear and distinct idea belonging either to motion or extension.

The universe which Descartes has postulated is one that predicates a fundamental dualism: soul and matter are irreconcilable opposites. If this be true, how does the body act upon the soul, or the soul upon the body? An answer was given by Descartes in his last work, *Les Passions de l'âme* (1650). The subject matter of this treatise is narrowly defined by Descartes. Accepting the ancient definition, he states that "everything that happens is called by the philosophers a *passion* in regard to the object to which it occurs, and an *action* in regard to what causes it to occur." Since nothing belongs to the soul except thought, "some thoughts are the actions of the soul, others are its passions. Those that I call its actions are our volitions, because we experience that these come directly from our soul and do not seem to depend upon anything else; while, on the contrary, one generally calls the passions all that sort of perception or experience that appears in us, and which often times are not made as they are by the action of the soul, and because the soul always is the *recipient* of these things that are represented by them." Apart from that passion which is nothing but the soul's awareness or experience of its own thinking, all the passions of the soul are caused by the body, which in turn is affected either by objects lying outside of it or by the state of its various organs.

All perceptions are passions in the broadest sense of the word. In a narrower meaning the passions of the soul are those perceptions of effects which seem to belong in the soul itself rather than in the body—the sensations of joy, anger, and other such emotions. So Descartes comes to a final definition of the passions of the soul as "perceptions, or feelings (sentiments), or emotions of the soul, that one refers specifically to the soul, and which are caused, sustained and fortified by some movement of the vital spirits." They are perceptions because they are not actions of the soul, and because, as ideas, they are not clear and direct knowledge;

they are feelings because they are received by the soul in the same way as the sensations provided by the external senses; they are emotions because they are changes of the soul, changes more violent than those caused by ordinary thoughts.

The soul receives its passions through the agency of the body, a machine subject to geometrical and mechanical laws that govern all physical matter. The link between the material body and the non-material soul is provided by the vital spirits. These are rarefied fractions of the blood extraordinarily sensitive to any sort of stimulus. They are formed by the heart which warms the blood circulating through it and, in so doing, "rarefies the most vital and most subtle parts of the blood." From the heart all blood passes through the great artery towards the brain. But only the most subtle and most agitated parts of the blood actually enter the brain's minute passages. There the vital spirits may act upon or be acted upon by the soul which Descartes locates in the pineal gland. They may be dispatched by the soul to contract or relax the muscles, thereby causing bodily motion, or they can communicate to the soul a form of motion received via the senses from outside the body.

The passions or emotions of the soul are always accompanied by distinctive physiological symptoms. Breathing may quicken or the heart may beat more rapidly or slow its pulse. Since these are forms of mechanical motion, the stimulus of the vital spirits that caused these things to happen must be of like motion. Therefore, by analyzing the physiological manifestations of the passions, it is possible to determine what kind of motions causes the emotions of the soul. According to Descartes there are only six basic emotions, though these may vary in intensity and may be combined in an infinite number of ways. The fundamental passions are wonder, love, hatred, joy, sadness, and desire. Of these wonder is the most important. It is, in the words of Descartes, "the sudden surprise of the soul which causes it to consider attentively whatever seems rare or extraordinary." In wonder the soul is aware of the object which causes the "shock of surprise," but does not take into account the good or ill inherent in the object as it does in the case of the other emotions. But wonder is the precondition of all other passions. Unless an object first engages our soul through the element of surprise we shall remain passionless. Only when the attention of the soul has been focussed by surprise can it respond to the stimulus of an object with an emotion commensurate with the benefit or harm that will accrue from it.

The passions, as seen by Descartes, are the link between the physical world and the soul. Through the volatile medium of the vital spirits external motion becomes internal emotion, the world of nature acts upon the soul, and the soul upon matter. The nature of their interaction can be known exactly, since the laws of motion are discoverable by reason. Consequently the once vague states of the soul can be analyzed and utilized by reason. Reason's laws have tamed the turbulent passions, mainsprings of human action.

The ideas of Descartes had a profound influence upon the men who followed him. Every branch of knowledge and of art was re-examined and reformulated in the light of reason and in the spirit of scientific method. The Cartesian attributes of truth, clarity and distinctness, became the standards of literature. Language was purged of its baroque pomp and verbosity and was transformed into the cool, measured verse of French Classicism. On the other hand, even the Baroque love of exaggerated effects could be justified in the light of Descartes' psychology. Was not wonder the precondition of all other emotions? The novelty and surprises in the magnificent operatic productions were, it seems, necessary in order that the attention of the audience might be gained and held.

The new conception of the passions required a reinterpretation of the aims of art: to teach, to delight, and to move the emotions. Among the first to do so was Bernard Lamy. In his *L'Art de bien parler* (1675) Lamy offered an interpretation of the art of oratory based upon the new philosophy. While accepting the traditional aim of oratory: to teach and to move the passions, he gave a special emphasis to the latter function. "Men are not to be acted upon but by motion of their passions: Every man is carried away by what he loves, and follows that which gives him most pleasure: For which reason there is no other natural way of prevailing upon men, than this we have proposed. . . . While we are without passion, we are without action; and nothing moves us from this indifference, but the agitation of some passion." The passions are the key to all we do: they are the moving force of our existence.

The passions of which Lamy speaks are the mechanical emotions formulated by Descartes. "Every motion that is made in the organs of sense, and communicated to the animal spirits (vital spirits) is joined by the God of Nature to some certain motion of the Soul. Sound can excite passions, and we may say that every passion answers to some sound or other, which excites in the animal spirits the motion wherewith it is allied. . . . To discover the particular causes of this sympathy, and explain how among the numbers, some produce sadness, some joy, we should consider the different motions of the animal spirits in each of our passions. It is easily conceived that if the impression of such a sound in the organs of hearing is followed by a motion in the animal spirits like that which they have in a fit of anger (that is, if they be moved violently and with inequality), it may raise choler and continue it. On the contrary, if the impression be doleful and melancholy, if the commotion it causes in the animal spirits be feeble and languishing, and in the same temper as commonly in melancholy, what we have said ought not to seem strange; especially if we reflect upon what has been told to us by many eminent authors relating to the strange effects of music."

If the different motions of sound stir different passions in the soul, it should also be true that the emotions affect the character of speech. "The discourse of a man that is moved cannot be equal. Sometimes it is diffuse, and describes exactly the thing that is the object of our passion. Another time it is short; his expression is abrupt; twenty things said at a time; twenty interrogations; twenty exclamations; twenty digressions together; he is altered by a hundred little particularities and new ways of signifying his mind, which ways are as different and distinguishable from his ordinary way, as the face of a man is when he is angry, from his face when he is quiet and serene. These ways of speaking (which are characters drawn by our passions in our discourse) are the famous figures mentioned by rhetoricians, and by them defined, *Manners of speaking, different and remote from the ways that are ordinary and natural.*"

The figures of which Lamy speaks must be distinguished from tropes which are also used by the orator. Tropes are devices of language, such as metaphors and similes, employed to explain an idea and "to signify the motions both of our will, and our thoughts." They are purely explicative and can instruct but not move us. Figures, on the other hand, are arrangements of speech, such as an exclamation or question, that signify some motion of the soul. They are manifestations of the soul perceptible in sound as accents or alterations of normal speech patterns. Exclamation, for example, "is a violent extension of the voice. When the soul comes to be disturbed, and agitated with a furious impulse, the animal spirits passing through all the parts of the body, and thronging into the muscles that are about the organs of the voice, swell them up in such a manner, that the passage being straitened, the voice comes forth with more impetuosity, by reason of the passion that propells it. Every ebullition of the soul is followed by an exclamation." Since the figures are a particular sound or quantity in motion, they are capable of imparting a certain motion to the vital spirits and of evoking a similar emotion in the souls of others. Therefore, if oratory is to arouse the passions which move men, figures rather than tropes must be used.

Such a reduction of the art of oratory to "scientific," mechanistic principles inevitably affected the theory and practice of music which had adopted oratory as its preceptor. The fusion of the doctrine of Musica Poetica and the mechanistic psychology of Descartes is most clearly revealed in a periodical, *Der critische Musicus* (*The Critical Musician*), founded by Johann Scheibe (1708–1776). Scheibe insists that the end of music is "to move the spirit, in particular to rouse or still the passions." To attain this goal we must study the principles of composition in a scientific way. The musician must first learn how the passions manifest themselves and what motions are involved in them. This he can learn from speech. "Speech makes use of different tones which Nature brings forth according to the characteristics of things and of the body itself without any help from art. We raise our voices without thinking about it; we let them fall. . . . It is the activity of the soul which causes all this." The sounds of emotional speech are equivalent to the tones of melody, in which the passions find their most immediate musical expression. Harmony is only a secondary, though necessary, factor which ennobles the melodic idea. "Harmony must add its expression to melody, if the Noble is to be created which will seize our understanding, charm our senses, and arouse passions in us similar to those represented."

The act of musical creation begins with the invention of a melodic motion capable of arousing an emotion. First the composer must find a theme from which the melody will evolve. "In all musical works a principal theme is necessary, from which the following music must originate. The remainder of the composition is only a working out of this idea and is therefore a question of style. It is in the principal idea that the inventiveness of the composer is manifested." The invention of the theme, the most important factor in artistic creation, is related entirely to the question of the passions. "In music one is most concerned with the emotions of the soul: the composer must express them, arouse them, or still them. He must, therefore, represent them through the force of his invention, just as if he found himself in the circumstances which he is to express. Pain, fear, anxiety and the like must move him; otherwise his expressions will be either artificial or dull."

To express the passions in his theme the composer, like the poet and orator, will use figures and tropes. The latter are employed only for ornamental purposes. They can embellish but not express the passions. The figures, on the other hand, are the very essence of music. "Everyone will agree with me, if I state that it is the figures which give the greatest impression to musical style and lend it an uncommon strength. It is the same in music as in oratory and poetry. Both of these liberal arts would possess neither fire nor the power to move, if one took away from them the use of figures. Could one indeed arouse and express the passions without them? By no means! The figures in fact are the speech of the affections."

The musical theme has become identical with the figure. Therefore the principal musical idea must be, like the rhetorical figure, a charac-

teristic arrangement of sound. It must be a specific type of musical motion, melodic, harmonic or rhythmic, related to the passion the composer
wishes to express. For anger the melody will use wide intervals and a
rapid rhythmic motion; for sadness, the smallest intervals, a subdued
tempo, and chromatic harmonies will be chosen. Since every passion has
a specific set of appearances, a particular motion, it is necessary to maintain the same type of motion as long as the passion is being expressed. The
principal theme, usually contained in the opening measures, will provide
the substance of the remainder of composition; all that follows will be
derived from it. This technique of composition is now called "the spinning out of a theme" (*Fortspinnung*).

By the beginning of the eighteenth century the art of creating music
had become almost entirely rationalized. The older humanistic conception
of the intimate relationship of words and tone still remained, but this relationship now rested upon physical laws. Music presented the passion contained in the words in terms of sound in motion. The musical metaphors or
tropes, which had played so large a part in the madrigalian style of the
sixteenth and early seventeenth centuries, tended to disappear. Only here
and there, as in the case of Bach, did the rich musical imagery of the early
Baroque still flourish in the eighteenth century. In its place there had arisen
a series of standardized formulas for the expression of the passions, and it
is quite possible today to analyze the types of eighteenth century arias in
terms of the passions contained in them. The music of this period utilizes a
single theme for a large section or even for an entire composition, and
simply spins it out for the remainder of the work. The resulting work of
art, though full of energetic motion, does not progress. It remains static in
spite of its rhythmic and melodic activity, for throughout its duration we
are sustained in the grip of a single emotion.

From the middle of the seventeenth to the middle of the eighteenth
century, opera dominated the international scene. Largely the work of
Italian composers, these musical dramas became increasingly stereotyped.
At their best, they explored the human passions in a series of arias adroitly
arranged to provide the maximum amount of contrast between them.
But generally the characters, though based on historical figures, existed
on the plane of allegory, as representations of the passions, rather than as
living beings. As a pastime of the aristocracy, the operas were staged
magnificently with many elaborate sets and astonishing effects created by
stage machines.

In this period the art of the singer reached unsurpassed heights.
The highest esteem was reserved for singers who could produce a grace-
fully or expressively modelled phrase with utmost vocal power, or embellish a line with intricate figurations. In the mastery of vocal virtuosity,

no one excelled the castrato, who enacted both male and female roles. The audience listened, enraptured, to the stylized perfection of this artificial voice as it expressed the passion contained in an aria. The insatiable demand for musical novelties for the singers taxed the creative powers of a vast number of composers and librettists. It forced the musician to set the same dramatic poem over and over again—frequently with little regard for its dramatic motivation or verisimilitude. Another understandable, if deplorable, result of this demand was the *pasticcio*, an opera written by several composers, or compiled with arias drawn from other operas.

The expression of the passions was also the chief concern of the dramatic cantatas and oratorios. It was particularly the chamber cantata performed in intimate surroundings for a small group of connoisseurs that challenged composers to display their highest talents. Hundreds of cantatas of the greatest beauty were created, only to be given a few performances. The majority of them have survived only in their original score or in manuscript copies. Some cantatas were written upon extended dramatic poems for performance at lavish fêtes. In time these became indistinguishable from oratorios on secular subjects through their use of the role of the narrator.

The vogue of Italian opera, oratorio, and cantata rapidly conquered the aristocratic circles of Europe. In the increasingly opulent courts the sumptuous presentations of these Italian forms became symbols of the political as well as the artistic pretensions of the ruler. Simultaneously, following the example of many of the smaller cities of Italy, public theatres mainly performing opera were opened in various northern cities such as Hamburg (1678). Here, after the opening years in which the works of German artists were performed, the repertory became Italianized.

In France the opera and the aesthetic principles on which it was founded at first made but slow headway. It was opposed by two French forms of the greatest vitality: the classical tragedy of Corneille and Racine, and the court ballet. In the former, stylized speech and action conveyed the passions of the drama without the assistance of music. In the latter, music cooperated in the orderly and eloquent figures and stylized gestures of the dance, or added sonorous magnificence to the spectacular scenes. Nevertheless a number of major Italian operas were performed at the French court, culminating in 1662 with Cavalli's *Ercole Amante* to celebrate the wedding of the young Louis XIV. This was the last Italian opera to be produced under the official patronage of the court, but many of the imported Italians settled in Paris, forming a nucleus for the growing enthusiasm for the music of Italy. Because of this, Italian opera continued to be produced in Paris in subsequent years.

Indirectly these early examples of Italian opera brought about the foundation of the Academie Royale de Musique in 1669. This institution for the production of French operas was soon taken over by a Florentine, Jean-Baptiste Lully (1632–1687), who created a truly French concept of opera, significantly described as *tragédie en musique* or *tragédie lyrique*. From years of experience with French taste Lully skilfully coordinated the dramatic elements most popular at the court of Versailles, including the ballet and spectacular stage effects, with a reticent, dignified musical style. The dramas themselves, modelled upon those of Corneille and Racine, do not provide for the constant recurrence of arias as in the Italian opera. Instead musical recitative occupies the center of interest. Adherence to the rhythmical stress and accent of the words rather than melodic variety distinguishes the style of Lully's recitative, which is clearly derived from that of contemporary spoken drama. The conflict between the rival passions, particularly those of la Gloire and l'Amour, controls the action of most of these tragédies lyriques. Lully established the essential form of French opera for approximately a century. French operas were performed from time to time in other countries and certain characteristics of their musical style were incorporated in the cosmopolitan language of Italian music. Notwithstanding the prestige of French culture, the influence of French opera never rivalled that of the Italians.

Italian opera never gained a real foothold in England. After a marvellous flowering during the reign of Elizabeth, musical activity was first seriously interrupted by the civil war and then discouraged by the triumph of Puritanism, which frequently regarded the art of music with suspicious eyes. The restoration of Charles the Second in 1660 abruptly re-established musical life at the court and in London, but the tastes of the monarch were French rather than Italian. As a result of these events, attempts to introduce Italian music were both sporadic and ineffectual. Even the genius of Henry Purcell (1658–1695) was channelled by the conservative taste of the aristocracy into the older tradition of the masque, in which speech was not joined to music in recitative, and where the affective power of music was confined primarily to scenes of fantasy and splendor. Not until the early eighteenth century did the rising tide of Italian music and musicians begin to sweep over London. The Royal Academy of Music was founded in 1719 for the production of Italian opera, and it was there that George Frideric Handel produced many of his operas that for a time captivated London. But the victory of Italian opera over the English audience was never really consolidated. As an "irrational and exotic form of entertainment," it was tolerated only because the passions might be moved by the beauty of the arias despite the absurdity of the drama.

While Italian opera was extending its influence over Europe, its techniques were also being applied to the settings of liturgical texts. The secularization of religious music gathered increasing momentum after 1650. The musical organizations of Catholic, Lutheran, and Anglican churches were modified and their personnel trained in the new operatic and instrumental styles. Royal chapels and the best endowed churches could often muster musical resources which vied with or even excelled in number those of an elaborately performed opera. But the voices of women and castrati were rarely utilized or tolerated in church services outside of Italy.

The musical portions of the liturgy, particularly those which challenged the composer by reason of the grandeur of the passions contained in the texts, took on the complexion of secular art. The texts of the Ordinary of the Mass, of Psalms and of Canticles were divided into sections in which a single passion predominates. These are set in the self-contained forms of secular music as choruses, ensembles or solos. Motets assume the appearance of cantatas, occasionally expanded by the use of full chorus and orchestra, as in the Grand Motet cultivated in France. The Lutheran gospel motet becomes the "sacred cantata," while the sacred oratorio increasingly resembles the opera.

Closely associated with the expansion of opera in Italy and Europe was the rapid development of various categories of instrumental music for solo, ensemble and orchestra. The suite, the sonata, and the concerto emerged as entities sharply defined by the unity of affection and the musical logic which characterized their individual movements as well as the totality of movements. These instrumental forms were readily transmitted to all parts of Europe by their Italian practitioners, and were emulated by native artists. Instrumental music, which, as Johann Scheibe remarks, "in regard to the affections is nothing but an imitation of vocal music," in time acquired a status that began to challenge the hitherto uncontested primacy of vocal music.

During the period in which Italian opera occupied the leading position in European music both its dramatic form and the music which clothes it underwent considerable alteration. When viewed in terms of the vast quantities of operas composed after 1650, the evolution of the dramatic and musical elements appears to be a gradual one, the product of many artists' creative imagination. Nevertheless, the distance between the characteristic works of Venetian composers of the mid-seventeenth century and the *opera seria* of the eighteenth century is considerable. The intense, contrasting and unruly passions whose various permutations had provided the mainstay of the former became systematized and formally controlled, both dramatically and musically, in the latter.

The poetic dramas favored by the Venetians followed the ideals of Giambattista Marino, who early in the seventeenth century had defined the aim of poetry as the marvelous, that is to say, the startling effect. They abounded with powerfully affective imagery and dramatic situations. The main dramatic material was drawn from episodes in Roman, ancient, or early western history, freely reworked to provide a maximum number of situations in which complex and contrasting emotions could be brought into sharp focus. In the succession of scenes, the amorous, the noble, and the tragic alternate abruptly with the comic and the bawdy. To concentrate attention upon the singers the orchestral accompaniment is reduced to little more than a nucleus of strings surrounding the continuo instruments.

At the very beginning of the eighteenth century the extravagances of this form of opera came under the attack of litterateurs led by members of the Arcadian Academy in Rome. It seemed to them that contemporary Italian opera suffered by comparison with the reasoned dramas of Racine. They wished for a more rational musico-dramatic form, purged of the excessive confusions of plot and the disorderly display of the passions. They also desired a purification of the poetry, which they felt "had been constrained to the uses of music, lost its purity and become full of idiocies." The first drama to embody these reforms seems to have been *La Forza del Virtù*, set to music in 1693, but subsequently composed many times by different writers of the eighteenth century. It was followed by similar works of Apostolo Zeno and of Pietro Metastasio, the most admired poet of the eighteenth century. Notwithstanding the literary pretensions of these authors, their dramas were invariably staged as operas, and were to a large extent shaped by musical considerations.

The reform opera excluded all comic scenes and personages, and hence was known as opera seria. Though "serious" in nature, the final tragedy upon which the plot converged was usually avoided by the divine intercession of the gods. The actions and personality of each of the leading characters were dominated by a single passion to the extent that they appear more as personifications of the passions than as real individuals. The action often maintained only the most tenuous relationship with the historical material upon which it was based, and disguises and mistaken identities became conventional devices to keep the plot moving. The libretto, written in verse, was divided into a series of scenes whose limits were determined by the entrance or exits of a character. Each scene was designed to lead up to the lyrical expression of a single passion in an aria.

Such a drama presented the composer with a series of individual scenes, each conceived as an entity in itself. The text of a scene consisted of a monologue or dialogue of considerable length in which the dramatic action took place. It was concluded by an expression of the passion evoked by the preceding action, customarily stated by the dramatist in one or two brief stanzas. The dimensions of this literary form are completely reversed when translated into music: the expository material is set in *secco* (dry) recitative, traversed very quickly in the rapid, perfunctory style of the *parlando* (speaking) vocal part, supported sparsely by the continuo only; the lyrical expression, on the other hand, is greatly extended in the elevated form of an aria which is generally accompanied by several instruments besides the continuo. In the interest of musical eloquence, such arias repeatedly interrupt the dramatic progression for extended periods of time.

This formula, in which the dynamic and the reflective aspects of the drama are clearly separated, replaces the continuous musical and dramatic motion achieved by early Baroque composers through the marriage of music and words in lyrical recitative. But by placing the emphasis upon the aria, this treatment of a scene conforms to the theories of contemporary psychology, and also satisfies popular taste. In order to express the passions the composer must set up a musical motion that will arouse a corresponding passion in the soul of the auditor. This he can do only within the expansive limits of an aria.

As the musical expression of the passions became increasingly formalized and stereotyped, so did the form of the aria in which they were voiced. In the latter part of the seventeenth century one form alone, the so-called *Da Capo* aria, became dominant in the opera and its related musical genres, the cantata and the oratorio. This form is based upon two poetic stanzas, the first of which presents the principal emotion, while the second contains a subsidiary or contrasting emotion. Each stanza is given an appropriate musical setting, creating a musical form of two independent but related sections. At the end of the second section the words Da Capo appear, directing the performers to return to the beginning and to repeat the first section. In performance it was customary for the singers to introduce extemporized ornaments and coloratura passages into the vocal melody in this repetition.

Such a form is wonderfully illustrative of the contemporary conception of the passions, for the Da Capo aria does not present them in dramatic evolution. Even when the middle section contains a contrasting affection, the return of the first part of the aria necessarily brings us back to the emotional state with which the aria had begun. The principal passion is thus emphasized by its repetition, and heightened by the contrast provided in the middle section. There has been no progression in such an aria but only a static presentation of the emotion gripping the soul of the dramatic personage.

In operas such as Alessandro Stradella's *Floridoro* (*c.* 1675), arias begin to take musical precedence over recitatives. The three-part form of the Da Capo aria is as yet not clearly articulated, because the harmonic cadences with which the first and second sections conclude are passed over without interruption of the regular musical motion. In an aria from this opera, "Stelle ingrate" (Illustration 1), the rhythmic motion is maintained continuously.

ILLUSTRATION   I

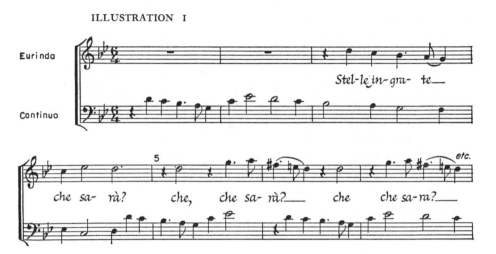

The initial two bar phrase of the continuo is a musical figure representing the amorous passion of Eurinda. It provides all the melodic material of the vocal part and of the instrumental ritornello which opens and closes the aria. At the same time the passion is intensified in the vocal part through the use of exclamatory phrases.

The disparity between the declamatory, musically insignificant substance of the typical secco recitative and the carefully organized musical rhetoric of the formal aria was ever present. But this gulf could be bridged at appropriate moments by a form of recitative called *recitativo accompagnato*. The accompanied recitative was frequently chosen for setting monologues occurring at a moment of dramatic climax and containing a succession of varied and agitated emotions. The declamatory phrases of the vocal part, supported by an orchestra of strings, alternate with orchestral punctuations of rhythmical or lyrical motifs, which provide a counterpart to the dramatic gestures of the actor.

Many of these resources for rendering the emotions of a text are to be found in the cantata *Su le sponde del Tebro* (On the banks of the Tiber) by Alessandro Scarlatti (1660–1725). The affective content of this anonymous pastoral poem has determined Scarlatti's musical treatment entirely. The shepherd Aminta's betrayal of Chloris is narrated in the opening lines and is therefore declaimed in secco recitative. The composer effectively emphasizes Aminta's despairing cry, "Io son tradito," (I am betrayed) by the arioso style of the concluding measures. Then the principal affections which dominate his love-torn soul are set forth in a succession of arias. From Aminta's words, likening his faithful thoughts to the armed guardians of his heart, Scarlatti abstracts an emotion of heroic restraint in the first Da Capo aria written in D major with a contrasting middle section in B minor. The change from a major to a minor tonality corresponds to the opposition between the faithful thoughts and the sorrow expressed in the text. The martial metaphor of the poet is echoed in the melismata of the vocal line and again in the concertante trumpet, traditional symbol of the warrior. The persistent sixteenth-note figuration of both sections is of course a form of motion corresponding to the vigorous passion of the text (Illustration 2).

ILLUSTRATION 2

A brief recitative forms a narrative translation to the acute grief depicted in the succeeding Largo section in A minor (Illustration 3). Here a single motif, in which a dissonant minor second formed by a suspension, portrays Aminta's anguish, dominates the voice, the continuo, and the two violin parts. The shape of the initial vocal phrase with its falling fifth succeeded by a minor sixth and a poignant diminished seventh is a classical example of the type of melodic succession created by Baroque composers for the expression of sorrow. The contour of this line with its wide intervals is in marked contrast to the vocal melodies of the past where step-

ILLUSTRATION 3

wise progressions predominated. Since only one emotion is expressed in the text, Scarlatti embodies it in a monothematic structure. This is also true of the aria in A minor (Illustration 4).

ILLUSTRATION 4

The falling line of the figure contained in the first two measures of the continuo part represents Aminta's tears and vain hopes. Extended throughout the composition by sequences this phrase establishes a musical and affective unity in much the same fashion as the basso ostinato had done in earlier compositions. While the basic affection is carried out by the continuo, the vocal line moves more or less independently, opposing its broken phrases to the persistent rhythms of the accompaniment.

The final recitative describes Aminta's determination to subdue his passions. Thus heroic resolution, the passion of the opening aria, is again portrayed in the concluding Da Capo aria for trumpet, voice, and strings. In the dramatic progression of feelings contained in the complete text, Scarlatti has perceived a symmetrical form in which the heroic encloses the softer passions of grief and despair. He reflects this symmetry in his music by balancing the opening sinfonia and aria with their brilliant obbligato trumpet by the concluding aria written in the same style and mood. The clarity and concision of this cantata and the generalized rather than particularized musical vocabulary are symptomatic of the universal tendency towards a reasoned art in which Cartesian ideals replace the earlier striving for unique and striking modes of expression.

The developments of the seventeenth century came to their richest fruition in the art of George Frideric Handel (1685–1759) and Johann Sebastian Bach (1685–1750). Though born in the same year and stemming from analogous Lutheran surroundings, their completely dissimilar careers represent the full diversity and grandeur of Baroque musical art in its final phase. By the second decade of the eighteenth century Handel, renowned as a composer of opera throughout Europe, was established permanently in the cosmopolitan city of London. Bach, on the contrary, was practicing his profound and distinctive craft in the provincial circles of Lutheran Germany. Outside of this limited milieu his name and his music were totally unknown. Handel had won his fame by working in the international category of opera, while Bach had deliberately turned his back upon a worldly reputation by choosing to place his art in the service of the Lutheran church. However different the careers of these two men of genius may have been, they are united in the common objective of their art: to move the passions.

Handel came to London in 1710 as an acknowledged master of Italian opera. During the next three decades he presented more than thirty operas there. Through the force of his genius the conventions of Italian opera, even its foreign tongue and the eccentricities of its performers, were accepted by the English audience. He wrote much other music during these years, some for the salon in the form of solo cantatas or instrumental suites and sonatas, some for royal occasions (such as the Water Music) and for ecclesiastical ceremonies. While many of these compositions reveal his art in all its beauty, assuredly none of them were as important to Handel as his operas.

Handel adopted unquestioningly the operatic ideals prevailing at the opening of the eighteenth century. The musical expression of the specific passions dominating the characters takes precedence over all other considerations. The recitative style used for dialogue or expository soliloquy is clearly of much less importance than the arias of emotion. In his operas the dramatic action proceeds in a succession of scenes, each culminating in the expression of the intense feeling of one character. Thus the opera as a whole consists of a succession of individual moments of feeling, which have meaning only because of the music which clothes them. Thoroughly sensitive to the rhetorical and emotional values of a text, Handel not infrequently invests his recitatives with dramatic and emotional excitement by expressive phraseology and by unexpected series of chords in the accompaniment. The recitative portions of scenes often increase in intensity until the introduction of the elaborate arias upon which the work as a whole depends.

The complementary function of recitative to the extended, symmetrical aria is admirably exemplified in Handel's *Sosarme* produced in 1732. The action of this opera, which unfolds like all opera seria in three acts, concerns the struggle between Argone and his father, Haliate, King of Lidia. Haliate, his wife Erenice, his daughter Elmira, who is betrothed to Sosarme the King of Media, and Melo, Haliate's illegitimate son, are all passionately torn by this family crisis. Altomaro, Haliate's counsellor, endeavors to bring matters to a bloody climax in order that Melo may be placed upon the throne of Lidia. All efforts to mediate between father and son fail until the deceitfulness of Altomaro is discovered, whereupon Argone gives in to his father and is forgiven. This resolution of a dramatic situation contrived for the exposition of the passions of the participants also permits Sosarme and Elmira to be united.

Typically, all the characters are sung by high voices: tenor (Haliate and Argone), counter-tenor (Sosarme), contralto (Erenice and Melo), and soprano (Elmira). Only Altomaro's part is written for a low voice to distinguish this man with his devious passions from all the others. The primary musical emphasis is placed upon the twenty-four arias and duets contained in the score. Differing distinctly in character because of the various passions they express, nearly all are arranged in the three-part symmetry of the Da Capo form. Consistency of rhythmical motion, often derived from the patterns of instrumental dance forms, provides a strong element of unity within each aria. The melodic material grows from the expressive shape of the opening phrase, which is generally announced by the solo or tutti instruments before it is taken up by the voice. From this initial idea a series of melodic phrases is spun out by means of melismatic extensions, by subtle alterations of the intervals which define the original motif, or frequently through the use of sequences wherein the phrase is repeated on successively higher or lower steps. These are so arranged that but one affective state of mind is represented.

The aria which concludes Act One, "Dite pace, e fulminate, crudi Cieli!" (You speak of peace and yet you thunder, cruel heavens!) typifies Handel's realization of the aesthetic principles of his age. Erenice and Elmira have sought unsuccessfully to restrain Argone from leading the attack against his father, and Elmira, alone after the departure of the others, soliloquizes upon the situation. In a brief recitative she recalls the prophecy of the goddess Hecate that peace will come only when royal blood is shed. In the following aria the essence of her thought is the paradox inherent in the attainment of peace through strife. The contrast of peace and raging violence is presented in the opening instrumental ritornello. The serene and simple melodic phrase of the adagio opening measures is opposed by six measures of furious figuration formed by spinning out two brief motifs by repetitions and sequences. These disparate materials are the sole ingredients of the first and last of the three sections of the aria. Shared by the concertante vocal and instrumental parts, they require of the singer the most accomplished vocal technique, from melodious bel canto to agile coloratura. The concentrated middle section of the aria intensifies the mixed emotions by changing to the minor mode, by utilizing chromatic progressions in the harmony, and by the arioso style of the vocal part (Illustration 5).

The enthusiasm of English society for the exotic Italian opera of Handel gradually disappeared during the 1730's, forcing him, reluctantly at first, to change his field of musical activity. His strenuous efforts to keep his opera company going culminated in a complete physical and nervous collapse in 1737. When he resumed his creative career in the following year, it was with the composition of the oratorios *Saul* and *Israel in Egypt*. In turning to the oratorio Handel was resorting to a category in which he had worked occasionally in the past. The dramatic oratorio had been steadily growing in favor since 1650, in part because of its assimilation of operatic techniques. In its increasingly popular guise the oratorio became an acceptable substitute for the operas which were prohibited during the Lenten season in Catholic regions. By the opening of the eighteenth century the oratorio had become so closely identified with operatic practices that it placed its primary emphasis upon a succession of solo arias, dispensing in many cases with the choruses which had formerly been one of its essential characteristics. The Italian oratorios written by Handel early in his career all belong to this secularized form.

In the series of oratorios that begins with the works of 1738 Handel created a new milieu for the oratorio. Though rooted in the fundamental aesthetics of their era, they expressed deep national and religious aspirations far removed from the world of opera. These were most powerfully expressed in *Israel in Egypt*. In this work Handel touched responsive chords in the hearts of Englishmen which his operas had never been able to reach. Through his choice of Old Testament subject matter, Handel revealed his understanding of its significance in the Protestant tradition of England, Anglican and nonconformist alike. A parallel between the Israelites, the people chosen to be the instruments of God's salvation of men, and the people of Protestant England had been preached about for well over a century. Thus the English audience was able to identify itself with this oratorio, whereas it had never felt quite at ease with the foreign figures of opera singing in an unintelligible tongue. In *Israel in Egypt* Handel restored the chorus to the oratorio, giving it a position

ILLUSTRATION 5

ILLUSTRATION 5 (*continued*)

surpassing that of the solo arias. By so doing he reinforced the audience's sense of identification with the subject matter, for he was drawing upon the English practice of performing elaborate choral works in religious services commemorating great national occasions.

In his famous oratorio, *The Messiah*, Handel propounds the meaning of the life and death of Christ. His text is a compilation of passages from the Old and New Testaments containing the most fundamental tenets of English morality and religion. In solos and in choruses Handel portrays the distinctive emotion of each section of the text. Unadorned recitatives are brief and infrequent, being generally reserved for texts of narrative or proclamatory content. The clarity of his interpretation of each verbal idea is one of the most impressive features of this oratorio. In each section of the text the words which contain the strongest affective meaning are detached from the surrounding context and given prominence by a melodic phrase or figure or by the particular accentuation he gives them.

Handel's procedure is strikingly illustrated in his treatment of the text, "His yoke is easy, His burthen is light." The antithesis implied in this short sentence is illuminated and clarified in the choral structure he builds upon the melody with which this text is first stated (Illustration 6). Above the persistent motion of the continuo, Handel weaves a transparent contrapuntal texture in which the effect of effortlessness is sustained by the device of allowing only two or three of the vocal lines to sound at once. At only one moment is this light movement interrupted (measures 38–40) when all four voices coincide briefly in slower note values to portray the gravity of the "burthen." But even this passage is but part of the design of the whole, serving to emphasize the synchronized vivacity of all the four parts with which the chorus concludes. The whole piece is built upon one theme announced at the beginning by the sopranos. It is divided into two motives, corresponding to the two phrases of the text, and the first of these is distinguished from the second by the facile melisma with which Handel graces the word "easy."

The religious subject matter and lofty ethos of Handel's oratorios suggest a kinship with the great body of sacred music written by J. S. Bach. But the Lutheranism of the latter is far removed from the English protestantism which nurtured the former. Handel's oratorios were conceived for performance outside of the church, and thus they are not identified with any liturgy. On the other hand, the hundreds of church cantatas and the Passion oratorios of Bach were conceived entirely within the Lutheran liturgy and for the religious practices of the communities in which he worked as a cantor. This fact accounts for many of the specific differences in the musical practices of the two men. Most notable is the use of the Lutheran chorale which figures prominently in the music of Bach, whereas its use by Handel is almost nonexistent.

ILLUSTRATION 6

ILLUSTRATION 6 (*continued*)

The chorale had been chosen by Luther and his colleagues two centuries earlier as a vehicle for the congregation's direct expression of faith. It had developed along various lines in the intervening years. By the first quarter of the seventeenth century, a very large number of hymns paraphrasing and enlarging upon sacred and liturgical texts had become firmly established within the practice of the liturgy. Beside these there came into being an ever expanding body of poems with or without melodies expressing in individualistic terms various attitudes and feelings of personal devotion. The growth of the pietistic spirit during the seventeenth century with its emphasis upon directness of emotional expression provided a continuing impetus for the writing of such devotional songs and hymns. Increasingly sentimental or rationalistic in character, the rising flood of hymns tended to modify or obliterate the functions and place of the earlier liturgical chorales.

When Bach began his career in the church, he found Lutheranism beset by continual controversies arising from the opposition of the various movements of rationalism, pietism, and orthodoxy. This situation made it necessary for a deeply religious, thoughtful man like Bach to find his own solutions to the problems of Christian life. The heir to a long-standing family tradition of musical service in the church, Bach early in his career made known his goal of creating "a well-regulated church music to the honor of God." As a craftsman of consummate skill and as an organist whose proficiency had made him famous in Germany, he was fully equipped to serve God with the means so highly regarded by Martin Luther himself. In his pursuit of this goal he absorbed all the various contemporary musical techniques of expressing the passions in order to apply them to the most profound elements of the Lutheran tradition.

To Bach, one of the most vital elements of a well-regulated church music was the liturgical cantata, since it provided the opportunity and the responsibility for the musical interpretation of the Word of God. The descendant of the Gospel motet sung between the Gospel and the sermon, the cantata had come to be the central and climactic moment of the musical liturgy, employing all the vocal and instrumental resources available to the cantor. The text of the cantata was closely related to the subject matter of the liturgy of the day. The composer's task was to interpret such a text with all the resources of musical rhetoric. In this function the composer occupied a position analogous to that of the preacher, whose sermon was also an interpretation of the prescribed texts of the day. During the latter half of the seventeenth century the theologically trained Lutheran composer compiled the texts of his cantatas by surrounding the Gospel text with appropriate quotations from the various books of the Bible, and with stanzas from chorales. The prose style of the former might be rendered appropriately by recitative, arioso, or chorus, while the chorale stanzas were seldom presented apart from the melodies that had become associated with them.

By the beginning of the eighteenth century it was clear to men like the Lutheran pastor Erdmann Neumeister of Hamburg, that one of the most powerful means of affective expression in the theatre, the aria, was inaccessible to church musicians. To remedy this deficiency he wrote cycles of ecclesiastical cantata texts in the style of operatic poetry, freely paraphrasing and amplifying the Biblical Word. His example was soon emulated by many devout, though frequently unskilful, poets and musicians. By the time Bach began the composition of his church cantatas both the form and the content of the texts had become largely a matter of the composer's discretion and choice.

A number of factors, practical as well as religious and aesthetic, account for the varied forms found in the more than two hundred cantatas written by Bach for liturgical use. The majority of them, however, conclude with a stanza of an appropriate chorale set in a straightforward four-part harmonization. The cantata, therefore, proceeds through a number of artistically sophisticated movements to an austere, unadorned conclusion that stands symbolically as the collective expression of the congregation. With the exception of the relatively small number of solo cantatas, the opening movement is one of large proportions written in an elaborate style for chorus and concerted instruments. In many cases, especially in the cantatas composed in Leipzig after 1727, the textual material for the opening section is a chorale stanza. Occasionally chorale stanzas and melodies are also interpolated within the body of the cantata. Sometimes they are combined in concertato style with solo vocal forms, as in cantatas No. 21 and No. 80. Between the opening and closing choral sections there appears a number of solo recitatives, ariosi, and arias in the contemporary dramatic idiom. By employing all the styles of sacred and secular music, both old and new, Bach created a synthetic art which summarizes all the developments of the Baroque era.

Like their secular prototypes, the textual materials of Bach's sacred cantatas are always arranged in dramatic form. Even when the substance of the Epistle and Gospel interpreted by a cantata is dogmatic rather than dramatic, Bach perceives it in terms of the central dramatic themes of Lutheran theology: the contrast between sin in its manifold forms and salvation; between the sorrow and suffering of the human soul removed from God and its ecstatic union with Christ. The progression of the former state to the latter is the dramatic pivot around which Bach's cantatas usually revolve. These themes form the substance of cantata No. 19, *Es erhub sich ein Streit* for the Feast of St. Michael. The Epistle and Gospel readings (Revelation 12:7–12 and Matthew 18:1–11) for that day deal respectively with the war of Michael and the angels

against the dragon of Hell, and with the admonition to become as innocent as children.

This cantata begins with a massive movement depicting the battle
of Heaven and Hell. To convey this grandiose scene Bach employs a four-
part chorus supplemented by two oboes, strings, continuo, and the

ILLUSTRATION 7

martial tones of three trumpets and a kettledrum. The movement is conceived in two distinct sections. The first is based only upon the words "Es erhub sich ein Streit" (There arose a strife) from which Bach derives a musical theme (Illustration 7) used throughout this whole sec-

ILLUSTRATION 7 *(continued)*

ILLUSTRATION 7 (*continued*)

tion. Bach's vivid but somewhat antiquated imagery is very apparent in his madrigalian handling of the text. He represents the word "arose" with a strenuous upward leap of an octave and the word "strife" with a writhing melisma of exceptional length. Upon this theme Bach builds a dense fugal structure. But even here, in his choice of a particular musical style, Bach reveals that he is thinking only of the meaning of the text. The independent musical lines of this imitative polyphony vie with one another as if in combat, and the successive entrance of the voices, from the lowest to the highest, is a symbol of this battle in which Hell rises against Heaven.

In the second section the words deal with Michael's defeat of the dragon, and once again Bach adapts his music to the meaning of the text. In this part (Illustration 8) he joins the three upper parts in homophonic declamation as a symbol of the united band of angels, against which the bass voice, representing the serpent of Hell, moves independently in raging melismata, and with words which never coincide in time with

ILLUSTRATION 8

ILLUSTRATION 8 (*continued*)

those of the upper voices. The movement does not conclude with the second section but returns to the beginning for a repetition of the first part. This use of the Da Capo form is anything but a meaningless acceptance of a conventional formula. On the contrary, Bach wishes to signify by the return to the opening text that the evil serpent, though defeated by Michael, still survives to make war upon mortals. Nothing perhaps could better illustrate the interrelationship of text and music in the creative thinking of Bach than this seemingly innocuous use of the most conventionalized form of his day. Through this simple repetition he has created the dramatic crux upon which the remainder of the cantata depends. The Da Capo form, instead of being a static, self-enclosed moment, has become the motivating force for the rest of the cantata.

The opening chorus is followed by two pairs of recitatives and arias. The first gives thanks for the victory of the angels, and the emotional mood is conveyed in the aria through the use of a major key and through the tones of the two concertante oboes d'amore. In the second recitative and aria the text becomes more introspective, dwelling upon the frailty and sinfulness of man, who, nevertheless, is protected by a host of angels through the mercy of God. These sentiments are reflected first of all in the recitative which is accompanied by a rich harmonization of the strings instead of the dry, meagre tones of a continuo instrument alone.

The aria which follows is one of Bach's most profound utterances. The strings continue to support the tenor voice while it implores the angels to remain with him. The adagio tempo and the minor key (E) together with the quasi-ostinato figure of the basso continuo, all serve to emphasize the timorous plea of the voice. Listening to the undulations of the vocal phrases it is only gradually borne in on one that a trumpet is making itself heard with the phrases of the chorale *Herzlich lieb hab ich dich* (Deepest love have I for thee), adding its connotative force to the explicit words of the singer. For all its apparent simplicity this aria is one of the most complex musical creations. Here Bach has fused the modern phraseology of the aria with the simple tones of the chorale and has placed the old device of a cantus firmus, represented by the trumpet melody, in the service of a contemporary rendition of the affection of the text. It is in such examples of technical virtuosity masked in seeming simplicity that one feels the magic of Bach's art. It is an art that contrives all its complexities not for the sake of vain display but only as means to enrich the significance of the text.

Following this aria a soprano recitative prays that our sins may not prevent us from attaining everlasting life, and serves as an introduction to the final chorale, which expresses the hope of reunion with God after death. Thus the cantata has progressed from the objective depiction of strife in the first movement to the subjective spirit of the chorale. As a mode of collective expression this chorale makes it clear that the message of this cantata is one having personal significance for each individual. Everything about this cantata, its forms and the details of its symbolic language, reveal that Bach has taken all the available resources of affective musical expression, and has used them to create a work whose sole purpose is to illuminate the truths of Christian doctrine.

Throughout the first half of the eighteenth century the highest goal of musical art continued to be the faithful and logical expression of the passions contained in the text. This aim, initiated in the Baroque era, and carried out to its fullest extent in the period of the Enlightenment, was pursued with increasingly systematic methods in accordance with the tenets of rationalism. The idea of codifying the passions of man as well as the means by which they might be expressed in music led to the development of methods by which the melodic and harmonic figures could be arranged in musically coherent forms. The codification of key relationships had begun with the appearance of the continuo upon the musical scene. These concepts were major factors in the emergence of instrumental music as an important artistic phenomenon of this period, for they established purely musical principles, as opposed to those derived from textual material, for the organization of instrumental forms.

The development of instrumental forms depended also upon the fact that the precise musical vocabulary worked out in vocal music could be transferred to instrumental music. The figures, whose specific meanings were known in vocal music, could be carried over into instrumental forms where "without any words they allow us to speak fierily,

expressively, and in the language of passion with mere musical tones."
The literalness of his statement must of course be modified by recognition of the fact that the idiomatic characteristics of the favorite instruments of the period—the violin, harpsichord, and organ—also played a
role in the formation of instrumental style.

In all of the instrumental categories of this period there is a consistent
evolution from the prolixity and looseness of the earlier forms of the
Baroque to tightly knit movements in which a single theme predominates.
This development is fully in accord with the prevailing aesthetic ideal of
a unified representation of the passions. The result may be discerned in
the *sonata da chiesa* of Arcangelo Corelli (1653–1713), Opus 3, No.
9 in F minor. This is one of four sets of sonatas published by him between
1681 and 1694. In this sonata, as in the others, four comparatively brief
but formally self-contained movements in the order of slow-fast-slow-
fast replace the numerous connected sections of differing tempi and
styles which characterized sonatas in the early part of the century. While
each of the movements is based upon the spinning out of a single theme,
the second and fourth movements carry out this procedure within a contrapuntal framework.

The second movement of Corelli's sonata provides a concise example
of a form in which the single theme presented in the first two measures is
worked out continuously in a fugal style. Here in miniature we may see
the elements of the fugue, a form which reached its most grandiose expression in the organ fugues of Bach. As a form the fugue represents a
rationalization of the imitative polyphony of earlier vocal forms by sys-
tematizing the successive entries of a theme. These are now determined
by key relationships instead of being introduced more or less at random
as was the case in the earlier music. The first entry of the theme (Illustration 9) is in the principal key (F minor in this movement), the next
entry in the key a fifth above the original (in this case C minor, measures
3–4), while the third returns to the original key (measures 6–8). Further
entries continue with this same alternation of keys, the number of entries
being determined by the number of parts to be introduced, or simply by
the discretion of the composer. A section of such alternate entries is
called an exposition. It may be followed by further expositions in related
keys but with the same alternation of keys determining the individual
entries of the fugue subject. Between entrances of the subject there are
episodes, or passages, in which the parts continue their melodic motion,
and sometimes modulate in preparation for the next key (measures 8–12).

The fourth movement is also of interest from a formal point of
view. Here the two violins work as a pair in opposition to the persistent

ILLUSTRATION 9

eighth-note figuration of the continuo (Illustration 10). This piece is divided into two sections separated by a double bar indicating that each section is to be repeated. By the end of the first section the music has modulated and comes to a cadence on C, the dominant of the original key, pausing, in other words, on a moment of suspense. In the second section the tension is released as the music proceeds to a conclusion on the tonic. This simple bi-sectional form, known as binary form, has been

ILLUSTRATION 10

borrowed by Corelli from dance movements. Next to the Da Capo form, it is the most widely utilized instrumental form of this era.

Corelli divided his published trio sonatas into two genres: *Sonate da chiesa*, and *Sonate da Camera*. The former, exemplified by the Sonata in F minor, were designed for performance in the church during portions of the Catholic liturgy, and were characterized by the seriousness and gravity of their subject matter and style. The latter are designated for chamber performance, and they differ markedly from the former in that they are made up of a succession of stylized dances. They thus correspond to the groups of dance pieces for keyboard instruments known as suites, ordres, or partitas of which the Partitas and the French and English Suites of Johann Sebastian Bach are supreme examples. In nearly all of these, four specific dances are central features: the moderately slow Allemande in quadruple meter; the "nimble" Courante or Corrente in triple meter; the grave and dignified Sarabande in slow triple time; and the lively Gigue in a compound triple time such as 6/8 or 12/8. These four dances are often preceded by an introductory movement and between the last two of them additional dances, such as the Minuet, Bourrée, or Gavotte, are frequently inserted.

These dances are all unified through the use of the same key and they all have analogous formal characteristics. Each has its own typical tempo and rhythmic motion which are maintained uninterruptedly. The melodic material grows out of the opening phrase or figure by additions and sequences; it is distributed freely throughout a polyphonic fabric except in the Sarabande and, in some instances, the Allemande, where an aria-like melody in the highest part is supported by harmonies in the lower parts. All of the dances utilize the binary form. Such standardization of musical expression is once again most typical of the love for reason and order. Drawn from every part of Europe, and even, in the case of the Sarabande, from Central America, the diversity of these dances has been smoothed away by the application of universal musical principles.

The last of the instrumental forms to become crystallized is the *concerto grosso* (large concerto). The instrumental concerto rests upon the systematic use of opposing bodies of sound as a decisive element of style and form. It thus represents an extension of the principle which had been so brilliantly developed in Venetian sacred music in the early Baroque period, and a continuation of Monteverdi's aesthetic premise that it is contrasts which most excite the human passions. The concerto exploits the dynamic contrasts afforded by a string orchestra of five parts (first and second violins, violas, and cellos with the double bass paralleling the latter at the sub-octave) called either the *ripieno* or *tutti*, and a solo instrument. In the concerto grosso a small group of solo instruments, called the *concertino*, replaces the single instrument. Naturally the ubiquitous continuo is the foundation of this ensemble. As worked out by Italian composers, the various possibilities of this form assume many profiles.

Some of the most typical features of the concerto grosso may be seen in the Concerto in B flat for oboe, violin and orchestra by Antonio Vivaldi (1678–1741). It is designed in a symmetrical form of three movements in which the element of contrast is already apparent through the opposition of the opening and closing Allegro movements to the middle Largo with its broad melodic contours. The contrast between the movements is heightened by the fact that the central movement is written for the solo instruments of the concertino alone, with only the accompaniment of a single violoncello duplicating the continuo line, and by the fact that the key of this movement is G minor. The form of the first and last movements provides the maximum amount of internal contrast. In essence it consists of an alternation of tutti and concertino sections which creates a striking contrast in tonal volumes. The full sound of the tutti passes abruptly into the smaller sound of the concertino in a contrived effect that has been given the name of "terrace" dynamics.

The opposition of the two bodies is further emphasized by assigning specific thematic material to each of them. To the tutti is given a complex of striking motifs with which it opens the movement. This material functions as a ritornello, which in shortened form recurs periodically throughout the movement in the related keys of F major, D minor, and G minor. A final complete re-statement in B flat balances the opening refrain. Between these recurrences of the ritornello, which resemble the spacing of the pillars of a portico, are passages of varying lengths for the concertino, in which brief melodic motifs derived from the original ritornello are used, but are elaborated in a distinctively soloistic style by the oboe and solo violin. Such a form again reveals the rational spirit of the eighteenth century at work. Contrast as such has here been carefully analyzed and exploited to achieve its maximum effect, and at the same time to create a form of almost flawless balance and symmetry.

Johann Sebastian Bach, whose mastery of the concerto was second to none, also brought the chorale prelude for organ to its final fruition. For one hundred and fifty years, chorales had been performed in the Lutheran liturgy in various ways. They had been sung by the congregation in unison, they had been sung by the choir arranged in the style of the sixteenth century cantus firmus motet, and they had been used by the organist for preludes whose style and structure were derived from the motet. The chorale preludes were an integral part of the liturgy; therefore Bach was particularly drawn to them. He embellished and interpreted the melody and the meaning of the Lutheran chorales with his greatest skill in such collections as the *Little Organ Book* (*Orgelbüchlein*) and the third part of the *Klavierübung*. In the latter he applied the most grandiose, intricate and abstract techniques to the problem of interpretation, while in the former the interpretation is presented in the most concentrated and direct form.

The *Little Organ Book* represents an unfulfilled plan of Bach to provide a prelude upon each of the chorales that he regarded as being essential within the liturgical year. Though he gives to each one a distinctive and unique interpretation transcending stylistic classification or grouping, there are some elements which all share in common. In each the integrity and dominance of the chorale melody is maintained, as well as the independence and musical significance of the pedal part. Aside from these similarities, Bach's evident intention to convey the core of meaning of each chorale produced the most varied settings. For example, in *Ich ruf zu dir, Herr Jesu Christ* (I call on thee, Lord Jesus Christ) the melody appears in simplest outline with only a few embellishments in the highest of the three parts. The middle voice within the trio texture is composed of long and undulating figuration, outlining the harmony, while the pedal part, supporting the structure, maintains its own identity through an uninterrupted series of pairs of repeated eighth notes. The pathetic supplication of the text is expressed by the simple contours of the melody and by the frequent dissonances formed by the middle figuration in combination with the melody and the pedal. The sorrow and pain conjured up by the text of another chorale, *O Mensch bewein dein' Sünde gross* (O Man bewail thy sins), is conveyed by the sensitive embellishments of the chorale melody, and by the rich chromaticism of the harmonic accompaniment (Illustration 11).

These chorale preludes demonstrate once again the cardinal principle of seventeenth- and eighteenth-century music that musical style is deter-

ILLUSTRATION 11

Adagio assai

mined by the passions or affections that the composer wishes to express. Everything that takes place within a composition should be there only because it enhances the basic emotion that the work expresses. For the men of this period the passions were neither amorphous nor ambiguous; they were emotions that could be analyzed and known by reason. Thus the musical style created to mirror the passions is rational and direct, a truly universal language.

X THE AGE OF GENIUS

Part I. The Classic Era

THE TRIUMPHANT MARCH of reason had arrived at a point in the mid-eighteenth century where it laid claim to sovereignty in every province of man's activity. But even then there were those who challenged its tyranny over the spirit. They recognized in the human mind an indefinable quality of originality and individuality that the materialistic terms of reason failed to explain. They felt that the cold precepts of rationalism could not account for the uniqueness of the products of the artist's imagination. The laws of reason, it was said, can only teach us how to imitate; they cannot show us how to be original. Are we to be chained forever to the past by reason's authority?

It was in England that the voice of artistic liberty first spoke out clearly. Lord Shaftesbury (1671–1713) in his essays "On the Imagination" and "On Enthusiasm" and Joseph Addison (1672–1719) in the essays on the "Pleasures of the Imagination" published in the *Spectator* pleaded the cause of originality and imagination. Natural geniuses, wrote Addison, are to be preferred before those "who have formed themselves by rules and submitted the greatness of their natural talents to the corrections and restraints of art . . . The great danger in these latter kind of geniuses, is lest they cramp their own abilities too much by imitation, and form themselves altogether upon models, without giving full play to their own natural parts. An imitation of the best authors is not to compare with a good original; and I believe we may observe that very few writers make an extraordinary figure in the world, who have not something in their way of thinking or expressing themselves that is peculiar to them, and entirely their own."

Even more outspoken was Edward Young in his *Conjectures on Original Composition* (1759). "Nature," he cried, "brings us into the world all originals. No two faces, no two minds, are just alike; but all bear nature's evident mark of separation on them. Born originals, how comes it to pass that we die copies?" The spark of originality should not be extinguished by the uniformity imposed by reason, but should be allowed to flourish in the free world of its own imagination. "In the fairyland of fancy, genius may wander wild; there it has a creative power, and may reign arbitrarily over its own empire of chimeras. The wide field of nature lies open before it, where it may range unconfined, make what discoveries it can, and sport with its infinite objects uncontrolled, as far as visible nature extends, painting them as wantonly as it will."

Recognize your own abilities, Young adjures: "Know thyself" and "Reverence thyself." "Dive deep into thy bosom; learn the depth, extent, bias, and full fort of thy mind; contract full intimacy with the stranger within thee; excite and cherish every spark of intellectual light and heat, however smothered under former negligence, or scattered through the dull, dark mass of common thoughts; and, collecting them into a body, let thy genius rise (if a genius thou hast) as the sun from chaos . . . This is the difference between those two luminaries in literature, the well-accomplished scholar and the divinely-inspired enthusiast: the first is as the bright morning star; the second, as the rising sun. The writer who neglects those two rules above, will never stand alone: he makes one of a group, and thinks in wretched unanimity with the throng. Incumbered with the notions of others, and impoverished by their abundance, he conceives not the least embryo of new thought; opens not the least vista through the gloom of ordinary writers into the bright walks of rare imagination and singular design. While the true genius is crossing all public roads into fresh untrodden ground, he, up to the knees in antiquity, is treading the sacred footsteps of great examples with the blind veneration of a bigot saluting the papal toe; comfortably hoping full absolution for the sins of his own understanding from the powerful charm of touching his idol's infallibility."

Thus exhorted to assert their originality, the men of the mid-eighteenth century increasingly turned away from reason to embrace the imagination. The ability of the human mind to invent new ideas was identified as genius, a special endowment of the individual enabling him to create new forms of art. Genius revealed itself in individuals as a peculiar sensibility or mode of perception differing from that of other men. The world was perceived and re-created through the emotions of the divinely inspired artist. But these emotions were not the schematized passions of the rationalists. Vague and imprecise, they arose spontaneously within the soul. Instead of being the product of a known mechanical stimulus, they were a form of sympathy or "feeling with" an object.

Under the influence of the idea of genius, a decisive reorientation of taste took place in the second half of the century. This is the period of tender sensibilities, the age of sentimentality or *Empfindsamkeit*, of which the European vogue of Richardson's *Pamela* is symptomatic. The new emotionalism, an indeterminate, instinctive movement of the heart, found utterance not within the carefully tended fields of tragedy and the epic but within the lyric forms of poetry.

The shift of emphasis to the expression of feeling in poetry and the growing interest in world-wide folk poetry brought about at last, late in the century, a definite dethronement of the drama and epic in favor of the lyric . . . The emotional effect which had always been the aim of rhetoric and of some poetry became, under the influence of sentimentalism, the *sine qua non* of all poetry, even of all literature. Romantic subjectivism was only a step away.*

In revolt against classical literature, which had been enthroned by the rationalists, the sentimentalists sought and found new fields of literature which they described variously as primitive or naïve. Homer was re-interpreted as a primitive bard; the Bible was appraised as primitive poetry; Germanic sagas, Shakespeare, Macpherson's *Ossian*, the poetry of Oriental nations, and the songs and ballads of the folk, all captured the imagination of the man of sentiment. These, it was felt, were poetic works untrammelled by the cold, sophisticated laws of reason. They were the product of men who had lived in times when they were free to voice their genius and emotions unrestrained by reason and convention.

The strain of irrationality and emotionalism grew stronger throughout the century, culminating finally in the movement known as Romanticism. But the ultimate triumph of Romanticism does not come until the very end of the century: the years preceding its final victory belong rather to men who sought a middle ground between reason and emotion. During this period Germany began to emerge as a leader in intellectual life, particularly in philosophy and music. There the new emotionalism had suddenly burst forth in the sixties in the movement of Storm and Stress, and just as suddenly had subsided into quieter channels. This tempering of violent emotional expression was due in part to the reassertion of the authority of reason by philosophers such as Immanuel Kant (1724–1804). But it was also brought about by a new movement of Classicism inspired

* René Wellek, *History of Modern Criticism*, I, 123–124.

by Johann Winckelmann (1717–1768) who had discovered in the art-
works of Greece a spirit of "noble simplicity and tranquil grandeur."
Germany's neo-Classicism is opposed to the older French Classicism in
that it does not see Greek art as a system of rules to be imitated, but
rather perceives in it certain emotional qualities, an element of grace and
an indefinable organic unity that were to be emulated.

The Classic Era in Germany includes such men as Goethe, Haydn,
Mozart, and Beethoven. Unfortunately the name of this epoch has given
rise to many misconceptions. A too rigid distinction has been drawn
between Classicism and Romanticism, and the two terms have even been
made to stand for eternal polarities in the art of all ages. Such distinctions
will not bear close scrutiny. German and European Romanticism were
well under way before Beethoven, a "Classic" composer, had written his
first major work; Byron, Keats, and Shelley, arch-Romantics, were dead
before Goethe had completed his monumental literary labors. Thus
German Classicism, while possessing definite and easily identifiable traits,
flourishes side by side with Romanticism, and actually shares many ideas
in common with it. In proper perspective the Classic Era should be seen
not as an age in eternal conflict with Romanticism but as a distinctive
and wholly German moment within the context of a wider European
movement of Romanticism.

It was during the eighteenth century that the recognition of a faculty
of the mind and a mode of perception which could not wholly be ac-
counted for by reason gave rise to the science of aesthetics. Beauty and
art, it came to be seen, could not be satisfactorily defined either through
pure sensationalism or through the schematic concepts of rationalism.
They were to be judged instead as a form of experience and activity
distinct from all others and having laws of their own. But the new science
of aesthetics, which was given its name by Alexander Baumgarten (1714–
1762), could not and did not reach a truly independent status until its
position within a philosophical system had been clearly defined. This was
finally accomplished by Immanuel Kant.

Kant investigated the nature of knowledge, using the transcendental
method, a form of inquiry that is concerned not with objects themselves
but with how we come to know them. He maintains that human cognition
is conditioned by its *a priori* postulation of time and space. These two
qualities, he asserts, are not truly parts of objects. They are instead something which the thinking subject has to presuppose in order that the
objects of his thought may be discerned as something apart from himself
and in a certain successive relationship with himself. Without these pre-
conceptions of time and space the thinking being could never separate

himself from the objects which surround him. Thus Kant maintains that we can never know the real world, the world of things in themselves, as God may know them; we see only a world of appearances as determined by our peculiarly human concepts of time and space.

The function of human thought, according to Kant, is to define or determine the manifold and chaotic appearances presented to the mind by the senses. This it does by means of certain universal laws of thought residing in the faculty of understanding. These laws are specific ways in which the understanding formulates relationships among the numberless appearances that crowd in upon us. Scanning the jumble of sense impressions, the understanding endeavors to make them coherent and orderly by assessing them in such forms of judgment as "This S is P," "Some S's are P." "All S's are P." Cognition or the act of knowing, therefore, is the act of forming a conclusion. It is accomplished when judgment brings the faculty of understanding to bear upon an image formed by the imagination from the objects brought to it by the senses.

Though the faculty of understanding creates concepts out of the amalgam of sense impressions, it is not the highest faculty of the mind. It is subject in turn to the faculty of reason which rises above the laws of the understanding and presupposes that there are still higher principles. Reason assumes *a priori* that there is a totality of all possible knowledge, an infinite knowledge never to be known in its entirety by finite man. The function of reason is to relate the individual judgments of the understanding to the higher principles which order and regulate the totality of knowledge. Moving entirely in the realm of concepts provided for it by the understanding, reason synthesizes these into transcendental ideas which "overstep the limits of all experience, [for] no object adequate to the transcendental idea can ever be found within experience." In limiting pure reason to the single function of regulating the concepts of the understanding, Kant has moved far away from the Enlightenment's faith in the all-embracing power of reason.

When Kant turned from his investigation of *pure* reason to that of *practical* reason, he found he had created a difficult problem concerning human freedom when he made the premise that the concept of time is a necessary precondition of knowing. Time is a succession of events, each of which must be the result of some cause. Thus the concept of time implies an infinite regression of cause and effect. How then can the individual act with any freedom? As long as his actions are motivated by the desire for some specific object, he cannot be free, for his actions have been caused by a foreknowledge of the end he wishes to attain. In nourishing himself or building a shelter for protection from the elements he may have a choice as to the manner in which these ends are accomplished, but still he is not free: these actions have been caused by the need for sustaining the body.

Since we cannot be free as long as our actions are guided by laws derived from experience—such as, we must eat to live—some law must be found that will admit at least the possibility of freedom of action. Because such a law cannot be framed with a specific object in view, it can only be the mere form of a law. It contains only an imperative: "thou must." However, all laws are legislated towards some end. Kant therefore concludes that the object of the mere form of a law must be something infinite and unconditioned. It can only be the Supreme Good which contains the sum of all that is good and which has no other cause than itself. For Kant, the only practical action in which the possibility of freedom exists is one undertaken to realize the Supreme Good.

Practical action is thus synonymous with moral action. It is governed by universally applicable precepts which we feel *must* be obeyed by everyone. Its fundamental law, called by Kant the Categorical Imperative, is: "Act so that the maxim of thy will can always at the same time hold good as a principle of universal law." Our freedom exists in the fact that we may choose to obey this law or not, and that we may choose to act according to the law even though its end may not be attained. The protest of a citizen against a tyrant may still be uttered, though his action can in no way end oppression and may even result in his own destruction. His action, however, remains as a concrete illustration of the moral law and may serve as an example to all other men. Kant's conception of moral law and practical action, in which men are given the liberty to act within the framework of a universal law residing in us, profoundly stirred his generation. Beethoven was moved to adopt it, exclaiming: "The moral law within us and the starry heaven above us. Kant ! ! !"

Kant has postulated two worlds, one the world of appearances regulated by the laws of the understanding, the other the suprasensible realm of things in themselves regulated by the moral law of pure practical reason. There is a great gulf between the two worlds of nature and moral freedom. Nevertheless "the latter is *meant* to influence the former—that is to say, the concept of freedom is meant to actualize in the sensible world the end proposed by its laws; and nature must consequently also be capable of being regarded in such a way that in the conformity to law of its form it at least harmonizes with the possibility of the ends to be effectuated in it according to the laws of freedom." We must, in other words, assume the unity of the two worlds.

Kant assigns the *a priori* conception of the unity of the two worlds to the faculty of reflective judgment, an aspect of judgment distinct from that employed in cognition. The latter is called determinant judgment, for its function is to determine a particular object by the laws of understanding: to subsume the particular under known universal laws. Reflective judgment approaches the natural world in quite another way. It assumes that the manifold appearances and laws of the natural world are subject to a higher unity and that this unity of natural laws was established by some intelligence for the purpose of making nature cognizable. While it is impossible to know the laws of this higher unity, we assume that they exist, as when we say, for example: "Nature takes the shortest way; yet it makes no leap." Such a maxim tells us not *how* we judge, but how we *ought* to judge. The function of reflective judgment then, as opposed to determinant judgment, is to subsume a particular under a universal law that is *not* known.

Since the universal law is unknown, how can we tell that we have made a reflective judgment? Kant replies that it is not by any precise thought but only by a sense of pleasure or displeasure, sensations that tell us that a particular object has been brought into line with the unknown laws of the understanding that are presumed to govern this higher unity. When any object awakens such a pleasurable sensation within us, we say of it that it is beautiful. The pleasure thus experienced must, however, be distinguished from the delight we feel in the gratification of some desire. It must be a disinterested pleasure, removed from any desire to possess the object in question. Since beauty is free from the element of desire associated with the useful and the good, it is not to be confused with either of these concepts. By this careful distinction Kant has marked out a special realm for beauty and aesthetics.

Kant's formulation of beauty has important implications for art. While the beautiful can and does exist in nature, it may also be brought into being by man. The products of fine art are created simply for the feeling of pleasure that will arise from them, apart from any moral or didactic purposes. Furthermore, the creation of beauty can never be accomplished by the application of specific laws, for the known rules of the understanding can only give us knowledge of an object: they cannot determine the subjective qualities of beauty. The rules of art themselves are not given by determinant judgment, but are only to be found by nature working through the individual: "Fine art is only possible as a product of genius."

This necessary quality of genius is defined by Kant as "the innate mental aptitude through which nature gives the rule to Art." It is a talent for producing that for which no definite rule can be given; consequently originality must be its primary quality. Although an original work of art is necessarily unique, the fact that it is beautiful is proof that it somehow embodies the hidden universal laws of the higher unity of nature. Therefore the products of genius may serve as examples for other artists and should be used as a standard for evaluating other works of art.

In the philosophy of Kant the conflicting ideals of reason and genius are reconciled. He had managed to incorporate the essentially irrational idea of genius into one of the most rigorously rational systems of philosophy ever created. But even more than this, he had made the realm of beauty over which genius presides a necessary and valid link between the world of appearances and the world of things in themselves. In this way he prepares the way for the exalted position that was to be accorded to art in the Romantic period.

The changing attitudes of the second half of the eighteenth century are accurately reflected in the music of this period. Most notable is the emergence of instrumental music as the primary mode of expression after centuries of subordination to vocal music. This development had been prepared by the Baroque era in which instrumental music in league with the doctrine of the passions had gained a musical language—meaningful without the aid of words. Now it acquired still greater independence, for the very indefiniteness and imprecision of the new sentiments and emotions could best be realized in the inexplicit language of instruments. The new emotionalism, moreover, seeks for unique and individual expression rather than for the universal and the general. The stereotyped figures of the passions must give way to ever more original musical ideas, so that each work may possess what men of this age call the "characteristic." In the seventies Joseph Haydn struggles to provide for his symphonies what he calls their moral character. But while the musician desires individuality for each of his works, it must be contained within universally valid forms. Thus the composers of the Classic Era choose to express their ideas within certain self-imposed musical forms, which, valid for all, still allow the greatest possible degree of latitude to the individual artist.

Another factor that played an important part in the musical evolution of this period was the fundamental change taking place in society itself. The eighteenth century marks the emergence of the middle class as an influential segment of society. As this increasingly wealthy bourgeois class pressed for recognition within a world dominated by the aristocracy, it strove to assimilate the culture and ideals of the court. Taste and learning no longer remained the exclusive property of the nobility but were ever more widely disseminated among the members of the middle class, who took pride in being designated as "Kenner und Liebhaber," connoisseur and dilettante. Their demands for increased participation in the musical life formerly confined almost entirely to courtly circles led to the establishment of new musical institutions. Informal associations of amateurs banded together to perform music for their own edification and amusement. But the primary means by which the musical appetite of this large new audience could be satisfied became the public concert. With this new institution came many of the features of musical life that still exist today. To fill the ample spaces of public halls with sound, larger ensembles of instruments were called for and the symphony orchestra was evolved. The newly invented pianoforte with its greater volume of sound soon replaced the harpsichord and clavichord. The touring virtuoso came upon the scene to dazzle and bewitch his listeners with his incredible technique. As a result new categories of composition appeared and old ones, unsuited to contemporary tastes, disappeared.

The ascendancy of instrumental music begins with the composers of the mid-eighteenth century. It differs sharply in character, style and structure from its antecedents, and also from the theatrical style which had so long dominated musical art. To be sure, many musicians continued to compose works which carried on the ideals and grandiose proportions of the late Baroque. Christoph Willibald Gluck (1714–1787), for example, whose interests were exclusively theatrical, created a series of operas largely based upon the Baroque *dramma per musica*, in which he partially overcame the static formalism of the conventional opera seria. Religious music, written for the Catholic liturgy or in the form of the dramatic oratorio, also continued to absorb the creative talents of many composers. It is not in these traditional categories but in the intimate, instrumental music of the salon that the ideals of sensibility found a suitable medium for the growth of a new musical style. Here, a small but important number of composers developed a means of expressing the fluctuations of emotion that typify the man of sensibility. The clavichord was at first the favorite instrument because the performer, in response to his sensitive feeling, could produce on it a varied and subtle range of dynamics by the pressure of his fingers. But it was soon supplanted by the newer, more powerful pianoforte and the quartet of stringed instruments.

The leading composer of this transitional stage was Carl Philipp Emanuel Bach (1714–1788), the second son of Johann Sebastian. Although he was an intelligent and devoted admirer of his father's music, Emanuel Bach's own instrumental music reveals a change in taste which far transcends that which is usually found between two generations. He continued to write in some of the categories in which his father had worked, such as the concerto, but in style and content these differ profoundly from those of Sebastian. At the same time he forsook the suite, so assiduously cultivated by his father, in favor of fantasies, rondos and sonatas for the clavichord, which were widely admired because of the eloquence with which they expressed the play of feeling. His sonatas were published in a series beginning with the "Prussian" sonatas of 1742, dedicated to his employer Frederick the Great, and concluding with the six sets of sonatas for "Kenner und Liebhaber" published between 1779 and 1787. In them his contemporaries recognized the qualities of originality and daring which are the marks of artistic genius.

An artistic ideal which stresses the spontaneous play of feeling does not favor consistency of style or form. In his own day Bach was particularly admired for his improvisations because of the startling variety of feeling they conveyed. In his sonatas, though he makes use of older styles, he combines them in novel and unfamiliar ways to express individualistic sentiment. The majority of his sonatas retain the symmetrical form of three movements favored by his immediate predecessors, but the content of each movement is often so striking as to upset the former balance of this form. Many of the first movements are arranged in the symetrical order of the *sonata form*, shortly to be described.

What makes these sonatas most striking are the idiosyncrasies of Bach's personal style: the interruption of the regular motion by unexpected and irregularly spaced caesuras, the flexibility of tempo, the unusual chord progressions mingled with sharp dissonances, the abrupt alternations between major and minor modes, and the melodic phrases pivoting upon wide, unvocal intervals. Bach also demands gradual increases or decreases in dynamics and abrupt alternations of loud and soft to underline nuances and changes of feeling. All of these elements are clearly at odds with the orderly, musical architecture practiced by the previous generations of composers. They prompted a writer of the Storm and Stress period, Reichardt, to say of Bach's music: "One heard with rapture the original and bold course of ideas as well as the great variety and novelty in form and modulations. Hardly ever did a musical composition of higher, more daring, and more humorous character flow from the soul of genius."

The sonatas of Emanuel Bach were a constant source of inspiration to his contemporaries and to the younger generation of German artists of the second half of the eighteenth century. In these works the greatest composers of the Classic Era, Joseph Haydn (1732–1809), Wolfgang Amadeus Mozart (1756–1791), and Ludwig van Beethoven (1770–1827), found the components of a new style of instrumental expression to which each in his own way aspired. It is through the achievements of these three men that the sonata for solo instruments or orchestra came to occupy the position of first importance that had formerly belonged to the opera. Between the early string quartets, symphonies, and piano sonatas of Haydn and those composed by Beethoven in the last years of his life an enormous development took place. Indeed this period may be seen as a continuous evolution in the morphology of instrumental form and style, an evolution brought about by a striving for originality in contrast to the universality of expression sought by the men of the Enlightenment. The fundamental qualities that distinguish the individual works of these three composers cannot be reduced to a collection of academic formulas without destroying their vitality. Here is a vast musical repertory whose coherence and meaning are no longer explicable through verbal factors, but solely through purely musical elements. Yet for all their incredible diversity and originality these works are still related to one another through their adherence to common forms and procedures.

In tracing the evolution of this instrumental repertory, certain phases of its growth will be examined, taking in succession illustrations from the music of Haydn, Mozart, and Beethoven. There is some justification for this procedure, since Mozart benefited from the achievements of Haydn, and Beethoven from both of his predecessors. The relationship of the three men is beautifully suggested in the prophetic statement made to Beethoven by Count Waldstein as Beethoven departed for Vienna in 1792 only a few months after the death of Mozart: "The genius of Mozart is mourning and weeping over the death of her pupil. She found a refuge but no occupation with the inexhaustible Haydn; through him she wishes to form a union with another. With the help of diligent labor you will receive Mozart's spirit from Haydn's hands."

The long career of Joseph Haydn embraces both the tentative beginnings of the instrumental sonata and its full maturity. Until 1790, when he was nearly sixty years old, Haydn's creative life, like that of the majority of his predecessors, was molded by his position as composer, performer, and director of music in the service of the aristocracy. From 1761 to 1791 he was employed by the wealthy Esterhazy family in their palaces at Vienna and Eisenstadt and above all at Esterhaza, the magnificent edifice built by Prince Nicholas to rival the splendors of Versailles. Although Haydn's fertile pen was sorely taxed by Prince Nicholas' incessant demand for new works in every musical medium, the long years of artistic isolation at Esterhaza were most conducive to the development of his genius. The stability of conditions at the court and the excellent musical organization at Haydn's disposal, to say nothing of the sympathetic encouragement of his employer, were positive advantages. They made it possible for Haydn to work out the new ideals of the instrumental sonata in a multitude of compositions for various media, particularly the string quartet and the orchestra.

It is no exaggeration to say that the string quartet is the decisive category in Haydn's development of the sonata. In it he evolved principles which were subsequently to be transferred to all types of instrumental music. Although a number of eighteenth-century composers had written for the medium of a quartet of two violins, viola and cello, this ensemble had acquired no unique features when Haydn began to work with it. In general, the group of four instruments was treated as if it were a trio in the Baroque manner by coupling the viola and violoncello in octaves, creating a texture of only three lines. These early quartets, moreover, borrowed their forms from the suite. No exception to this practice, Haydn's very earliest quartets generally consist of five movements whose order retains the Baroque principle of symmetry and contrast. The first and last movements are alike in their rapid motion and character, the second and fourth are balancing minuets, and these in turn flank the central movement, a lyrical adagio. All of the movements, with the exception of the middle one, are in the same key. These characteristics are all to be found in Haydn's string quartet, Opus 1, no. 1. It is worth while pausing to examine the structure of the first movement of this work (Illustration 1), for here may be seen in embryo the form which was to grow until it reached the awe-inspiring proportions of the first movement of Beethoven's Ninth Symphony.

At first glance this movement seems to preserve the elementary binary form of the dances of the past. If it is compared with the fourth movement of Corelli's sonata da chiesa, however (see Chapter IX, p. 282), some significant differences will be discovered. Where Corelli's movement is absolutely symmetrical, with the same number of measures in each of the two sections, there is a certain imbalance in this piece of Haydn's, for the second section is longer than the first. Moreover, differences are to be discerned in the handling of the two sections. Corelli simply comes to a conclusion on the dominant chord at the end of the first section, but Haydn makes the dominant serve as the basis of a new key. Starting in measure 9, Haydn consistently writes an E natural thereby establishing the key of F (the dominant of the original B flat) for the remainder of this section. In this way he establishes two opposing tonal areas within the first section.

Haydn clearly distinguishes and articulates these two areas by his handling of the thematic material. A sharply defined theme is presented in the first eight measures.* It consists of a two-measure phrase in forte dynamics in which the instruments spell out in unison the chord of B flat, firmly establishing the tonality of this movement. This aggressively rising figure is answered by two subdued phrases in piano dynamics, each of which is one measure in length. The first of these is given a characteristic profile by joining together the F and B flat of the first violin with a slur (a curved line which signifies that the notes joined together should

---

* In counting measures one does not include the initial incomplete measure.

ILLUSTRATION I

ILLUSTRATION I (*continued*)

ILLUSTRATION I (*continued*)

ILLUSTRATION I (*continued*)

be played smoothly). The following G is separated from its neighboring notes by a dot above it, which indicates that the note is to be played staccato. This phrase is echoed in the next measure, but its force is lessened because the slur now extends over three notes, and a decreasing tonal volume is called for by the two converging lines which are the sign of a diminuendo. The effect of the first four measures is that of a breaking wave which spends its force as it falls. The next four measures repeat this idea with some slight modifications of pitch. It is obvious that this theme has been given its form and coherence through the use of purely musical factors such as melodic direction, dynamics, and phrase marks, and that its careful periodicity is the result of balancing and complementary phrases of two and four measures. These are to be characteristic features of the music of the Classic Era.

Having established the key of F in measure 9, Haydn works for eight measures with a figure which can be identified through its phrase marks with the melodic idea of measure 3. In the last two and a half measures of this period the two violins detach themselves from the other instruments and rise impetuously to the highest note reached in this section. From here, after the briefest of pauses, the first violin begins to plunge downward in a new arpeggio figure, which in turn is followed by four concluding measures bringing this section to a momentarily subdued ending. The first section of this movement is thus divided into three parts: measures 1–8 present a theme in the tonic key; measures 9–16 establish the dominant key while using material derived from the first theme; and measures 17–24 introduce a new idea and a concluding passage also in the dominant key. Here in essence are the elements that are to be exploited by Haydn and his successors. This first section is to become what is now called the *exposition*, consisting of three parts: the presentation of a first theme in the tonic key; a passage called the bridge, which modulates to the dominant or relative key; and the presentation of a new theme with a concluding passage in this new key.

After repeating the first section, Haydn in the beginning of the second part of his movement detaches certain thematic motifs from their original context in the exposition, rearranging them and modifying the harmonic accompaniment. Thus the descending arpeggio of the second theme reappears in measure 25 transposed and answered by the concluding motif of the main theme (measures 4 and 8), now harmonized in C minor. Similar rearrangements occur in the next fourteen measures in which the music progresses from B flat major through B flat minor, coming finally to rest on an F chord in measure 40. This functions as a dominant chord bringing back the original tonic. There is a caesura at this moment, which separates this section from the next. From this point to the end of the movement the musical material is a reproduction of that found in the exposition, modified, however, so that the movement may come to a satisfactory conclusion in the original key. For this reason the bridge after moving to F major and E flat major returns to B flat. In this key the subordinate theme now makes its concluding appearance. But the movement is not yet at an end: the whole section from measure 25 onward is repeated immediately.

The first part of this second section up to the caesura is now known as the *development*, and the restatement of the themes is called the *recapitulation*. If we were to draw a diagram of the form of this movement and that of its ancestor, the dance form, the asymmetry of the one and the balance of the other would be easily perceptible:

A	A		B	B		DANCE FORM

a	b	a	b		c	a	b	c	a	b		SONATA FORM

In the diagram of the sonata form the small *a* represents the tonic thematic area; *b* stands for the second thematic area, which in the exposition is presented in the dominant, and in the recapitulation appears in the tonic; and *c* represents the development section.

Here, presented in the simplest terms, is a structural principle which is capable of almost unlimited development and extension. It offers the possibility of associating contrasting thematic materials of strong emotional tensions in the two thematic areas of the exposition, the further intensification of these melodic and harmonic tensions in the development and their resolution in the recapitulation. It would be wrong, however, to think that Haydn in his Opus 1 was at all aware of these potentialities. The spirit of the Baroque still breathes in this quartet, particularly in the minuets where the viola and cello move together in octaves in a line resembling a continuo against which the two violins form a duet.

In the years following the appearance of his Opus 1 Haydn worked continually in the field of the quartet, striving to establish it as an art form capable of conveying profound and original feeling. He had to find the means to transform its graceful, charming, but fundamentally superficial character to one which would demand serious and sensitive concentration on the part of those to whom it was addressed. His first step was to establish a sequence of four movements as the norm. The first movement is invariably an allegro, in an increasingly expanded version of the sonata form. This movement, which carries the greatest weight, is followed by a slow lyrical movement in a related key. Then comes the minuet. In reality the minuet movement consists of two individual minuets, the second of which is called a trio. After the two are concluded the first minuet is performed once again. Finally a closing Allegro rounds off the quartet with a rousing finale. The last movement is invariably in the same key as the first and the minuet is usually so.

Such a sequence of movements is a dramatic departure from the practices of the preceding age. Instead of a symmetrical, and therefore static, succession of movements, the grouping is asymmetrical, producing a dynamic, organic progression from first to last. The vitality of the first movement subsides into the reflective lyricism of the second. From this point the work again begins to generate moving power in the pleasant sociability of the minuet which in turn propels us into the exuberance of the final allegro.

This progression can be described in general terms, but it cannot be exactly formulated for it differs in each work according to the type of themes and the forms employed. If Haydn creates a first movement which is less energetic than usual, he reverses the order of the two inner movements. In this fashion the animation of the minuet intervenes between the seriousness of the opening movement and the languor of the slow movement. The succession of movements is planned in accordance with the function of each in the emotional progression of the quartet as a whole. We have entered a new world of art in which emotions have become less particularized and precise than the carefully analyzed passions of the Baroque, and where the form of a work of art depends not upon rules sanctioned by reason but upon the individual genius of the composer. The four-movement form, universally accepted by the men of this era, is no straitjacket. In its flexibility it reflects the ideal of this age: to express the individual and unique within certain universal principles. The essence of the sonata is a continuous and varied emotional experience which is perceptible intuitively; thus its only constants are formal procedures.

To enrich the content of the quartet, Haydn enlarges the role of the lower instruments. At first he experiments in Opus 20 with the "learned" polyphony of the fugue to create equality among the instruments. Later he achieves a sort of free polyphony in which the thematic materials pass from one instrument to another, nevertheless assigning the largest share of melodic materials to the first violin and the cello, with its rich lyrical tone and intensity of expression. The dimensions of the sonata form are enlarged. Themes capable of expressing deep and turbulent feelings are given rich, complex harmonic support by widening the concept of tonality to include chords suggesting the minor mode in a major context and vice versa. The character of the minuet is sometimes changed by folk-like melodies whose exuberance denies the decorous spirit of this dance. Thus Haydn gradually transformed the nature of the quartet, eliminating with the variety of melodic and harmonic materials the easy consistency of the earlier quartet.

The Russian Quartets, Opus 33, published in 1781, mark the first complete realization of Haydn's aims. By this time he had established the organic nature of the sonata and its appropriate style. In this collection he presents a new method of working with thematic materials, and he describes these quartets as being written "in an entirely new and particular manner." The substance of a movement is now generated throughout by the evolution and modification of the initial phrases of the themes. This may be illustrated by an examination of Opus 76, No. 3, the so-called "Emperor" quartet (Illustration 2), one of a set of six composed in 1797–1798.

The kernel of the entire first movement is to be found in the opening four measures. The first theme, symmetrical in form, consists of four compact phrases, of which the first two provide the fundamental material for the whole process of development. The initial sharp upbeat imparts dynamic energy to the first phrase, but the principal melody of the first violin releases this energy in a falling third and a further descent after the slight rise to F. At the same time the two quarter notes of this phrase, falling on the primary accents of the measure, are harmonized with the tonic chord of C, from which the phrase acquires a certain immobility despite its dynamic inflection. This is then overcome by the second phrase with its staccato eighth notes ending upon a G chord, the dominant of C major. The expected resolution comes in the third phrase, with its reiteration of the initial phrase by the viola. Its original clarity is, however, obscured in this repetition by the introduction of the B flat in the

ILLUSTRATION 2

ILLUSTRATION 2 *(continued)*

ILLUSTRATION 2 (*continued*)

ILLUSTRATION 2 (*continued*)

ILLUSTRATION 2 *(continued)*

second violin, and by the syncopation of the first violin. Three decisive chords resolve the ambiguity of this phrase, bringing the theme unequivocally to an end. Haydn now proceeds to break apart the hard shell of this self-contained theme and to unfold the life within it.

The first phrase is heard again in the viola and the second violin, (measures 5 and 6) but against it a countermelody in the form of an ascending scale of dotted sixteenth and thirty-second notes makes its appearance. The animated rhythmic motion of the scale soon engages each of the instruments until all are involved with it in measures 11 and 12. Throughout this passage Haydn does not depart from the key of C, but in measure 8 a definite tension is set up between the cello and the upper instruments. While the cello insists upon the tonic C the other instruments assert a dominant seventh chord on G. Unable to withstand the pressure, the cello yields in measure 11 and joins the other instruments in their headlong motion and their reiteration of the dominant chord. A resolution must be found for this insistent demand and it comes, after a sudden silence of all the instruments in measure 12, when the soft assertion of the first phrase begins the bridge passage.

Haydn begins to modulate immediately, still using the first phrase in a contrapuntal interchange. In measure 18 this phrase is somewhat modified by replacing the first quarter note with a trilled dotted eighth note followed by two thirty-seconds. In this same measure the cello begins a rapid tremolo on D, asserting the dominant of the key of G towards which Haydn is modulating. For five measures, while the rhythmic excitement and the volume climbs to a fortissimo, this dominant harmony clamors for a resolution. At the height of this excitement (measure 22) the first violin suddenly breaks into a rapid arpeggio, and then all the instruments pause in the typical caesura by which the composer marks off the structural members of his composition.

We are now prepared for the entrance of the second theme in G major, but we are confronted instead with E minor. The harmony passes rapidly to A minor and then comes to rest in the anticipated key of G. The melody of the second theme appears at first to be new, but examination reveals it to be a derivative of the opening material of the movement. In measure 23 the second violin carries the familiar phrase of measure 1 and, beginning with the last note of the same measure, the first violin sings a melody built out of the first three notes of this same phrase. The second theme continues in measure 26 with a melody derived from the second phrase of the original theme. Once again the rhythmic motion begins to quicken as the sixteenth notes of the accompaniment spread to all four instruments, and a new tension arises as the harmony veers into G minor (measure 29) and then into E flat. Again a caesura (measure 32) interrupts the exposition peremptorily, separating the forte dynamics of the massed instruments and the solitary entrance of the cello which follows. In this remote key the first phrase is treated polyphonically, and just as it seems about to lose all its force and motion (measures 35–37) a modulation carries it back to G major and to a section corresponding to measures 26–28. This time, however, this passage does not slip into the minor key but ends with a triumphant assertion of the dominant tonality. Motion does not, though, come to a complete halt. Scarcely have the firm closing chords been heard, when a rhythmic, melodic motif of only two notes carries us back to the repeat of the exposition. This motif is obviously the dropping third with which the first phrase begins, and thus even the repeat of the exposition has been generated from an element of the original thematic material.

In the development section which follows, the two motifs of the main theme continue to produce new ideas, such as the imitative dialogue between pairs of instruments using only the two jaunty notes of the beginning of the first phrase, and the extended passage in dotted rhythms over the monotonous drone of open fifths in the cello and viola, which recalls the popular bagpipe. In the recapitulation all the distinctive features of the exposition are presented in the same order but with a number of alterations necessary to prepare for the final C major repetition of the subordinate theme.

Everything in this movement has evolved logically from the four opening measures, and all that follows is also the product of its emotional premises. The second movement is an adagio cantabile in the key of G in the form of a theme and variations. In this quiet sequel Haydn explores the expressive lyricism of the melody now known as the Austrian National Anthem, which he had composed in honor of the Emperor. Here, as in many of his other quartets, the simplest improvisatory scheme replaces the complex formal factors with which the first movement abounds. Each of the four variations, however, increases in intensity until the full harmony of the fourth, where the melody soars in the highest register of the first violin. The following minuet and trio in C major is cast in a lighter vein, but even here the harmonic ambiguity of major and minor that had characterized the first movement is to be found. To conclude the entire work Haydn composes a movement which parallels the first movement in form, proportions, and compact developmental technique. But this movement is written in an impassioned C minor: the tonal ambiguities of the preceding movements are apparently to be resolved into a tragic finale. It is only in the last two pages that Haydn allows the clear tones of C major to return, averting the unhappy ending suggested by the previous events.

Haydn fashioned the coherent, deeply expressive sonata in the medium of the quartet, a medium intended only for the cultivated and discerning ears of skillful amateur performers and small audiences of connoisseurs. But he transferred the stylistic achievements of the quartet to other categories of composition, especially to the symphony. When Prince Nicholas died in 1791, releasing Haydn from the constant and demanding obligations of his musical establishment, the composer embarked upon the new life of the free artist in the service of the public and the impressario-manager. In this status he composed between 1791 and 1795 the twelve London symphonies, which represent the summit of Haydn's symphonic achievement, revealing his mastery of this medium acquired in the ninety-odd works of this genre preceding them.

The symphony orchestra, like the quartet, had become a stabilized group of instruments. The center of the orchestral ensemble is the string section of two bodies of violins, together with violas, cellos, and double basses, which double the cellos at the lower octave, thus providing solid foundations for the vertical harmony. This string choir carries the main burden of the music and dominates all the most forceful passages with its vigorous and brilliant style. The wind choir, consisting of pairs of flutes, oboes, clarinets, horns, and bassoons, plays a highly important complementary role. The winds are sometimes treated soloistically, imparting their expressive color to thematic material which they share in dialogues with the strings. As a body they also re-enforce and fill out the harmony in fortissimo passages. A third component of this instrumental complex consists of trumpets and kettle drums to emphasize rhythmic accents, and to add volume and splendor to loud passages. Thus the orchestra, as opposed to the rather limited possibilities of the quartet, is an instrument capable of a wide range of dynamics. With its extensive palette of instrumental color it can create textures by turns sombre and brilliant, and can depict a wider range of emotion than the quartet.

Haydn's London Symphony, No. 104 in D major, may serve as an illustration of the sonata for orchestra. Like all his later symphonies, it is arranged in the four movement sequence exemplified by the "Emperor" quartet, but it is distinguished by a very evident attempt to achieve a higher unity within the total work by using thematic relationships between the movements. A slow introduction in D minor, consisting of pompous fanfare-like figures alternating with plaintive lyrical phrases, precedes the first allegro movement. By its serious and intense atmosphere and by the contrast of mode and emotion it dramatizes the entrance of the first theme of the allegro in D major. The first two phrases of the sixteen-measure theme not only present the principal material for this movement but also foreshadow the themes of the following movements. In the illustration they are identified by asterisks and zeros respectively as are their thematic derivations with which the second and third movements commence. The relationship between the first themes of the first and last movements is less obvious: the phrases comprising the latter pivot upon intervals which are prominent in the former, but the dactylic rhythm of the first movement is transformed into an anapest in the last movement (Illustration 3).

ILLUSTRATION 3

Throughout this symphony Haydn makes extensive use of the wind instruments. They come to the fore in the slow movement, a tripartite structure skillfully blending the two techniques of development and variation. They also dominate the minuet and trio. Here Haydn completely removes the social connotations of this form by distorting the rhythm with heavy, displaced accents on the third beat of the measure, and by the amusing caesura in the middle of a phrase at the end of the minuet. The use of winds to establish the character of a theme is particularly evident in the last movement (Illustration 4).

A drone bass sustained by horns and cellos accompanies the first violin melody which is later reinforced by the bucolic tones of the oboe. The effect is that of a bagpipe. This sound coupled with the heavy-footed, square-cut rhythm of the melody creates a theme suggesting a jovial peasant dance. In measures 19–20 and following, the winds are used as a body to give the continuation of the first theme its distinctive character of exaggerated accents. Such treatments of the winds reveal

ILLUSTRATION 4

ILLUSTRATION 4 (*continued*)

the extent to which the tonal resources of the orchestra have become a means of heightening the expressive qualities of the instrumental sonata. Now they enable the composer to express in tones ideas which formerly could be conveyed only through the explicit language of words.

In many respects the enormous output of the younger Mozart complements that of Haydn. Indeed, intimate contact with each other's quartets in the early 80's contributed vitally to the development of the personal style of both composers. But differences in personality and training served at the same time to separate and distinguish the musical thought of the two men. As a child genius, Mozart's extraordinary talents had been carefully nurtured by his father, Leopold, a highly competent court musician. He had been exposed to every aspect of the contemporary musical scene from Italian opera to the learned contrapuntal exercises of Padre Martini in the hopes that his incomparable creative power would gain for him a position in one of the most distinguished courts. But young Mozart was too conscious of the privileges and responsibilities of genius to accept with equanimity the role of a court musician with its connotations of menial servitude and restricted freedom.

In 1781 he escaped from the service of Archbishop Colloredo of Salzburg to begin the life of an independent artist—a life that was to end tragically in poverty and premature death. During his eleven years of independence in Vienna Mozart never abandoned hope of a high appointment in the Imperial service. Meanwhile he endeavored to sustain himself and his family by giving piano lessons and by accepting commissions for various occasional compositions. He saw, however, that the surest way to fame and fortune lay in the theatre or in the flourishing public concert life, where he could display his talents both as a performer and as a composer. For this reason he centered his artistic energy in these years primarily upon the opera and the piano concerto.

The conflict between the ideals of two ages can be seen most dramatically in the concerto. The concerto had embodied the Baroque ideal of symmetry attained through the balance of opposites. Some modifications had been made in its form and expression after the middle of the century, but no way had yet been found to reconcile this category with the ideals of the new age. Clearly the concerto represented a problem still to be solved. Of all the instrumental categories employed in the Classic Era, it is the one with the strongest tradition of the past behind it. It is indicative of the strength of this tradition that the concerto obstinately withstood the four-movement form of all classical music and clung to its standard three-movement form. (There had been concertos in the past with more or less than three movements, to be sure, but these were the exception rather than the rule.)

As its name implies, the element of contrast and of opposition between tutti and solo are inherent in the concerto. From its inception the concerto was almost always associated with virtuosity: the solo instrument was distinguished from the ensemble through its greater technical display and scintillating thematic materials. Thus the problem that faced Mozart was how to reconcile the element of contrast with the new thematic technique of his age. Still another challenge was the problem of reconciling the element of virtuosity with the contemporary demand for musical expressiveness. Soloistic figuration must be made something more than a superficial means of attaining brilliance.

Mozart's piano concertos offered various solutions to these problems. Throughout he maintains the sequence of three movements in the order fast, slow, fast, favored by the Baroque. However, the first of these movements is now invariably in sonata form, the second is usually a lyric andante, while the third is in most cases a rondo or rondo-sonata. From a formal standpoint the first movement is the most interesting of the three, for here one can see how structural principles of the Baroque concerto have been modified by those of the sonata form. It will be remem-

bered that the first movement of the Baroque concerto had been constructed out of an alternation between tutti and solo, each with its own
thematic material (see Chapter IX, p. 283). Such a plan would obviously
not be satisfactory for the sonata form with its two themes. If it were
followed, it is evident that the principal theme would be the exclusive
property of the orchestra while the soloist would be allotted only the
less important second theme. Thus he would be denied a significant role
in the presentation and development of the musical material.

To overcome this dilemma without completely destroying the distinctive roles of the tutti and solo, Mozart made use of a double exposition. The first exposition is the exclusive property of the orchestra, presenting the principal theme of the movement as well as a subsidiary
theme. This orchestral exposition functions in the same way as the initial
large ritornello of the Baroque concerto. That Mozart intends it to have
the same function is very evident in the fact that he does not modulate
to the second theme. Instead he presents it in the tonic, so that this first
exposition adheres to the older practice of stating the first ritornello
entirely in the tonic key.

The solo instrument makes its appearance at the beginning of the
second exposition, restating the principal theme of the movement. This
is followed by another theme in a related key which is the exclusive property of the soloist. In this way Mozart preserves something of the older
distinction between tutti and solo themes. Then the soloist continues with
the subsidiary theme, which may be the same as that already given in the
first exposition or may be a new one. In either case it is presented in the
normal key expected in a sonata, i.e., in the dominant or relative major. The usual development section follows the second exposition and
this in turn is succeeded by the recapitulation, where the thematic materials of the two expositions are now combined in a single statement by
the orchestra and soloist together.

When the movement seems about to end, the piano embarks upon
an improvisatory *cadenza*. Mozart's lofty conception of the concerto
required that the cadenza be more than the mere display of technical
virtuosity. Improvisation was to Mozart and to his contemporaries an
essential element of creative expression. The cadenza was intended for
further development of the thematic materials, and an opportunity to
display the taste and sensibility of the performer as well as his grasp of
the structural design of the movement. A conventional prolonged trill
concludes the cadenza, and the orchestra brings the movement to a close
with a few vigorous measures.

The remaining two movements did not present such formal difficulties. The slow movement was dominated by the lyricism of the piano's

melodic phrases, while the last movement resorted to the rondo form which with its schematic alternation of refrain and couplets or episodes was admirably adapted to the principle of opposition between tutti and solo that is the essential feature of the concerto. Although each of the piano concertos of Mozart has a distinctive personality of its own and represents a unique solution to the problems inherent in this category, certain characteristic features of Mozart's genius may be exemplified by the Concerto in C Major, K. 503.*

Written for an unusually large orchestra, this concerto reveals in its dimensions and in its complexity Mozart's elevated conception of this category. With a prodigality that sharply contrasts with Haydn's parsimony, Mozart lavishes upon the first movement a number of distinct musical ideas. The majestic first theme (Illustration 5) is intoned with the full sonority of the orchestra.

ILLUSTRATION 5

* Mozart's works are customarily referred to by a number preceded by the letter K, the number being that given to the work in the systematic catalog of Mozart's compositions made by Köchel.

ILLUSTRATION 5 (*continued*)

It consists of a series of chords declaimed in a decisive rhythm, and an appended motif presented by the bassoons and the oboes (measures 7–8). A balancing phrase continues the theme and leads to still another musical idea which, in a way that is highly characteristic of Mozart, has slipped mysteriously into the minor (Illustration 6). An extensive section

ILLUSTRATION 6

working with this motif leads to a decisive G major cadence (measures 44–50), followed by the appearance of the subsidiary theme of the exposition, which again veers between C minor and C major (measure 50 ff.). (Illustration 7) This in turn is followed by still another idea (measure 70 ff.) (Illustration 8), which forms an epilogue to the first exposition.

ILLUSTRATION 7

ILLUSTRATION 8

At the end of the orchestral exposition the piano makes its entrance (measure 91), tentatively and hesitantly, as if afraid to enter the dramatic pageant of this massive movement. Only slowly does it gain confidence and then, after a series of runs, restates the first theme. At this moment we can see a wonderful example of Mozart's sensitivity to musical style. Obviously he was aware that the forceful tones of the first theme could not be reproduced with the comparatively small volume of his instrument. To avoid the incongruity resulting from the piano's attempt to reproduce the sonorities of the full orchestra, he entrusts the first part of the theme to the orchestra while the piano replies with a filigree above the motifs of the winds. In the second part of the theme the piano echoes

ILLUSTRATION 9

ILLUSTRATION 9 (*continued*)

the resounding chords of the orchestra (Illustration 9). Such a detail reveals how intimate is the relationship of musical idea and instrumental style, for here Mozart has adapted the piano to the requirements of an essentially orchestral theme.

In measure 146 the piano introduces the solo theme in the key of E flat and then in measure 170 a new subsidiary theme in the dominant key of G (Illustration 10).

ILLUSTRATION 10

ILLUSTRATION 10 (*continued*)

With so many different melodic ideas it might appear that this movement would suffer from discursiveness, but Mozart has overcome this danger by establishing an affinity between the various motifs through a pattern of three eighth notes at the beginning of each of them. (Compare Illustrations 6, 7 and 10.) The importance of this figure as a unifying device is also to be seen in the fact that Mozart devotes the whole of his rather brief development to it, as it appears in the subsidiary theme of the first exposition.

The seriousness of this movement is maintained in the following movements, for even in the lyric second movement and the jovial finale the principles of the sonata form are to be found. The slow movement has all the elements of the sonata form, though the development section is little more than an extended quasi-improvisatory passage on a dominant pedal point. The last movement modifies the rondo form within the outlines of a sonata movement. Usually a rondo consists of a refrain alternating with episodes which introduce new thematic material, producing the following scheme:

$$R \ E_1 \ R \ E_2 \ R \ E_3 \ R$$

With its schematic opposition of recurrent refrain and new themes the rondo resembles the form utilized in the Baroque concerto. Whereas the ritornello of the Baroque concerto appears in various related keys, the rondo refrain is always stated in the tonic.

To bring this somewhat discursive form into line with contemporary ideals of organic unity Mozart frequently introduces elements of the sonata form, imposing upon the sequence of refrains and episodes the outlines of exposition, development and recapitulation. In this concerto, for instance, the first refrain (measures 1–32) is followed by a solo episode in which the piano presents two themes, the first (measures 33–48) in C and the second (measures 75–83) in the dominant G, the accepted key relationship of an exposition. After the solo episode the refrain returns in the tonic, serving to separate the exposition from the development section. The return to the tonic at this point is, of course, a deviation from the normal procedures of the sonata form.

The next episode, beginning in measure 145, introduces two new themes, one in A minor, the other in F major. The introduction of new themes at this point follows the procedures of the rondo form, but the second of the themes is submitted to an extensive development in conformity with the sonata form. The return of the tutti refrain in measure 237 heralds the beginning of the recapitulation. The solo episode following it re-presents the two themes of the first episode, the first in a curtailed and modified form, the second in the tonic key establishing the normal key relationships of a recapitulation. In measure 307 a fragmentary statement of the refrain initiates a concluding coda for piano and orchestra in which some of the preceding ideas are expanded upon. The adaptation of the rondo in this movement is an eloquent witness to the pervasive power of the sonata form and the ideals which it embodies.

Mozart's achievements in the concertos written for the concert-hall public are matched by his operas composed for the devotees of the musical theatre. Mozart's operas represent every phase and category of the contemporary operatic scene, from the declining opera seria to the ascendant opera buffa, from the grandiose French opera to the popular German Singspiel. Since the middle of the eighteenth century the opera buffa, or comic opera, had been growing in favor with the public. Although it borrowed the musical practices of recitative and aria from the well-established opera seria, it was totally removed in spirit from it. It consists of two rather than three acts, and the arias are written in simpler, more popular forms. The world of opera buffa was populated by comic figures, the buffoons of the *commedia dell' arte*, scheming servants, swaggering captains, and foolish pedants. The roles were sung by natural voices, including the bass voice which had not been tolerated in opera seria. Unlike the latter where the noble hero might be sung by a soprano, the opera buffa matched the voices to the personage, and the bass voice in particular was used in a comic manner (the *basso buffo*) for comic servants and the like.

A special feature of the opera buffa came to be the finale at the end of each act. Instead of the schematic alternation of recitative and aria of the older opera, this lively final scene involves most or all of the characters. The action progresses in consecutive musical numbers, including ensemble singing. Mozart's librettist, Da Ponte, has described the requirements of such a scene:

This *finale*, which has to be closely connected with the rest of the opera, is a sort of little comedy in itself and requires a fresh plot and a special interest of its own. This is the great occasion for showing off the genius of the composer, the ability of the singers, and the most effective "situation" of the drama. Recitative is excluded from it; everything is sung, and every style of singing must find a place in it—*adagio, allegro, andante, amabile, armonioso, strepitoso, arcistrepitoso, strepitosissimo,* and with this the said finale generally ends. This in the musicians' slang is called the *chiusa* or *stretta*—I suppose because it gives not one twinge but a hundred to the unhappy brain of the poet who has to write the words. In this finale it is a dogma of theatrical theology that all the singers should appear on the stage, even if there were three hundred of them, by ones, by twos, by threes, by sixes, by tens, by sixties, to sing solos, duets, trios, sextets, sessantets; and if the plot of the play does not allow of it, the poet must find some way of making the plot allow of it, in defiance of his judgment, of his reason, or of all the Aristotles on earth; and if he then finds his play going badly, so much the worse for him! *

Originally conceived as a form of ludicrous comedy, the opera buffa rapidly began to change its character in the middle of the century through the introduction of sentimental elements. Drawing its characters from everyday life, however much it might travesty them, the opera buffa seemed much closer to reality than the opera seria. Soon its figures were transformed into more or less serious individuals capable of experiencing the tender emotions of the world of sensibility. As a result, the opera buffa became less and less comic and increasingly moral and pathetic. Richardson's virtuous but persecuted Pamela, transplanted into the world of opera buffa as *La buona figliuola* by Piccinni in 1760, left scarcely a dry eye in all of Europe.

Mozart was intimately concerned with the changes taking place in comic opera. Indeed in *Don Giovanni* (1787) he carries his subject to emotional heights that actually transcend the limits of the category. In the Don Juan legend, Mozart and his librettist Da Ponte had chosen a theme that eighteenth-century society, to whom the rake was a familiar social type, found suitable for comic treatment. But the figure of Don Giovanni is transformed by Mozart and his poet from that of a mere profligate into a demonic being whose vital force no human power could withstand, a being that could meet its fate only through the intervention of some supernatural force. Effected in part by Da Ponte's handling of the libretto, this change is primarily accomplished by Mozart's musical characterization.

To represent the objects of Don Giovanni's unquenchable desire, Da Ponte chose three feminine figures from different stations in life: the aristocratic Donna Anna, the middle-class Donna Elvira, and the peasant lass Zerlina. Don Giovanni becomes involved with each of these in a series of attempted seductions, but the central action evolves from the opening scene in which Don Giovanni slays the Commendatore, the father of Donna Anna. Indifferent to his heinous crime, Don Giovanni

* Trans. E. J. Dent, *Mozart's Operas,* pp. 104–105.

continues his amorous adventures hindered only by the intervention of Elvira, Donna Anna, and her lover, Ottavio. Since none of these have the power to bring him to justice for the murder, the ghost of the Commendatore himself appears before Don Giovanni. Given an opportunity to repent, Don Giovanni, true to his character, still refuses, and is dragged down to Hell. The drama thus begins and ends with scenes of violence and theatrical horror. The intervening scenes, both comic and sentimental, serve to reveal the principal characters under the stress of different emotions and, above all, in their relationship to the irresistible Don.

The characters and action are brought to life not so much by Da Ponte's words as they are by Mozart's music. Insisting that a well-constructed libretto was essential to the success of a musical drama, Mozart maintained that "in an opera the poetry must be altogether the obedient daughter of the music." Here, surely, is remarkable evidence of the change in musical ideals that has taken place since Monteverdi stated that it was his intention "to make the words the mistress of the harmony and not the servant." To express the inner life of his characters Mozart utilizes every musical means at his disposal. To establish their individualities he assigns to each a specific musical style. Thus the noble Anna and the passionate Elvira are clothed in the elevated musical style of the opera seria, while Zerlina sings the simple ariettas of opera buffa and Singspiel. Leporello, Don Giovanni's comic servant, chatters away in the tones of the basso buffo. Don Giovanni's character, significantly, is not associated with any specific style, and this perhaps is one of Mozart's greatest strokes of genius. In making the Don sing in the style of the various characters he comes into contact with, the protean nature of this man is revealed. Forever changing and yet ever the same, Don Giovanni is at one moment the courtly lover as he serenades Elvira and in the next he has become a simple, unsophisticated man as he sings to Zerlina in the folk-like tones of the famous duet "La ci darem la mano" (Now give me your hand).

Although much of the action in this opera is presented in the conventional secco recitatives, Mozart also utilizes arias and ensembles to further the dramatic progression. Instead of being static moments as they were in opera of the past, the arias now serve to illuminate psychological changes and to carry the action on into its next phase. To achieve this effect Mozart frequently employs a form composed of two distinct parts joined by a half-cadence. The final part, in a faster tempo or meter than the previous one, intensifies or develops the emotional substance of the aria. This is exemplified by "La ci darem la mano" where in the second part the united voices, and the new tempo and meter reveal Zerlina's sudden acquiescence to the blandishments of Don Giovanni. This duet portrays the transformation of Zerlina's reluctance into willing compliance, and likewise begins a new episode in the history of the Don's attempted seductions.

The use of the formal principles of music to carry on the organic evolution of the drama is particularly apparent in the ensemble finales. The dramatic climax of the opera occurs during the last part of Act II as Don Giovanni confronts the ghost of the Commendatore. Mozart sets this scene and the concluding moral as a musical whole. At the opening of this finale the Don sits down to dine, having invited the statue of the murdered man to join him. Served by Leporello, he commences to eat while his private band entertains him with excerpts from three current operas. His banter with Leporello is interrupted unexpectedly by Elvira who has come to beg the Don to repent. Rudely rejected, she angrily quits the room. Suddenly she screams, and Leporello is sent after her, but he too cries out in terror and returns, trembling and incoherent at the sight of the approaching apparition. Since he refuses to open the door to the insistent series of knocks, the Don himself opens it to reveal the marble statue at the threshold. The Commendatore announces he has come to summon Don Giovanni to Hell in payment of his wrongdoing, bidding him repent while there is still time. Don Giovanni heroically refuses to bow even to supernatural forces and, as the apparition fades from his view, is carried off to the infernal regions amid lightning, thunder and the chanting of an invisible chorus. After his final cry is heard, the lights go up upon all the other characters. Once Leporello has described the catastrophe, each briefly states his future course of action, and all together join in singing the moral of the piece.

Each episode, gay and ironic, tragic and terrifying, tender and brilliant, contained in this climactic solution to the drama is defined as an entity by specific musical materials. The uninterrupted flow of music is organized in four main divisions, set apart from each other by tempo, key, and rhythm. Each together with its clearly articulated subordinate parts is tied to its neighbor by harmonic relationships so as to form a diversified but organic unity, analogous to the structure of a symphony, the focal center of which is the solemn dialogue in D minor between the two protagonists. Mozart's sensitive perception of musical values has endowed the personages and the dramatic events with emotional qualities that unite the characteristic within the universal.

Just as Mozart had been led by his individual genius to expand the musical principles of the older Haydn, so Beethoven carried the premises of his predecessors to new conclusions. The character and the ideals of Beethoven, which were to have a decisive effect upon his musical work, had already been firmly fixed before his arrival in Vienna in 1792. In the enlightened city of Bonn, where Beethoven had spent his youth as one of the court musicians, he had absorbed the spirit of Kant's philosophy and Schiller's enthusiasm for art as a force to elevate mankind. From Kant he took over the conception of freedom within law—the necessity and yet the freedom of moral action stated in Kant's Categorical Imperative. Beethoven coupled this idea with the concept of genius, holding that genius, having been endowed with unique talents by the Creator, must not abuse its powers but must employ them for the benefit of mankind. Through his art the man of genius must ennoble and transform mankind.

Beethoven expresses his feeling of duty and obligation towards his creative gifts very movingly in the "Heiligenstadt Testament" of 1802. In this most personal document, written in the depths of despair over his increasing deafness, he confesses: "I almost reached the point of putting an end to my life—only art it was that held me back, ah, it seemed impossible to leave the world until I had brought forth all that I felt called up to produce. . . . It was virtue that upheld me in misery, to it next to my art I owe the fact that I did not end my life by my own hand." From this it is apparent that art and morality were the sustaining forces in Beethoven's life. Indeed, it might be said that they are in reality only one inseparable power. Throughout his life Beethoven struggled to impart through his music ideas of a moral or ethical nature. Works, such as the *Eroica Symphony*, the *Missa Solemnis*, and the *Ninth Symphony*, were created to embody concepts of moral or ethical import that transcend the realm of the personal and individual and enter the region of universal law.

Beethoven's adherence to the Classical ideal of the artwork as an expression of the particular within the universal is demonstrated by his choice of the instrumental sonata as the vehicle for his thought. So completely did the progressive order of the sonata conform to the aesthetic ideals of Beethoven that it remained valid for his entire creative career. The history of Beethoven's art is the history of his unceasing effort to create an art form that intensifies the contrast within and between its movements while increasing the unity of the whole—a unity that seems to be the product of a natural, organic growth.

His struggle to attain this ideal can be traced in his sketchbooks. They bear witness to the genesis of his musical themes, and to the long process of evolution during which Beethoven shapes and modifies the original idea to conform to his mental picture of the complete work. But his artistic aims are most clearly revealed in his finished works of art which, for all their diversity, manifest a single-minded purpose. In following the sequence of Beethoven's musical compositions it becomes apparent that the innovations in successive works are the result of two separate, yet intimately related musical ideals: to attain a musical form in which the process of development begins with the opening notes and continues without interruption to the end of the movement; and to create a sequence of movements which proceeds to a climactic conclusion in the finale.

In the thirty-two piano sonatas the evolution of Beethoven's musical style may be discerned. This category was of central importance to Beethoven, in all probability because he was himself a virtuoso performer on the pianoforte. Like Mozart, he first captured the Viennese public in his role as a concert performer. To sustain himself in this position he wrote, in the first decade of his life in Vienna, no less than twenty of his thirty-two piano sonatas and three of his five piano concertos.

From the outset his piano sonatas reveal signs of experimentation to find the proper solution to his artistic demands. In the first sonatas Beethoven fluctuates between three- and four-movement forms, as if seeking the ideal succession. It is not until his opus 26 (1801) that he begins to experiment with different forms for the individual movements. In this sonata we find an unusual sequence: theme and variations, scherzo, funeral march on the death of a hero, and rondo. An even more radical solution is to be found in the two sonatas of opus 27, both of which are designated as *Sonata quasi una fantasia*. In both of these sonatas the initial movements are made to proceed without a pause into the finale. To create a work which moves organically to a climax he increases the weight and importance of the final movement. At the same time the quasi-improvisatory nature of the initial movement bears the same relation to the finale as the Baroque prelude bore to the fugue.

The fantasie sonatas, however, had led Beethoven away from the accepted standards of the sonata form. Realizing this, he returns to a more normal grouping of movements in the three sonatas of opus 31 without abandoning the advances made in the preceding sonatas. In the second of these sonatas, the so-called "Tempest" sonata, Beethoven successfully reconciles the element of free improvisation with the classical concept of thematic development. At the same time he unifies all three movements through the use of the sonata form. The thematic material of the entire sonata is contained in the opening measures of the first movement, where two contrasting motifs are presented. The first of these is nothing but an arpeggio, only the last four notes of which are given specific rhythmic values. The effect of this arpeggio is as if the performer were preludizing before the movement begins. Its dreamlike, indecisive quality is emphasized by the fact that the arpeggio begins not upon the root of the chord (A) but upon the third (C♯). This motif is followed by one of violent contrast, but of equally elemental substance, for it consists of nothing but descending seconds (Illustration 11).

ILLUSTRATION 11

This fragmentary, unbalanced material bears little resemblance to themes as conceived by Haydn or Mozart for their sonatas. By comparison with the opening theme of Haydn's quartet (Illustration 2), Beethoven's musical idea is neither symmetrical, nor self-enclosed. The two elements of which it is composed seem to have nothing to do with one another, and neither is resolved. This is a theme which takes on meaning only as it begins to grow and evolve in the hands of the composer. Its condition and nature demand development, and by this process Beethoven derives the fully formed themes of this movement. It first takes the form shown in Illustration 12. Here the arpeggio forms the rising figure in the

ILLUSTRATION 12

left hand. It is balanced by the phrase in the treble clef in which the minor seconds of the second motif are especially prominent. The two segments forming the subordinate theme in the dominant are derived from the second motif (Illustration 13).

It thus appears that the exposition has become in fact a developmental section. The process of growth is continued without a pause in the development section proper, where three long arpeggios initiate the working out of the themes. Nor does it end even here. In the recapitulation the material of the section linking the opening theme with the subsidiary theme is entirely reworked. Most notable of all is the expansion

ILLUSTRATION 13

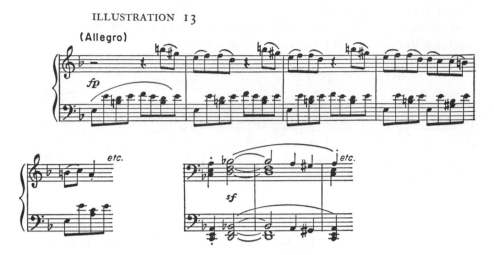

of the initial arpeggio into a poignant recitative marked *con espressione e semplice* (to be played with expression and simply). It is as if the burden of emotion had become too much for the inarticulate tones of the piano, necessitating the vocal accents of recitative to communicate its meaning (Illustration 14).

ILLUSTRATION 14

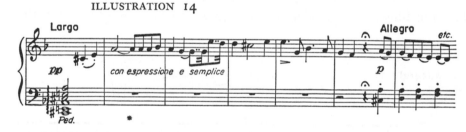

The movement ends with the rumble of the arpeggio dying away in the lower register of the piano, but its force is not yet spent. It provides the initial impetus for the first theme of the Adagio movement, and the rhythmic figure which dominates the first theme of the finale. The second motif of the opening movement also reappears in measure 43 of the finale to form the subsidiary theme (Illustration 15).

In the Tempest Sonata Beethoven formulates an ideal of development and integration that he was to uphold in most of his subsequent compositions. This sonata anticipates the *Eroica Symphony* (1803) which, with its idealized expression of heroism and its enormously expanded developmental sections, marks the beginning of his artistic maturity. In his continuing quest to deepen the content of his works and to establish the finale as the climax of the movement, Beethoven renewed his study of the

ILLUSTRATION 15

fugues of Johann Sebastian Bach. The fruits of this study are visible in the piano sonatas and string quartets written after 1815 in which fugal techniques are introduced into the final movements to give them the desired profundity and emphasis. The reversion to polyphonic techniques did not lead to an empty imitation of the past. On the contrary, Beethoven transformed them into a type of expression uniquely his own. As he once said, "To make fugues requires no particular skill. In my student days I made dozens of them. But the fancy wishes also to assert its privileges, and today a new and really poetical element must be introduced into the old traditional form." An examination of these late works reveals how freely and with what licenses Beethoven has bent the rigid structure of the fugue to fit the needs of his own form of expressiveness.

The desire to create works that progress with an inexorable emotional logic to a climactic finale led Beethoven to compose the most astonishing of all his masterpieces, the monumental and epoch-making *Ninth Symphony*, opus 125. Although this symphony was not completed until 1823, sketches for it may be found in notebooks going as far back as 1815. While its themes were still in the process of gestation, he conceived the idea of another symphony, one which would introduce a choral piece as a finale. But as the first three movements of what was to become the *Ninth Symphony* began to take shape in his mind, he came to the realization that their grandiose proportions required a finale of extraordinary power and drama. Thus he decided to make this symphony his choral symphony, choosing as a text for the finale Schiller's *Ode to Joy*. In the pursuit of an aesthetic ideal, Beethoven was thus led to break down the barriers which separated instrumental and vocal music. The introduction of voices into a category which had been purely instrumental was to have far-reaching consequences in the Romantic era. Indeed this symphony was hailed as the dawn of a new musical epoch in which the limitations and restrictions of the separate categories of vocal and instrumental music were to be transcended in a new synthesis of the arts.

The dimensions of the Ninth Symphony are such that the movements defy description in our limited space. The first movement, as long as an entire symphony of the early Classical period, is constructed as a sonata form with exposition, development, and recapitulation. The process of development continues through a final coda of unprecedented proportions. The first theme grows out of a germinal motif, an open fifth (A–E) lacking definition as either a major or minor chord and imbued with a sense of mystery by the *tremolando* of the strings. Against this murmur the theme gradually takes shape, a plunging fifth and fourth (E–A–E), gathering rhythmic force until it gives birth to the definitive form of the first theme in the tonic key of D minor with the last note of measure 16 (Illustration 16).

The tremendous force of the first movement is continued in the Gargantuan humor of the scherzo which follows it. But the intense seriousness of the scherzo's artistic form is seen in the use of the sonata form and in the fugal handling of the first theme. Beethoven then introduces the expressive slow movement, reversing the order of the two inner move-

ILLUSTRATION 16

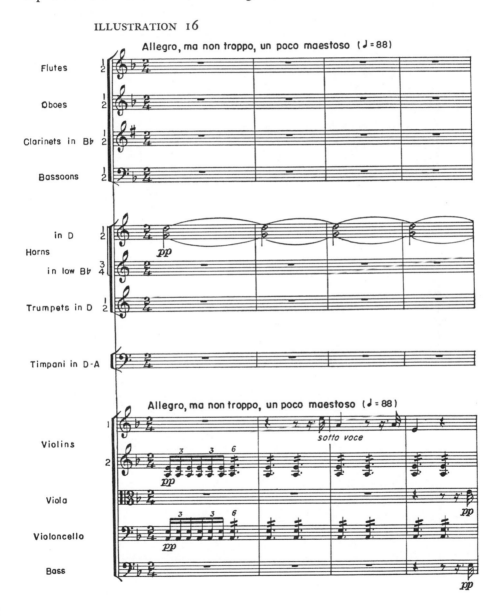

ILLUSTRATION 16 (*continued*)

ILLUSTRATION 16 (*continued*)

ments in order that the lyric melodies of this Adagio movement may subtly prepare us for the appearance of the human voices in the last movement.

The problem of how to introduce the voices in the final movement caused Beethoven endless anguish before he found a perfect solution. He recognized that he must somehow justify the introduction of voices in a work which has up to this moment remained wholly within the sphere of a purely instrumental symphony. The appearance of the voices must

ILLUSTRATION 16 (*continued*)

be made both meaningful and necessary. His solution to this problem is so successful that one would readily believe that he had had this movement in mind from the moment when he first began the Ninth Symphony.

The movement begins abruptly with a harsh, dissonant chord followed by an agitated clamor of wind instruments. It would appear, after all, that the last movement is to be an instrumental piece and furthermore that it is to be tragic in nature. But suddenly the winds are stilled by the entrance of the cellos and double basses who declaim a melodic line marked "to be performed in the character of a recitative." They are trying to say something, but the winds misunderstand and resume their dissonant tones, only to be interrupted once again by the instrumental recitative.

The message of the low strings is known from Beethoven's sketchbook; they are urging the winds to abandon their unhappy cries and to sing a more joyous theme: "Not these tones, they remind us of our doubts." As if understanding the plea of the strings, the orchestra softly suggests the theme of the first movement. But this too is rejected: "Oh no, not this theme either! I want something more pleasing." Then the orchestra suggests the scherzo theme, which is refused as well as the theme of the Adagio. Finally the winds introduce the first phrases of a new theme, which is enthusiastically hailed by the cellos and basses: "Yes, this is it; now we have found it. Joy!" Taking up the new theme, the low strings sing the famous Ode to Joy melody (Illustration 17), upon which the final movement is to be built. Gradually they are joined by the entire orchestra.

ILLUSTRATION 17

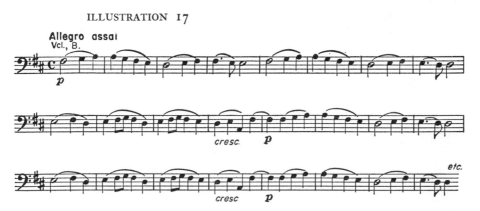

After this dramatic introduction we are prepared for the unprecedented choral movement that now begins. The orchestra once again returns to its discordant theme, but this time it is interrupted by the *human* voice, a baritone who declaims: "O friends, not these tones! Let us sing something more pleasing and more joyous!" and he begins to sing the words of Schiller's poem. Beethoven had been drawn to this ode as early as 1793 because it envisages the Utopia to be gained by humanity, if men will love one another and experience the joy that such love will bring. Schiller had conceived his poem as a series of stanzas with choral refrain. Beethoven preserves the poetic form of solo and choral response, though he uses only part of Schiller's text and changes the order of the stanzas to suit his own purposes.

This massive movement is divided into four large sections. In the first, the baritone soloist describes what joy will accomplish: the brotherhood of man and the attainment of the Elysian community. The lower voices repeat this goal in a refain and then the quartet of soloists inform us what conditions are necessary to attain this Elysium: only those who have known the power of love and joy may reach this state. Again the chorus repeats the lesson and then the quartet goes on to speak of the highest joy of all, the attainment of God through love (*und der Cherub steht vor Gott*), an idea that is stressed through climactic repetition by the chorus. All of the first section has been constructed upon the joy theme.

ILLUSTRATION 18

The next section is marked by an abrupt change of key (to B flat) and of meter (to 6/8) and the joy theme is transformed into a march rhythm. This section is devoted to an exhortation by the tenor soloist, echoed by a male chorus, to strive like heroes to reach Elysium. Beethoven's choice of men's voices and a march rhythm was obviously made to emphasize the heroic nature of this struggle. An interesting sound effect in this section is the "Turkish" music of the orchestra, a distinctive quality of tone created by the addition of a piccolo to the orchestra and the use of triangle, cymbals and bass drum. Beethoven's intention in using this peculiar tonal color is clear: having chosen a march to portray the heroic idea, he must somehow still convey the essential idea of joy. So he utilizes the light-hearted sounds of the "Turkish" music, which were very popular at this time. After the men have finished singing, the orchestra develops the march theme until the section concludes with the chorus once again singing the joy theme in the original key of D major.

The third section is initiated in the key of G major and an *andante maestoso* tempo. The text stresses the union of all mankind with one another and with God. Beethoven expresses this idea with a new theme sung only by the chorus (Illustration 18), a theme that suggests with its great upward leap of a ninth the vastness of this concept.

The fourth section begins with a double fugue based on the joy theme and the theme of the preceding section. In thus joining the two, Beethoven conveys the idea that the brotherhood of man, the future Utopia, has grown out of the concept of love and joy. The movement then culminates in a rhapsodic repetition of previous ideas in which chorus, soloists and orchestra join together to praise and exalt this glorious vision.

In this symphony Beethoven has carried the ideals of the Classic Era to their ultimate limit. Yet he has not violated them, for all the vast dimensions and novel finale of this work. The unprecedented size of this symphony is, after all is said, only the result of the Classical conception that the working out of an idea depends upon its intrinsic nature. Beethoven's titanic concept demanded a correspondingly vast canvas. But even when dealing with this highly individual subject matter, Beethoven did not forsake the principles of universality. He expresses his ideas within the confines of the sonata form and even the chorale finale is erected upon the generalized principles of the rondo, as the alternation of joy theme and episodes reveals. Beethoven's Romantic successors, however, perceived in this work not its universality but its uniqueness and individuality, interpreting it as the signpost pointing to the future, to the new age of subjective individualism.

XI THE AGE OF GENIUS

Part II. Romanticism

THE BASIC MEANING of the verb "define" is to establish the boundaries or limits of something. It would therefore seem paradoxical to attempt a definition of Romanticism, for there is not *a* Romanticism but only Romanticism*s*. What common denominator is there between a Wordsworth and a Byron, or between a Chopin and a Berlioz? How is it possible to reconcile those two antithetical figures, Wagner and Brahms? Yet even as we raise these questions we feel no hesitation in calling all of these men Romantics. Indeed the very fact that we do see differences between them provides us with a clue to the meaning of Romanticism: its essence lies in the universal belief in the necessity of originality and hence of difference.

We are confronted here with a movement unique in history. Unlike the other ages studied thus far which had a core of accepted beliefs drawing men together, Romanticism has as its centrum a single idea driving men in opposite directions. Whereas other epochs may be described as being ruled by centripetal force, Romanticism is by nature a centrifugal movement. Therefore the only way to know Romanticism fully is to trace the trajectory described by each individual as he pursues his course of independence and difference. Such a method is patently impossible within the limited scope of a history of this size. But an alternative approach is open to us, and this is the way we must choose. The idea of differentness and individuation is accompanied by certain corollaries and implications that appear in one guise or another through the Romantic era. If we follow these ideas, we shall gain a partial insight into the nature of Romanticism and the influences at work upon the individual artist.

The door to Romantic philosophy had been opened by Kant with his supposition that the sources of human knowledge could be traced back to certain purely subjective a priori premises of the faculties of the mind. From here it is only a short distance to the position that what we know is the creation of our own thinking. Since in the act of knowing we impose upon the world the patterns of our thought, does it not follow that the world we know has been produced by our own ego? One might describe this world created by the thinking being as a circle within which lies all that the ego has thought and outside of which lies the world of finite appearances. The area of this circle is limited only by the ability of the individual ego to assert itself. Theoretically its perimeter could be pushed outward to infinity by the power of thought. It is only as we extend our consciousness that the world comes into being, and for this reason the only valid world is not that of objective reality but that of ideas.

Now there are two ways in which the world of ideas can be made known to others. One is by intellection, and this is the way of the philosopher. The other is by materializing the idea in physical form, and this is the way of the artist. Thus the artist and the philosopher are essentially one and the same, differing only in their modes of operation. Each creates his world of ideas, but the philosopher works wholly within the realm of concepts, while the artist engages in the paradoxical task of attempting to reveal the Ideal within the Real. But who is this artist who is philosopher and law giver, prophet and seer? He is, of course, the divinely inspired genius, the individual uniquely endowed with a temperament and ability to intuit the invisible world of the Ideal and to capture it with the silken threads of his art. Without the guidance of rules—for he himself frames the laws that govern his created world— he brings back from each expedition into the limitless regions of the mind a unique and different trophy, a fresh and original work of art.

The artist does not endeavor to reproduce the real appearance of things, but to re-create them in the form in which his imagination has represented them. This subjective art was early given the name "Romantic" by the Germans. It is an adjective originally derived from the old French "roman," a tale of chivalric deeds lavishly strewn with magical events. During the seventeenth and eighteenth centuries this adjective was used in a derisive sense for literary works in which the wonderful and improbable prevail over reality. However, a more favorable connotation began to creep into the word in the eighteenth century. Increasingly it was applied to scenery and objects that seemed to possess some indefinable quality of charm and grace. It became synonymous with the adjectives, interesting, charming, or exciting. In this way it assumed a subjective character, for it describes not a quality of the object, but the reaction of the beholder to the object. The subjective element implicit in the word "romantic" makes it an apt term for the new movement arising at the end of the eighteenth century.

Romantic art is an instinctive art. The artist cannot explain how he has created his masterpiece, for in a very real sense it is the product of nature working through genius. He must wait for inspiration to seize him in order to create. The tools of reason which had aided the artist of the Enlightenment are useless to the Romanticist except perhaps for the secondary task of weighing and polishing the pure ore of the imagination. The reliance upon inspiration and instinctive invention is revealed in some of Chopin's remarks about his own compositions.

The *Adagio* of the new concerto is in E major. It is not meant to be loud, it's more of a romance, quiet, melancholy; it should give the impression of gazing tenderly at a place which brings to the mind a thousand dear memories. It is a sort of meditation in beautiful spring weather, but by moonlight. That is why I have *muted* the accompaniment. . . . Perhaps that's bad, but why should one be ashamed of writing badly in spite of knowing better—it's results that show errors. Here you doubtless observe my tendency to do wrong against my will. . . . Sometimes I am satisfied with my violoncello sonata, sometimes not. I throw it into the corner, then take it up again. . . . When one does a thing, it appears good, otherwise one would not write it. Only later comes reflection, and one discards or accepts the thing. Time is the best censor, and patience a most excellent teacher.*

The creativity of the genius is also conditioned by the special qualities of soul and mind that nature has bestowed upon him. He can only follow the bent of his own peculiar talent. For this reason the Romantic musician is frequently a specialist. He may, like Chopin, write only for the pianoforte, or he may, like Hugo Wolf, compose songs almost exclusively. Even when his genius has sufficient range to give him freedom in all fields of music, the Romantic composer frequently does not approach all forms simultaneously but is drawn to one or another of them as the circumstances of his life may dictate. Thus the first period of Robert Schumann's life as a composer was devoted almost entirely to music for the piano, a preoccupation occasioned by his intense, though thwarted, desire to become a piano virtuoso. This rather narrow concentration of his energies was finally broken by a sudden outpouring of

* *Chopin's Letters,* collected by Henryk Opieński, tr. E. L. Voynich, pp. 88–89; 311–312,

song inspired by his love for Clara Wieck. Only after his marriage to Clara did Schumann begin to compose in all categories of music. Even then the Romantic predicament was still apparent, for almost without exception his first essay in a new category proved to be his best. The power of inspiration seemed to exhaust itself after the initial excitement and challenge of a new musical form had been met. Schumann himself recognized this, confessing: "One never composes so freshly as when one first begins to cultivate a new category."

The Romantic dependence upon the lightning bolt of inspiration has important consequences for music. It leads on the one hand to brief, aphoristic compositions, the product of a sudden communion with the Ideal. These fleeting moments of imagination are the *Impromptus*, the *Moments Musicals* (in Schubert's impromptu spelling), the *Leaves from an Album*, that occupy so large a place in the musical repertory of the nineteenth century. On the other hand, larger compositions tend to become loose, sprawling works, patchworks or mosaics of individual inspirations. Instead of the tight, cohesive unity of the Classical composers we find a new beauty of prolixity, the "heavenly lengths" that Schumann discovers in the symphonies of Schubert.

With such an ideal of composition the Classical conception of thematic development is no longer valid. A theme is not something to be worked with, a substance to be shaped by the hand of the artist. On the contrary, it is something divinely given, and it is not to be mangled on the Procrustean bed of reason. The Romantic artist does not develop his theme, for it is already complete; instead he displays it in different lights and in new settings. The colors of his gem seem to change as he exposes it to the beam of his imagination, but he would not dream of cutting new surfaces in it. On this matter nothing is more revealing than a comparison of the working methods of Beethoven and Chopin. From the notebooks of Beethoven we are able to trace the process by which he shapes and re-shapes his first crude musical idea until it takes the form of the theme we know in the finished composition. A conscious intelligence is at work upon the theme, modifying it to meet the demands of its creator. How different this is from Chopin who can only wait in solitude for further inspiration to complete the deficiencies of his first-born.

The art of the Romanticist is the product of his spiritual and emotional condition. He sees in things the aspects of his own being. Nature moves in the rhythms of the artist's jubilation or despair and reveals the hues of his imagination: an autumn leaf becomes something feverish and pestilential; a drop of rain is transformed into a tear. Romantic art is thus an effusion of the emotions, which finds its most characteristic expression in both literature and music in the form of lyricism. As a consequence the song or *lied* becomes one of the most important forms of musical utterance in the nineteenth century. Song-like melody also permeates all types of instrumental music. One needs only to cite the numerous instrumental works of Schubert built upon material drawn from his songs, the *Songs without Words* that Mendelssohn wrote for the piano, or, late in the century, the symphonies of Gustav Mahler who strove for a synthesis of the lyric and the monumental.

The emphasis on melody profoundly affects what a composer can do in his compositions, for melody is something which must have a certain cohesion and unity in itself. Melody is self-enclosed, and phrase must follow phrase with a certain logic; there must be inner correspondences and points of repose. For this reason themes conceived primarily as melodies are unsuited for development, because they would lose their identity in the process. Accordingly the Romantic predilection for the lyrical means an abdication of the Classical ideal of development. Repetition takes its place: the melody may be restated in new instrumental and harmonic colors, but it is not changed.

The desire of the Romantic artist to portray the Ideal within the Real, the Infinite within the Finite, influenced his choice of subject matter. For the men of the nineteenth century there was an open contradiction between the world of the Ideal to which they aspired and the increasingly materialistic society in which they lived. Finding it difficult to obscure or deny the insistent factuality of everyday existence, they turned to remote historical epochs and far-away lands which they could re-create in their own image, unhampered by the unyielding surfaces of reality. "Everything distant becomes poetry," said Novalis, "remote mountains, distant men and far-off events. Everything becomes Romantic." And Wordsworth's Solitary Reaper dreams of "old, unhappy, far-off things, and battles long ago." The Romanticist is drawn to the myths of antiquity and the legends of mediaeval chivalry. He is fascinated by the Orient and the unexplored regions of the American continents. The literature of foreign countries, the folksongs and hoary tales of the people, the mysteries of the Catholic church, all these provide grist for the romantic imagination.

To suggest his content the Romantic musician may utilize musical idioms for their evocative qualities. Frequently he models his songs upon ancient ballads or tries to capture the naïveté of the folk song. In his instrumental works he is inclined to use descriptive titles which help to orient the imagination of the listener. He may, like Chopin, call his works *ballades* or *nocturnes*, the latter title being quintessentially Romantic, for the Romanticist loves to look on what he calls the night-side of things, the shadowy world that lies behind reality. Or he may use more specific titles: "The Wild Huntsman," "St. Francis Feeding the Birds," "In a Gondola"; and may publish collections of such works under a title such as *Carnaval* (Schumann) or *Années de Pèlerinage* (Liszt). He may compose an overture on Byron's *Manfred* (Schumann), Shakespeare's *Romeo and Juliet* (Tchaikowski), or on a natural scene such as *Fingal's Cave* (Mendelssohn). These are not overtures in the proper sense of the word, for they are not an introduction to anything: they are instead a musical evocation of the subject matter indicated by the title.

Intent upon presenting his idea, the Romantic musician refuses to be shackled by any preconceived notions of musical form. On the contrary, his idea must have its own particular form: the sequence of musical ideas must obey the demands of the idea to be expressed. For this reason the Romantic composers eschewed the titles of the older categories of music, such as the sonata or rondo, which imply a certain standardized progression. Even when they chose to call their works symphonies or sonatas, they frequently departed from the expected forms and sequences of movements to accommodate their unique ideas.

Though the musicians of the nineteenth century may give titles to their works, this does not mean that they intend to present a realistic portrayal of the subject. Their musical realization is meant to penetrate to its inner meaning which cannot be apprehended by reason but only by an unconscious response in the souls of the auditors. "The artwork is not that which is presented to thought, but is that which stirs the heart through perceiving it" (Kleist). Music, the Romanticists held, was the art most suited to the expression of the Ideal because of the very imprecision of its language. Speaking immediately to the spirit in images that need no definition, music can transcend literature and the visual arts which must use precise and limited symbols.

"Music," said Tieck, "is the ultimate breath of the spirit, the finest element, out of which the most secret dreams of the soul are drawn as out of an invisible brook. . . . It is an organ, finer than speech, perhaps more tender than man's thoughts; it enables one to think thoughts without that tiresome circumlocution of words. Here feeling, fantasy, and force of thought are one and the same . . . : the soul is at home in the artwork; the artwork lives and rules in our innermost spirit; we are in agreement—our spirit plays the same melody as that of the artist; and we deem it unnecessary to add further proofs and to conduct long-winded speeches about it." With such a conception of music the composer of the nineteenth century felt justified and even obliged to reveal the inner essence of works of literature through the purer language of music.

In seeking to reveal the Infinite and Ideal within the Real, the composer found himself in a paradoxical situation. His task was to depict something which by definition could never be known in the world of reality. Seemingly then the musical material should be vague and ambiguous, as it sometimes is. But the composer's desire to realize the Ideal as fully as possible led him to do so as explicitly as possible. The rhythmic and melodic contours and the individual harmonies of his thematic material must all conspire to reveal the image in the mind of the creator. He draws upon every suggestive resource at his disposal: the galloping hoofs of horses are caught in a driving rhythm; the call of a bird and the murmuring of water are suggested in the tones of a flute or clarinet; the sound of a harp opens heavenly vistas before us, while the tones of a hunting horn evoke the mysterious life of the forest. In creating such a full vocabulary of musical symbols, the Romantic musician opened the door to the crassest realism. Before the era draws to a close we are to hear a severed head bounce down the steps of the scaffold in the *Symphonie Fantastique* of Berlioz, and we are to listen to the homely sounds of family life in Richard Strauss's *Sinfonia domestica.*

The composers who came of age during the flood tide of the romantic movement around 1830 did not turn entirely against the forms and categories cultivated by their predecessors. Instead they attempted to carry them on, modifying them in accordance with their personal visions. Clearly the instrumental sonata, whether composed for media suitable to the intimacy of the middle-class drawing rooms or to the larger confines of the concert hall, offered the most immediate means of communication. Above all other categories in power and prestige towered the symphony.

But how was the intensity of feeling, the fleeting perceptions of infinity, the exaltation of revelation to be conveyed within the confines of this universal form? Was it possible to express the uniqueness, the indefinable mystery of personal experience within the exemplary formalism of the sonata? Were not the clear lines and the carefully conceived "classical" proportions of the instrumental works of Haydn and Mozart at odds with the expression of romantic feelings? On the other hand, the innovations of Beethoven seemed to point to a more promising path. For were not the sharp rhythmic motifs, the syncopations, the startlingly abrupt changes in dynamics, the liberal use of dissonances, the juxtaposition of distant tonalities, and, above all, the violence of Beethoven's music romantic? To many of his successors these qualities were esteemed more than the magnificently coordinated structure of his symphonies. Together with his eccentric behavior they seemed to constitute the features of a romantic revolutionary artist—an irresistible but bewildering model to emulate.

Closest in all ways to the geographical and spiritual center of the

symphony was Franz Schubert (1797–1828). Living in the very shadow
of Beethoven he felt himself inhibited by the force and stature of his
music, observing on one occasion, "After Beethoven, who can achieve
any more?" In only his last two symphonies (the "Unfinished" in B minor
and the Symphony in C major) does he succeed in creating masterpieces
which speak in his own personal style. In the work of the younger
generation of German composers such as Felix Mendelssohn (1809–1847)
and Robert Schumann (1810–1856), the symphony and the instrumental
sonata declined even further in prominence. A man of conservative,
aristocratic culture, with a delicate, sensitive temperament, Mendelssohn
seems to have been largely impervious to the work of Beethoven other
than the Pastorale Symphony. His own symphonies are more closely
related in proportions and formal clarity to those of the earlier Viennese
composers, though they abound with lyrical melodies. Their character
is also modified by an association with extra-musical subject matter—
the picturesque in the *Italian* or *Scotch Symphonies*, the historical in the
Reformation Symphony. Beethoven's *Sixth Symphony* with its combination of expression and tone-painting inspired by pastoral scenes also
provided the most congenial model for the symphonies of Schumann. But
the problem of reconciling the ethical legacy of Beethoven's symphonies
with his own introspective muse became increasingly insoluble to him.
Alone among the composers of this generation, Hector Berlioz (1803–
1869) in France accepted the full implications of Beethoven's symphonic
achievement when composing his intensely subjective symphonies.

The desire to express the uniqueness of emotional experience found
new outlets in the small, intimate forms of the lied and the piano genre
pieces. Instead of the sonata or symphony, the further development of
which seemed at once so desirable and so difficult, the majority of composers lavished their finest talents upon these new categories. Unlike the
sonata neither of them possessed any "ideal" form or dimensions. Both are
the product of direct inspiration rather than considered or extensive reflection. A poem, an external image or event, even a momentary emotion
or mood may provide the impetus for an internal experience of which
music may be the concrete, if ephemeral, evidence. Such music is addressed to an intimate audience of sensitive spirits—as "ideal" in its own
very different way as the universal audience to whom Beethoven addressed his symphonies.

The qualities of the genre compositions are controlled by the composer's vision of the resources and potentialities of the instrument for
which he is writing. More than any other instrument, the pianoforte
seemed to afford the most enchanting possibilities. Its rapid mechanical
development during the early years of the century increased its range

of sonorities, providing the creative performer with endless new resources. Its richness and volume seemed to rival that of the full orchestra,
while in incandescent brilliance it had no equal. Its variety of tone colors
was capable of suggesting unusual moods or evoking mysterious sensations. The creative thought of all but a few composers throughout the
nineteenth century was profoundly influenced by the sound of the piano.

In addition to its use as a poetic, solo instrument, the piano rapidly
supplanted the harpsichord as the accompaniment of the solo voice in
the second half of the eighteenth century. At the same time, the solo song
or lied began to appear in great quantities as the Baroque chamber
cantata became outmoded. Already in the middle years of the eighteenth
century many collections of simple, strophic songs for domestic performance were published in Berlin. And in the later years of the century
many anthologies of folk-song texts provided new romantic materials
for settings for voice and keyboard instrument. The freedom of style,
straightforward sentiment, and picturesque qualities of this folk-poetry,
in the form of ballad or short lyric, set it apart from conventional
literary forms. Its appearance was one of the many stimuli which produced an ever-growing quantity of lyrical poetry from the pens of German poets from 1790 onwards. These poetic materials, both new and
old, so varied in proportions, scope and content, seemed to demand
musical settings, a situation to which many composers were quick to
respond.

Generally speaking, composers set individual poems to music rather
than related groups or cycles. When a folk-text was published with an
existing melody they were content to arrange a simple accompaniment,
which, together with the melody, was repeated for each stanza of the
poem. Yet North German composers like Johann Friedrich Reichardt
(1752–1814) were not always content with this strophic form, but frequently introduced melodic embellishments, alternations of tonality and
simple descriptive details in the accompaniment. A more dramatic style
was cultivated by his contemporary, Johann Rudolph Zumsteeg (1760–
1802) for the setting of ballads. These may be described as through-
composed, since, in contrast to the strophic form, the changing subject
matter of these narrative poems is expressed by new melodic and accompanying materials.

The first composer to discover the many facets of the romantic lied
was Franz Schubert. None of his successors ever surpassed his ability to
capture in immediate musical terms the emotional essence of a poem. And
in none was spontaneous creation more natural or more rapid: more than
six hundred songs poured from his pen during his brief life. These include
at one extreme such brief songs as Goethe's *Wanderers Nachtlied* whose
setting entails but fourteen measures of music within which Schubert

unforgettably expresses the serenity of the nocturnal singer. At the other extreme are the lengthy song cycles, such as *Winterreise* based on poems of Wilhelm Müller. Each of the twenty-four songs in the *Winter's Journey* possesses its own individuality, while representing at the same time but a single aspect of the introspective melancholy which permeates the whole cycle.

It is not easy to define the stylistic characteristics of Schubert's lyricism, for it assumes many forms. Certainly it depends upon a feeling for the beauty of the human voice as it moves through phrases conforming to the singer's natural breathing capacity. It is thus founded upon different aesthetic premises than the long, intricately curving lines, spun out from an initial motif, of late Baroque melodies. It is also very different, as a rule, from the melodic style of the symphony or sonata evolved by Schubert's predecessors. Most of all it differs from that of Beethoven, whose greatest works were appearing at the same time. In all but his lyrical slow movements, Beethoven's melodies, whether brief and compact or of relative length, consist of sharply defined motifs. These, like organisms, are capable of growth without losing their basic identity. Schubert's melodies, however, are generally as long as the stanza of the poem for which they are written. And the phrases of which they consist are such closely interrelated parts of the whole that they may not be isolated as materials for thematic development.

In Schubert's songs words and melody are united indissolubly. But the relationship between them differs from that found in Baroque music. What now determines the shape of the vocal melody and the substance of the piano accompaniment is the unique, intuitive insight of the composer. Illustrative details are not used for their external meaning or their structural value, but serve to illuminate the subtle, inner content of the poem divined by the composer. Each song is an expression of his own originality, and thus differs from all other settings of the same poem.

Two songs of Schubert composed as early as 1814–1815 already reveal the essential qualities of the lied as it was to be cultivated throughout the nineteenth century. Both are settings of poems by Goethe. Profoundly different in form and content, Schubert's music is perfectly matched to each. *Der Erlkönig* (The Erlking) is a narrative ballad. The poem tells of a father bearing his dying son on horseback through a storm. In the central portion of the poem the contest between the father and the Erlking for possession of the child is portrayed in a dialogue that conveys an ever mounting sense of horror and anguish.

The impetuous triplet rhythm in octaves with which the song opens (Illustration 1) immediately suggests the headlong pace of the rider, while the stormy rising and falling motif in the bass, which recurs violently from time to time, adds to the feeling of terror. The triplet rhythm is never interrupted as the song progresses, but it assumes a more menacing quality when its chords are broken up into soft figurations accompanying the Erlkönig. Though seemingly realistic in its analogy to the rhythm of the galloping horse, this rhythmic accompaniment expresses the changing feelings of the individuals as well as the indescribable terror of the scene by the different harmonic forms and dynamic levels it assumes.

ILLUSTRATION I

Schubert's music characterizes the three protagonists in a number of ways while keeping the melodic substance of the entire song within the capacities of a solo voice (Illustration 2). The lowest register is reserved for the father's part, and the shape of his melodic phrases imparts a certain solidity and strength. Sung softly, the Erlkönig's melodies occupy the middle range, and in their smooth, uninterrupted flow underline the seductive quality of his terrifying image. The appeals of the child are projected in the upper register. His breathless phrases are sung each time at a higher pitch, and his hysterical fear is vividly portrayed in the shrill discord that opens each of his appeals. The underlying harmony modulates through a number of keys, but only the Erlkönig's parts are sung in the major tonalities.

Gretchen am Spinnrade, drawn from Goethe's *Faust,* is a lyric poem of three stanzas expressing Gretchen's love for Faust. Each stanza begins with a refrain of two lines, "My peace is gone, my heart is sad," a formal feature Schubert reproduces in his musical setting. From the same initial phrase Schubert draws out a differently shaped melody for each stanza. With acute feeling for the rise in emotional tension, the melodies of the second and third stanzas reach quite different climaxes. The former comes to an indecisive conclusion on a high, sustained tone as Gretchen is rapt in ecstasy at the recollection of Faust's kiss. In the latter the melodic phrases rise sequentially to a decisive conclusion as Gretchen affirms her love. But Schubert's concluding repetition of the opening lines in their original melodic dress expresses the tragic aspect of this love more profoundly than the words themselves.

The accompaniment consisting of a persistent rhythm and harmonic figuration throughout has the same artistic importance as that of *Der*

Erlkönig. Its pliability makes it more than an obvious description of the whirring spinning wheel that only comes to a halt when Gretchen remembers Faust's kiss. Instead it reflects the uneasiness brought about by the obsessive quality of her love which has destroyed her peace of mind forever. Such a combination of sensitively modelled melody and ex-

ILLUSTRATION 2

ILLUSTRATION 2 (*continued*)

(Child)

Mein Va- ter, mein Va- ter jetzt fasst er mich an!

pressive accompaniment distinguishes the greatest of Schubert's lieder. Other composers who were drawn to this romantic art form, from Schumann to Brahms and Hugo Wolf, achieved similar results by various means. Seldom, however, was the equilibrium established by Schubert between voice and accompaniment so perfectly maintained.

Gretchen am Spinnrade illustrates a melodic style in which each phrase makes an indispensable contribution to the unity of the entire organism. This style is so much a part of Schubert's artistry that he instinctively seeks to use it in the composition of sonatas, quartets and symphonies. Its appropriateness for the variation form is to be expected, and may be observed in movements such as the fourth in the *Quintet* for *piano and strings* in A major, opus 114 (*Die Forelle*). But Schubert also uses melodies of this sort in sonata-form movements in works such as the *Eighth Symphony* (*Unfinished*), the unique *Quartet movement* in C minor and the *Quartet in A minor*, opus 29. The opening movement of this last work is a magnificent example of the effect such materials have upon the structure and meaning of the sonata form. The main theme (Illustration 3), 32 measures in length, is an exceptionally expressive song-melody played by the first violin with a stereotyped accompaniment divided among the other instruments.

The theme is made up of three strains (measures 3–10, 11–22, and 23–32). The motivic content and shape is similar in each, but the third strain is presented in the parallel major mode, a means Schubert often chooses to intensify the emotional content of a melody. Perfect in proportion and complete in meaning, the theme is more reflective than dynamic in character. Indeed the bridge and subordinate sections of the exposition and recapitulation, though clearly marked, assume the character of episodes between recurrences of this lyrical theme. It dominates the development section, which is a free and expressive extemporization on this melody in the subdominant tonality of D minor.

ILLUSTRATION 3

ILLUSTRATION 3 (*continued*)

The final harmonic modulation of this passage reintroduces the melody in its original form as the first part of the recapitulation; after a moment of hesitation, it reappears as the coda in a somewhat abbreviated version. The tightly-knit, dynamic structure of the earlier Viennese composers gives way here to one consisting of six semi-independent entities, whose unity is less the result of organic development than of feeling and mood.

In contrast to that of Schubert, the genius of Schumann, Chopin and Liszt found its most characteristic expression in their music for the piano. In writing for this instrument it seemed possible to develop a completely personal style and mode of expression unhampered by traditional theory and practice. Robert Schumann as a youth was torn by the rival attractions of literature and music. (Later in life he found a means of serving both muses by the foundation in 1834 of his musical journal, *Neue Zeitschrift für Musik*.) In the face of the constant opposition of his mother, he found increasing solace in musical activities. In 1830 he decided to devote his entire efforts to developing his proficiency as a virtuoso of the pianoforte. Although this goal was abruptly shattered by an injury to his hand two years later, his passion for this instrument absorbed his entire creative energies until 1840. In rapid succession he created a series of piano works whose episodic plan and fantastic content bear no resemblance to the integrated structure of the sonata. The finest of these, the *Papillons, Carnaval, Davidsbündler* and the *Phantasiestücke*, seem to be spontaneous products of the imagination. Unfettered by any preconceived ideal of form and structure, the music progresses in a series of individual pieces which seem to be as unrelated in mood and feeling as they are in musical materials and style.

In *Carnaval*, the free play of the imagination seems at first to be channeled into a more specific realm of fantasy than in the others. This is due to its title, and to the fact that some of its twenty pieces are headed by carnivalesque names, such as "Pierrot," "Arlequin," and "Pantalon et Colombine." But next to these are "Reconnaissance," "Florestan," "Eusebius," "Chopin," and "Paganini," and it becomes clear that the carnival Schumann envisages is entirely of the imagination. Each piece, written in a tonality which is never distant from the central key of A flat major, occupies but a minute or two and yet is complete in itself. In all of them Schumann contrives to incorporate the tones of A or A flat, E flat, C and B in one arrangement or another. The importance of these notes is underscored by their mysterious appearance as the three "Sphinxes" quoted midway through the work (Illustration 4). The first, E flat–C–B–A, are the only letters of Schumann's name which possess notational equivalents in German (S–C–H–A). Both the second and third represent the letters ASCH, the name of a small town in which there lived a young lady with whom the composer was currently in love. Nothing indicates more clearly the subjective nature of Schumann's art than

ILLUSTRATION 4

these three motifs. Even when the riddle of the Sphinxes is deciphered, the answer has meaning only for Schumann. And yet this intensely personal material has been made the subject of a work which is to be performed before an audience which could not possibly grasp its significance.

The tones of the Sphinxes do not obtrude as an obvious basis of structural unity, for they appear mostly as veiled allusions, now embedded in the inner parts ("Pierrot"), now as details of the melodic figuration ("Papillons"), or as a melodic cadence ("Chopin") (Illustration 5). Each piece contrasts with its neighbors because of the different styles in which they are cast. One may be a parody of remarkable subtlety and sensitivity, as in the case of "Chopin," while others express temperamental opposites as in "Florestan" and "Eusebius," the names Schumann attached to the two sides of his own personality. The first is impulsive, quixotic, and passionate in quick waltz rhythm, and the second, dreamy, indecisive, and lyrical, with deliberately vague, irregular rhythm.

Frédéric Chopin (1810–1849) virtually ignored the large forms of Viennese composers, confining his creative efforts to the piano upon

ILLUSTRATION 5

ILLUSTRATION 5 (continued)

which he could display his personal talents as a poetic musician and performer. With the exception of two piano sonatas and two concertos he seldom composed works of more than one movement. To the fashionable aristocracy of Paris, where his creative life was mainly spent, Chopin was the symbol of a poetic hero in exile from an oppressed land, his native Poland. This conception was strengthened by his melancholy mazurkas and brilliant polonaises with their distinctive Polish rhythms. The originality of his many genre compositions—ballades, nocturnes, waltzes, études, impromptus and preludes—lies in his highly personal approach to the piano, which emphasizes its unique qualities of sound. Possessing a stronger, more systematic technique as a performer than Schumann, he developed a style requiring both brilliant virtuosity and delicate control of the most subtle nuances of the piano.

Chopin's style is molded from many different elements, ranging from the elegant vocal embellishments of coloratura arias in the contemporary operas of Rossini and Bellini to the contrapuntal part-writing of Bach. Along with many other characteristics, these features are very prominent in his *Nocturnes* and *Preludes,* the "poetic" qualities of which were highly admired by his contemporaries. In the former (Illustration 6), a rhythmic accompaniment of regular figurations or successions of chords, provides the foundation for extended cantilena melodies. The melodies soar throughout a wide range of the piano, and are sustained by its singing qualities. The more important melodic phrases are often repeated many times, but rarely in identical shape or disposition. Slight alterations of meter, exquisite details of ornamentation and elaborate, widespread coloratura arpeggios or scales, underlined by rich, subtly colored harmonizations, give them constantly fresh expressive values. The flexibility of *tempo rubato* displaces the constancy of meter and rhythm characteristic of pre-nineteenth-century music. The accelerations and delays of rubato performance are governed by the feeling and punctuation of the melody. The beauty of such "bel canto" material is generally thrown into relief by a passionate, turbulent section; this section becomes the center of a musical form that is symmetrically conceived.

Chopin's *Preludes* are a romantic tribute to J. S. Bach. In fact, their inspiration comes directly from his *Well-tempered Clavier*, in which Bach defined the affective nature of each of the major and minor keys in a prelude and fugue. Chopin was guided by Bach's conception of the nature of a prelude, but not by its function. To distinguish each of the keys Bach had employed a great variety of forms and materials for his

ILLUSTRATION 6

preludes which serve as introductons to his fugues. Diversity of style and freedom of form are also attributes of Chopin's twenty-four preludes. But they are preludes in name only, for they are followed by no other pieces—least of all by fugues, whose logical structure and intricate counterpoint were for him objects of studious admiration but not models to be copied.

The Preludes are set forth in orderly fashion resembling, but not identical with that of Bach. The first Prelude is written in C major, the second in its related key, A minor. Hereafter they appear in pairs of major and related minor keys each a fifth higher than the preceding one. But the improvisatory character and self-sufficiency of each Prelude, however short, contradicts the logic of this systematic design. In the first Prelude, for example, an arabesque composed of three interlocking figures is pursued with a consistency reminiscent of the first of Bach's preludes. In the second, the center of interest is a descending, declamatory melody accompanied by regular patterns of persistently dissonant chords. As the melody and its accompaniment progress sequentially the tonal orientation remains ambiguous. Only when the accompaniment disintegrates at the very end does the melody take a decisive turn leading to the long delayed cadence in A minor.

To Franz Liszt (1811–1886) each one of these Preludes was "the fruit of but a short period of reflection, which sufficed to reproduce the tears and dreams of a day." Liszt could not have known the long hours of reflection that Chopin spent upon these pieces. In comparison to his own expansive canvasses Chopin's miniatures must have seemed ephemeral sketches. The incomparable virtuosity of Liszt's playing made him the most famous composer-performer of his time. Such instrumental virtuosity seemed to the romantic generation evidence of a mysterious power, divine or demonic rather than rational. The new middle-class audience had been in turn terrified, exhilarated and reduced to tears by the consummate skill of the violinist Niccolo Paganini (1782–1840). At the same time the contortions assumed by his gaunt, attenuated face and figure gave him the appearance of a man possessed.

The elegance of the strikingly handsome Liszt rivalled the satanic qualities of Paganini, and so did the exuberance of his playing. Schumann described Liszt's genius as a concert pianist perceptively. "It is one thing when the artist is playing before the public, and another, when he is playing before a small group—even the artist changes. The beautiful illuminated hall, the glow of candlelight, the handsomely dressed audience—all this tends to elevate the frame of mind of the giver as well as the receiver. And now the daemon began to stir in him; first he played with the public as if to try it, then gave it something more profound, until he had enmeshed every member of the audience with his art and did with them as he willed."

The music with which Liszt stunned audiences throughout Europe between 1830 and 1848 was mainly of his own making. Transcriptions of orchestral works or improvisations on contemporary songs and arias formed a large part of his repertory. The massive, glittering transformations of these materials by Liszt, as well as by his lesser contemporaries, are evidence of the vulgarity of contemporary tastes. But Liszt displayed a sensitive taste in his transcriptions of many songs by Schubert.

The heroic stature of the transcendent pianist is nowhere more brilliantly displayed than in his two piano concertos. Here the relationship between soloist and orchestra becomes particularly dramatic, for the concert grand piano, as handled by Liszt, was able to match the sonorities and volume of the orchestra, and even at times to triumph over it. The *Concerto in E flat* (1855) has a truly unique form. Liszt has divided it into three movements, as if bowing to convention, but the second movement contains two distinct parts. Thus this work actually contains four sections which are clearly related to the movements of the instrumental sonata in mood if not in form. Liszt's first movement is built, like the exposition of the sonata movement, on two contrasting motifs. The two sections of the middle movement correspond to the slow movement and scherzo of a conventional symphony, while the last movement is a triumphant conclusion based upon themes of the preceding movements. Since the four sections follow one another without a pause, one might even describe this concerto as a first movement sonata form containing within itself all four movements of a symphony. The first movement represents the exposition; the two interior sections supplant the development; and the final movement represents the recapitulation. In this novel synthesis, one discerns the romantic desire to fuse opposing ideas into a higher unity.

The piano plays the leading part throughout this concerto. This is established at the outset where it responds to the menacing motif announced by the whole orchestra with grandiose octaves and chords surpassing in weight and brilliance those of its rival. An extended solo passage follows which confirms the ascendancy of the piano (Illustration 7). Sounding like the spontaneous improvisation customarily found in a cadenza at the conclusion of the first movement in the older concertos, it emphasizes the bravura qualities of piano technique, and focuses the attention of the audience immediately and dramatically upon the soloist.

Liszt did not confine his piano compositions solely to music for the concert stage, however. During sojourns in Switzerland and Italy, he composed individual pieces for the pleasure of his intimates and himself.

ILLUSTRATION 7

They are musical analogues of the pen and ink drawings and water color sketches of romantic, picturesque scenes with which many of his contemporaries filled their private journals and letters containing their most personal feelings and experiences. Later he published them in two series with the Byronic title, *Années de Pèlerinage* (Years of Pilgrimage). In pieces of modest proportions like *Au bord d'une Source* and *Gondoliera*, Liszt obtains picturesque and colorful effects by sustained tones in the

ILLUSTRATION 7 (*continued*)

bass, unusual combinations of harmonies in the middle register, and delicate arabesques of rapid arpeggios, scales and trills in the highest register,
whose sounds mingle and dissolve like images reflected in running water.

Though Romantic ideals were at first most clearly expressed in the
smaller forms of the piano and the lied, they also began to appear in

older categories such as the opera. In French and Italian opera whose forms and styles had long been clearly defined and stabilized, novelty was at first confined to the choice of picturesque subject matter and Romantic situations. Italian opera continued to dominate the repertory, but alongside it the grave style and classical subjects exemplified by the operas of Gluck, Spontini and Cherubini, held the stage in Paris during the Napoleonic era and its conservative aftermath. Like the rest of Europe, however, the French were unable to resist the opera buffa of Gioacchino Rossini (1792–1868) appearing in profusion during the twenties. Rossini was equally skillful, if not as popular, in the opera seria. He employed romantic subject matter occasionally before *William Tell* (1829) but it is only in this final work that romantic elements stand out prominently. Written for Paris, as were so many of the most important works of his Italian confreres, it also includes the spectacular choral and stage effects so greatly admired in France at that time.

In Germany Romantic subject matter was first successfully introduced into opera by Carl Maria von Weber (1786–1826). *Der Freischütz* entranced a responsive Berlin audience when first produced in 1821. The drama takes place in seventeenth-century Bohemia. Instead of aristocratic or mythological personages its characters are gamekeepers and foresters, whose lives are dominated by the mysterious forest in which the supernatural forces of good and evil are all-powerful. The plot has the naïveté and simplicity of a fairy-tale: a gamekeeper's assistant, Max, may win the hand of his beloved Agatha only if he is victorious in a shooting match. Fearful of losing, he is persuaded to seek supernatural assistance by a comrade, Caspar, who has long since sold his soul to the devil. In a scene of terror in which the devil himself, Samiel, is invoked amid a variety of supernatural phenomena, the two conspirators cast seven enchanted bullets. In the subsequent contest Max's seventh bullet is turned by Samiel against Agatha, but, thanks to the protection of the consecrated wreath she is wearing, it is deflected to the heart of the villain, Caspar!

The action reaches its dramatic climax in the scene in the Wolf Glen where the powers of evil are invoked. To capture the horror of this scene it is entirely set to music. It is the orchestra which carries the main burden of musical expression, for the words of Max, Caspar, and the invisible Samiel are either declaimed or sung in recitative style. The mood of foreboding and terror is established at the very beginning by the mysterious sounds of low-pitched, agitated tremolos in the strings. These progress above a chromatically descending bass to a sudden fortissimo on a diminished seventh chord, whose distinctive sound is emphasized by the howls of a hidden chorus (Illustration 8). As the action progresses it is punctuated alternately by sudden explosions of sound and irregular in-

ILLUSTRATION 8

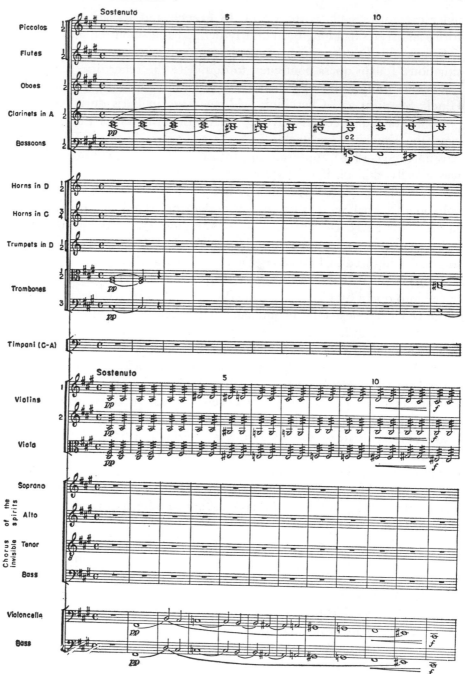

ILLUSTRATION 8 (*continued*)

ILLUSTRATION 8 (*continued*)

tervals of silence. The primary means of investing each episode with its
characteristic atmosphere and feeling is the instrumentation. Each of the
supernatural events which occur with the casting of the magic bullets is
described in a short passage of vivid orchestral tone-painting. To express
the nature and feelings of each of the participants, Weber composes instrumental motifs sharply differentiated by their harmony, pitch and
orchestration. Among the most original of these is the motif of Samiel
(Illustration 9). It consists only of the notes of a diminished seventh

ILLUSTRATION 9

chord, sustained by the sinister, low-pitched tones of clarinets and strings,
and punctuated by three ominous, syncopated beats of the kettledrum.
Its instrumental color is so striking that its appearance here and elsewhere
in the opera immediately implies the demonic. In this scene and in the
dramatic overture as well, Weber revealed to his contemporaries a new
possibility for Romantic expression—the power of the diverse timbres and
tone colors of the symphonic orchestra to stimulate the imagination.

The manifold resources of the symphony orchestra for the expressive portrayal of personal feeling was fully exploited for the first time by
Hector Berlioz (1803–1869). In 1821 Berlioz, the son of a physician, was
sent to Paris to study medicine, but he soon abandoned his medical training to study music at the Conservatoire. There the originality of his
musical ideas was at odds with the academic precepts of his teachers.

His artistic growth was nourished by a series of experiences which
occurred in Paris in the later twenties. First and most dramatic was his
discovery of Shakespeare. At the opening performance of *Hamlet* in
1827 by an English company, whose repertory also included *Romeo and*

Juliet, Berlioz was completely overwhelmed. "The lightning flash of [Shakespeare's] genius," he wrote, "revealed the whole heaven of art to me, illuminating its remotest depths in a single flash. I recognized the meaning of real grandeur, real beauty and real dramatic truth. . . ." His admiration for Shakespeare was extended in the following year to Goethe's *Faust*. Together with Virgil whose poetry he had known since earliest youth, these men influenced Berlioz' later compositions.

The performance of Beethoven's symphonies in Paris in 1828 opened a new world to Berlioz. Before that year the French had felt that instrumental music was a form of artistic expression inferior to both the opera and drama. This view was challenged after the full extent of Beethoven's genius was discovered by them in a series of concerts devoted to his music. Berlioz found in these works an inspired union of instrumental sound and dramatic content that could only be compared in their effect to the plays of Shakespeare.

Stemming from these experiences, the artistic goal of Berlioz became to unite the dramatic with the musical. This objective is evident not only in his two operas, *Benvenuto Cellini*, 1838, and *Les Troyens* (completed in 1858), but also in his treatment of the text of the *Requiem* (1837) and *La Damnation de Faust*, which received its final form in 1846. And it is responsible for the uniqueness of his three symphonies—the works in which the originality of his style appears most vividly. The first is the *Symphonie Fantastique*, composed in 1829–30. Subsequently he appended to it the explanatory subtitle "Episodes d'une vie de l'artiste," and added a bizarre sequel, *Lélio*. In 1834 he completed the second symphony, *Harold en Italie*, and, five years later, *Roméo et Juliette*.

All three of these works are symphonies, but symphonies modified by content since each springs from literary materials. This is particularly true of the last of them. Shakespeare's *Romeo and Juliet* had obsessed the composer ever since he first witnessed the play. He felt that "everything in it is designed for music," and was inspired by it to create a "dramatic" symphony which "by itself and without the accessories of Shakespeare's play [would] make known . . . the sum of passion contained in the original." He assumed that the dramatic and emotional content of a literary work could be transformed into a musical quintessence, more powerfully affecting than the original.

The complete design of this symphony suggests that to Berlioz two different problems were involved in translating the essence of Shakespeare's tragedy into music. The first was how to distill the passions of this drama into musical elements that could be used within the framework of a symphony. The second was the creation of a dramatic setting for them which would also summarize the action of the play in musical terms.

To this latter end he composed a long introductory section in which the particular circumstances of the love affair between Romeo and Juliet are described. Balancing this and forming a brilliant finale is an equally extended section depicting the renewal of the feud between the two families and the reconciliation effected by Friar Laurence. Both of these are composed for solo voices, chorus and orchestra to texts not written by Shakespeare but by the poet Emile Deschamps.

Within the frame created by these introductory and closing sections are four large instrumental movements expressing the contrasting emotions of this romantic love affair. These correspond to the four movements of a normal symphony. In the first, Romeo's melancholy contemplation of his love for Juliet provides the slow introduction to an Allegro expressing the exuberant gaiety of the festivities at Capulet's house. The two central movements are entitled respectively "Scène d'amour" and "Scherzo," the latter being inspired by Mercutio's reference to Queen Mab, the fairy of dreams. The form of the fourth movement resembles that of the first, beginning with a slow funeral march which is followed by an agitated Allegro depicting the violent emotions of the lovers in the tomb and their tragic death.

The *Symphonie Dramatique* bears direct comparison with Beethoven's *Ninth Symphony* in its huge proportions and in its use of the voice within the symphonic style and form. It is transparently evident that Berlioz found in Beethoven's symphony a precedent for his own work and that his introductory movement is modelled upon the Finale of the *Ninth Symphony*. The opening instrumental section in fugal style depicting the street fight with which the play commences corresponds to the agitated beginning of Beethoven's Finale. Just as in the latter's work, it is interrupted by an instrumental recitative, representing the intervention of the Prince of Verona. This gives way to a choral recitative, followed by a solo song and a return to the chorus. Here, as the chorus narrates the principal events of the drama, Berlioz illustrates them with the themes of the succeeding instrumental movements. Where Beethoven had used this device to recall the themes and emotions of past movements, Berlioz employs it to reveal the meaning of movements yet to come.

The task of expressing the "sum of passions" contained in Shakespeare's *Romeo and Juliet* challenged the musical imagination and technical skill of the composer to the uttermost. Berlioz achieved his most impressive results not through the massed resources of voices and orchestra but in those movements in which he is working purely with the many possibilities of orchestral color. The degree to which his style is wedded to the coloristic values of the different instruments is heard most impressively in the contrasting "Love Scene" and "Scherzo" movements. Berlioz, fully conscious of the novelty of a love scene expressed by wordless instruments instead of by solo voices, explains this innovation in the preface to the score. The Adagio is instrumental, he writes, because "the sublimity of the love itself made its expression so full of danger for the composer that he preferred to give a wider latitude to his imagination than would have been possible with words. He had recourse to the instrumental idiom, a richer, more varied, less limited language, and by its very vagueness infinitely more powerful."

In the absence of human voices Berlioz focuses the musical interest upon the unfolding of smoothly flowing melodies orchestrated to emphasize the lyricism of the various instruments. His underlying design is that of a dialogue in which the higher instruments—first violins, flutes, clarinets, English horn, in unison or harmonic combinations—alternate with muted violas and cellos in unison. To accompany the higher instruments the lower string sections are muted and subdivided into various numbers of parts, while the *pizzicato* double-basses repeat a gentle but persistent rhythmic figure. In the *Scherzo* the musical materials are as delicate and ethereal as Shakespeare's image of Queen Mab:

> . . . the Fairies' midwife; and she comes
> In shape no bigger than an agate-stone
> On the forefinger of an alderman,
> Drawn with a team of little atomies
> Athwart men's noses as they lie asleep. . . .

Nimble melodic figurations, transparent instrumentation, soft dynamics, the fastest possible tempo—these and many other details create a sonorous tissue from which all weight and volume have been removed. The elusive instrumental colors of which this piece is composed are well exemplified in the Trio. Here flute and English horn initiate tentative thematic figuration against a high-pitched pianissimo trill played by half the first violins and the sustained, bodiless harmonics of the remaining violins divided into three parts (Illustration 10).

Ideals similar to those of Berlioz led Franz Liszt to create his *Symphonic Poems*, which began to appear during the middle years of the century. But there is a considerable difference between Berlioz' dramatic symphonies and Liszt's new genre. Berlioz always portrays the essence of his subject in a dramatic succession of movements corresponding with the succession of events in a real or implied story. Liszt, on the other hand, portrays only the central theme of the work of art which inspired his composition. The result is a work of but one movement, whose sections are linked by a single motif. Convinced that music may express the essence of an idea which eludes other forms of art, Liszt recast a variety of subjects, from the *Tasso* of Goethe to the *Meditations* of Lamartine, from Gluck's opera, *Orpheus*, to Kaulbach's painting, *The Triumph of the Huns*. Though the auditor is expected to be familiar with the subject that inspired the composer, Liszt envisaged music as the catalyst by which its full meaning is at last revealed. But since the composer is the poetic agent of this process, it is, in truth, his own perception of the given subject that he presents to us.

ILLUSTRATION 10

The imaginative process by which a work comes into being, and the idealistic message it is intended to convey is described by Liszt in his preface to *Orpheus*, the fourth in the series of "poèmes symphoniques" completed in 1854. While rehearsing Gluck's opera he was reminded of an Etruscan vase in the Louvre on which is represented "the first musician, his lips open for the utterance of divine words and songs, and his lyre resounding under the touch of his long and graceful fingers." In his imagination he sees all nature enraptured, "yielding before those accents which reveal to Humanity the beneficent power of art, its glorious light and civilizing harmony. Instructed by the purest morality, taught by the most sublime dogma, enlightened by the torch of science, influenced by the philosophic reasoning of the intellect, surrounded with the refinements of Civilization, Humanity, now as formerly and ever, has within itself those instincts of ferocity, brutality and sensuality, which it is the mission of Art to soften, to mitigate, to ennoble. Now as formerly and ever

Orpheus, viz. Art, should pour forth his melodious waves, their chords vibrating like a soft and irresistible light over the conflicting elements. . . . Orpheus weeps for Euridice, the emblem of the ideal overwhelmed by griefs and misfortunes, whom he is permitted to snatch from the monsters of Erebus, to bring from the depths of Cimmerian darkness, but whom, alas! he knows not how to keep on earth. . . ." Liszt then suggests the essential theme of his music. "If I had been going to work out my idea in full, I should like to have portrayed the tranquil civilizing character of the songs, their powerful empire, their grandly voluptuous tones, their undulations sweet as the breezes of Elysium, their gradual uplifting like clouds of incense, their clear and heavenly spirit enveloping the world and the entire universe as in an atmosphere, as in a transparent vesture of ineffable and mysterious harmony."

The music of *Orpheus* springs from the initial tone, G, softly intoned by two horns an octave apart. A literal representation of "the primeval tone," it gains poetic perspective when joined by the soft harmonies of wind instruments supporting the languishing arpeggios of two harps, representing the lyre of Orpheus. This introduction of fourteen measures appears as though spontaneously improvised, since the two sustained harmonies of E flat major and a dominant seventh chord on A appear and dissolve with no harmonic relationship between them except their common tone, G. The same note is then transformed into the dominant of C major, the true key of the composition. In this fashion the one tone G seems to generate magically the harmonic material of this paean to the power of music. It also serves as the initial tone of each of the principal melodic ideas of *Orpheus*. Hymnlike in their regular motion and sustained quality, these melodic phrases take on different expressive values as the piece progresses.

Liszt's technique of thematic transformation is derived from the symphonic principle of thematic development. But it consists primarily of harmonic alterations, progressions to unusual tonalities by chromatic or enharmonic modulations, and by variety of orchestral color. The music moves in ascending and descending curves to two climaxes in C major, marked by the splendor of the full orchestra. Its energies dissipated, it sinks down to a thrice-repeated C minor cadence, only to rise again in a succession of gentle chords for divided strings, echoed by wind instruments, to a serene cadence in C major. The chromatic and enharmonic modulations which endow this conclusion with such an elevated tone stretch the concept of tonality to extreme limits (Illustration 11).

The initial appearance of the melodic material in *Orpheus* establishes the mood and character of the entire work. The tones of the melody

ILLUSTRATION 11

have been chosen solely for their suggestive quality, not for purely musical reasons. The harmonies and orchestral colors which clothe the successive appearance of the melody have no raison d'être other than to intensify and illuminate its expressive content. Thus *Orpheus* discloses the paradox in Romantic music: in asserting its superior powers of expression, music may become the slave of that which it seeks to express.

XII THE AGE OF GENIUS

Part III. The Twilight of the Gods

ROMANTICISM is essentially a movement of youth. Its fervor and aspiring spirit, its courage and idealism are fragile qualities, difficult to carry into later years. It has been well said that the greatest good fortune to befall a Romantic is an early death, "to cease upon the midnight with no pain." The roster of those who died before the blight of middle age fell upon them is truly impressive: Keats, Byron and Shelley in England, Novalis, Wackenroder and Kleist in Germany, Weber, Schubert and Chopin—to cite only the most familiar names. It would almost appear that they had pressed on to that ultimate victory of Romanticism, the final and complete merger with the Infinite through death. But it was not everyone's lot to be granted such a romantic demise, and by the middle of the nineteenth century Romanticism as a movement had become middle-aged. Its fresh enthusiasms and bold, though ill-defined, projects now tended to become programs and formulas. The inspirations of yesterday had become the standards of today.

The phenomenon of nineteenth-century Romanticism may be likened to a current conception of the creation of the universe. A nucleus of mass and energy suddenly explodes, hurling clouds of gaseous vapors throughout limitless heavens. Rushing away from each other with tremendous speeds, some of these clouds or nebulae have slowly congealed into galaxies of stars and planets caught up in an eternal revolution around

376

one another. Just so did the explosive force of the Romantic ideal of difference and originality drive men in opposing directions. But as the white-hot energy of the first period expended itself, it began to coalesce into fixed attitudes and to form schools. Men began to revolve in planetary orbits around central ideas or around dominant personalities. This is the age of the Wagnerite, the Brahmsian, the Franckist, and the Debussyite. This too is the era of nationalism in music, when composers strove to create music expressive of ethnic or national groups. Programs and manifestos were issued, exposing the tenets of individual artistic creeds and summoning adherents to the one true faith. But of all the credos of the second half of the nineteenth century none attracted more proselytes than that of Richard Wagner (1813–1883). Few indeed were the composers in the latter half of the century who were not influenced in one way or another by the attraction or repulsion of the mighty star of Wagner's art and theories.

Wagner is a true Romantic in that his art and his ego are as one: his personal and artistic aims are in many instances synonymous. For the Romanticist, life itself is a work of art, the product of his own creative consciousness. The unfolding of the personality is simultaneously a poem or novel, the fiction of the ego. So Wordsworth records his psychological development in the *Prelude;* Byron becomes Childe Harold and Don Juan; Hector Berlioz lives not only in his *Memoirs,* but also as *Lélio* in the sequel to the *Symphonie Fantastique.*

In the case of Wagner the history of his art is at the same time the history of his personality. Born of middle-class parents, he was educated in schools in Dresden and Leipzig before entering the University of Leipzig in 1831. There he imbibed the idealistic philosophy of Friedrich Schelling and participated in the student movement known as "Das junge Deutschland" which opposed the reactionary government with ideals of infinite progress and social reforms that would disregard national boundaries. At the University Wagner also decided to abandon a literary career in favor of music which he had been studying in a desultory fashion for a few years. This decision was prompted in part by his enthusiastic reaction to the music of Beethoven, whose symphonies he had heard in a series of concerts. Thus the skein of his future beliefs and activities was spun in these university years. Romantic philosophy, revolutionary politics, literature, and the symphonic art of Beethoven were to be woven into the fabric of his life and works.

Between 1834 and 1839 Wagner functioned as an opera conductor and composed his first operatic works. In the latter year, having been living in Riga beyond his means, Wagner fled from his creditors and found asylum in Paris. Here he lived in direst poverty, sustaining himself as best he could by making piano arrangements and by writing articles for the Paris and Dresden newspapers. Unable to gain access to the Parisian theater, Wagner began to theorize upon the conditions of his day which had brought him to this pass. It was because of his personal situation that he began to speculate seriously upon the relationship of artistic and social aims, a problem that was to engage his interest in one way or another throughout the remainder of his life.

Release from his drastic poverty and frustration came finally in 1843 when he was appointed chapelmaster at Dresden. For six years all went well with him until he took the side of the rebels in the Revolution of 1849. When the uprising was quelled, Wagner was forced to flee once again, this time to Switzerland. Finding it impossible to do any creative work, he took this time of enforced leisure to write three works in which he spelled out his theory of art, and laid the course for the future development of music. These treatises written between 1849 and 1851 are extraordinary documents. Though there are few original ideas to be found in them, they are at once a synthesis of the Romantic conceptions of the first half of the century and an apologia for the operatic revolution upon which Wagner was about to embark. In the first treatise, *Art and Revolution*, Wagner examines the function of the artwork within society, while in the other two, *The Artwork of the Future* and *Opera and Drama*, he formulates the role of art in the future.

The starting point of Wagner's theories is his belief that art is an expression of society and consequently suffers when the state itself is corrupt. Contemporary civilization, he felt, had made commerce its god, sacrificing all idealistic aims before the idol of gold. In such surroundings the modern artist had been forced to "squander his creative powers for gain, and make his art a handicraft." * The dramatist in particular had suffered, for "a work of dramatic art can only enter life upon the stage; but what are our theatrical institutions of today?—Industrial undertakings: yes, even when supported by a special subsidy from Prince or State."

But art had not always been the slave of the money-changers. In ancient Greece the drama had been the perfect expression of religion and the state. It had been performed before the entire populace instead of before the privileged few. The spirit of the "fair, strong manhood of freedom," embodied in the god Apollo, had breathed forth in those public spectacles.

The deeds of gods and men, their sufferings, their delights . . . lay disclosed in the nature of Apollo himself; here they became actual and true. For all that

* This and the following translations are from W. Ashton Ellis: *Richard Wagner's Prose Works.*

in them moved and lived, as it moved and lived in the beholders, here found its perfected expression; where ear and eye, as soul and heart, lifelike and actual, seized and perceived all, and saw all in spirit and in body revealed; so that the imagination need no longer vex itself with the attempt to conjure up the image. Such a tragedy-day was a Feast of the God; for here the god spoke clearly and intelligently forth, and the poet, as his high priest, stood real and embodied in his artwork, led the measures of the dance, raised the voices to a choir, and in ringing words proclaimed the utterances of godlike wisdom.

With the fall of Hellas the ancient drama was destroyed. What had once been the indissoluble union of all the arts was now dismembered into the separate arts of poetry, music, dance, and architecture. Since that time they had never been reunited. "Each one of these dissevered arts, nursed and luxuriously tended for the entertainment of the rich, has filled the world to overflowing with its products; in each, great minds have brought forth marvels; but the one true Art has not been born again, either in or since the Renaissance. The perfect Artwork, the great united utterance of a free and lovely public life, the *Drama, Tragedy*—howsoever great the poets who have here and there indited tragedies—is not yet born again: for reason that it cannot be *re-born*, but must be *born anew*."

Ostensibly the new birth of the united artwork would have to wait until a free society had been created, but Wagner would brook no delay. It must be born immediately, even though its ideals were not yet realized in society. Perhaps it would even inspire a renovation of society. It must then be a revolutionary art, for it will oppose the political institutions of the contemporary world. "Art remains in its essence what it ever was; we have only to say that it is not present in our modern public system. It lives, however, and has ever lived in the individual conscience, as the one, fair, indivisible Art. Thus the only difference is this: with the Greeks it lived in the public conscience, whereas today it lives alone in the conscience of private persons. Therefore in its flowering time the Grecian Art was *conservative*, because it was a worthy and adequate expression of the public conscience; with us true Art is *revolutionary*, because its very existence is opposed to the ruling spirit of the community."

The nature of the revolutionary artwork was revealed by Wagner in his two subsequent essays. "As Man stands to Nature," he begins, "so stands Art to Man. When Nature had developed in herself those attributes which included the conditions for the existence of Man, then Man spontaneously evolved. In like manner, as soon as human life had engendered from itself the conditions for the manifestment of Art-work, this too stepped self-begotten into life." Working unconsciously and yet according to inner laws of necessity, Nature has produced her myriad forms of which Man is the highest expression. Through Man Nature finally attains consciousness of her own activity, but "from the moment when Man perceived the difference between himself and Nature, and thus commenced his own development as *man*, by breaking loose from the unconsciousness of natural life and passing over into conscious life . . . , from that moment did Error begin, as the earliest utterance of consciousness."

Misunderstanding the workings of Nature, taking the "endless harmony of her unconscious, instinctive energy for the arbitrary demeanour of disconnected finite forces," Man has shaped his life by artificial, arbitrary powers, the maxims of this or that religion, nationality or state. Not until "Man recognizes the essence of Nature as his very own" will he attain true knowledge. "The real Man will therefore never be forthcoming until true Human Nature, and not the arbitrary statutes of the State, shall model and order his Life; while real Art will never live, until its embodiments need be subject only to the laws of Nature, and not to the despotic whims of Mode. For as Man only then becomes free, when he gains the glad consciousness of his oneness with Nature; so does Art only then gain freedom, when she has no more to blush for her affinity with actual life."

When Man recognizes his identity with Nature, his art will no longer depict the egocentric whims of the individual, but the collective wants of the People, the unconscious and instinctive life-needs of humanity. These are most fully revealed when presented in physical reality and not just as intellectual abstractions. In the immediate physical portrayal of the Art-work "we shall all be *one*—heralds and supporters of Necessity, knowers of the unconscious, willers of the unwilful, betokeners of Nature—blissful men." The Artwork of the Future will therefore be a communal affair in which all will participate. It will lay before the People the truth of their common life-force embodied in a form that speaks to all the senses and faculties of Man. It must be a Total Artwork (*Gesamtkunstwerk*) that will "embrace all the genres of art and to some degree undo each of them in order to use it as a means to an end, to annul it in order to attain the common aim of *all*, namely, the unconditioned, immediate, representation of perfected human nature—this great united artwork we cannot recognize as the arbitrary need of the individual, but only as the inevitable communal work of the humanity of the future."

In the Total Artwork the individual arts, dissevered since the disappearance of Greek tragedy, will be reunited. Upon a stage prepared by the architect and painter, Man, complete and free, will step forth portrayed by the united arts of poetry, music and the dance (pantomime). Through the union of these three arts Man will be completely represented, for each expresses an aspect of his being. The body expresses itself in gesture (dance); the heart or feeling finds utterance in tone (music); while the intellect reveals itself through speech (poetry). When these arts join forces in common purposes, the living artwork will make its appearance once again.

Though the opera would seem to fulfill the requirements of the Total Artwork, Wagner denies that any opera up to his day had matched the standards of the true drama. "The error in the Operatic consisted in that a Means of expression (music) had been made the end, while the End of expression (the Drama) had been made a means." In opera the drama had only served as a vehicle for arias; the plot functioned only to provide the arrogant singer with a number of opportunities to display his vocal prowess. To become Drama the opera must abandon its emphasis upon absolute music and must restore the balance between the arts. But before this can be accomplished Drama itself must be reformed. According to Wagner the modern drama has evolved from two forms of the past: "the one a natural, and peculiar to our historic evolution, namely, the Romance—the other an alien, and grafted on our evolution by reflection, namely the Greek Drama as looked at through the misunderstood rules of Aristotle. The topmost flower of the Drama which sprang directly from Romance, we have in the plays of Shakespeare; in the farthest removal from his Drama, we find its diametrical opposite in the 'Tragédie' of Racine." Both dramas fail to represent the whole man. That derived from Romance creates only a semblance of life through its multiplicity of actions. Dramas based upon Greek models are artificial imitations, possessing an outward unity of action but failing to express the life of the People.

If the drama is to return to its true birthright, it must learn to represent the aspirations and needs of the People, revealing these in living, breathing figures. "Art, by the very meaning of the term, is nothing but the fulfillment of a longing to know oneself in the likeness of an object of one's love or adoration. Thus did the Folk poetry portray in Mythos to itself its *God;* thus its *Hero;* and thus, at last, its *Man*." The subject matter of drama must therefore be myth which represents in a compressed form the communal beliefs of a people. The myth, revealing Man's community with Nature, addresses itself not to our intellect but to our feelings. Its truths are of such a nature that they can never be known by reason, but only through feeling. "In the Drama, we must become knowers through Feeling."

To give the myth its most sensuous and emotional expression, the poet must resort to "tone-speech," which surpasses mere "word-speech." "Tone-speech is the beginning and end of Word-speech: as Feeling is beginning and end of the Understanding, as Mythos is beginning and end of History, the Lyric beginning and end of Poetry." Wagner's theory of tone-speech is borrowed from a widely disseminated notion that the first utterances of Man were simple vowel sounds, cries born of his emotional response to the things about him. Thus language is born of emotions. Only subsequently did man learn to make his articulations more precise and definite by enclosing the open vowel sounds with consonants, and this was the work of the intellect.

The vowel, immediately related to emotion, is the root of language as well as the root of music through its quality as tone. Accordingly the poet must make emotion apparent by re-enforcing the vowel sound with assonance and alliteration. Through this device of "stem-rhyme" words of the same primal feeling will be associated. Wagner is demanding that the poet should abandon the artificial convention of end-rhyme which is the product of cold reason rather than emotion. Not only must he forsake conventional rhyme schemes, he must also give up conventional meters. In their place he will employ a rhythm derived from the rise and fall of speech accent, a rhythm that will become a musical rhythm when equated with the strong and weak beats of the musical measure. There will be no predetermined number of accents in the poetic line; instead their number will increase or diminish in response to the emotional situation. Wagner is here proposing a drastic revision of poetic practices. Instead of a standard libretto divided into recitative and aria, there will be a poem whose form is dictated not by musical exigencies but by the emotional progression of the subject matter.

After the poet has expressed his subject in tone-speech, it is the obligation of the musician to convert this into melody. Just as the poet has used stem-rhyme to show the emotional kinship of his words, so the musician will use keys to the same end. Every key, whether major or minor, establishes relationships between its tones, creating a unity out of diverse elements, just as stem-rhyme reveals the inner unity of words of seemingly opposite emotional connotations. As long as the words are all associated with the same emotion there will be no need to depart from the chosen key, but when the emotion changes, a modulation must be effected. This will be accomplished by a tone functioning as a leading tone, one "that urges from one key into another, and by this very urgency discloses its kinship with that other key."

Wagner illustrates how this is to be done with the following example.

If we take, for instance, a stem-rhymed verse of completely like emotional-content, such as: "Liebe giebt Lust zum Leben" (Love gives joy to living), then, as a like emotion is physically disclosed in the Accents' stem-rhymed roots, the musician would here receive no natural incitement to step outside the once selected key, but would completely satisfy the Feeling by keeping the various inflections of the musical tone to that one key alone. On the contrary, if we take a verse of mixed emotion, such as: "die Liebe bringt Lust und Leid" (Love brings joy and sorrow), then here, where the stem-rhyme combines two opposite emotions, the musician would feel incited to pass across from the key first struck in keeping with the first emotion, to another key in keeping with the second emotion, and determined by the latter's relation to the emotion rendered in the earlier key. The word "Lust" (joy)— which, as the climax of the first emotion, appears to thrust onward to the second—would have in this phrase to obtain an emphasis quite other than in that: "die Liebe giebt Lust zum Leben"; the note sung to it would instinctively become the determinant leading-tone, and necessarily thrust onward to the other key, in which the word "Leid" (sorrow) should be delivered.

ILLUSTRATION I

As the tones of the melody will evolve from the emotional connotation of the poetry, so will the musical rhythm and phrasing grow out of the accents of the text and the length of the poetic line. The melody will therefore develop from the words and will no longer be constructed by means of artificial principles derived from absolute music. It will no longer be constrained by the repetitions and balanced phraseology that condition melodic progression in absolute music, but will obey only the laws of emotion, and move freely in one, never-ending, "infinite" melody. Such a conception of melody means, of course, the complete denial of the conventional division of operatic scenes into sharply differentiated sections of recitative and aria.

To reinforce the meaning of the melody the composer will add harmony to the vocal line. Each tone of the melody will be intensified by the harmonic structure upon which it rests. The harmonic sounds will not, of course, result from any arbitrary rules of progression, but will be the product of the emotion contained in the melody. Wagner visualizes these harmonies as arising not from any abstract vertical alignments, such as those taught in theory books, but from the combination of melodies. "Harmony is in itself a mere thing of thought: to the Senses it becomes first actually discernible as *polyphony*, or, to define it more closely, as *polyphonic symphony*." This harmony, arising from polyphony, will be entrusted to the orchestra whose instruments possess in their tone colors the pure, elemental vowel, which is the root of all emotion. "The orchestra indisputably possesses a *faculty* of *speech*, and the creations of modern Instrumental-music have disclosed it to us. In the Symphonies of Beethoven we have seen this faculty develop to a height whence it felt thrust on to speak out That which, by its very nature, it can not speak out. We have plainly to denote this Speaking-faculty of the Orchestra as the faculty of uttering the *unspeakable*."

With its indefinite language of interwoven melodies the orchestra will support the vocal melody with harmonies, portraying the illimitable emotions that words cannot fully depict. To accomplish this, the orchestra will ally itself with gesture by employing short pregnant phrases or motifs related to the action on the stage. At other times the *leitmotif* (leading motif) will bring up remembrances of past emotions or will foreshadow emotions still to come. Thus the orchestra will sustain the emotional level without cease, even when the action on the stage must of necessity descend to more prosaic levels. The orchestra will no longer serve as a mere accompaniment to the voice; it will be an equal partner in the depiction of the dramatic truth.

Before Wagner had completed these essays, he had already begun work upon the operas which were to convert his theories into practice. Wherever they were performed, his operas created an extraordinary impression through the power of the music and the novelty of the dramatic presentation. Each new musical drama that came from his pen seemed to justify the theories expounded in his essays, and his influence extended in ever widening circles throughout the century. His most ardent disciples were naturally to be found among the Germans, men such as Richard Strauss and Gustav Mahler. But even in France, where anti-German feeling ran high after the defeat in the Franco-Prussian War, Wagner was to become the adopted figurehead of the symbolist movement.

The core of Wagner's musical work is the cycle of dramas, the *Ring of the Nibelungen*. He had begun the poetic text for a single tragedy, *The Death of Siegfried*, in 1848. Increasingly absorbed in the philosophical and dramatic implications of the Nordic myths, from which he drew his materials, Wagner expanded his original plan to recount the chain of events leading to the birth as well as the death of Siegfried. This entailed the writing of two dramas, *Die Walküre* and *Siegfried,* to precede the tragic finale, re-entitled *Die Götterdämmerung,* and eventually a self-contained, expository introduction, *Das Rheingold.* The music for the first two of the dramas and half of the third, *Siegfried,* was composed by 1857. But in that year he turned to *Tristan und Isolde,* and the final pages of the entire *Ring* cycle were not scored until 1876.

The stem-rhyme, in which these dramas are written, no longer preserves the long-standing distinctions between recitative and aria. To match its freedom Wagner created a continuously flowing melody in which declamatory and lyrical elements are mingled in accordance with the emotional content of the text. Customarily he reproduces the metrical accents of the poetry in the rhythmic values of the melody; only rarely does he underline the content of an individual word by drawing out a single syllable in a melismatic curve. The metrical lines of stem-rhyme are directly reflected in the length of the musical phrases. Heretofore melodic symmetry and formal design had been achieved by the repetitions of phrases or entire sections together with the words to which they had first been heard. But in denying the dramatic propriety of even verbal repetitions, Wagner had likewise ruled out melodic repetitions based upon any consideration of an arbitrary musical form. Since his arioso-like vocal style thus lacks the means of producing formal unity, this function is taken over by the orchestra.

The symphonic orchestra, with its many timbres, its different instrumental choirs and immense range of dynamics, seemed ideally suited to express the violent passions of love and lust, of greed and valor, by which his characters are torn. But how could the dramatic progression of these emotions be reconciled with the principles of architectonic structure? Wagner found the answer to this dilemma in the technique of thematic development by which, in his opinion, Beethoven "burst through the bounds of the old absolute forms." A theme or group of themes could be used to provide structural unity to the various sections of the opera, while at the same time admitting infinite nuances of emotion through their modification or development. It is with this in mind that Wagner invented the series of leitmotifs of which the orchestral fabric of the dramas is woven.

The majority of these motifs are brief and incisive, consisting of the successive tones in a chord (Siegfried's sword, for example) or a striking succession of harmonies (Fate). Others consist of entire melodic sentences, such as the Song of the Rhine-maidens, or the motif of Valhalla

(Illustration 2). When the appearance of a leitmotif in the orchestra corresponds with the entrance of a person, a specific action, or with the words of a singer its extra-musical meaning is immediately established. Each motif is projected initially by a distinctive register and orchestra-

ILLUSTRATION 2

tion, both of which are capable of subsequent alteration. Before it is developed in accordance with a change in dramatic circumstances or feeling the entire motif or its initial phrase is usually isolated and impressed upon the listener by repetition.

In the first half of the *Ring of the Nibelungen*, the leitmotifs are mainly diatonic, both melodically and harmonically. They occur so persistently and under such transparent circumstances that they easily absorb the primary attention of the listener, and provide him with a running commentary in terms of specific, extra-musical symbols. In *Das Rheingold* a great many events are enacted on the stage, and the motifs provide direct links between visual and musical action. They operate on the symbolic level of exterior rather than interior action. Later, and particularly in the concluding drama, the motifs tend to become symbols of inner experiences. At times they are merged together or superimposed upon one another in reference to chains of previous events, or complexes of internal feeling.

Nowhere are Wagner's musical principles realized with greater eloquence and consistency than in *Tristan and Isolde*. Their legendary story is one of the mediaeval romances beloved by the Romantic movement.

Wagner was drawn to this Celtic myth for several reasons. It is first of all a legend, and hence of the "Volk," one of Wagner's prerequisites for a great work of art. But in characteristically Romantic fashion he chose it also because of a very personal experience. He began to compose both text and music at the beginning of his love affair with Matthilde Wesendonck, the wife of one of his most generous patrons. The opera portrays a love affair so passionate that it transcends all earthly standards of honor and morality.

Tristan is fetching the Irish Princess, Isolde, to Cornwall to be the bride of his sovereign, King Mark. Driven by conflicting motives of passion, hatred and despair, Isolde invites Tristan to drink a cup of forgiveness which she has secretly poisoned as the ship nears the shore. But Brangaene, her handmaiden, substitutes a love potion for the poison, which causes them to fall helplessly in love. After Isolde's marriage to Mark, their all-consuming passion is discovered by the king when he returns unexpectedly from a nocturnal hunt to find them together in the garden of the castle. Wounded, Tristan returns to his own castle to die. Isolde, arriving as he expires, seeks death herself as the means of eternal union with Tristan.

Wagner's version of this legend endows it with Romantic meanings and symbols. Love, like death, is eternal, whereas hate is equated with life. Night becomes the symbol of love and death, while the lovers regard day as the symbol of life and all that is hateful. As the drama progresses towards its tragic climax, they discover that only in the infinite oblivion of death will the barriers separating them disappear. Only in the realm of eternal night can they find eternal life.

In such an interpretation the fundamental theme of the drama becomes the yearning for the infinite. To express this Wagner exploited a striking phenomenon of music. In the major and minor diatonic scales, each of the tones with the exception of the tonic itself possesses an attraction for a neighboring tone. The "pull" of one tone towards another is particularly strong between the semitone of the seventh and eighth steps and the fourth and third steps in major scales, and between the second and third and seventh and eighth steps in harmonic minor scales. In tonal music the fundamental melodic and harmonic cadences, the means by which tonal areas are clearly established and defined, depend upon this phenomenon. Indeed it has long been customary to refer to the seventh step of these scales as the "leading tone," in the sense that it is felt to possess an inexorable tendency to lead a succession of tones to its nearest neighbor, which is, of course, the tonic. The leading tone thus possesses considerable tension which will be released by the expected resolution. A similar attraction exists between certain chords, especially between

those which are built upon the dominant and tonic notes, because of the
prominence of the leading tone in the former. Wagner discovered in this
relationship between tones or chords a way to express the meaning of his
opera. By continually denying a resolution to the leading tones, he could
create a sense of longing ever unfulfilled, a yearning forever unsatisfied.

The first three bars of the Prelude foreshadow all that is to come.
In this one phrase Wagner has compressed the meaning of the entire
opera, the "infinite yearning" of a love which can find fulfillment only
in death (Illustration 3).

ILLUSTRATION 3

Despite its brevity, this is an amazingly complex theme. The vibrant tones of the cellos sing the first notes, an upward leap of a sixth, the energy of which is immediately expended as it sinks by semitones to D♯. As it reaches this last tone, the winds enter on a wholly unexpected chord which functions as a dominant seventh chord on B. The oboes push upwards by semitones in search of resolution, but the cadence in the third measure does not bring the triad on E promised by the preceding chord. In its stead a dominant seventh chord built on E is found, which prevents the phrase from ending conclusively. In measure 4 the cello again rises a sixth, this time from B to G♯, both of which are notes found in the final chord of the preceding phrase. But once more they are denied the goal to which they aspire, for the winds repeat the sequence of the first measures only to reach a dominant seventh chord built on G. Striving still higher, the cellos rise from D to B, but still find no satisfaction as the winds move from one dominant seventh chord to another. The chromatic idiom established by the movement of the parts in these opening measures is carried through the entire opera; from beginning to end Wagner's score is saturated with unresolved leading tones.

The sweep of this vast orchestral score is animated by leitmotifs, which express internal emotions, thoughts and aspirations—the significance of Tristan's glance, Isolde's desire for vengeance, the meanings of death. As psychological symbols they are transformed and developed by harmonic alterations and melodic extensions, becoming increasingly suggestive in the process. By interrupting or avoiding anticipated cadences, and by the constant use of chords of the seventh and ninth, Wagner creates a mobile, surging sea of orchestral sound which interprets and underscores the rise and fall of emotional tensions.

In this luxuriant musical fabric the vocal parts form only one of many strands. This is especially true in the most ecstatic sections of the love scene of Act II, and the conclusion of Act III, Isolde's "Love-Death." Here the vocal lines become indistinguishable from those of the orchestra. Typical of this novel relationship between voice and orchestra are the passages for Brangaene during the love duet. As Tristan and Isolde embrace, the orchestra expresses their feelings, and Brangaene, keeping her lonely watch, warns of the approaching day and reality. Her voice, however, provides but one of the many melodic curves which tie together the succession of voluptuous harmonies (Illustration 4).

The aesthetic ideal of Wagner's Gesamtkunstwerk is the fusion of the arts of painting, poetry, mime and music. But in *Tristan and Isolde* and his other mature works, music and particularly orchestral music occupies the leading role. Wagner's opulent orchestration blends the various instrumental sounds into a rich, powerful euphony. To accom-

ILLUSTRATION 4

ILLUSTRATION 4 (*continued*)

ILLUSTRATION 4 (*continued*)

ILLUSTRATION 4 (*continued*)

plish this objective more completely, the composer designed a sunken orchestral pit, the first of its kind, for his Festival Theatre at Bayreuth. From the invisible source of this "mystic abyss" the sounds emerge, enveloping and overwhelming the audience with their Dionysiac eloquence, fully realizing Wagner's aim of disclosing the inner life of feeling in a physical form that speaks directly to the emotions of the auditor.

The majority of younger German composers, among them Richard

Strauss (1864–1949) and Gustav Mahler (1860–1911), eagerly grasped
Wagner's powerful weapons. Strauss at first confined his creative talents
to the symphonic poem, composing seven of them between 1889 and
1898. In these works which won him immediate fame, he marshaled his
huge orchestral forces with the same force and brilliance which distinguished Wagner's music dramas. In addition he took over the principle of
the leitmotif and Wagner's complex harmony. His thematic materials are
invented to express clear-cut extra-musical meanings: the irrepressible
humor of Till Eulenspiegel is realistically painted by a jaunty, melodic
figure, followed unexpectedly by a sharp fortissimo chord; and the failing
pulse of the protagonist in *Death and Transfiguration* is depicted in monotonously repeated chords of irregular rhythmic grouping. In his concern for realistic details Strauss goes so far as to employ devices such as
the wind-machine.

The explicitness of Strauss' tone poems distinguishes them from
those of Franz Liszt. They also differ in their exploitation of existing
musical forms. Strauss, like a true Romantic, does not utilize these because of their abstract qualities, but because he finds in them a correspondence to his subject matter. The program of *Don Quixote*, for example, describes a series of tragi-comic adventures in which the knight
becomes involved because of his misplaced chivalry. Accordingly Strauss
constructs his symphonic poem in the form of a theme (of "knightly
character") and variations, interspersed with interludes of highly realistic
tone-painting.

The *Life of a Hero* brings the series of tone poems to a climax. With
disarming self-esteem Strauss identifies himself as the Hero by quoting
themes from his previous works. The events in this autobiographical
essay are portrayed in six sections succeeding one another without interruption. The resulting musical structure, while combining certain formal
characteristics of the sonata form and the symphony as a whole, never
quite overcomes the episodic form of a discursive narrative. The opening
section, depicting the Hero, functions as exposition; the next two are
analogous to scherzo and adagio movements, while the fourth, describing
the battle between the Hero and his adversaries, corresponds to the development section of the sonata form. The fifth, the "Hero's peaceful
works," consists of a recapitulation of the contents of the exposition as
well as of the leading motifs and themes of Strauss' earlier symphonic
poems. The concluding section, a majestic summation, functions as the
coda. In this fashion Strauss associates the purely musical techniques and
formal principles of the instrumental sonata explicitly with the expression
and description of "real" events and feelings. This realism is greatly en-
hanced by the assurance with which he combines striking effects of

orchestration with dramatic modulations, juxtaposition of distant tonalities, and various styles of melody.

In order to intensify the expressive properties of functional harmony, Strauss goes beyond the chromaticism of Wagner's *Tristan and Isolde* to exploit the possibilities of enharmonic modulations. The abrupt but smooth transition between tonalities as remote as E flat and E major is exemplified in the opening measures of the *Life of a Hero* (Illustration 5). The upward thrust of the heroic theme, propelled by wide leaps and energetic rhythm, carries it from E flat two octaves below middle C to the same tone four octaves higher during the first sixteen measures. Progressing confidently upon the tones of the E flat major triad, announced by the horns, cellos and violas, the tonality suddenly becomes blurred in measure seven with four notes which may be construed as part of the scale of E major. This ambiguity is overcome by a return to E flat in the next measure, but in measures eleven and twelve E major triumphantly breaks through only to be vanquished again in the next measure. This theme contains a superabundance of elements associated with the expression of heroic feelings in nineteenth-century music. It illustrates Strauss' tendency to overstatement and his talent for parody. A more powerful repetition of this theme is interrupted at the beginning of the twenty-first measure by a sudden change in dynamics, orchestration and key. The tonic E♭ has become D♯, the third tone in the scale of B major. The smooth lyricism of this new theme, emphasized by the succession of parallel sixths, serves as a sentimental foil to the initial heroics. The succeeding passage exemplifies Strauss' ability to create tension and excitement. Elements from both themes form an intricate polyphonic texture, which progresses by a chain of sequences through a rapid succession of modulations.

Strauss' symphonic poetry pushes musical realism to extremes that lead logically to the theatre. After an interval of reflection and experimentation, he accomplished this artistic progression in 1906 with his opera *Salomé*. To capture the morbidly sensuous quality of Oscar Wilde's play, he utilizes the full resources of the Wagnerian orchestra with an enlarged percussion section, animating it with a many-voiced tissue of motifs embedded in thick, chromatic harmony. The vocal style includes at one extreme the stylized declamation of Herod, and, at the other, the lyrical phrases of Salomé filled with chromatic and augmented intervals derived from the harmony. The opera reaches its climax in Salomé's soliloquy upon the severed head of John the Baptist. Her pathological feelings are expressed in the enormous range and tortured phraseology of her melody supported by the full orchestra.

Strauss' penchant for expressing violent and perverse emotions led

ILLUSTRATION 5

ILLUSTRATION 5 *(continued)*

ILLUSTRATION 5 (*continued*)

By permission of F. E. C. Leuckart, Munich-Leipzig.

him next to Hugo von Hofmannsthal's tragedy, *Elektra*. To produce effects of crude realism and clashing colors, Strauss in this opera resorts at times to multiple dissonances created by superimposing chords of opposing tonalities upon one another. Despite such passages of tonal confusion resulting from the multiplication of harmonic resources, the musical structure is still grounded upon the diatonic system of functional harmony. But the last assets of traditional harmony have been discovered and expended in these works. The bankruptcy of a harmonic system reaching back to the seventeenth century is at hand.

Gustav Mahler was known during his lifetime primarily as a conductor, and Director of the Imperial Opera in Vienna. In the repertory of this theatre the music dramas of Wagner occupied the most prominent position. From them Mahler drew many of the resources for his own compositions. Though he shared with Wagner the ideal of expressing the infinite by means of music, he did not pursue the path of the music drama. He sought instead to reconcile the polar elements of musical Romanticism, the lied and the symphony, to fuse the lyricism of subjective emotions with the brilliant colors of the orchestra. The series of symphonic works written between 1888 and 1909 bears witness to his goal of uniting the lied—so intimate in character, and so simple in style and form—with the symphony bequeathed by Beethoven to the nineteenth century.

A program is present in each of Mahler's nine symphonies, either explicitly because of the use of words, or implicitly because of the expressive nature of the movements. His attitude towards the ambivalent aspects of programmatic music is revealed in a letter of 1896 where he states that "beginning with Beethoven there exists no modern music which hasn't its inner program." He adds, however, that "no music is worth anything when the listener has to be instructed as to what is experienced in it." To account for the fact that he had provided a detailed explanation of his second symphony, first performed in this year, he continues: "For myself I know that as long as I can sum up my experiences in words, I can certainly not create music about it. My need to express myself in music begins precisely where dark feelings hold sway. . . . Just as it seems trivial to me to invent music to a preconceived programme, I find it unsatisfactory and sterile to add one to an existing musical composition. That does not alter the fact that the motive for a musical picture is certainly an experience of the author, which should be concrete enough to be expressible in words."

Wagner had solved the problem of expressing ideas in music by uniting the opera and the symphony in the Gesamtkunstwerk. But his solution did not satisfy Mahler who wished to express himself as a symphonist and not as a dramatist. "We stand now . . . at the great cross-roads which divides forever the diverging paths of symphonic and dramatic music so easily visible to the eye of one who is clear about the direction of music. Even now, should you hold up a Beethoven symphony against the tone pictures of Wagner you will easily recognize the essential difference between them. Indeed, Wagner made the means of expression of symphonic music his own, just as now the symphonist, fully qualified in and completely conscious of his medium, will profit by the wealth of expression which music gained through Wagner's efforts." *

To profit from Wagner's wealth of musical expression meant for Mahler the further expansion of harmonic resources, and the further growth of the techniques of thematic development and orchestration. It also entailed the extension of the orchestral apparatus, adding to the huge symphony orchestra the sonorities of organ and massed choirs of voices and brass instruments. With this went a corresponding expansion of the proportions of individual movements. This process reaches its climax in his Eighth Symphony, somewhat inaccurately referred to as the "Symphony of a Thousand." Consisting of but two enormous movements, it is written throughout for large chorus and orchestra, to which are joined additional vocal and instrumental groups in the second movement. Mahler composed the first movement to the ancient Christian hymn, *Veni Creator Spiritus*, and for the second he took the final visionary scenes from Part Two of Goethe's *Faust*. Only a profoundly Romantic artist would have conceived of uniting these disparate subjects in a single musical work.

The extension of musical expression does not always require the magnification of sound. It can also be attained through the refinement of instrumental tone color, by combinations of solo instruments in place of massive sonorities. Mahler only succeeded in reaching this ideal consistently in one of his last works, *Das Lied von der Erde*, though it is reflected in individual movements in his other symphonies. Composed for contralto, tenor, and orchestra, *The Song of the Earth* unites the concept of the song with that of the symphony. The six songs are poems translated from the Chinese, which contrast the eternal beauties of nature with the transience of life. Mahler's subtitle, "a Symphony," is justified not only by the unity of subject matter, the use of the orchestra, and the extensive proportions, but also because of the imaginative development of a single, incisive theme carried on throughout each movement (Illustration 6). The most prominent feature of this theme, which is sounded emphatically by four horns in the opening measures, is the interval of the fourth. Its concluding four tones suggest the pentatonic, or primitive

* Alma Mahler, *Gustav Mahler: Briefe*, p. 187.

five-tone scale (C D E G A), which provides both harmonic and melodic materials for many subsequent sections.

By means of rhythmic alterations this theme generates flowing melodic lines, as in the second song; provides ostinato rhythmic figures, as in the final song; or becomes the half-concealed basis for the deriva-

ILLUSTRATION 6

ILLUSTRATION 6 (*continued*)

tion of new themes and motifs. The frequent proximity of major and minor triads for the expression of pathos characterizes the harmonic style, and provides a strong element of continuity throughout the score. Its predominantly contrapuntal texture is projected with exceptional clarity because Mahler exploits the many contrasting tone colors of all the instruments by treating them soloistically, and often placing them in unusual registers and combinations. The extremely personal character of this work, so pessimistic in spirit despite its passages of vigorous affirmation, marks it as a late-blooming flower of Romanticism, while its technical novelties have made it the inspiration of many orchestral songs in the twentieth century.

The host of recruits flocking to Wagner's standard found few opponents. But in Vienna, a small but sturdy band led by Eduard Hanslick, a music critic, strove to turn the tide of battle. From the middle of the century until his death in 1904, Hanslick unrelentingly attacked Romantic enthusiasts in general and the Wagnerites in particular. "Instead of closely following the course of music," he writes in *The Beautiful in Music,*

these enthusiasts, reclining in their seats and only half awake, suffer themselves to be rocked and lulled by the mere flow of sound. The sound, now waxing and now diminishing in strength, now rising up in jubilant strains and now softly dying away, produces in them a series of vague sensations which they in their simplicity fancy to be the result of intellectual action. . . . For their ear the aesthetic criterion of intelligent gratification is wanting, and a good cigar, some exquisite dainty, or a warm bath yields them the same enjoyment as a symphony, though they may not be aware of the fact. In the indolent and apathetic attitude of some and the hysterical raptures of others, the active principle is the same—delight in the *elementary* property of music.

The true understanding of music, he asserts, demands the active participation of the contemplative mind. In good music it is not the sentiment or spirit of the composition but the specifically musical element which matters.

The form (the musical structure) is the real substance (subject of music)— in fact is the music itself, in antithesis to the feeling, its alleged subject, which can be called neither its subject nor its form, but simply the effect produced.

But more than words were needed to combat Wagner: a composer had to be found to lead the attack with musical weapons. The composer chosen, against his will, was Johannes Brahms (1833–1897). Like Wagner, Brahms had an unbounded admiration for the symphonies of Beethoven. Unlike Wagner, who saw Beethoven's *Ninth Symphony* as the end of the instrumental sonata, and the forerunner of his own musical dramas, Brahms sought to maintain the integrity and universality of the symphony. It was not easy for him to revert to the symphonic ideal of the Classic Era because of his own Romantic tendencies. Only in his thirty-ninth year did he finally complete his first symphony. In the meantime he found an outlet for the melancholy introspection of his spirit in the lied and in genre pieces for the piano.

The underlying romanticism of Brahms' nature is unmistakably reflected in his symphonic works notwithstanding the degree of his success

in fusing lyrical thematic materials and unusual harmony with the processes and techniques of thematic development. The expressive element so
prominent in the *First Symphony*, completed in 1877, is no less pronounced in the *Fourth* and last of 1886. Though this *Symphony in E
minor* is accompanied by no stated subject or program, the content and
sequence of movements conveys an intensely personal meaning. Brahms'
nostalgic feeling for the lost values and ideals of the past here receives its
most eloquent statement. In the first movement it is manifested in the
skillfully worked out sonata form culminating in a stern coda. It appears
in the fatalistic mood of the second movement for which the expressive
contrast of E minor, E major and the Phrygian mode with its lowered
seventh step is responsible. The C major Allegro of the third movement
in sonata form defies, as it were, the tragic content of the previous movements. But its heroic energy has nothing in common with the brusque
wit and straightforward humor of the scherzos of older symphonies.
Denying the promise of this movement and confirming the tragic content of the opening movements, Brahms turns in his finale to an archaic
form, the *chaconne*. Here Brahms' suppressed Romanticism breaks its
bonds. He chooses this dance, remote from the tradition of the symphony, not for the stringency of its form, but for its connotations. With
its variations upon a brief, persistently repeated theme the chaconne is
used to bring the symphony to a close with the resigned tones of a fatalistic Dance of Death.

The opening theme of the first movement (Illustration 7) is stamped
with Brahms' individual style to a marked degree. Its lyrical contours
extend over nineteen measures, divided into two unequal sections (measures 1–8, and 9–19). In the first section the thematic material consists of
pairs of quarter and half notes spanning thirds, sixths and octaves. The
accompaniment consists of chordal figurations in the lower strings, with
a canonic echo of the theme by the wind instruments. This section of the
first theme constitutes the "motto" of the symphony, recurring throughout the first movement and towards the end of the last. A restatement of
the theme begins at the end of measure 18 before the first statement has
come to a close. It is a masterly recasting of the original material. The
violins now break their phrases into eighth-note octave leaps; the canon
of the winds is transferred to the cellos and double basses in a modified
form; and new countermelodies are added to the original theme by the
violas and winds. Only after this second statement does the bridge begin.
The second theme brings no relief from the tragic minor tonality. Instead of choosing the key of the relative major, Brahms goes to B minor.
The lyricism of this cello melody is belied by the sweep of its phrases
and by the heroic rhythm of the accompaniment derived from the martial

ILLUSTRATION 7

405

ILLUSTRATION 7 *(continued)*

ILLUSTRATION 7 *(continued)*

horn motif that precedes the entrance of the second theme. The tragic tone of the symphony has been set in these first two themes, and it is sustained throughout Brahms' thoroughly classical development, recapitulation, and coda in the first movement.

The final movement is the most "original" feature of this symphony. Following the tradition of the chaconne, Brahms composes a theme of eight measures which is both a melody and a sequence of harmonies. In the thirty variations which follow it, the melody appears at times in the top voices and at times as an ostinato bass. In many variations the top melody vanishes, but its accompanying sequence of chords is found in its place. This theme climbs from the tonic E to the dominant B, only to plunge down an octave and from thence relentlessly back to its starting point. Both its shape and its recurrence suggest the remorseless will of fate. Brahms groups the variations in sections corresponding roughly to exposition, development and recapitulation. In the middle section the variations recall the spirit of the second and third movements by modulating to their tonalities. In the concluding variation, above the ostinato theme he introduces a sequence of descending thirds derived from the motto theme of the first movement in a canon between the upper and lower stringed instruments. In this subtle manner Brahms recapitulates the events of the entire symphony within the archaic form of the chaconne, and confirms their meaning.

The music and ideas of German composers dominated Western music throughout the nineteenth century much as Italian music had done two centuries earlier. But the history of Europe in this period is characterized by the growing strength of nationalism in culture as well as in politics. This is mirrored in the mounting enthusiasm for native folk songs and rhythms, and indigenous musical traditions. Musical nationalism does not appear in the same form in the different countries where political and cultural aspirations favored its growth. In Italy, for example, it is represented almost exclusively by the personality and the operas of Giuseppe Verdi (1813–1901). An ardent patriot and fighter for the political unification of Italy, Verdi's rise to artistic fame coincides with the events which led eventually to the realization of Italian nationalism.

Verdi's identification with this cause did not manifest itself in his art as a discovery and display of Italian folk song but as a renewal of an art form intimately related to Italian life for three centuries, the opera. His acceptance and continuation of the traditional tenets of Italian opera made him undeniably an adversary of Richard Wagner. Verdi's idealism was as tenacious as Wagner's, but it was applied to the task of invigorating and refining the longstanding conventions and forms of opera.

The subjects of his many operas are indicative of his Romantic literary taste. They range from the plays of Schiller, Alexandre Dumas, Victor Hugo and Eugène Scribe to the mediaeval romance *Il Trovatore*. Above all these stand the plays of Shakespeare for which he possessed a veneration as passionate as that of Berlioz, the arch-romanticist of earlier years. But his adaptation of *Othello* (1887) and *Falstaff* (1895) is not carried out by Romantic musical transliteration in the manner of Berlioz. To the Italian Verdi the human voice is the supreme instrument of human expression, and the numerous emotions of individuals may be fully conveyed by the various styles of recitative and aria. The orchestra with its increasingly subtle, varied instrumentation may comment upon a situation by means of expressive motifs, but its role remains complementary to the dramatic action in conformity with the tradition of Italian opera. Verdi asserts his national pride by bringing a native art form to a peak of perfection that challenges the supremacy of the Wagnerian Gesamtkunstwerk.

National musical aspirations are directly responsible for the appearance of a Russian school of composers in the second half of the nineteenth century. Since the early eighteenth century Russian aristocratic circles had favored the music and musicians of Italy. These in turn had been supplanted in their esteem by the products of nineteenth-century German composers. The impact of German musical styles and forms upon Russian composers is eloquently exemplified in the symphonic poems and symphonies of Peter Ilyich Tchaikowski (1840–1893). But beneath this musical overlay, an extremely rich and varied repertory of folk melodies and a copious liturgy combining Byzantine and Oriental elements continued to flourish. These became the rallying point for the leaders of the Russian national school, Balakirev, Borodin, Cui, Rimski-Korsakov and Musorgsky, the "Russian Five." They used these native elements to give the forms cultivated by Romantic European composers a nationalistic flavor. Their music is more colorful and bizarre than genuinely national, however, for a successful reconciliation between the idiom of folk melodies and rhythms and the harmonic and thematic techniques of the symphonic style is not effected.

Modeste Musorgsky (1839–1881) alone among this group succeeded in creating music in which native Russian elements play an essential rather than a decorative role. The Romantic ideals of his earlier works give way progressively to those of direct, realistic expression in his masterpiece, *Boris Godunov*, an opera composed between 1868 and 1872. The subtitle, "a musical Folk-Drama," accurately describes the nature of this work. In a letter of 1876 Musorgsky defined the artistic aim that guided him in his musical creations: "My present intention . . . is directed towards the melody that partakes of life, not toward Classical melody. . . .

I explore human speech; thus I arrive at the melody created by this speech, arriving at the embodiment of recitative in melody (excepting, of course, the passages of dramatic action, where each interjection may become important). One might call this a melody justified by sense."

This ideal, which recalls after many centuries the original premises of Monteverdi's *dramma per musica*, is founded upon a sensitive appreciation of the idiomatic elements of the Russian language. It is realized by translating the speech rhythms and accentuations into a free-flowing declamatory style. The limited range of his melodies, their irregular rhythms and asymmetrical phrases, often monotonously repeated, are virtually indistinguishable from the Russian folk melodies with which they alternate. Throughout the opera the latter are employed to epitomize the deepest feelings of the diverse groups and personages who populate the scenes, linking them in a common idiom. The people voice their pleas for mercy or their rejoicing in Boris' coronation with folk melodies, just as the barmaid expresses her loneliness, the nurse diverts Boris' children, or the Simpleton bewails the lot of Russia. Sometimes these melodies appear to be integral parts of the musical fabric, as though they were invoked instinctively, while elsewhere they erupt suddenly and violently.

The characteristics which differentiate the Russian melodies from those of western Europe stand out sharply in the song of the vagabond friar, Varlaam, in the second scene of Act I. It is a ballad describing Tsar Ivan's victory over the Tartars at the city of Kazan (Illustration 8). Each of its five stanzas are sung to the same brief melody of only two strains. A twice-repeated phrase of five measures forms the first half of the melody. After an upward leap of a perfect fifth it descends stepwise in a scale which is not the conventional minor of western Europe but the old Phrygian mode. In the second strain, a different phrase of four measures begins from a new tonal center, A natural. It too is repeated, and then concluded with an abrupt fall from a sustained D to G as its final tone. The unequal length of the phrases and the modal character of the melody contrast sharply with the symmetry and the major-minor tonality of contemporary European music.

Here, as in much of the opera, the accompaniment consists of simple triads based upon the formulas of the ecclesiastical modes. Since many of the chords are in root position a succession of parallel octaves and fifths is produced, creating a sturdy, crude quality completely at variance with conventional harmonic procedures. At other times, to underline violent expressions of passionate feelings or to paint a picture of barbaric splendor as in the Coronation scene, Musorgsky invents dissonant chords or unusual mixtures of tones which sound both primitive and novel by comparison with the musical language of his day.

ILLUSTRATION 8

In France during the second half of the nineteenth century musical activity was carried on by a number of composers of the second rank, each of whom tended to develop his style in accordance with the various currents of musical Romanticism which criss-crossed in Paris. The doctrines and music of Wagner attracted more and more attention, and after 1880 Wagnerism became a dominant force in French artistic thought. The subject matter of his dramas sired a number of imitations by both writers and musicians. His aesthetic doctrines reinforced by the emotional impact of his music won the adulation of a number of notable literary figures who founded the *Revue Wagnérienne* in 1885. Among them were Mallarmé, Verlaine and Swinburne, men who felt—to quote one of the founders of the periodical, Dujardin—that Wagner "was one of the masters of symbolism; his conception of art, his philosophy, even his formula belonged in their origin to symbolism and it was impossible to go to the root of Wagnerism without discovering there symbolism."

Wagner's influence had a particularly strong impact upon the symbolist poetry and poetic theory of Stéphane Mallarmé. By no means a trained musician, Mallarmé felt music to be more spiritual than sensual, an intrinsic mystery of the human soul, "because each soul is a melody which must be renewed." The substance of Wagner's dramas, the bric-a-brac of Gods and heroes, did not impress him, though he was moved by their symbolic meanings. But in common with other symbolist poets, Mallarmé regarded music, particularly the music of Wagner, as the ideal medium to arouse images and feelings. Words, too, he felt, are capable of evoking mysterious and powerful feelings if their symbolic meanings and musical sonorities are fused. The recognition of these mysterious musical values carried with it a heightened appreciation of nuance. To Paul Verlaine "nuance alone marries dream to dream and flute to horn."

The poetry of suggestion and the elusive theories of the symbolists played an important part in forming the musical style of Claude Debussy (1862–1918). As a young man, Debussy was as little attracted by the academic principles of the art of music as Berlioz had been. At the Conservatoire, he was known for his habit of improvising bold successions of chords out of context with their conventional relationships. He was borne on the fashionable tide of Wagnerism until he attended the official productions of the music dramas at Bayreuth in 1888 and 1889. Here he perceived sharp discrepancies between Wagner's idealistic theories and their musical realization. In particular, the system of leading motifs seemed to him as tyrannical as the thematic formulas and techniques of development in the sonata form. His disenchantment was subsequently increased by the contrast he discovered between the elaborate machinery of Wagnerian musical forces and the small but effective resources of the Javanese music he heard at the International Exposition of 1890. Penetrating beneath the surface exoticism of this music he found a means of release from what he was coming to think of as outmoded melodic and harmonic conventions. In the Javanese music he encountered the pentatonic and whole-tone scales, which contain no semitones (Illustration 9). Devoid of

ILLUSTRATION 9

any pull of leading tone, these scales, like many of the old church modes, have a vagueness and a freedom that Debussy could exploit for his own purposes.

Debussy's first work to reflect his musical aspirations is the *Prélude à l'Après-midi d'un faune*, completed in 1892, but later revised. An instrumental composition inspired by a poem of Mallarmé, its genealogical descent from the symphonic poem is obvious. But the obscure content of the poetry precludes as direct a relationship between the poetic subject and music as that found in the symphonic poems of Liszt or Strauss. Debussy seeks only to capture the vague imagery of Mallarmé in an equally vague musical language. The theme with which the work opens (Illustration 10) lacks any regularity of rhythmic stresses in its undulating contours. It suggests no specific tonality for it is partly based upon the whole-tone scale. Its indecisive conclusion is supported by the harmonies of two seventh chords, whose succession is not determined by recognizable harmonic relations, and whose clarity is blurred by the shimmer of a harp arpeggio and the interlocking wind and string instrumentation.

In the *Nocturnes* and *Images* for orchestra, and the preludes and genre compositions for piano, which appeared in subsequent years, the unique features of Debussy's style, frequently described as "impressionistic," become distinct and consistent. Fragmentary motifs replace symmetrical, balanced melodies. To produce nuances instead of sharply defined tones, they are frequently enunciated by several instruments of

ILLUSTRATION 10

ILLUSTRATION 10 *(continued)*

dissimilar tone color in unison. Often concluding indecisively by two or three descending whole tones, these motifs possess little dynamic energy. The harmonic fabric, by turns luminous and misty, is composed of parallel chords of simple or complex structure, progressing freely without any orientation to definite tonal centers. Sections of monotonously regular rhythmic values without rhythmic accents alternate with passages in which the rhythm is fluid and irregular. The outlines of Romantic forms dissolve in vagueness and ambiguity.

Debussy's style is most completely realized in his opera, *Pelléas et Mélisande*. In composing this work, which occupied him almost exclusively between 1892 and 1902, Debussy made but minor revisions in the play of Maurice Maeterlinck, which was an attempt to translate the aims of the symbolist poets into dramatic form. Superficially the central action of the play bears a resemblance to Wagner's *Tristan and Isolde*.

Golaud, a middle-aged man, discovers Mélisande weeping in the forest, marries her and brings her home to the castle of his grandfather, blind King Arkel. There she meets Golaud's half brother, Pelléas, who is as young as she is. They gradually fall in love, a development Golaud suspects but cannot prove. Driven by jealousy, he murders Pelléas, and Mélisande dies after giving birth to a child. These events are only shadows of inner feelings. Maeterlinck is more interested in suggesting the "vast ocean of the unconscious which lies beneath all human thoughts, volitions, passions and actions," and his characters pursue their destiny through a forest of symbols which are but the visible signs of an inward, spiritual reality.

Debussy's objective was to compose a musical score whose function was to suggest rather than to underline the meaning of the text, and which would maintain the continuous flow of dialogue and action envisaged

ILLUSTRATION 11

ILLUSTRATION 11 (*continued*)

ILLUSTRATION 11 *(continued)*

Permission for reprint granted by Durant et Cie, Paris, France, copyright owners; Elkan-Vogel Co., Inc. Philadelphia, Pa., agents.

by the playwright. His first concern was the creation of a vocal style which would pursue the inflection of each word and the shape and rhythm of each phrase. In the first scene where Golaud encounters the mysterious Mélisande, the distinctive qualities of this style appear immediately (Illustration 11). The vocal lines are as free from the repetitions and symmetries of traditional melody as they are restricted in their range. In conformity with the vague, indefinite nature of Maeterlinck's text their phraseology seldom takes on the musical curves of lyricism as a means of intensifying or expanding upon passages of strong feeling. Nor are the brief phrases of the text bridged over to form long or continuous melodic arches. Many of the musical periods hover around a single tone, but their irregular shapes add expressive overtones to the disjointed, unfinished sentences of the characters.

The orchestra alternately underlines a phrase, supplies punctuation, or provides a comment as the action progresses. It seems to be, in the words of Erik Satie, "musical scenery . . . in which the characters move and talk." Debussy accomplishes this effect by the use of ecclesiastical modes and the whole-tone and pentatonic scales in place of major and minor keys, by spreading the harmonies thinly through portions of the orchestral choirs, and by maintaining a low dynamic level of sound. The repetition of brief motifs provides some continuity to a harmonic panorama, which is momentarily immobile, then ephemeral. Its chords may be dwelt upon without any resolution, or may give way unexpectedly to new, unrelated harmonies. Debussy's acute sensitivity to subtle differences of tone brings to this music expressive nuances of every sort.

All these innovations earned for Debussy's music the term "modern." For he had replaced the grandiose pathos of Wagnerian and post-Wagnerian music with the suggestive powers of understatement, and created a style in which both melody and harmony depart radically from the procedures of nineteenth-century music. Yet many of the ideals of Romanticism, refined, attenuated and diffuse, still lie beneath these novelties. His music seems to mark both the concluding phase of musical Romanticism and the beginning of a new era.

XIII THE TWENTIETH CENTURY

The Search for Reality

TO FIND THEIR VISIONS of life and reality the men of the nineteenth century had probed deeply into the most secret recesses of the soul. The Romantic artist had striven, in the words of Browning, to

> Drag into day
> The abysmal bottom-growth, ambiguous thing
> Unbroken of branch, palpitating
> With limbs' play and life's semblance!

To plumb the mysteries of existence the men of this era had also turned to the past, to the forgotten events of history; and the scientist had explored the arcana of the physical universe.

As his knowledge of the past and of the natural world expanded and deepened, man was confronted with troubling doubts about the reality of his own being. Was he a creature so firmly bound in evolutionary processes that his actions were in a sense determined by events of the past or by physical reflexes over which he had no control? Were all his thoughts and actions written by an inexorable hand upon the wall of time? Or was it possible that they were a matter of his own choice? Could he determine his own relationship to past and present, to material and immaterial reality? To affirm the latter possibility would require a courageous willingness to penetrate to depths of the soul undreamed of

419

by the Romantics. The necessity of such a course, urged by Kierkegaard and others during the nineteenth century, was reasserted by Freud, when he concluded that the one positive means of controlling man's brief span of time lay in the Self.

The desire to assert his own reality, to triumph over time and history, stimulated the artist to find new ways of conceptualizing his inner vision. Reality to a Proust lies in the remembrance of things past; to a Joyce it consists in the attempt to apprehend the simultaneous existence of different levels of human experience; to a Picasso it may be revealed by viewing an object from all sides at the same time. At the artist's disposal were techniques, styles, and forms reaching back from the present to the most primitive times. Yet each must be scrutinized and evaluated before being made to serve his will. Some techniques and forms might be adopted almost unchanged, or details from many different sources might be assembled in wholly new combinations. Moreover, the artist may continually discover new ways of expressing himself, so that he works in various styles at different times, or may even cultivate different idioms simultaneously. Relativity, a new term for describing the nature of the universe, seems an apt characterization for the creative activity of the twentieth century.

The search for new means of expression, even though related to new aesthetic ideals, is a continuation of the Romantic quest for the individual and the unique. The desire for originality in music prompted the radical innovations of Debussy, just as it inspired the empirical experimentation of America's Charles Ives (1874–1954). But younger composers were increasingly aware of the fact that the limits of the musical language of the nineteenth century had been reached. In seeking to intensify music's expressiveness, their predecessors had centered their attention upon harmony more than any other element of music. The frontiers of harmonic practice had been continually extended by the use of chords of ever-increasing complexity and by the frequency and novelty of modulations. This led in many instances to an obscuring of key relationships and to the disappearance of well-defined tonalities as the means of articulating musical structures.

If the nineteenth century had exhausted its most admired musical resource, were not its aesthetic premises also vitiated? The possibility of other worlds than that defined by the symphonies of Beethoven and the music-dramas of Wagner encouraged composers to abandon long-established values and traditions of music. The tempo of this change was accelerated by the war of 1914–1918, which profoundly altered the institutions of the Western world. After the war, the development of media of mass communication, the radio, cinema, and phonograph, also had an important, though negative, effect upon the composer. The mass audience, possessing only a casual knowledge of the nature of music and instinctively drawn to the familiar, did not welcome innovations. Finding no audience for his works, the composer increasingly tended to write for an "ideal" audience of the future. Freed from the dictates of the public's taste, his experimentations were guided only by his own desires.

The rapidly changing status of music raised many questions about the nature of this art. Many attempts were made to clarify its purpose, ranging from the prescriptions of politicians, such as Hitler and the members of the Politburo, to the disillusioned panaceas of writers such as Jean Cocteau. But the most important answers had to be found by composers themselves. Many of them, facing the question of how the vitality and meaning of music might best be renewed, initiated a searching examination of the basic materials of music. One who did so was Bela Bartok (1881–1945).

Bartok grew up in a musical environment where the conflicting values of Hungarian nationalism and nineteenth-century German music produced extreme tensions. Drawn at first to both of them, Bartok, as his knowledge of European music expanded, became increasingly unsure of the fundamental bases of musical art. His uncertainty helped to stimulate his interest in Hungarian peasant music, and, in turn, the primitive music of the Balkan peninsula, Asia Minor and North Africa. His researches made him increasingly aware of the artistic value of elemental musical materials, and stimulated the growth of his own style and his respect for impeccable craftsmanship rather than inspiration. "The conception that attributes so much importance to the invention of a theme originated in the nineteenth century," he wrote in 1931. "It is a romantic conception which values originality above all. . . . In music, as in poetry and painting, it does not matter what themes we use. It is the form into which we mould them that makes the essence of our work. This form reveals the knowledge, the creative power, the individuality of the artist."

Mastery of the craft of musical composition was also the solution to the problems of contemporary music advocated by Paul Hindemith. Born in 1895, he became a leader among the young radicals of music after World War I, and experimented widely and daringly in the decade of the twenties. At the same time he sought to uncover fundamental laws of musical composition in the aesthetic and practical treatises of the past, and by scientific analysis of the acoustical properties and physical laws of sound. In 1937 he published the first of a series of textbooks on composition (*The Craft of Musical Composition*). Comparing his role to that of Johann Josef Fux, whose *Gradus ad Parnassum* published in 1725 was intended to conserve the traditional style of vocal polyphony, Hindemith wrote: "A musician who feels called upon in these times to contribute to the preservation and transmission of the craft of musical composition is . . . on the defensive. He is, in fact, even more so than Fux, for in no other field of artistic activity has a period of overdevelopment of materials and of their application been followed by such confusion as reigns in this one . . . Now something that cannot be understood by the analysis of a musician . . . cannot possibly be more convincing to the naive listener. . . . The initiated know that most of the music that is produced every day represents everything except the composer: memory, cheap compilation, mental indolence, habit, imitation, and above all the obstinacy of the tones themselves. Our principal task is to overcome the latter. To do this we need precise knowledge of the tones and of the forces that reside in them, free from aesthetic dogma and stylistic exercises . . . but leading the composer rather to natural laws and technical experience." And he points out that from early antiquity through the Middle Ages up to modern times farsighted composers have held firmly to such views and sought to pass them on.

The artistic achievements of Bartok and the teaching of Hindemith each contributed to a clarification of the meaning and direction of music in the first half of the twentieth century. But neither had as profound an impact upon the nature of musical art in this period as did the ideas and music of Arnold Schoenberg (1874–1951) and Igor Stravinsky (born 1882). Both have presented concepts of music between which it is difficult to discern any points of agreement. Stravinsky's influence has been asserted primarily through his music, for he is one of the few major composers of the twentieth century who has not joined teaching with composition. But Schoenberg began teaching very early in his career, and his importance must be measured as much by the work of his most gifted disciples as by his own compositions and his writings on music.

Schoenberg's conception of music went through a rapid and violent evolution during the first decades of the century. Like the German expressionist painters, with whom he was closely associated, he was profoundly affected by Siegmund Freud's analysis of the unconscious.

In the words of Thomas Mann, Freud's "discovery of the great role played by the unconscious, the Id, in the soul-life of man challenged and challenges classical psychology, to which the unconscious and psyche are one and the same, as offensively as once Schopenhauer's doctrine of the will challenged philosophical belief in reason and the intellect." In his *Anatomy of the Mental Personality*, Freud asserts that "the domain of the Id is the dark, inaccessible part of our personality; the little we know of it we have learned through the study of dreams and of the formation of neurotic symptoms." He describes the Id as a chaos, a melting pot of compulsions and of seething excitations received from physical experience. The Id's energy provided by these forces struggles to achieve satisfaction for the conflicting impulses. "Contradictory stimuli exist alongside each other without cancelling each other out or even detracting from each other; at most they unite in compromise forms under the compulsion of the controlling economy for the release of energy." In this subconscious world no laws of thought are valid, for the unconscious is dynamic, primitive, irrational. It knows no values, no good or evil, no morality. It knows no time, nor any effect of time upon its psychic process. "Wish stimuli, which have never overpassed the Id, and impressions which have been repressed into its depths," Freud concludes, "are virtually indestructible, they survive decade after decade as though they had just happened."

The Ego, according to Freud, is that part of the Id which is modified by contact with the outer world. It strives to distinguish the objectively real from the accretions of its inward sources of stimulation. The Id has entrusted the Ego with the lever of action; but between impulse and action there is interposed the delay of the thought process, during which experience is summoned to its aid. Thus the Ego possesses a certain regulative authority over the unconscious, correcting its impulses by means of the principle of reality. But since it is hemmed in between the unconscious, the outer world, and what Freud calls the Super-Ego, the existence of the Ego is neither stable nor serene. Torn between contradictory forces it is responsible for the irrational element in man's thought and action.

Freud's ideas began to affect Western thought profoundly after the turn of the century. Nowhere was their impact greater than in Vienna, where Freud was practicing his profession, and where insoluble social and spiritual conflicts seemed to lead inevitably towards calamity. In Freud's nocturnal world of the unconscious, more irrational and haunted than the Romantics had ever imagined, Arnold Schoenberg and his Viennese colleagues discovered the psychoneurotic subject matter of their astonishing works created in the epoch of the First World War. The generation of Expressionist artists strove to depict the self as the repository of the hidden, nameless horrors that lurk beneath the surface of life. Painters found appropriate means of expression in the use of rough, clashing surfaces and the technique of the palette brush. Musicians utilized asymmetrical, distorted rhythms and jagged melodic lines. Above all they exploited the values of dissonance, avoiding consonance because of its association with the external world of conventional beauty.

"Destiny or the Supreme Commander," as he put it, seemed to force Arnold Schoenberg into this uncharted world of sound and expression.

Schoenberg came of age during the high tide of Wagnerism. His first major work, *Verklärte Nacht* (1899), though written as a string sextet, is in all respects a symphonic poem in the chromatic idiom of Wagner's *Tristan and Isolde*. Its subject is a psychological conflict and resolution described in a poem *Zwei Menschen* (*Two People*) by Richard Dehmel. During the succeeding decade his penetration into the world of total chromaticism was paced by his growing absorption with the inner world of the subconscious. The aim of the *Five Orchestral Pieces* of 1909 was subsequently described as an attempt to find the expression of "all that dwells in us subconsciously like a dream, which is a great fluctuant power, and is built upon none of the lines that are familiar to us. . . . In it all technical craft is submerged, made one and indivisible with the content of the work."

In an essay, *The Relationship to the Text*, published in 1912, Schoenberg questions the assumption that music must summon up images of any sort, or even that it must be rationally comprehensible: "Even Schopenhauer, who at first says something really exhaustive about the essence of music in his wonderful thought, 'the composer reveals the inmost essence of the world and utters the most profound wisdom in a language which his reason does not understand, just as a magnetic somnambulist gives disclosures about things which she has no idea of when awake'— even he loses himself later when he tries to translate details of this language *which the reason does not understand* into our terms." Music, the language of the inmost world should remain instinctive, felt, rather than understood. From this it follows, Schoenberg asserts, that the work of art ought to be an organism so homogeneous in its composition that it reveals its essence in every detail. It comes into being not because of the ability of the artist but of necessity. "What is innate in a practicing artist he can develop. What he wills, good or bad, shallow or profound, modern or antiquated, he can do. But he cannot influence what he produces. Necessity drives him, not his will." Schoenberg is arguing like a Romantic—like Kant!—that the work of art is produced by nature working through genius. But there is an essential difference: the Romantic held that the works of genius should contribute to the moral and spiritual welfare of mankind; Schoenberg maintained that the work of art has no aim other than the realization of Self by artistic necessity.

Art for art's sake is raised by Schoenberg to a position of extreme exclusiveness. The composer's goal is simply the presentation of his own idea, by which he does not mean themes or motifs as expressions of explicit ideas, but the "totality of the piece" as the composer conceived it. "If everything is done that this idea demands, the external appearance, that is to say the style, will be adequate." Thus style, in Schoenberg's view, grows naturally from the artist's idea. "Only a master who is sure of himself, of his sense of form and balance, can renounce conscious control in favor of the dictates of his imagination." Only he may venture safely into the world of sound where distinctions between dissonance and consonance no longer exist. "From these premises," as Theodore Adorno points out, "it follows that music is no longer to present the appearance of passions; instead, shocks and traumata, which are tangible manifestations of the unconscious, are registered in the medium of music."

Schoenberg was thoroughly aware of the revolutionary implications of these conclusions, but he felt that the evolutionary process of history made them inevitable. Man had always been sensitive to the differences in meaning between consonance and dissonance. But creative artists had taught him to accept as pleasing harmonic combinations and progressions that other epochs had regarded as dissonant. During the nineteenth century the increasing demands of personal expression had greatly enlarged the number of acceptable dissonances by the exploitation of chromaticism. Inevitably this process imposed an increasing strain upon the rational, systematic understanding of the behavior of harmonic progressions.

Schoenberg points out that "the idea that one basic tone, the root, dominated the construction of chords and regulated their succession— the concept of *tonality*—had to develop first into the concept of *extended tonality*. Very soon it became doubtful whether such a root still remained the center to which every harmony and harmonic succession must be referred." Wagner's practices had led to the "so-called impressionistic use of harmonies, . . . without constructive meaning, [which] often served the coloristic purpose of expressing moods and pictures. Moods and pictures, though extra-musical, thus became constructive elements, incorporated in the musical functions; they produced a sort of emotional comprehensibility. In this way, tonality was already dethroned in practice, if not in theory. This alone would perhaps not have caused a radical change in compositional technique. However, such a change became necessary when there occurred simultaneously a development which ended in what I call the *emancipation of the dissonance*."

The premise underlying this last conclusion is that the twelve tones of the octave possess no natural or inherent relationships with each other. If that is the case, consonance and dissonance are terms which no longer have meaning, for consonance is predicated upon a relationship, a congruence of tones, and dissonance, upon the deviation from such relationships. With such an assumption conventional tonality disappears as a factor of musical composition. The emancipation of the dissonance can be realized only by the elimination of tonal centers defined by preconceived ideas of the relationship of tones.

The principles of *atonality* were slowly worked out by Schoenberg in his works composed between 1908 and 1912. Only two of these were written for instruments alone, the *Five Pieces for Orchestra*, Opus 16, and the *Six Little Piano Pieces*, Opus 19. The orchestral pieces bear a tenuous relationship to the symphonic poem of the nineteenth century, for each has an expressive, extra-musical title. The arrangement of the chromatic materials of the first and last two pieces is controlled by fluctuations of emotional paroxysms rather than by considerations of musical form, as the music oscillates between extremes of dynamics and pitch. Frequently enormous numbers of harmonic dissonances accumulate through the superimposing of a number of nonsynchronized polyphonic lines. The third piece appears in contrast to its surroundings as a study of suspended motion. It consists entirely of the chromatic permutations of a single complex chord. Removed from the perspective of tonality, this chord functions as neither consonance nor dissonance, but as an indeterminate combination of sounds. Because of the meticulously conceived instrumentation in these changing "Colors" of *Summer Morning by a Lake*, the sensuous qualities of conventionally unrelated harmonic intervals seem deceptively placid (Illustration 1).

Schoenberg employs the style of the *Five Pieces* in another work of 1909, the monodrama *Erwartung*, in which a woman in the extremities of terror gropes her way through an impenetrable forest seeking her lover, whose dead body is ultimately disclosed by the moon. But the atonal idiom reaches a new stage of refinement in Schoenberg's setting of *Pierrot Lunaire* (1912), a cycle of twenty-one poems by Albert Giraud. In these the distraught and dimly perceived figure of Pierrot, the itinerant minstrel and clown of tradition, apostrophizes the moon in images that are in turn nostalgic, bizarre or ghastly. The music is written for soprano and an ensemble of five instruments, piano, cello, violin (at times replaced by viola), clarinet (and bass-clarinet), and flute, for which a piccolo is sometimes substituted. The combination of instruments is altered from song to song. The poetic texts are set in a species of musical declamation, the *Sprechgesang* (spoken melody) which Schoenberg had previously devised for the woman of *Erwartung*. Its manner of execution requires that the notated rhythm must be observed as in conventional singing. But unlike a sung melody in which the tones are to be exactly rendered in pitch, the singer is merely to approximate them, so that the inflections of the voice conform to the contours of the written musical phrase.

ILLUSTRATION I

ILLUSTRATION 2

Schoenberg scrupulously observes the musical values of the words, their rhythms, the sonorous qualities of vowels and consonants, now liquescent, now harsh. Though the vocal pitch has no relationship to the tuning of the instruments except where exact pitches are occasionally indicated, the voice is intended to blend with the instrumental ensemble, providing an additional polyphonic line. The vocal part is not supposed to dominate the performance despite the fact that the content of the texts dictates the musical setting. "Whenever it seemed important . . . to

ILLUSTRATION 2 *(continued)*

render the events and sentiments of the text, this is done by the music itself," Schoenberg writes. As in the Romantic lied, the composer builds his musical settings upon an expressive detail, an image or psychological motif. In the first poem, "the wine . . . which pours from the moon in waves at night-time" generates a wave-like pattern of sounds, first heard in the piano, but then taken up sporadically by the other instruments. It supports or surrounds a rhapsodic melody of wide intervals and irregular phraseology initiated by the flute (Illustration 2).

In contrast to the transparent texture of this song, the obscure and tortured obsession of the eighteenth poem, in which Pierrot tries to rub off a spot of moonlight, provokes a setting of great complexity: a pair of canons, whose direction is reversed in the second half of the piece, unites piccolo with clarinet, and violin with cello, while the piano simultaneously pursues a three-voiced fugue.

For ten years after the completion of *Pierrot Lunaire*, Schoenberg remained mute. Apart from the disruptive effects of the war upon his creative activities, he was confronted with the necessity of carrying his musical thought beyond the stage it had reached by 1912. The emancipation of the dissonance from the principles of functional harmony had been won on the premise that all combinations of musical intervals are equally comprehensible. Such a postulate denies the hierarchic order of the chords of functional harmony, and posits a need for a new method of organizing tones and harmonies. The anarchic freedom of the new musical language must somehow be brought under control.

Reviewing his evolution in 1941, Schoenberg describes this problem as follows: "Formerly the harmony had served not only as a source of beauty, but, more important, as a means of distinguishing the features of the form. For instance, only a consonance was considered suitable for an ending. Establishing functions demanded different successions of harmonies than roving functions; a bridge, a transition, demanded other successions than a codetta. . . . Fulfillment of all these functions—comparable to the effect of punctuation in the construction of sentences, of subdivision into paragraphs, and of fusion into chapters—could scarcely be assured with chords whose constructive values had not as yet been explored. Hence, it seemed at first impossible to compose pieces of complicated organization or of great length. A little later I discovered how to construct larger forms by following a text or poem. The differences in size and shape of its parts and the change in character and mood were mirrored in the shape and size of the composition, in its dynamics and tempo, figuration and accentuation, instrumentation and orchestration."

But the problem of achieving order, logic, and comprehensibility in large-scale works without a text still had to be worked out. It was solved by the invention of the "Method of composing with twelve tones which are related only with one another," exemplified in his music from 1923 on. This method, commonly called the *serial* or *tone-row* method, starts with an arbitrary arrangement of the twelve tones of the octave, described as the Basic Series, Tone Row, or Series of Tones. This arrangement provides the materials for an entire composition. The series may be regarded as the *Gestalt*, the spiritual and formal essence of the work of art, from which every detail, large or small, is derived.

The validity of this principle, Schoenberg argues, lies in the fact that "the two-or-more dimensional space in which musical ideas are presented is a unit . . . [which] demands an absolute and unitary perception. In this space, . . . there is no absolute down, no right or left, forward or backward. Every musical configuration, every movement of tones has to be comprehended primarily as a mutual relation of sounds, of oscillatory vibrations, appearing at different places and times. . . . Just as our mind always recognizes, for instance, a knife, a bottle or a watch, regardless of its position, and can reproduce it in the imagination in every possible position, even so a musical creator's mind can operate subconsciously with a row of tones, regardless of their duration, regardless of the way in which a mirror might show the mutual relations, which remain a given quantity."

It is through the use of certain rational procedures, analogous to some of the more rigorous canonic techniques of the Flemish composers of the fifteenth century, that Schoenberg learned how to manipulate the Tone Row. Like an object in space, the Tone Row may be perceived and recognized in different positions. A Basic Series of twelve tones may exist in four horizontal versions: its original form, its inversion, its retrograde form, and the latter's inversion. Each of these may be stated at any degree of pitch, and each may be subdivided into smaller motifs (Illustration 3).

ILLUSTRATION 3

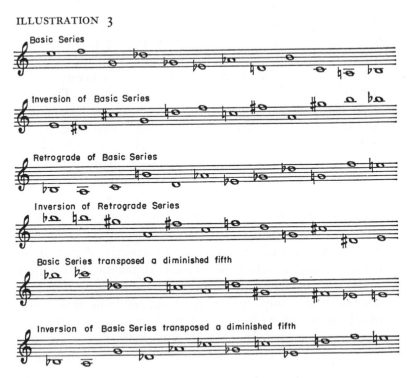

Further variety is assured because the individual tones in a given series may be presented at other pitch levels. The basis for this procedure, known as the principle of octave displacement, is that the identity of a tone within a series is unmistakable whether it occurs in its original position or at any octave above or below this position. The tones of the Basic Series, all together or in smaller groups, may also be presented vertically in the form of a chord. In this fashion, the Basic Series may provide all the harmonic as well as the melodic materials required for the attainment of absolute unity of form.

Schoenberg's original preoccupation with the irrational features of the unconscious has led him finally to an abstract conception of music. In 1912 he had read with "great joy" Kandinsky's *On the Spiritual in Art*. Kandinsky asserted there that though music is by nature the most abstract, spiritual, and least material of the arts, nineteenth century music had failed to achieve this ideal. In common with its sister arts, it had attempted to be both realistic and materialistic, concerning itself wholly with features of external beauty. He declared that an unbridgeable gulf lies between external, material beauty and internal, spiritual beauty, between that which appeals to the ear and that which penetrates the soul. The higher beauty may be attained only through abstraction, he asserted, and the final abstract expression of art is number. "Abstraction is the reaction of man confronted by the abyss of nothingness," Herbert Read states in his *Philosophy of Modern Art*, "the expression of Angst (anguish) which distrusts or renounces the organic principle, and affirms the creative freedom of the human mind in such a situation."

Schoenberg's idea that a work of art may be created upon a "Gestalt" of twelve tones rests upon two abstract premises. The equality of the twelve tones of the *tempered* scale is already a "practical" abstraction from the *natural* scale. The second premise is that these twelve tones have no relationship to one another other than that established by their position within a Tone Row. In the past it had been assumed that tones have certain specific relationships and functions determined either by the ratio of their vibrations or by the conventions of usage (e. g., the quality and function of the "leading tone"). Schoenberg's method of composition with twelve tones denies such relationships. A Basic Series may be conceived therefore without reference to criteria of human sensibility or, for that matter, the nature of the musical medium to be employed.

By 1923 Schoenberg's theory of composing with a series of twelve tones had been completely worked out, and the first fruits of his new method had begun to appear. For the rest of his life the process of continuous variation of a Basic Series by complex techniques of canonic imitation provides the musical substance of works in the "absolute" instrumental forms, such as the quartet, concerto, or variations, as well as the dramatic and representational categories such as the opera *Moses and Aron* and the *Accompaniment to a Cinematographic Scene*. The features of this style are revealed nowhere more precisely and distinctively than in the *Suite for Piano*, Opus 25 (1924). This is one of his first extended works in which a single series of twelve tones provides all the musical ingredients.

This work reveals that Schoenberg was aware of the fact that a Basic Series does not in itself possess all the elements of form necessary to insure comprehensibility. For this reason Schoenberg turned to the instrumental forms of the past for his architectonic models. In the case of the *Suite for Piano* he used the formal principles of the Baroque keyboard suite. Each of the pieces in such a suite (Schoenberg's contains a Prelude, Gavotte with Musette, Intermezzo, Minuet, and Gigue) possesses a stereotyped character, dictating the rhythm, tempo, order of thematic materials and certain other features. The Prelude, which functions as an introductory piece, has traditionally the "freest" form. This freedom is reflected in Schoenberg's Prelude by its episodic character. Nevertheless the twelve tones of the Basic Series are presented at the outset in the right hand (Illustration 4). This Tone Row is the same as the one presented in Illustration 3. Here it assumes thematic character because of the temporal values assigned to the individual tones, and because the Series is so phrased that it falls into three groups or motifs of four tones each.

ILLUSTRATION 4

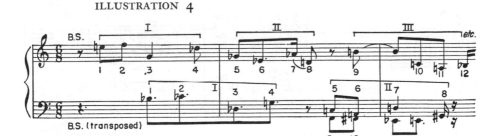

Copyright 1925, renewed 1952 by Universal Edition A.G., Vienna. By permission of Associated Music Publishers, Inc., New York.

Because each of these motifs has its own distinctive contour, Schoenberg treats them subsequently as thematic units which may function as counterpoints to each other or against the Series as a whole. The Basic Series and each of its three motifs are also transposed to various pitches. It appears in the left hand, for example, transposed a diminished fifth. The second and third motifs of this transposed version are here played simultaneously.

In the Gavotte the twelve tones of the Basic Series are again divided into three groups (Illustration 5). The first group provides the opening melodic material in the right hand, while the third group appears as the accompaniment in the left hand before the second group is heard in the right. Schoenberg justifies this "deviation" in the established order of the tones in the series on the ground that the Series and its subdivisions

ILLUSTRATION 5

have already become familiar in the Prelude and therefore may be used somewhat more freely. Following upon this initial statement, the Series reappears, transposed a diminished fifth and inverted (second half of measure two to four). It is followed by a passage in which the Basic Series, presented at the same transposed pitch, is used harmonically; it is now broken up into three groups of three tones superimposed upon one another to provide three-voiced broken chords. This in turn is succeeded by an inversion and a transposed arrangement of this same grouping, etc.

Schoenberg also achieves continuous variation by the device of octave displacement: tones seven and eight are initially separated by the interval of a diminished fifth plus two octaves, but in the next appearance of the Series, they are only a diminished fifth apart. The varied appearances of the Basic Series are contrived to define the bipartite musical structure of the original dance form. The use of only one transposition of the Basic Series—at the interval of a diminished fifth—is the most important element for articulating this design. The original series and its transpositions are used as an analogue to the tonic and dominant relationships that regulated Baroque polyphony. Nothing, perhaps, could better demonstrate the abstract nature of Schoenberg's art than this arbitrary choice of the interval of a diminished fifth to control the entrances and repetitions of the theme. The first part of this Gavotte concludes with a version of the Basic Series proceeding from B flat (the "dominant") while a retrograde version of the Series brings it to a close on E, the tone with which the Series begins.

Schoenberg was the leader and inspiration of a group of younger composers who studied under him in Vienna during the first decades of the century. Though the musical development of his most gifted pupils, Alban Berg (1885–1935) and Anton von Webern (1883–1945) parallels Schoenberg's evolution from "free" atonalism to the "strict" technique of composition upon a twelve-tone series, each of these men found highly individual means of expression for themselves. As they explored the regions of harmonic dissonance, they were confronted, as Schoenberg had been, with the difficulty of organizing their musical ideas into forms of large proportions. Unlike Webern, who developed the most radical potentialities of the dodecaphonic (twelve-tone) style in pieces of utmost brevity, Berg introduced musical expressionism into the large-scale forms of the past.

From his earliest years as a composer he was interested in the dramatic combination of words and music. Until 1914 he had confined himself almost exclusively to the composition of songs. In that year he attended a revival of *Wozzeck*, the unfinished drama of Georg Büchner, a liberal writer and revolutionary of the 1830s. In twenty-six brief scenes

Büchner had depicted the fate of the poor soldier, Wozzeck. Driven to insanity by the taunts of his captain, the dietary experiments of the regimental doctor, and the infidelity of his mistress, Marie, Wozzeck drowns himself after murdering Marie. Büchner's stark language contains neither moral nor subjective meditations upon the brutalized society which had made Wozzeck its victim.

Berg found in this dramatic torso a subject for a music drama of strong contemporary meaning. Büchner's melodramatic scenes which mount to a sordid climax seemed to document the plight of modern man, cut off from his fellows by mutual indifference, and absorbed in his own ego to the point of monomania. None of Büchner's characters possess compassion or understanding for each other, or even for themselves. Each, in his own way, is driven close to the abyss of mental and spiritual chaos. To Berg, heir to a whole century of music which had sought to express the emotional truth beneath the surface of poetry, and deeply aware of the discoveries of psychoanalysis, the only appropriate means of expressing their tortured psyches was the new language of atonality. Through the agency of music, he felt, it may be possible for the audience to be stirred to compassion.

In his opera Berg applies the dialect of atonality to both traditional and contemporary vocal styles, from *bel canto* to *Sprechgesang*. Furthermore he establishes an unusual relationship between the musical and dramatic substance of each scene, utilizing traditional instrumental forms and procedures, whose musical meaning is analogous to that of the dramatic episode. He found it necessary to rearrange and combine the many brief scenes of the original play into fifteen, equally divided within three acts. The five scenes of Act One acquaint us with the world of Wozzeck and his mistress Marie. Since the order in which the scenes occur is not dictated by dramatic development but only the requirements of clear exposition, Berg organizes each with an independent, unrelated form. The five scenes of Act Two, however, progress towards the dramatic climax. Their sequence in Berg's conception is similar to the succession of contrasting but interrelated movements of an instrumental sonata. Thus the music of the first scene is in sonata form, and the second consists of an Invention and Fugue. The middle scene of the act is a Largo for chamber orchestra, while the concluding scenes are composed respectively as a Scherzo and an Introduction and Rondo. In the third act each scene builds to an individual climax, and here Berg applies the principle of variation to give each unity and mounting intensity. Berg also uses the blackouts which separate the scenes to continue the orchestral commentary upon the preceding scene as well as to introduce the following one.

By the opening of the third act (Illustration 6) the final catastrophe
has become inescapable. Wozzeck's psychological deterioration has disrupted his personal relationship with Marie. Humiliated and distracted by
the inhumanity of his Captain, and by the scientific experiments of the
Doctor, he has learned of Marie's infidelity with the handsome Drum
Major, who has given him a brutal beating. In the first scene of this act,
Marie, bewildered by the course of events, turns over the pages of the

ILLUSTRATION 6

Bible, seeking an answer to her problems. As she reads, talks to her child, and reflects upon Christ's compassion for Mary Magdalene, Berg delineates her feelings by alternate passages of declamation, *Sprechgesang* and lyrical melody. These are projected above a succession of inventions on a theme, which reaches a climax of complexity and intensity after the curtain has descended.

The terminal invention concludes as the music sinks down to a foreboding, dimly discerned tone—low B. This tone becomes a psychological and musical pedal point for the ensuing scene. The curtain rises to disclose Wozzeck and Marie strolling in the twilight at the edge of a pond. The obsessive tone B, recurring in various octaves, is the only ominous note as the two people converse. Then the sudden appearance of the blood-red moon maddens Wozzeck. As the tone beats gradually louder and faster in the drums, he stabs Marie. In the subsequent blackout, the same tone pervades the entire orchestra in two cataclysmic crescendi, a musical counterpart to Wozzeck's mad obsession. For each of the remaining scenes, a different principle of variation provides unity, psychological commentary, and even, as Wozzeck drowns himself in the fourth scene, vivid tone painting. Between the cruel conclusion of this scene and the ironic epilogue, Berg inserts the longest and most important interlude. This is designed as a musical commentary, removed from and yet involved with the foregoing events. In the manner of a nineteenth-century symphonic poem, even to the point of using tonality, the composer develops and superimposes upon one another the motifs associated with Wozzeck. Here through the perspective of instrumental sound, as the shifting sands of atonality are replaced by the sombre tonality of D minor, the meaningless fate of the ineffectual Wozzeck is raised to the heights of universal tragedy.

Berg's use of atonality differs from Schoenberg's in that for him it is primarily an extension of tonality. It thus assumes its expressive power within the perspective of tonal harmony. The primary characteristic of this technique is not its tendency toward musical abstraction, but its power to intensify the sensuous distinctions between dissonant and consonant harmonies. Berg's last completed work, the *Violin Concerto* of 1935, reflects a deeply felt personal experience, the sudden, tragic death of young Manon Gropius to whom he was devoted. The Concerto is composed upon a twelve-note series of strong tonal character consisting of four interlocking minor and major triads and three whole tones. Later in the concerto Berg dramatically identifies the last four notes of the Basic Series with the opening tones of the Lutheran chorale *Es ist genug*, which is presented in the rich harmonization of J. S. Bach (Illustration 7). It was not so much the musical relationship of the chorale to the Basic Series that led Berg to choose the chorale for the climax of the concerto as its poetic content expressing serene resignation in the face of death. Upon this chorale Berg creates a series of variations to conclude his concerto, achieving great intensity of expression by contrasting his contorted melodies and atonal harmony with Bach's tonally stable, though chromatically harmonized setting of the chorale.

If works such as the *Violin Concerto* appear in some respects to be extensions of the nineteenth-century concept of "symphonic poetry," this cannot be said of the music of Webern. Beginning with his *Six*

ILLUSTRATION 7

Pieces for Orchestra of 1910, Webern pursued a radical, solitary path increasingly remote from that of either of his colleagues. He was as quick to employ the serial method of composition as Schoenberg, but for him the abstract, quasi-mathematical relationships of the twelve tones of a series took precedence over all other considerations. At the same time the compositions which appeared from 1910 onward indicate his fascination with the multifarious qualities of individual sounds in themselves. In the *Six Pieces* his musical speech is already characterized by extreme brevity and by the use of unique instrumental timbres thrown into sharp relief by the transparent orchestral texture and the frequent silences with which the pieces are interspersed. This technique of melodic instrumentation, called *Klangfarbenmelodien* (tone-color melodies), was anticipated by Schoenberg's *Summer Morning by a Lake* where the continuous evolution of new instrumental colors supersedes all other artistic factors. Webern applied this principle of continuous coloristic change to the successive tones in a melody.

Webern's only *Symphony*, composed in 1928, is a superb example of the application of these two principles—serial composition and coloristic melody. Consisting of two unequal movements, it bears no relationship to the form of the traditional symphony. The first movement of this work consists of two equal parts, each of which is repeated. It is constructed according to an intricate technique of canonic imitation, the second part being the note-for-note retrograde of the first. Imitative counterpoint also controls the texture of the second movement, which is a series of variations upon a twelve-tone row. Because of the pitch and color of each tone in the contrapuntal fabric a luminescent mosaic of sound is produced. Even with the score in front of him the listener cannot easily discern the melodic lines of the tone row with which this fabric is woven. The intervals in each appearance of the Basic Series are widely separated in pitch; they are usually not heard successively in the same instrumental timbre; and moments of silence frequently intervene between each tone of a melodic line. Thus the pair of two-voiced canons of the first movement (Illustration 8) produces successions of sound which bear comparison with the pointillists' seemingly fortuitous arrangements of colors on a canvas.

Webern treats musical sound as totally nonreferential. It is not related to poetic, dramatic or visual images; it expresses no literary program, nor can one be applied to it. In its mathematical logic it contains no identifiable feeling, attitude of mind nor psychological mood. It is an abstract design composed of purely musical elements—sounds and time. The music of Webern was rarely heard and but little known until after the Second World War. Since then its technical features have provoked in-

ILLUSTRATION 8

creasing interest among a wide number of composers. Recently its principles have inspired the creation of music based only upon the components of electronically produced sound.

Among those who have been attracted to Webern's music in recent years is Igor Stravinsky. Nevertheless Stravinsky's music stems from ideals which differ markedly from those of the Viennese composers. Stravinsky defines music as communication through sound. This generalization is sharply qualified by the distinction he makes between communication and self-expression. "Music," he writes, "is, by its very nature, essentially powerless to express anything at all, whether a feeling, an attitude of mind, a psychological mood, a phenomenon of nature. . . . Expression has never been an inherent property of music. If music appears to express something this is only an illusion and not a reality. It is simply an additional attribute which, unconsciously, only by force of habit we have come to confuse with its essential being."

If music is not essentially the communication of expressive feelings, what then does it communicate? Order, says Stravinsky.

Music is the sole domain in which man realizes the present. By the imperfection of his nature, man is doomed to submit to the passage of time—to its categories of past and future—without ever being able to give substance, and therefore stability to the category of the present. The phenomenon of music is given to us with the sole purpose of establishing an order in things, including, in particular, the coordination between man and time.

Its indispensable and single requirement is construction. Construction once completed, this order has been attained; and "it is precisely this achieved order," he concludes, "which produces in us a unique emotion having nothing in common with our ordinary sensations and our responses to the feelings and impressions of daily life."

This discussion of the nature of music, which is found in Stravinsky's *Autobiography*, is considerably amplified in the group of essays published as *The Poetics of Music* in 1942. Here he speaks of music as "nothing other than a phenomenon of speculation: . . . the basis of musical creation is a preliminary feeling out, a will moving first in an abstract realm with the object of giving shape to something concrete. The elements at which this speculation necessarily aims are those of *sound* and *time*." The understanding and employment of the element of time is of utmost importance. "Time passes at a rate which varies according to the inner dispositions of the subject and to the events that come to affect his consciousness," he states.

Expectation, boredom, anguish, pleasure and pain, contemplation—all of these thus come to appear as different categories in the midst of which our life unfolds, and each of these determines a special psychological process, a particular tempo. These variations in psychological time are perceptible only as they are related to the primary sensation—whether conscious or unconscious—of real time, ontological time. What gives the concept of musical time its special stamp is that this concept is born and develops as well outside of the categories of psychological time as it does simultaneously with them.

It follows then that there are two kinds of music:

one which evolves parallel to the process of ontological time, embracing and penetrating it, inducing in the mind of the listener a feeling of euphoria, and, so to speak, of "dynamic calm." The other kind runs ahead of, or counter to, this process. It is not self-contained in each momentary tonal unit. It dislocates the centers of attraction and gravity and sets itself up in the unstable; and this fact makes it particularly adaptable to the translation of the composer's emotive impulses. All music in which the will to expression is dominant belongs to the second type. . . . Music that is based on ontological time is generally dominated by the principle of similarity. The music that adheres to psychological time likes to proceed by contrast. To these two principles which dominate the creative process correspond the fundamental concepts of variety and unity.

Stravinsky concludes that it is more satisfactory to proceed by similarity than by contrast, for while "contrast produces an immediate effect . . . similarity is born of striving for unity. The need to seek variety is perfectly legitimate, but we should forget that the One precedes the Many."

In establishing order, music must also take tradition into account.

A real tradition is not the relic of a past that is irretrievably gone; it is a living force that animates and informs the present. . . . Far from implying the repetition of what has been, tradition presupposes the reality of what endures. It appears as an heirloom, a heritage that one receives on condition of making it bear fruit before passing it on to one's descendants.

The artist, whenever he exercises his creative imagination, has a responsibility to a series of values and concepts which are above and beyond the idea of mere self-expression.

Stravinsky's attitude toward tradition is close to that expressed by T. S. Eliot in his essay, "Tradition and the Individual Talent":

[A true understanding of tradition] involves, in the first place, the historical sense, which we may call nearly indispensable to any one who would continue to be a poet beyond his twenty-fifth year; and the historical sense involves a perception, not only of the pastness of the past, but of its presence; the historical sense compels a man to write not merely with his own generation in his bones, but with a feeling that the whole of the literature of Europe from Homer and within it the whole of the literature of his own country has a simultaneous existence and composes a simultaneous order. This historical sense, which is a sense of the timeless as well as of the temporal and of the timeless and of the temporal together, is what makes a writer traditional. And it is at the same time what makes a writer most acutely conscious of his place in time, of his own contemporaneity.

Related to the awareness of tradition is a second principle, that of style. "Style," asserts Stravinsky,

is the particular way a composer organizes his conceptions and speaks the language of his craft. This musical language is the element common to the composers of a particular school or epoch. . . . The style of an epoch results from the combination of individual styles, a combination which is dominated by the methods of the composers who have exerted a preponderant influence on their time. We can notice, going back to the example of Mozart and Haydn, that they benefited from the same culture, drew on the same sources, and borrowed each other's discoveries. . . . [Such masters] appear as powerful signal-fires . . . by whose light and warmth is developed a sum of tendencies that most of their successors will share and that contributes to form the parcel of traditions which make up a culture.

The concept of style means that the subject or musical category which inspires the artist imposes by its very nature certain limits upon the language he uses. But far from restricting his freedom, awareness of these disciplines provides him with confidence and strength, "because they provide a sure means of achieving the purpose of music, which is the establishing of order in things." Within the limits imposed by tradition, there is still room for the imaginative exploration of new methods of organizing sound and for original modes of expression. These are the natural concomitants of musical "speculation."

Stravinsky's speculative activity may be said to have begun during the four years (1909–1913) in which he was entirely occupied in composing for the Ballet Russe in Paris. His musical style had been formed in his early years in Russia by his experiences of Italian opera, the music of the Russian nationalists, and the brilliantly orchestrated works of Rimski-Korsakov with whom he had studied. His first ballet, *L'Oiseau de Feu,* with its colorful orchestral effects and its straightforward use of numerous folk melodies reveals his complete mastery of these elements. It also contains passages, such as Katschei's dance, in which the dynamic quality of rhythm assumes a role of great importance.

It is in the *Sacre du Printemps* of 1913 that Stravinsky begins to transcend the influences and traditions of the past. According to the aesthetic tradition of the narrative ballet, the functions of music are to provide rhythmic accompaniment and descriptive gestures, and to underscore the dramatic and emotional climaxes of the dance. This presupposes the existence of a dramatic and pictorial frame within which the music may paint a picture. Such was not the case with the *Sacre du Printemps.* The inspiration for this ballet, Stravinsky wrote, "was a musical theme that came to me when I had completed the *Firebird.* As this theme, with that which followed, was conceived in a strong, brutal manner, I took as a pretext for developments, for the evocation of this music, the Russian prehistoric period. But note well this idea came from the music, the music did not come from the idea. My work is architectonic, not anecdotal; objective, not descriptive." In other words, the music was conceived apart from the stage picture or dramatic plot, and contains all its essential meaning in itself.

One of the features which strikes the ear most forcefully in the *Rite of Spring* is the quantity and quality of sounds invented by Stravinsky. They range from the delicate sonorities of impressionism to effects of primitive force and barbaric violence. His huge orchestra includes twice the conventional number of wind and brass instruments and percussion, as well as rarely used instruments such as the bass trumpet. Yet the massive resources of this nineteenth century orchestra are employed for purposes of rhythmic accentuation and to articulate the musical structure rather than for Romantic expressiveness.

The *Rite of Spring* is organized in two parts, each containing an introduction and a series of dances. The dances follow one another without pause so that they progress in each part towards a final dynamic climax. Nevertheless each dance is given a distinctive character by the pervasive recurrence of a small number of chords, rhythmic patterns, and thematic figures. The few themes employed by Stravinsky, closely resembling each other in their brevity and restricted range, produce a sense of the concentration and unity of the whole work. Though each may be repeated many times, monotony is tempered by variety of treatment. Thus the theme with which the introduction commences (Illustration 9) consists essentially of a stereotyped figure of only six tones. In the space of the first four measures, each containing a different number of beats, this theme is repeated five times. Always recognizable, its shape is modified each time not so much by ornaments or embellishments as by rhythmic alterations.

ILLUSTRATION 9

Copyright 1921 by Edition Russe de Musique. Assigned 1947 to Boosey & Hawkes. Reprinted by permission of Boosey & Hawkes Inc.

The element of rhythm dominates the *Rite of Spring*. The many new treatments of this element tend to fall into two comprehensive techniques. The opening dance, "Les Augures Printaniers," illustrates the first of these (Illustration 10). Here the meter embodied in the succession of eighth-note chords set forth in four-beat measures establishes a regular ostinato. Sharp accents reinforced by the weight of eight horns impose upon these regular pulsations a succession of irregular rhythmic patterns consisting of various numbers of beats, counted as follows:

```
>              > >           >     >     >       >
1 2 3 4   5 6 7 8   9 1 2 1   2 3 4 5   6 1 2 3   1 2 3 4   1 2 3 4   5 1 2 3
```

Throughout the dance passages such as this contrast with sections in regular quadruple rhythm, producing a series of roughly symmetrical periods. The second technique is exemplified by the final "Danse Sacrale,"

ILLUSTRATION 10

where the metre itself is not constant but shifts as irregular rhythms succeed one another. At the same time melodic materials have been eliminated entirely so that the jagged, irregular rhythms completely absorb the attention.

Massive, novel chords in which dissonances predominate, underline these rhythmic patterns. They are most frequently created by the superimposition of diatonic chords drawn from distinctly different tonalities. A simple instance of the harmonic ambiguity resulting from this technique may be observed in the chord repeated thirty-two times in the opening portion of the first dance (Illustration 10). Consisting of eight tones, the upper four compose a seventh chord on E flat major, while the lower four are those of the major triad of F flat (E natural) with the root doubled. The diatonic components of such a "polychord" clash sharply because of the presence of no less than three minor seconds. Yet Stravinsky treats it as a harmonic center of gravity which defines the shape of this dance. Because of the fashion in which he arranges the instrumentation here and elsewhere these dissonances take on no expressionistic connotations whatsoever.

Many of these stylistic elements reappear in *L'Histoire du Soldat* of 1918, though the form of this work differs enormously from that of the *Sacre du Printemps*. Based upon a Russian folk story, the *Soldier's Tale* narrates a series of encounters between the Soldier and the Devil, in which the supernatural powers of a violin play a crucial part. It is presented by means of declamation, pantomime and dance, with all the participants, including a small instrumental ensemble, occupying portions of the stage in full view of the audience. The musical forces are reduced here to a handful of solo instruments: violin, clarinet, cornet, bassoon and double bass, with drums and cymbals. This ensemble is analogous to the American jazz bands which at this time were fascinating many Europeans with their rhythmic novelties and their strident instrumental timbres.

Stravinsky's orchestra plays no part in narration or description. The individual pieces and dances function as a musical decoration of various episodes in the story, and provide the propulsive accompaniment for the occasional dances. Yet the music with its tone of ironic gaiety clearly has a leading role, particularly at the moment when the soldier, having regained possession of his violin from the Devil, uses its powers to restore a beautiful Princess to health. For this scene Stravinsky composes a suite of three dances, Tango, Waltz, and Ragtime.

Each of these popular dance forms is characterized by an underlying rhythmic pattern which accompanies the melody. The pattern is usually expressed by percussion instruments, but it also appears in the accompanying harmonies. Almost always only a single harmony is used for each measure. The simple 1, 2, 3 pattern of the waltz, for instance, normally is found in the accompaniment in the form of a single note, the root of the chord, on the first, accented beat of the measure, and a complete realization of the chord on both the second and third beats. The tango has as its basic patterns the rhythm: ♩♪♪♫, but its melody is also characterized by certain stereotyped syncopated figures:

In each of his three dances, Stravinsky assembles their conventional components in novel ways, disrupting their normal relationships. The typical rhythmic pattern of the tango (Illustration 11) appears in the percussion instruments, but it does not always coincide with the measure, as it normally would. It first begins on the second half of the measure; next, on the first beat of the measure; then, on the last eighth note of the measure. Against these dislocated figures, the violin moves in syncopation typical of the tango, but disregards the regular periodicity of the dance. In this arbitrary rearrangement of recognizable elements one finds a musical equivalent to the contemporary paintings of Picasso where natural objects are broken down into their individual elements which are then placed, as the artist wills, upon the canvas.

Though it is clear that this ballet has stylistic features in common with the *Sacre du Printemps*, the nature of the ensemble for which *L'Histoire du Soldat* was written modifies their appearance and function. The individual qualities and timbres of each instrument, whether alone or in ensemble, stand out vividly. For the first time an attitude towards the means of making music, which has been described as "objective realism," emerges clearly in Stravinsky's work. Here the idiomatic pecularities and characteristics of the chosen musical resources determine the stylistic qualities of the musical composition.

The ballet, *Pulcinella*, written in 1919 in collaboration with Picasso, seemed to mark a distinct deviation from the path Stravinsky had previously followed. In it the two artists sought to evoke the atmosphere of eighteenth-century Neapolitan culture, exemplified in the music of Giovanni Battista Pergolesi (1710–1736). Instead of a simple "arrangement" of the fragments of Pergolesi's music, Stravinsky amalgamated the long-flowing curves of Italianate vocal melody with his own distinctive harmony, instrumentation, and rhythm. The importance of this work is often overlooked. Working with Pergolesi's music the composer became aware of an additional objective factor in the invention of music: the stylistic propriety and consistency, which Pergolesi shared with his contemporaries. Though Stravinsky translates Pergolesi's idiom into his own language, Pergolesi's style imposes certain limitations and obligations

ILLUSTRATION II

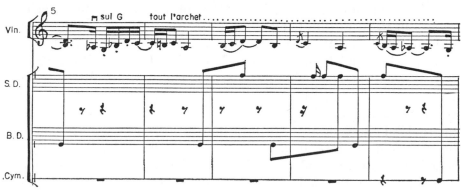

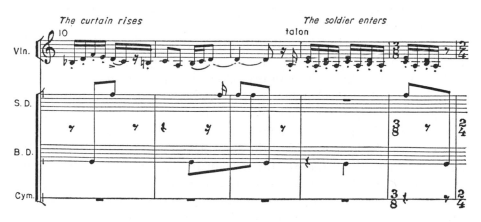

ILLUSTRATION 11 (*continued*)

upon him. *Pulcinella* then is an especially graphic illustration of the role of style as an impersonal factor in the creation of works of art.

A recent description by Stravinsky of the process by which he creates an art work calls to mind the observations on music of both Aristotle and Zarlino. "When my main theme has been decided I know in general what kind of material it will require. I start to look for this material sometimes playing old masters (to put myself in motion) sometimes starting directly to improvise rhythmic units or a provisional series of notes (which can become a final series). I thus form my building material." This statement may well stand for the process by which all his compositions since 1919 have been materialized. By "main theme" Stravinsky means the subject and idea of the work of art in gestation. Just as it dictates the kind of musical materials required, it also effects the choice of musical forces, the variety of medium, and consequently many details of style.

A commission by the Boston Symphony for the celebration of its fiftieth anniversary suggested the theme of religious commemoration, and, in turn, the three stages in orthodox Christian worship: repentance, absolution, and grateful praise. So Stravinsky was drawn to the Psalms and psalmody where these ideas are repeatedly and eloquently expressed. The musical characteristics of psalmody are the narrowness and monotony of its melodic lines within the formulas of the ecclesiastical modes, and a rhythm which follows the declamation of the Latin text. These elements shaped the total construction of a *Symphony of Psalms*, for chorus and orchestra. In like manner, *Orpheus*, a ballet of 1947, is a restatement of one of the most deeply felt and pervasive myths of the Western World. To the Greeks, Orpheus embodied the united gifts of music and poetry, which symbolize the divine, creative spark in man.

The idea of Orpheus, the immortal singer, led Stravinsky to employ musical elements of the Baroque era where melody had reigned supreme; and the idea of classical antiquity induced him to begin the ballet with the symbolic tones of the Greek Dorian mode.

All of Stravinsky's works rest upon the stability of diatonic tonal centers and consequently the discriminating use of chromaticism. In none is this more true than the *Cantata* of 1952, where the centrality of C major becomes increasingly pronounced in each refrain by contrast with the chromaticism of the verses. Stravinsky's speculative but sensitive investigation of the traditions of Western art has led him finally to a scrutiny of contemporary usage. Recently the language of total chromaticism, including the techniques of composition with twelve-tone rows has made its appearance in his music. But Stravinsky's appropriation of this style reflects no change in his antagonism to the aesthetic assumptions of Viennese expressionism exemplified by the music of Schoenberg. Stravinsky's point of contact with dodecaphony is provided by the music of Webern, the twelve-tone composer whose conception of music most resembles his own. The results are increasingly apparent in the *Ode to Dylan Thomas*, the *Canticum Sacrum*, and the ballet, *Agon*.

First performed in 1957, *Agon* is designed to accompany the "challenge," a dance contest. It presents no story or sentiment, only a suite of dances testing the skill of a dozen dancers in solos and various groupings. The whole contest is framed by a reprise of the opening prelude at the conclusion. The dances are arranged in four sections separated by the same interlude of stylized trumpet fanfares. These five stage "signals," extended in the prelude and reprise to take on the importance of independent compositions, are the regularly disposed piers of a highly symmetrical structure. Their stability and solidity result from the prominence of the tonic-dominant harmonies centering upon C. The intricacy, complexity and ordered disorder of the twelve-tone idiom is reserved for the dances constituting the contest of skill. Following the increasingly intense rivalry of the contestants, the music of the dances becomes increasingly dodecaphonic, the tone rows more pervasive, and the polyphony more dense. But the transparency of the pointillist musical texture throws the intricate rhythmic forms and gestures into bold relief.

The first Basic Series appears in the coda of Part II (see Illustration 12). Its twelve tones are distributed in pairs between the harp, plucked sharply, and the cello played *glissando*. Thereafter it is repeated by the staccato tones of the piano and trombone. It thus assumes the character of an ostinato, whose rhythmic components are unpredictable rests as well as percussive tones. While this nontonal series functions as the unitary foundation for this dance the musical surroundings remain tonal.

The row is sounded first against a fifth (C-G) sustained by two trumpets and a mandolin strumming on one note. After this introduction, the melodic interest is centered upon the solo violin which with its character-istic tonal figures in parallel sixths moves in the rhythm of a gigue

ILLUSTRATION 12

towards a cadence on F. The prevailing sounds of this piece and those that follow it are those of dodecaphony. Nevertheless the context still remains tonal, because here as elsewhere, Stravinsky balances his music upon that most solid of consonant intervals—the fifth.

In *Agon* many worlds meet. The title recalls the great athletic and musical contests, the *agones*, that the Greek city-states had celebrated hundreds of years before the birth of Christ. Dances of the Renaissance

ILLUSTRATION 12 *(continued)*

and the Baroque are found here, the *bransle* and *gaillarde*, inspired by descriptions in a dance manual of the seventeenth century and in Marin Mersenne's *L'Harmonie Universelle*. The polyphony and canons of the Middle Ages and Renaissance reappear, transformed into the idiom of dodecaphony, which in turn is contained within tonal concepts of the eighteenth and nineteenth centuries. It is impossible to speak of this as an eclectic work, for each of these elements has undergone metamorphosis in the process of assimilation. Such a work, with its many layers of meaning, its association of ideas, makes enormous demands on us. Here the past becomes the present, style becomes idea.

APPENDIX: BASIC PRINCIPLES OF MUSIC

IN ITS SIMPLEST FORM music is a succession of tone in time. The temporal values of the tones provide music with the element of *rhythm*. If the tones rise and fall in pitch instead of remaining on a single pitch, *melody* will result. Melody might be called a horizontal motion similar to an undulating line on a piece of paper. When two or more tones are sounded simultaneously, music gains a vertical dimension called *harmony*. Today these primary elements of musical speech are handled in many ways. But the most widely disseminated repertory of music is based upon principles formulated in the seventeenth century and embodied in the leading musical categories of the last two centuries. The following definitions and examples of musical principles apply specifically to this music which is the most familiar. They are set forth in order that the reader may familiarize himself with some fundamental terms employed throughout this book.

I. Rhythm

A. The division of sound into various durations of time is one of the basic characteristics of any musical composition. Sounds grouped together into identical units of stressed and unstressed, equal beats produce *meter*. *Rhythm* refers to the grouping of notes of different durations into recurrent and non-recurrent patterns which generally exist within the framework of an implied meter. The rhythm of a given composition may be identical with, complementary to, or different from the meter. The

455

speed at which the notes (representing measured durations of time) are to be sounded is called the *tempo* of a composition.

B. The notation of meter, rhythm and tempo is indicated as follows:

1. All notes are mathematical subdivisions of the *whole note*. The *half note* has half the time-value of the whole note. The *quarter note* has half the time-value of the half note; the *eighth note* half the value of the quarter note, and so on through the smaller subdivisions of the *sixteenth, thirty-second,* and *sixty-fourth notes.* A dot placed after a note means that the tone is to be sustained its regular value plus one half its face value. A whole note, for example, is equivalent to four quarter notes. When a dot is added to a whole note, it will have a value of six quarter notes.

Other temporal values can be indicated by joining two notes of the same pitch with a curved line called a *tie.* The group of half note tied to eighth

note, for example, means that the tone is to be held for the value of a half note plus an eighth note.

2. An equivalent set of symbols called *rests* exists for the measurement of silence. Thus there are the *whole rest,* the *half rest,* the *quarter rest,* the *eighth rest,* the *sixteenth rest,* the *thirty-second rest,* and the *sixty-fourth rest.*

3. The most frequently used musical meters are duple, triple or quadruple, and they may be notated as follows (the strong beats are indicated by the accent mark >):

4. These metrical units are marked off from one another by bar-lines to form measures, with the implied accent falling on the note immediately following each bar-line:

There are also compound measures containing two or more duple or triple units. A measure of six beats, for example, is subdivided into two groups of three by accenting the first and fourth beat:

The second accent is stressed less emphatically than the first one, however.

5. In most compositions a single meter will dominate the entire work, or at least large sections of it. In order to establish this unit at the beginning of a composition, the *time-signature* (meter) is given thus:

If the metrical unit is two half notes, the time signature is $\frac{2}{2}$. The lower number indicates the type of note representing the beat (in this case the half note), while the upper digit specifies the number of such notes in a measure. If it is two quarter notes, the time signature is $\frac{2}{4}$. If it is four quarter notes, the time signature is $\frac{4}{4}$. $\frac{2}{2}$ and $\frac{4}{4}$ time are sometimes represented by ¢ and c, respectively, symbols carried over from earlier forms of notation.

6. In a melody the sounding rhythm will be affected by the accents implied by the meter. The meter of a March is $\frac{4}{4}$, but the March rhythm (in the melody) might be as follows:

Even though the four equal beats of the meter may not literally be sounded, the accent on the first beat of the measure implied by the meter will be transferred to the corresponding note of the rhythmic succession.

7. Frequently a melody will begin with a tone preceding the first beat of a measure. Such a note is called an *upbeat* and it has the effect of throwing added emphasis upon the following note.

8. Some of the terms used at the beginning of compositions to indicate the tempo at which they are to be performed are as follows:

Largo   very slowly and broadly
Adagio   very slowly
Lento   slowly
Andante   moving along very moderately

Moderato	moderately fast
Allegretto	less fast than Allegro
Allegro	fast
Vivace	very fast
Presto	extremely rapidly

Because these terms are by no means precise it is customary in modern notation to indicate the tempo also by a metronomic indication.

II. Melody

A. Tones are distinguished from one another by pitch. Starting at any given tone and moving upwards or downwards in pitch we will ultimately arrive at a tone which we recognize as the seeming reproduction of the original tone at a higher or lower pitch. This natural phenomenon is called the *octave*. In our contemporary musical system the range from a given tone to its octave is divided into twelve so-called *half tones* or *semitones*. Figure 1 represents the central segment of the piano keyboard, illustrating the characteristic arrangement of the semitones in white and black keys, the letters of the alphabet used customarily to identify each tone or key, and the octaves a to a′ and c to c′. It is to be noted that only the first seven letters of the alphabet are used and that these are allocated only to the white keys. The black keys are identified by the letters of the keys adjacent to them, with either the sharp sign (♯) or flat sign (♭) designating the pitch as a semitone above or below the adjoining white keys.

FIGURE 1

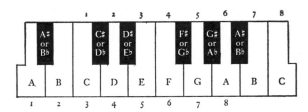

B. Most melodies consist of a selection and arrangement of tones contained within the compass of an octave. The distance between two tones of different pitch is called an *interval*. Intervals are named by ordinal numbers calculated from the first of the two tones. The interval E to F, for example, is called a second because F is the second in the series of notes that begins with E. The precise dimensions of an interval are indicated by the adjectives major, minor, perfect, diminished and augmented. The dimensions and names of the commonly used intervals are listed below:

E–F	1/2 tone	minor second
C–D	1 whole tone	major second
D–F	1 1/2 tones	minor third
C–E	2 whole tones	major third
D–G♭	1 tone, 2 semitones	diminished fourth
C–F	2 1/2 tones	perfect fourth
F–B	3 whole tones	augmented fourth or tritone
C–G♭	2 tones, 2 semitones	diminished fifth
C–G	3 1/2 tones	perfect fifth
C–G♯	4 whole tones	augmented fifth
E–C	3 tones, 2 semitones	minor sixth
C–A	4 1/2 tones	major sixth
E–D♭	3 tones, 3 semitones	diminished seventh
E–D	4 tones, 2 semitones	minor seventh
C–B	5 1/2 tones	major seventh
C–C′	5 tones, 2 semitones	octave

C. The pitch of tones is written down as follows: on a sheet of music paper the group of five parallel lines is called the *staff*. Each of the 5 lines and the 4 spaces between them indicates a pitch, so that a note written upon a line or space means that a tone of a specific pitch is to be sounded. Additional lines and spaces may be placed above or below a staff to accommodate pitches not contained within it.

D. On the staff a symbol called the *clef* fixes the pitch of a given line. The three commonly used clefs are the C-clef, the G-clef, and the F-clef. Originally these clefs could be affixed to any line, but in current usage they appear in only one position (see Figure 2). The C-clef designates the middle line of the staff as Middle C.

FIGURE 2

C-CLEF   G-CLEF   F-CLEF

The G-clef designates the second line from the bottom of the staff as the G above middle C. The F-clef designates the second line from the top of the staff as the F below middle C. Once a line is given a specific pitch by a clef sign, the pitch of the remaining lines and spaces is also determined. The space above the middle line in the C-clef will be D; the line above that, E, etc.

E. The lines and spaces of the staff designate only seven of the twelve tones into which the octave is divided, specifically the "natural" tones, A, B, C, D, E, F, G. The remaining five tones can be represented only with the aid of "accidental" signs, the sharp and the flat. These are placed before the note which is to be raised or lowered a semitone, and on the line or space of the note to which they refer. Figure 3 represents the notation of the tones of the keyboard contained in Figure 1.

FIGURE 3

F. In earlier Western music most melodies were written within the range of an octave, which comprised only the "natural" tones. Because the succession of half steps and whole steps differs within each octave, melodies written in the compass of different octaves will have different characters or "modes." Since the seventeenth century, only two of these modes, the *major* and *minor scales*, have commonly been used. These are represented by the succession of tones sounded by the white keys of the piano within the octaves C to C and A to A respectively, as indicated in Figure 3. Such scales are called *diatonic* scales, meaning "through the (natural) tones."

G. The character of each scale depends upon the order of whole tones (T) and semitones (S). For the major diatonic scale the succession of intervals proceeding from its tone of origin (the *tonic*) is shown in Figure 4. It should be noted that the fourth and fifth steps of this scale form with the tonic a perfect fourth and fifth respectively, and that the seventh step is only a semitone from the eighth. In singing the scale the seventh tone seems to "pull" to the eighth tone. For this reason it is called the *leading tone*.

FIGURE 4

```
 1   2   3   4   5   6   7   8
 C   D   E   F   G   A   B   C
   T   T   S   T   T   T   S
```

The minor scale is represented by the succession shown in Figure 5.

FIGURE 5

```
 1   2   3   4   5   6   7   8
 A   B   C   D   E   F   G   A
   T   S   T   T   S   T   T
```

In practice it is customary to employ different versions of this scale in ascending and descending. In the latter the tones are those given in Figure 5. In ascending it is customary to raise the sixth and seventh steps by a semitone respectively, making the final steps of the minor scale similar to those of the major, as shown in Figure 6.

FIGURE 6

1	2	3	4	5	6	7	8
A	B	C	D	E	F♯	G♯	A
	T	S	T	T	T	T	S

H. The major and minor diatonic scales may be reproduced within any octave by the use of sharps and flats. For example, if a scale is written with G as its tonic, it will be found that the tones proceeding upwards in succession fall into the same pattern of tones and semitones exemplified in the scale of C-major with the exception of the seventh step. To make the G-scale conform to the pattern of the C-major scale it is necessary to sharp F, thus making it a semitone from the final G. By similar alterations it is possible to construct major or minor scales on any of the twelve tones.

Music written according to the diatonic scale system may be composed in any one of 12 major or 12 minor keys, each of which is identified by a key-signature placed at the beginning of the staff: *

FIGURE 7

From this it appears that C-major and A-minor have the same key-signature, for they use the same eight tones, though they stem from different tonics. So likewise G-major and E-minor, etc. Because of this similarity they are considered to be related keys and A-minor is spoken of as the *relative minor* of C-major. In order to determine whether a piece is written in a major key or its relative minor it is necessary to examine the final chord which is customarily constructed upon the tonic. Since the tones of G-major and F-major differ from C-major by but one tone (F♯ and B♭ respectively) these keys are also closely related to C-

* The C♯-major and D♭-major scales are of course identical despite their appearance.

major. On the other hand the relationship between B-major and C-major is considered to be very distant since they possess but two tones in common.

III. Harmony

Western music became clearly differentiated from the music of other civilizations when, around the ninth century, two or more melodies were rationally combined to sound simultaneously. Such a combination of melodic lines is called *polyphony*. It will be easily perceived that notes sounded simultaneously will produce an effect quite different from that which results from playing notes consecutively in a melody. If we play the notes C, E, and G, one after another, we have a rudimentary melody; but if we play them simultaneously, we receive an entirely different auditory impression, a complex sound which is called a *chord*. When several melodies are combined in polyphony, the result is a series of chords which is commonly termed harmony.

To even the most untrained listener some chords seem more pleasing or stable than others. These chords are generally described as consonant, while those which seem harsher or to have a certain degree of tension are called dissonant chords. During the course of musical history the conception of which chords are dissonant or consonant has changed radically. But the basis of this distinction may be discerned from an examination of the acoustical phenomenon called the overtone series.

When a string is sounded or a column of air is caused to vibrate in a pipe, a principal or *fundamental tone* is produced, and in addition to it a series of higher, less audible tones as well. For example, when a string tuned to low C is sounded, the series of overtones shown in Figure 8 will

FIGURE 8

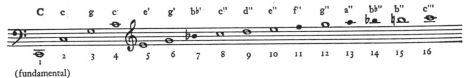

(fundamental)

result. Numbers 7, 11, 13, and 14—represented by black notes—are only approximations of the pitches indicated. Each of the overtones is related arithmetically to the fundamental tone C. If we divide the string exactly in half, each segment, when sounded, will produce a tone one octave higher than the fundamental tone C. This octave note, c, is identical with the first overtone. Its relationship to the fundamental tone is that of half the string to the whole string, or, in mathematical terms, 1:2. The second overtone, g, is found when the string is divided into three equal segments, and therefore possesses the ratio 1:3 with the fundamental tone. Each of the other overtones may be produced by further subdivisions of the string, and thus may be described by other mathematical ratios. The more distant the overtone from the fundamental, however, the more involved is the ratio.

The phenomenon of consonance and dissonance seems to be related to the overtone series. If a tone of the overtone series is produced by another instrument or voice simultaneously with the original fundamental, a chord of varying degrees of tension will result. If the octave or first overtone is sounded with the fundamental we do not receive the impression of a harmony, but merely a repetition or reinforcement of the fundamental tone at a higher pitch, as when a group of men and women sing the same melody at the interval of the octave. But if any other interval, either of the overtone series or outside of it, is sounded with the fundamental, we instantly perceive that two different tones are sounded simultaneously. When the added tone is at the same time one of the first few overtones, the chord will seem consonant. The farther removed it is from the fundamental, the more dissonant it will sound when combined with the fundamental.

In the first six notes of the overtone series there are three C's a G and an E. If we consider two of the C's as duplications of the fundamental, we have three notes, C G E, which when sounded together, produce the common chord, or major *triad*. If we include the seventh note of the series with this chord the resulting chord seems more dissonant and less stable than the triad.

The simple triad forms the basis of the conventional harmonic system, because it is the most consonant and stable of chords. The tones of the triad normally are arranged in thirds above the basic tone. If the first third is major and the second minor the chord is called a major triad. If the first third is minor and the second major, the triad is called minor. If both thirds are minor, the chord is called diminished. Triads may be readily constructed with the available tones of major or minor scales on every step of the scale (see Figure 9). Harmony generally consists of an alternation of simple, consonant chords and more dissonant ones.

FIGURE 9

major minor minor major major minor diminished

While the tones which are the regular components of any triad remain the same, they may be doubled and their position with respect to each other may be rearranged. In their normal or "root" position the fundamental tone will be the lowest in pitch. When any other tone of the triad is lowest, each chord is described as inverted. The number of possible inversions depends upon the number of different tones in a chord (see Figure 10).

FIGURE 10

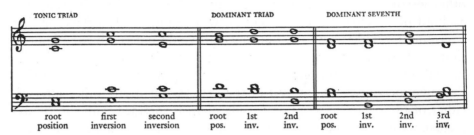

In traditional harmony the most important chord is the triad built upon the first note of the scale or key in which a piece is written. Called the tonic triad, all other chords revolve around it. Next in importance are the triads built upon the fifth above the tonic, called the *dominant* chord, and on the fifth below, called the *subdominant* chord. It will be noted that the seventh or leading tone of any diatonic scale is one of the three tones in the dominant triad, and likewise in the dominant seventh chord. One of the most characteristic endings or *cadences* in a piece of music is the progression from the dominant (or dominant seventh) chord to the tonic (see Figure 11). This cadence also serves to establish the tonal center of a piece.

FIGURE 11

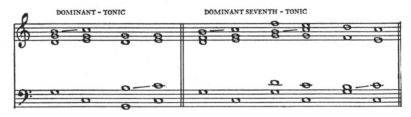

In the course of long compositions, and even short pieces, the music may depart from the tonic key and modulate to another key or tonality. We are conscious of harmonic modulations when chords appear containing notes not found in the tonic key in which the piece began. A modulation or change of key is effected when the harmony progresses to a cadence such as the one above consisting of the dominant and tonic chords of the new key. If such a modulation is between closely related keys it may not be very noticeable unless it is from a major to its related minor key, or vice versa. Modulations between the major and minor modes and between distantly related keys may often suggest distinct changes in feeling.

The interaction of the horizontal motion of melody and the vertical feeling of harmony creates what might be called the texture of a composition. At times the harmony consists of chords supporting a melody and moving in the same time-values as the melody. This is called *homophony*. At other times the harmony is created by combining two or more melodic lines, each having a distinctive rhythm. The resulting texture is more animated and complex than homophony and is called *polyphony*. The texture of both homophony and polyphony may be described as rich or thin, depending upon the greater or lesser number of tones involved.

INDEX

INDEX